JOURNAL FOR THE STUDY OF THE OLD TESTAMENT SUPPLEMENT SERIES
258

Sheffield Academic Press

The Psalms of the Return (Book V, Psalms 107–150)

Studies in the Psalter, IV

Michael D. Goulder

Journal for the Study of the Old Testament
Supplement Series 258

Copyright © 1998 Sheffield Academic Press

Published by
Sheffield Academic Press Ltd
Mansion House
19 Kingfield Road
Sheffield S11 9AS
England

Typeset by Sheffield Academic Press
and
Printed on acid-free paper in Great Britain
by Bookcraft Ltd
Midsomer Norton, Bath

British Library Cataloguing in Publication Data

A catalogue record for this book is available
from the British Library

ISBN 1-85075-866-2

CONTENTS

Part III
PSALMS 135–150 AND EZRA

The earliest commentary on the psalms is the Psalter. Some ancient Jews, probably before 200 BCE, ascribed the psalms to certain collections—two major David collections, psalms of the sons of Korah, Asaph psalms, Songs of the Ascents, and others; set them apart in five Books; arranged them in the order in which we have received them; prefaced them with Headings, and appended other notes and indications, often obscure to us. These old comments are faithfully recorded in the introductions to the standard commentaries, but it is rare for commentators to allow them to affect, let alone shape, their exegesis of the individual psalms. Rather, since Gunkel, the tendency has been to assemble collections under modern categories, such as royal psalms, or individual laments.

It is certainly possible that the ancient indicators are all misleading. Some are, for sure: Psalm 52 has nothing to do with Doeg the Edomite. It might be that the Asaph and Korah collections were just florilegia made by fourth-century Levites—like *The Methodist Hymn Book*, or *Songs of Praise*. But it cannot be sensible to *assume* that this is so. Indeed, when so many psalms are without headings, it might seem likely that the collections were preserved as being significant. Order was also important in earlier manuals of worship: the collects, epistles and gospels in the Breviary or the Book of Common Prayer are not set out at random, but follow a liturgical cycle.

I have attempted to write a series of *Studies in the Psalter*, of which this is the fourth (as my subtitle implies). Sheffield Academic Press published my *The Psalms of the Sons of Korah* in 1982, *The Prayers of David (Psalms 51–72)* in 1990, and *The Psalms of Asaph and the Pentateuch* in 1996. The present volume covers Book V, which has fewer explicit headings: 18 of the psalms have no heading, and there are not many *Selah*s, *Maschil*s, and so on. Nevertheless the pattern of the psalms' arrangement is once again suggestive, and yields an understanding of the individual psalms different from those normally

canvassed. An exegesis which gives a rationale to the ancient interpretative indicators should be its own recommendation.

As in the earlier volumes, I have, with one exception, printed the
translation of the Revised Version margin (1881): that is, the version
proposed by the minority of the panel, usually the scholars. RVmg is
as close as we have to a literal rendering of the Hebrew, and I give it
so that the reader can see at a glance where I diverge from accepted
interpretation. Now and again I have deserted RVmg, and these places
are marked either with (RVtext) or with the Hebrew. RV uses italic
print for words not in the Hebrew. In my comments, *per contra*, I use
italics for words which are.

The exception that I have made is Psalm 119, for which I have
printed no translation. The book is an argument for interpreting the
psalms in line with their place in the Psalter, and this involves in most
cases a close analysis of the text. But my theory does not affect the
interpretation of 119 as a text, and there are already too many repetitive treatments of the psalm. I have indeed a new hypothesis to propose for its original setting, but this may be set out without adding to
the bulk and cost of the present volume.

In preparing these books, I have begun the work on each psalm by
reading twelve commentaries, and I should like to record my debt to
men who have become my old friends: especially to Franz Delitzsch
for his amazing learning; to Alexander Kirkpatrick for his insight into
the historical setting of many psalms; to Hermann Gunkel and Sig-
mund Mowinckel, the giants of the century; to Leslie Allen for his
wide-ranging bibliographies, and comments on the Hebrew; and to my
friend and teacher, John Eaton, whose kindly influence is, I hope,
apparent in what I write. Mowinckel, *si magna licet componere parvis*,
wrote six volumes of *Psalmenstudien*, and showed the potential of
liturgical theories; but it was Eaton who taught me to think of the
Psalter.

The secondary literature on the psalms is large, and I have limited
references to those works that I thought relevant to my discussion.
There is a fairly comprehensive list of articles up to the mid-1980s in
Allen's commentary; thereafter I have been a little more generous.
But I am sceptical of 'structural' analysis of psalms, especially of
alleged chiasmus, and of proposals to emend the MT. It is likely that
the psalms were in as much use as any books in the Bible, and so the
MT Psalter is especially reliable. I have almost always defended its

text, and thought the variations in the versions and the Qumran writings to be easier readings, adaptations.

July, 1997
Michael Goulder

ABBREVIATIONS

AJSL	*American Journal of Semitic Languages and Literatures*
AnBib	Analecta biblica
BA	*Biblical Archaeologist*
BDB	Francis Brown, S.R. Driver and Charles A. Briggs, *A Hebrew and English Lexicon of the Old Testament* (Oxford: Clarendon Press, 1907)
BETL	Bibliotheca ephemeridum theologicarum lovaniensium
BHS	*Biblia hebraica stuttgartensia*
Bib	*Biblica*
BKAT	Biblischer Kommentar: Altes Testament
BZ	*Biblische Zeitschrift*
BZAW	Beihefte zur *ZAW*
CBQ	*Catholic Biblical Quarterly*
DCH	David J.A. Clines (ed.), *The Dictionary of Classical Hebrew* (Sheffield: Sheffield Academic Press, 1993–)
DJD	Discoveries in the Judaean Desert
GKC	*Gesenius' Hebrew Grammar* (ed. E. Kautzsch, revised and trans. A.E. Cowley; Oxford: Clarendon Press, 1910)
HAT	Handbuch zum Alten Testament
HKAT	Handkommentar zum Alten Testament
JBL	*Journal of Biblical Literature*
JSOT	*Journal for the Study of the Old Testament*
JSS	*Journal of Semitic Studies*
JTS	*Journal of Theological Studies*
KB	Ludwig Koehler and Walter Baumgartner (eds.), *Lexicon in Veteris Testamenti libros* (Leiden: E.J. Brill, 1953)
LD	Lectio divina
MT	Massoretic Text
NCB	New Century Bible
NEB	*New English Bible*
OBO	Orbis biblicus et orientalis
OTL	Old Testament Library
RB	*Revue biblique*
RevQ	*Revue de Qumran*
RSR	*Recherches de science religieuse*
RV	Revised Version
RVmg	Revised Version margin translation
SBLDS	SBL Dissertation Series
SUNVAO	Skrifter utgitt av Det Norske Videnskaps-Akademi i Oslo

TLZ	*Theologische Literaturzeitung*
VT	*Vetus Testamentun*
WBC	Word Biblical Commentary
ZAW	*Zeitschrift für die alttestamentliche Wissenschaft*

In the Massoretic Text, the Fifth Book of the Psalter comprises 44 psalms, 107–150; numerically the longest unit in the book.[1] However, the headings of the individual psalms suggest a sub-division into

1. LXX has 45 psalms. As it has MT's 9 and 10 combined into a single psalm 9 (as its acrostic pattern shows it originally to have been), its numbering is one ahead of MT for most of the Psalter, and it would have ended with 149 psalms had it not divided its 146 (= MT 147) into two after 146.11. There is a further complication in that LXX treats MT's 114 and 115 as a single psalm (113), and divides MT's 116 after v. 9 to make LXX 114 and 115. I comment on these differences below, pp. 167, 170, 292, but for the moment follow most scholars in giving priority to MT.

The discovery of the text of many psalms in Cave 11 at Qumran (11QPs[a]) has posed problems for which there is as yet no clear solution. The psalms include most of those between 101 and 151, but the order is markedly different from MT: for example, 119 is placed after 132 and before 135. The text is available in J.A. Sanders, *The Psalms Scroll of Qumran*, and in Y. Yadin, 'Another Fragment (E) of the Psalms Scroll from Qumran Cave II (IIQ Ps[a])', *Textus* 5 (1966), pp. 1–10, with plates. It is possible that the variant order is related to liturgical use following the Qumran calendar. Such a suggestion has been made by M.H. Goshen-Gottstein, 'The Psalms Scroll (IIQ Ps[a]): A Problem of Canon and Text', *Textus* 5 (1966), pp. 22-33; P.W. Skehan, 'A Liturgical Complex in 11Q Ps[a]', *CBQ* 35 (1973), pp. 195-205; and *idem*, 'Qumran and Old Testament Criticism', in M. Delcor (ed.), *Qumran: Sa piété, sa théologie et son milieu* (BETL, 46; Paris: Duculot, 1978), pp. 163-82; E. Tov, 'Excerpted and Abbreviated Texts from Qumran', *RevQ* 16 (1995), pp. 581-600; and R.T. Beckwith, *Calendar and Chronology, Jewish and Christian: Biblical, Intertestamental and Patristic Studies* (Leiden: E.J. Brill, 1996).

In general the MT offers a harder text than either LXX or Qumran. This may be explained on the one side by the desire to avoid difficult readings, and on the other by the perseverance of psalm texts because of their use in devotion or worship. Many older Christians defy modernizers and English teachers by beginning the Lord's Prayer, 'Our Father which art in heaven'; and the text of the psalms may have been similarly conservative. But naturally there are late additions to the MT: the headings 'For David, For Solomon', for example, in 122, 124, 127 and 131, are missing from most MSS of LXX, from the Vulgate and the Targum, and are probably late glosses in the MT.

three, for Psalms 120–134 each bear the title *A Song of [the] Ascents*, (שׁיר למעלות 121) שׁיר המעלות.[2] These are the only psalms in the Psalter with this title, so they constitute a complete collection. Book V thus falls into three sections: (1) 107–119, thirteen psalms, (2) 120–134, the Songs of the Ascents, fifteen psalms, (3) 135–150, sixteen psalms.

The validity of this subdivision is confirmed by further features in the first and third groups. In the first, Psalms 113–118 are spoken of in Jewish tradition as the Egyptian Hallel.[3] In fact, in the MT 111, 112, 113 begin 'Hallelujah', and 113, 115, 116, 117 end 'Hallelujah'.[4] In the third group all the Psalms 146–150 both begin and end 'Hallelujah'; they constitute the Little Hallel, with the introductory 145, whose heading speaks of it as תהלה. Leading into these two Hallel sequences there are alphabetic acrostic psalms, 111 and 112, and 145. Before these, in turn, stand short David sequences: 108–110 are headed 'For David', and so are 138–145. 107 is widely (though not universally) interpreted as a psalm of exiles returning from Babylonia; and 137 begins, 'By the waters of Babylon, there we sat down, yea, we wept, When we remembered Zion'. So we have a simple parallelism, mostly given by the Headings in the text:

107	psalm for the exiles returned from Babylon	137
108–110	psalms for David	138–145
111, 112	alphabetic psalms	145
113–118	Hallel psalms	146–150

The parallel is not balanced, for there are more alphabetic psalms in the first group, and more David psalms in the second.

2.   RV and other traditional translations render *A Song of Ascents*, but Heb. has ה, *A Song of the Ascents*.

3.   The most common Jewish usage is 'the Hallel' (*m. Pes.* 5.7; 9.3, etc.), sometimes 'the Hallelujah' (*m. Pes.* 10.6). But there are also 'the little Hallel' (Pss. 145–150) and the controverted Great Hallel; and for clarity rabbinic tradition spoke of 'the Egyptian Hallel', as in *b. Ber.* 56a, הללא מצראה. The Tosefta prescribes the use of this Hallel on eighteen days and one night in the year; but it is especially associated with Passover, as in the Mishnah references above. Cf. M. Millard, *Die Komposition des Psalters* (FAT, 9; Tübingen: J.C.B. Mohr, 1994), pp. 30-35.

4.   The school of Hillel prescribed the recital of the Hallel at the Passover meal with a break after Ps. 114 (*m. Pes.* 10.6): hence the Hallelujahs in the MT function as markers between psalms which are being chanted continuously, but with a pause. The school of Shammai had the pause after 113: this would involve a serious imbalance, and may be related to the Hallelujahs before 111 and 112.

A learned consensus invites us to extend the parallel in two directions. It is often noted that 107 does not stand on its own, but shares both theme and language with the two historical psalms which precede it, 105 and 106, at the end of Book IV.[5] These psalms recite Yahweh's wonders for Israel from Abraham to the Settlement (105), and from the Exodus to the Exile (106). The latter stresses Israel's constant sinfulness, and ends with a prayer that God will 'save us…and gather us from among the nations'; and 107 calls for thanks that the LORD has done just that. All three psalms open, 'O give thanks unto the LORD', and 106 and 107 continue, 'for he is good: For his mercy [endureth] for ever'. It is therefore generally thought that 105–107 belong together.

There is only one other pair of historical psalms in the Psalter, and they are numbers 135 and 136; and 136 opens, 'O give thanks unto the LORD; for he is good: For his mercy [endureth] for ever'. Indeed, the latter clause forms the refrain to every verse of the psalm. So we may think that there is a fuller parallel:[6]

105–106	historical psalms	135–136
107	return from Exile	137
108–110	David psalms	138–145
111, 112	alphabetic psalms	145
113–118	Hallel psalms	146–150

It may have been noticed that Psalm 119 has been quietly left out of these neat tables; and 119 is in many ways *sui generis*, being by far the longest psalm in the Psalter with 176 verses. Unlike any of the other psalms I have considered, it is, in one aspect, entirely devoted to the

---

5. So for example F. Delitzsch, *Biblical Commentary on the Psalms* (ET; 3 vols.; London: Hodder & Stoughton, 1888), III, pp. 136-37, A.F. Kirkpatrick, *The Book of Psalms (Psalms XC–CL)* (The Cambridge Bible for Schools and Colleges; Cambridge: Cambridge University Press, 1903), III, p. 638, J.W. Rogerson and J.W. McKay, *Psalms 101–150* (The Cambridge Commentary on the New English Bible; Cambridge: Cambridge University Press, 1979), III, p. 48, Millard, *Komposition*, p. 82, P.D. Miller, 'The Beginning of the Psalter', in J.C. McCann (ed.), *The Shape and Shaping of the Psalter* (JSOTSup, 159; Sheffield: JSOT Press, 1993), p. 89; form critics have been less interested in the sequence of psalms.

6. The parallel may be read slightly differently. 135 and 136 have been thought to be a response to the brief 134; and it is also sometimes supposed that 120–136 were thought of as a unity, the Great Hallel. In that case 120–136 would comprise seventeen psalms ending in two historical psalms, like the seventeen psalms in Book IV, 90–106, ending in two historical psalms; and 137–150 would parallel 107–119 as in the first table above. For further discussion see pp. 194-96.

glorification of the Law. There is only one other psalm in the Psalter that is totally given to this topic, and it is Psalm 1: indeed, 1 opens as 119 does, 'Blessed...'. We might therefore bear in mind the possibility that the Jews of the fourth century BCE viewed the Psalter as a cycle, in the same way that the Torah is traditionally read as a cycle, with Genesis 1 overlapping Deuteronomy 34 at the end of Sukkot. We should then have:

105–106	historical psalms	135–136
107	return from Exile	137
108–110	David psalms	138–145
111, 112	alphabetic psalms	145
113–118	Hallel psalms	146–150
119	praise of the Law	1

Under this arrangement, there would be 15 psalms in the first group as well as in the Songs of Ascents; and there would be 17 psalms in the third group. There are also 17 psalms in Book III, 73–89, and in the present Book IV, 90–106. Of course, if we sever 105–106 and attach them to 107–119, the rump of Book IV, 90–104, will consist of only 15 psalms. The significance of these numbers may be left over for the moment: they are indeed significant, and are discussed on pp. 108-11, 192-96 and 301-305.

The presence of two such similar series of psalms poses the question of why anyone should compose, or arrange such sequences. There would appear to be a thread of thought running through the two of them. God called the patriarchs (105.8-23: 135.4)/created the world (136.5-9). He delivered Israel from Egypt (105.24-38/106.7-12: 135.8-9/136.10-15). He led Israel, despite their sins, through the wilderness (105.40-42/106.13-33). He gave them the land (105.43-44/106.34: 135.10-12/136.16-22). Because of their sins he exiled them (106.35-43). But he remembered his covenant and delivered his people (106.44-46: 136.23-24). He has brought us back from Babylon (107: 137). We have suffered dire difficulties since (108–110: 138–145). But now we can thank and praise God (111–118: 146–150); and devote ourselves to his Torah (105.45/119.1–176: 1). The last two sentences are an inference from the parallel structure of the two sequences.[7]

7.   It is widely observed that most of the David psalms, especially in the second series, 51–70, are so-called Individual Laments. The David psalms in Book V frequently draw on these earlier David collections (most obviously in 108, which is

It would appear then that Book V as a whole belongs after the Exile, and that the first and third sections of the Book have been arranged in what, for the editors or authors, was a meaningful pattern. It would be understandable, for example, if those responsible for the third section saw meaning in the first, and framed their own series in parallel. But this in turn raises questions about the middle section, the Songs of Ascents. The only practicable policy must be to take the three sections independently, and study them, with the aim of comparing the three at the end. For this purpose I propose to take the Songs of Ascents first, because I wish to lay to rest any anxieties among my more sceptical readers. The Songs are a collection in the Massoretic text, and furthermore they share a number of obvious features in common. With them I am going with tradition, and going reasonably with tradition. I intend to suggest a similar original interpretation of all three groups, and should prefer to build upon the least controversial base if I can. Scepsis is a virtue: the imaginative need to build upon what rock they may if they hope to gain trust and to win conviction.

---

virtually composed of sections of Pss. 60 and 57). Later sufferers might well draw on language believed to go back to David, especially if they were national representatives; and editors drew attention to this with a heading note, לדוד.

Part I

THE SONGS OF THE ASCENTS AND NEHEMIAH

INTRODUCTION

'The Goings Up'

Each of the central group, Psalms 120–134, carries the heading
שִׁיר הַמַּעֲלוֹת, with the slight exception of 121, where the wording is
שִׁיר לַמַּעֲלוֹת: 'Song of/for the goings up'. The word מַעֲלָה is common
for a *step*; but it is also used at Ezra 7.9 for an expedition of exiles
returning to Palestine: 'upon the first *day* of the first month, that was
the foundation of the going up from Babylon'. The word is never used
for an ordinary *pilgrimage* for one of the three annual feasts,
although the verb עלה is so used frequently.

The understanding of מַעֲלָה as a *return of exiles* probably underlies
the translations of Aquila, Symmachus and Theodotion, each of whom
renders with ἀναβάσεις. LXX translates מַעֲלָה at Ezra 7.9 with
ἀνάβασις; it renders 'step' with ἀναβαθμός, which is also its translation for our Headings, and it uses ἑορτή both for a pilgrimage-feast
(חג), and for those attending it (מועד). The *Midrash Tehillim* takes
מַעֲלָה to mean 'a going up from captivity'; but the plural is interpreted
as of a series of such goings-up, first from Babylon, until finally 'the
last ascent whereto thou shalt raise us from among the kingdoms'.[1]
There is a similar tradition in the Syriac Church: the Peshitta gives a
heading to 120, 'The First Song of the Ascent: the people in Babylon
pray that they may be delivered', and the 'Ascents' reach their climax
with Christ's manifestation in 132. R. David Kimḥi knows four interpretations of מַעֲלוֹת, none of which is 'pilgrimages': it had been
thought to refer to the 'fifteen steps' on which the Levites were said to
have sung the Songs; or to the legend that the 'deep' sank and then
'rose' when David founded the Temple; or to their being sung 'on a
high note' (Saadia); or (Kimḥi's own preference) to 'ascents from

---

1.   W.G. Braude (trans.), *Midrash of the Psalms* (Yale Jewish Studies, 13; 2
vols.; New Haven: Yale University Press, 1959), II, p. 289, *ad* Ps. 120.

exile', in the future.[2] Thus tradition mainly supports the 'ascent from exile' tradition, in one form or another, and has nothing for 'pilgrimage'.

Objections to this understanding are weak. C.C. Keet says that in Ezra 7.9 the *going up* is specified as 'from Babylon', and the plural would be strange for such a momentous turning point in Israel's history.[3] But the Book of Ezra–Nehemiah describes three separate 'goings up', under Sheshbazzar, Ezra and Nehemiah; and it is likely that the success of these three expeditions will have been reported in the east, and that further supplementary caravans may have followed. Nehemiah's expedition came from Susa, so 'from Babylon' (or any other starting point) would be unsuitable. It might well be then that a group of psalms celebrating the Return could be brought together under the title 'The Songs of the Goings Up'.

Keet's 'more important point' is that 'we should expect the subject of the deliverance from Babylon to be one of their most salient features', which in his view is not so. Furthermore, Psalms 122 and 134 presuppose that the Temple and its services are fully operative.[4] These objections are the more curious because Kirkpatrick's commentary, written six decades before Keet's, carefully draws out points for every psalm that seem to place them in the period of (Ezra–) Nehemiah. The Temple had been rebuilt in the 510s, and its operation is presupposed in the times of Ezra and Nehemiah, whose goings-up took place in the second half of the fifth century. The Songs are in many ways a celebration of Jerusalem, now 'builded as a city that is joined together' (122.3), with its walls and towers (122.7): they contain many prayers for its peace and prosperity and triumphant thanks for deliverance (124.7, 126.1-3, 129.4), often understood as deliverance from Babylon. There is even the hope of the budding of the horn of David (132.17). So there seems to be no obvious difficulty in taking the Songs as the products of 'goings up' of the fifth century.

2.   J. Baker and E.W. Nicholson (eds. and trans.), *The Commentary of Rabbi David Kimḥi on Psalms CXX–CL* (University of Cambridge Oriental Publications, 22; Cambridge: Cambridge University Press, 1973), pp. 2-3: 'It is also possible to interpret the meaning of המעלות as being מעלות הגלות—the ascents from the exile—that is, the ascents whereby Israel will at some future time go up from the lands of the exile to the land of Israel'.

3.   C.C. Keet, *A Study of the Psalms of Ascents: A Critical and Exegetical Commentary upon Psalms CXX to CXXXIV* (London: Mitre Press, 1969), p. 11.

4.   Keet, *A Study of the Psalms*, p. 12.

Theories of the Collection

Nineteenth-century exegetes often attempted to link the Songs with a common setting, and Ewald, in the first edition of his *Poesie* (1839), and Kirkpatrick (1899) are commentators who took the fifth-century option and understood מעלות in this sense. But with the rise of form-criticism interest in the collections ebbed. To Gunkel and his many followers, the 'I' of the Songs was the individual, lamenting or thanking God or expressing his trust; and the inconvenient appeals to Israel might be later liturgical adaptations. To Mowinckel and Eaton the 'I' was the national leader at the pilgrimage feast of Tabernacles; very many of the psalms were in this category. מעלה might never be found meaning a 'pilgrimage', but the dangerous justification was widely offered that עלה was used for 'go up on pilgrimage'. But then in English we speak of going up to London, or going up to Scotland, or going up to the University, but we do not speak of an 'ascent' to the capital, or to North Britain, or to Oxford. James Barr has been wise to warn us against such philological short cuts.[5]

The last 30 years have seen a return to interest in the Collection. Keet's book in 1969 isolated the Songs, but is an odd combination of exegetical conservatism and explanatory speculation. The detailed commentary often follows Gunkel, and contains some interesting comments on the Hebrew, and on the traditions of interpretation; but the hypothesis proposed is a surprising one—the Songs were put together as a liturgical setting for the offering of *Bikkurim*.[6] It is difficult to find any sustained argument in the book supporting this conclusion, and the two descriptions of *Bikkurim* processions from Delitzsch[7] do little to advance the suggestion.

From the next decade we have Klaus Seybold's *Die Wallfahrts-psalmen* (1978). Seybold also begins with a criticism of the *Return expeditions* interpretation of מעלות, similar to Keet's, and concludes also that the Heading should be understood as 'pilgrimage psalms', as his title implies. If so, then we have a possible insight into the piety of ordinary Israelite farmers and *petit-bourgeoisie* on their annual

---

5.   'The semantic value of words therefore... has to be determined from the current usage, and not from the derivation', J. Barr, *The Semantics of Biblical Language* (Oxford: Oxford University Press, 1961), p. 107, cf. pp. 107-60.

6.   Barr, *Semantics,* p. 17.

7.   Delitzsch, *Biblical Commentary*, III, pp. 165-68.

pilgrimages. But alongside many homely phrases expressing an attractive and direct faith, there is an official Zion theology. Seybold accordingly sees almost every Song as an original piece of popular devotion later overlaid with some Temple piety. The originally independent prayers, greetings and curses were put together into 'a kind of *Vade Mecum* for pilgrims',[8] to cover the expedition from start to finish. 120 sees the party setting out from the Syrian–Arabian Diaspora (v. 5); 121–122 cover their journey and arrival in Jerusalem; 123–129 are their laments, prayers, thanks, and so on for their deliverance; 130–131 are their confessions; 132–134 are the climax of the sequence, with a farewell blessing in the Temple.[9] The overlong 132 is an especial instance of official theology.

Seybold is learned and ingenious, but not convincing. The basis of the theory, that מעלה means a 'pilgrimage psalm', is without evidence. The criteria for distinguishing lay devotion from Temple piety are sometimes circular, sometimes arbitrary: why should lay people not have held a 'Zion theology', or national leaders used homely phrasing? Leslie Allen is constantly critical of the way in which Seybold's proposed expansions destroy the poetic balance of the Songs. Also, what would the ordinary Israelite farmer do with his *Vade mecum*? Meshech is not on the Syrian–Arabian border, nor would most groups of Diaspora pilgrims come from there. The explanations for the order of 123–129 are vague. 134 does not seem to be a farewell blessing.

A similar two-layer theory is proposed more recently by Loren Crow, *The Songs of Ascents* (1996). Crow gives a full history of interpretation, exposing the weaknesses of the mystical (patristic), step-poetry (Gesenius and Delitzsch), and other now disregarded theories to explain the collection; and since the work is thorough and recent, it is unnecessary to duplicate it here. But he sees a problem in that the Songs are both a unity and also diverse, most importantly in genre, some being laments, some thanksgivings, some blessings, and so on. He explains this on the basis of certain Repeated Formulae, such as 'the maker of heaven and earth': he suggests five possible explanations for these, and concludes that they are signs of the hand of a

8. K. Seybold, *Die Wallfahrtspsalmen: Studien zur Entstehungsgeschichte von Psalmen 120–134* (Neukirchen–Vluyn: Neukirchener Verlag, 1978), p. 73.

9. A rather similar progressive structure for the Songs is proposed by Louis Jacquet, *Les Psaumes et le coeur de l'homme: Etude textuelle, littéraire et doctrinale. III. Psaumes 101 à 150* (Paris: Duculot, 1979), pp. 401-405.

Jerusalem redactor, which can then be traced in further traits. The original Songs (120, 123–131) came from northern Israel, and the Heading, as with Seybold and most critics, means 'pilgrimage psalms'.

It is difficult to follow Crow's logic, though his diversity argument is lamentably common. Why should we think that a collection of psalms is not a unity because it contains pieces from different *Gattungen*? Have such critics never attended a church service that began with a confession, included lessons of instruction, hymns of praise and prayers, and ended perhaps with the General Thanksgiving? If we found a book of sermons whose first four homilies expounded the themes of Advent, and then moved on to the Incarnation and the Epiphany, should we conclude that a redactor had succeeded a prophet of doom? Surely, on Mowinckel's hypothesis, say, we should expect a series of psalms for the autumn festival to cover a series of moods, with different genres? The Repeated Formulae argument is equally flawed: Crow's five explanations do not include the possibility that these were favourite phrases of a single author or group of authors! It is true that one of Crow's Formulae mentions Zion, but the others do not, nor is there any reliable sign of a northern underlay. Such theories of redaction bear an *onus probandi* they cannot carry.[10]

Features Common to the Songs

Seybold and Crow are certainly right to justify 120–134 as a unity, which they do on several grounds that we may amplify.[11] First, the Songs are notably *brief* in comparison with the Psalter generally. They occupy just over six pages of *BHS*, 0.4 of a page on the average, including 132, which is notably longer than the others (a page). The remaining 135 psalms occupy 134 pages of *BHS*, a page apiece on average, two and a half times as long as the Songs. The exclusion of

10. Another recent suggestion is made by Mathias Millard in his *Komposition*, pp. 76-81: the Songs were arranged in three fives, with climaxes for the first two in 124 and 129 ('Let Israel now say...'), and the turning point of the last five 132. The sequence is said to be similar to that proposed for the Korah psalms, but it is not very similar, nor are the three fives very similar; nor are they marked in the text; nor is any motive evident for the arrangement in such a way.

11. H. Viviers, 'The Coherence of the Ma῾alot Psalms (Psalms 120–134)', *ZAW* 106 (1994), pp. 275-89, offers a good statement of the many features which show the Songs to be a unity; but he does not refer to the imagery, and his conclusion is that the Songs are a book of devotion.

119 (eight pages) would make little difference, nor does any of the other collections (Korah, Asaph, David) much diverge from this picture.

Secondly, there is the so-called 'step parallelism':

> *He that keepeth thee will not slumber.*
> *Behold, he that keepeth Israel*
> *Shall neither slumber nor sleep* (121.3-4).
> *Except the LORD build the house,*
> *They labour in vain that build it:*
> *Except the LORD keep the city,*
> *The watchman waketh but in vain* (127.1).
> *Many a time have they afflicted me from my youth up,*
> *Let Israel now say;*
> *Many a time have they afflicted me from my youth up,*
> *But they have not prevailed against me* (129.1-2).
> *Surely I have stilled and quieted my soul:*
> *Like a weaned child with his mother,*
> *My soul is with me like a weaned child* (131.2).

Parallelism is the basis of Hebrew poetry, and this often involves some repetition and modification; but the regularity of such repetitions in succeeding verses, and their artistic force, are peculiar to the Songs generally. Here again 132 is an exception, as is 134: there are repetitions in 132 ('the mighty one of Jacob'; much of the second half of the psalm echoes the first), but the carrying over of whole phrases from one verse to the next, so characteristic of the other Songs, is absent here.

Thirdly, we have Crow's repeated phrases:

> *Maker of heaven and earth* (121.2, 124.8, 134.3)
> *From this time forth and for evermore* (121.8, 125.2, 131.3)
> *Let Israel now say* (124.1, 129.1)
> *Peace upon Israel* (125.5, 128.5)
> *The LORD bless thee out of Zion* (128.5, 134.3)
> *O Israel, hope in the LORD* (130.7, 131.3).

We might add a variety of very close phrases, such as:

> *My soul hath long dwelt* (רבת שכנה־לה נפשי)...(120.6)
> *Our soul is exceedingly filled* (רבת שבעה־לה נפשנו)...(123.4)

Scholars such as Delitzsch and Duhm have suggested that such close phrasing is an indication of common authorship, though others like Gunkel have denied this. But alongside other unitary signals we may think that the repeated phrases have their weight. When different parables and sections of Matthew's Gospel display repeated phrases, 'You offspring of vipers', 'there shall be weeping and gnashing of teeth', 'you of little faith', they are generally taken as indications of the hand of the evangelist.

A fourth indication is the frequency of *similes*, and especially of *homely similes*, in the Songs. While metaphorical language is ubiquitous in Hebrew psalmody, similes are not so common; but they are in the Songs. Sometimes these are related to women and children, which would be hard to parallel:

> *Like a weaned child with his mother,*
> *My soul is with me like a weaned child* (131.2).
> *Thy wife shall be as a fruitful vine...*
> *Thy children like olive plants...* (128.3)
> *As arrows in the hand of a mighty man,*
> *So are the children of youth* (127.4).
> *As the eyes of a maiden unto the hand of her mistress* (123.2b).

Also from the home (quite a well-to-do home) comes 123.2a:

> *as the eyes of servants [look] unto the hand of their master*

and the brilliant image of happiness:

> *We were like unto them that dream* (126.1);

and from any flat-roofed Palestinian house:

> *as the grass upon the housetops,*
> *Which withereth afore it be plucked up* (129.7).

The psalmist loves Jerusalem:

> *Jerusalem that art builded*
> *As a city that is compact together* (122.3);
> *They that trust in the LORD*
> *Are as mount Zion, which cannot be moved* (125.1)
> *As the mountains are about Jerusalem,*
> *So the LORD is round about his people* (125.2);
> *My soul [looketh] for the LORD,*
> *More than watchmen [look] for the morning,*
> *[Yea, more than] watchmen for the morning* (130.6).

He loves the Temple ritual too:

> *It is like the precious oil upon the head,*
> *That ran down upon the beard,*
> *Even Aaron's beard;*
> *That came down upon the collar of his garments* (133.2).

For agriculture, I have noted the *fruitful vine* and the *olive plants* in 128.3; and from 133.3 we have

> Like the dew of Hermon
> That cometh down upon the mountains of Zion;

and from outside the farming areas:

> As the streams in the South (126.4).

Farming included trapping animals too:

> as a bird out of the snare of the fowlers (124.7).

That is 16 similes in a collection of 97 verses. We may contrast the relatively large number of similes in the second David collection (51–72, the Prayers of David), where there are 27 similes in 329 verses: one in twelve verses against one in six. The difference of tone in the similes is even more noticeable. *Arrows* occur once in the Songs as an image of children, but otherwise there are no war similes, nor anything unpleasant. The images in 51–72 are: a razor, an olive tree, bread, a dove, oil, butter, venom, an adder, failing water, grass, a snail, an abortion, dogs (×2), a leaning wall, swords, arrows, silver, smoke, wax, hairs, an ox, a bull, rain, showers, Lebanon and grass. The imagination behind these psalms is full of fear, violence and hatred, far removed from the serenity and domesticity of the Songs.

In view of these four elements common to the Songs—their brevity, their so-called step-parallelism, their repeated use of a number of simple phrases, their love of homely, positive similes—there seems to be a good *prima facie* case for regarding the Songs as a genuine unity. The only, and striking, exception to this case is 132, which is not included on any of the counts: it is not brief, it has no step-parallelism, it contains none of the repeated phrases and it has no simile. It will therefore need to be treated with caution. It *is* one of the Songs, and we should not be quick to dismiss it as a later intrusion, with Ewald and Duhm; but some good arguments are required to include it as the creation of the same community as the others.

A Setting for the Songs

Most critics note the presence of a range of late Hebrew words and 'Aramaisms' in each of the Songs: the use of שֶׁ־, 'that', for example, ten times, or רַבַּת, 'much, many times' (×3), or the Aramaic spelling

שׁנא, 'sleep'. I shall give details of these in the exegesis of the individual psalms, but it may suffice here to say that such a linguistic pattern
is noticeable in all the Songs, again with the partial exception of 132,
and that the normal explanation offered for it is that the psalms are
postexilic. This is not a necessary inference, for such traits might be a
sign of northern provenance (Dahood, Crow), and Mowinckel, Eaton
and others have thought the Songs belong in the monarchy. However,
they share Book V with other clearly late psalms that exhibit similar
linguistic peculiarities; and this may incline us to think of them as
psalms of the Return, particularly as שׁיר המעלות may be thought to
specify this.

The Songs cannot belong with the Returns of the sixth century, for
the Temple is in operation, and the walls are clearly in place: *For the
sake of the house of the LORD our God* (122.9); *This is my resting
place for ever* (132.14); *Which by night stand in the house of the
LORD* (134.1); *Peace be within thy walls, And prosperity within thy
towers* (122.7); *Except the LORD keep the city, The watchman waketh
but in vain* (127.1). Indeed 122.3 may imply some pride in their
recent completion: *Jerusalem that art builded As a city that is joined
together* (שׁחברה־לה יחדו).

The Songs cannot be earlier than 445 BCE, then, if the linguistic
argument holds; and they must have been composed some time before
the Chronicler, for he alters Solomon's Prayer of 1 Kings 8 to bring
it into line with Psalms 130 and 132:

> Now, O my God, let, I beseech thee, thine eyes be open, and *let thine
> ears be attentive* unto the prayer that is made in this place. Now therefore
> *arise*, O LORD God, *into thy* resting place, *thou and the ark of thy
> strength: let thy priests,* O LORD God, *be clothed with salvation, and let
> thy saints* rejoice in good. O LORD God, *turn not away the face of thine
> anointed: remember* the mercies of *David thy servant* (2 Chron. 6.40-42).

> *Let thine ears be attentive To the voice of my supplications* (Ps. 130.2).

> LORD, *remember for David. . .*
> *Arise,* O LORD, *into thy resting place;*
> *Thou and the ark of thy strength.*
> *Let thy priests be clothed with righteousness/salvation,*
> *And let thy saints shout for joy.*
> *For thy servant David's sake,*
> *Turn not away the face of thine anointed* (Ps. 132.1, 8-10).

The Songs are familiar to the Chronicler, and seem suitable to him in Solomon's mouth at the Temple consecration.

For their general tone we may think the Songs belong earlier rather than later in the period 445–350 BCE. Nehemiah's 'Memoir' is marked by a spirit of irenic optimism. The Songs similarly are full of prayers for the peace of Jerusalem, for its prosperity, for the birth of children; Yahweh is its defence like the hills surrounding it, he blesses it with his dew, and so on. There are enemies who are for war, men of lying lips and a deceitful tongue (like Sanballat and Tobiah); but the psalmist is for peace, like others in a weak military position. This is in sharp contrast both with earlier and with later Jerusalem sentiment. When hopes of empire were high in early times, Yahweh would give the king the nations for his inheritance; he would break them with a rod of iron, and dash them in pieces like a potter's vessel (Ps. 2.8-9). Princes would come out of Egypt, and Ethiopia would run to stretch out hands to God (68.32). Even in more modest times, perhaps in the seventh century, it was to be told out among the heathen that Yahweh was king (Pss. 96, 98). Nor is this aggressive spirit quenched by the Exile. The late Psalm 149 (pp. 297-300) has the saints with two-edged swords in their hands, intent to bind their enemies' kings in chains, and their nobles with links of iron; the Chronicler describes many an imaginary Judaean victory with spirit, and his beloved Levites are the inspiration of the battle line. But people wanted peace in Nehemiah's days, for the place was barely defensible.

If the Songs stemmed from Nehemiah's time, we should expect them to display some triumph in having begun to reverse the Exile, and considerable devotion to Jerusalem, the newly fortified capital. It is precisely these things that we do find: *Our feet are standing Within thy gates, O Jerusalem* (122.2); *Blessed be the LORD, Who hath not given us as a prey to their teeth. Our soul is escaped as a bird out of the snare of the fowlers: The snare is broken, and we are escaped* (124.7-8); *When the LORD turned the fortunes of Zion, We were like unto them that dream... Then said they among the nations, The LORD hath done great things for them.* Jerusalem and Zion are the constant themes of thought and prayer (Pss. 122, 125, 126, 128, 129, 132, 133); they are mentioned 12 times in the Songs, far more frequently than elsewhere in the Psalter. Israel often seemed coterminous with the city and its environs.

Kirkpatrick was impressed by the frequency with which phrases and details in the Songs corresponded with the book of Nehemiah. In ch. 1 Nehemiah prays in distress at the news of Jerusalem's plight, 'Let thine ear now be attentive, and let thine eye be open...': cf. Ps. 120.1: *In my distress I cried unto the LORD*; 130.2: *Let thine ears be attentive.* In Neh. 2.10 Israel's enemies grieve 'that there was come a man to seek the good of the children of Israel': cf. 122.9, *I will seek thy good.* In Neh. 2.19 and 3.33-8 Sanballat and his friends 'laughed us to scorn and despised us': compare 123.3-4, *Our soul is exceedingly filled with the scorning of those that are at ease, And with the contempt of the proud.* In Nehemiah 4 it takes all the governor's resolution and prudence to prevent an attack on the still open city, under the providence of 'our God who fights for us': see 124.7-8: *The snare is broken and we are escaped. Our help is in the name of the LORD.*

In Nehemiah 6 the wall is completed, and the nations 'perceived that this work was wrought by our God': see 126.2, *Then said they among the nations, The LORD hath done great things for them.* In ch. 7.1-4, Nehemiah sets watches on the gates, and plans for the rebuilding of houses: see Ps. 127.1, *Except the LORD build the house, They labour in vain that build it: Except the LORD keep the city, The watchman waketh but in vain.* In Neh. 7.5a and 11.1-2 there are traces of a policy to repopulate the city: compare Psalm 128, with its hope of children and grandchildren. In Neh. 12.27-43 the governor leads a double procession to the Temple: compare Psalm 132, which recalls David's bringing of the ark to the Temple.

We may think that Kirkpatrick was right to be impressed by so many parallels; but what Kirkpatrick did not observe (at least in words) was that *these parallels are in the same order in the Songs and in the Nehemiah 'Memoir'.* It is this striking fact that suggests a solution to many longstanding puzzles, and so forms the basis of the hypothesis argued in Part I of this book: *The 'I' passages in Nehemiah were Nehemiah's testimonies at the Tabernacles celebration in 445 BCE, in the weeks after the wall had been completed. They were delivered in short units, and the Songs were responses to them, chanted by a leading Levite who was a loyal follower of the Governor, sometimes addressing him, often identifying himself with his plans and policies.*

Nehemiah's Testimonies

We are fortunate that critics are largely of one mind about the book of Nehemiah.[12] Underlying the present text is a narrative in the first person singular, comprising most of Neh. 1.1-7.5a (less the list of wall-builders in 3.1-32) and of Neh. 13.4-31; also perhaps 11.1-2 (rewritten) and 12.27-43 (expanded with names). This I-narrative has been heavily over-written after 7.5a with extraneous material in the third person. It has been normal to speak of the I-narrative as 'the Nehemiah Memoir'.

This label is unfortunate, for it invokes the suggestion of the many memoirs written for quite different purposes in the last two centuries; and Mowinckel has been concerned to expose its unsuitable and misleading nature (*Nehemia*, II, 50-56). Although there are scholars, like Hugh Williamson[13] and Joseph Blenkinsopp,[14] who still think the narrative was intended as a report to King Artaxerxes, of which a copy was deposited in the Temple, the form of the narrative suggests rather a report to God: for many of the episodes end with a short prayer opening with the word 'Remember' (5.19; 6.14; 13.14, 22, 29, 31; cf. 3.36-37).

A better description might be The Nehemiah Testimonies. There is evidence in the Psalter that the king, or other leading national figure, used to give his testimony, probably at a festival. The speaker of Psalm 71 for example says, 'My mouth shall tell of thy righteousness, Of thy salvation all the day. I will come in the strength of the mighty acts of the Lord GOD: I will make mention of thy righteousness, even of thine only...hitherto have I declared thy wondrous works. Yea, even unto old age and gray hairs, O God, forsake me not, Until I have declared thine arm unto *the next* generation, Thy might to every one that is to come' (71.15-18). The speaker promises praise on the

---

12. I have relied on S. Mowinckel, *Studien zu dem Buche Esra–Nehemia*. II. *Die Nehemia-Denkschrift* (SUNVAO NS 2.7; Oslo: Universitetsforlaget, 1964); U. Kellermann, *Nehemia: Quellen, Überlieferung und Geschichte* (BZAW, 102; Berlin: Alfred Töpelmann, 1967); and commentaries by W. Rudolph (*Esra und Nehemia* [HAT, 20; Tübingen: J.C.B. Mohr, 1949]); H.G.M. Williamson (*Ezra, Nehemiah* [WBC; Waco, TX: Word Books, 1985]), and J. Blenkinsopp (*Ezra–Nehemiah: A Commentary* [OTL; Philadelphia: Westminster Press, 1988]).

13. Williamson, *Ezra, Nehemiah*, pp. xxvii-xxviii.

14. Blenkinsopp, *Ezra–Nehemiah*, pp. 47, 210, and *passim*.

psaltery and harp, and his tongue will talk of God's righteousness all the day long (vv. 22-24); so he is unlikely to be a private individual. John Eaton has been at pains to describe the king's duty to give testimony;[15] partly to God's mighty deeds of old, no doubt, but partly also to his current mercies. In this respect he is rather like a President of the United States giving his state-of-the-Union address: a comforting blend of realism, rhetoric and religiosity.

Nehemiah's narrative is a testimony in this sense. He constantly tells what 'my God' has done for him (2.8, 18; 4.3, 8, 9, 14; 6.12; 7.5), and in the 'Remember' prayers asks that he will take further appropriate action. The whole narrative reads like an account of the events of the past year, spoken in the Temple arena before the crowd of festal worshippers in the presence of their God. But a salient feature of the narrative is its division into episodes. Many of these, as I have noted, close with a 'Remember' prayer; but many of them also open with something of a formula such as 2.10, 'And when Sanballat...heard of it...' (cf. 2.19, 3.33, 4.1, 6.1, 16); or 'In those days...' (13.15, 22). There is accordingly fairly widespread agreement among commentators that the Nehemiah Testimonies divide into episodes which can be delimited both by topic and by the opening and closing formulae.

There is also broad agreement that the first part of the Nehemiah Testimonies follows a chronological order: the report in Susa, Nehemiah's petition, his survey of the city by night, the building of the walls, the repopulation problem (though there may be some doubt over details in ch. 6). Over the second part of the work there is less agreement. I have argued below that the chronological sequence was followed throughout: that some version of 11.1-2 and 7.26-33 described the repopulation; that the four incidents in ch.13 followed this before the dedication procession in 12.27-43 ('Now before this...', 13.4); and that the Dedication was the climax of the work. I leave the argument over to be settled in detail below.

The result of such an analysis is that the Nehemiah Testimonies break into fourteen episodes, and these may then be set against the fifteen Songs. In the exegesis below I have printed the episodes of the Nehemiah Testimonies on the left-hand page with the relevant Song opposite, and have attempted to show that the Song yields a full sense

15. J.H. Eaton, *Kingship and the Psalms* (The Biblical Seminar, 3; Sheffield: JSOT Press, 2nd edn, 1980), pp. 181-95.

when it is seen as a comment on the Testimonies. There is one Song over at the end, the brief 134 that terminates the series. It is not an accident that there are 14 testimonies, nor that there are 14 Songs plus one; and I will offer an explanation for this at the end of the exposition (pp. 108-11). My theory is an ambitious one, what philosophers of Popper's school called a baroque hypothesis: the more ambitious and elaborate, the easier it should be to falsify.[16] Proof and disproof are not granted to Old Testament scholars: but I hope to persuade my readers of its sustained plausibility, and to convince them.

16. J. Rodwell, 'Myth and Truth in Scientific Enquiry', in M.D. Goulder (ed.), *Incarnation and Myth* (London: SCM Press, 1979), pp. 64-75 (66-67).

PSALM 120

Nehemiah 1.1-11a

[1][The words of Nehemiah the son of Hacaliah.]
Now it came to pass in the month Chislev, in the twentieth year, as I was in Shushan the castle, [2]that Hanani, one of my brethren, came, he and certain men, out of Judah; and I asked them concerning the Jews that had escaped, which were left of the captivity, and concerning Jerusalem. [3]And they said unto me, The remnant that are left of the captivity there in the province are in great affliction and reproach: the wall of Jerusalem also is broken down, And the gates thereof are burned with fire. [4]And it came to pass, when I heard these words, that I sat down and wept, and mourned certain days; and I fasted and prayed before the God of heaven, [5]and said,

I beseech thee, O LORD, the God of heaven, the great and terrible God, that keepeth covenant and mercy with them that love him and keep his commandments: [6]let thine ear be attentive, and thine eyes open, that thou mayest hearken unto the prayer of thy servant, which I pray before thee at this time, day and night, for the children of Israel thy servants, and while I confess the sins of the children of Israel, which we have sinned against thee: yea, I and my father's house have sinned. [7]We have dealt very corruptly against thee, and have not kept the commandments, nor the statutes, nor the judgements, which thou commandedst thy servant Moses. [8]Remember, I beseech thee, the commandment which thou commandedst thy servant Moses, saying, If ye trespass, I will scatter you abroad among the peoples: [9]but if ye return unto me, and keep my commandments and do them, though your outcasts were in the uttermost part of the heaven, yet will I gather them from thence, and will bring them unto the place that I have chosen to cause my name to dwell there. [10]Now these are thy servants and thy people, whom thou hast redeemed by thy great power, and by thy strong hand. [11]O Lord, I beseech thee, let now thine ear be attentive to the prayer of thy servant, and to the prayer of thy servants, who delight to fear thy name: and prosper, I pray thee, thy servant this day, and grant him mercy in the sight of this man.

It is the opening evening of the festival of Tabernacles, 445 BCE, and Nehemiah rises, as chief executive, to give his testimony. As it is a Jewish festival, he uses the Jewish calendar, with its third month Chislev in the previous winter, and its long established Jewish year running up to the present feast as its climax. The whole year, from the

1   A Song of the Ascents (המעלות).
     In my distress I cried unto the LORD,
     And he answered me.
2   Deliver my soul, O LORD, from lying lips,
     And from a deceitful tongue.
3   What shall be given unto thee, and what shall be done more unto thee,
     Thou deceitful tongue?
4   Sharp arrows of the mighty, (RVtext)
     With coals of juniper.
5   Woe is me, that I sojourn in Meshech,
     That I dwell among the tents of Kedar!
6   My soul hath long had her dwelling
     With him that hateth peace.
7   I am *for* peace:
     But when I speak, they are for battle.

end of the previous Tishri, has been Year Twenty, that is the twentieth year of the current reign, that of Artaxerxes I: they might count regnal years in Susa, and start their calendar in the spring, but this is Jerusalem.

For comments on various puzzles associated with the dates see Mowinckel, *Nehemia*, II, 17-19; Williamson, *Ezra, Nehemiah*, pp. 169-70; Blenkinsopp, *Ezra–Nehemiah*, p. 205; E.J. Bickerman, 'En marge' (1981). I limit my comments on the Nehemiah Testimonies to those matters that are relevant to the exegesis of the Songs.

Nehemiah had risen to a high position in the Persian court, which he could not have done if he had lived in Palestine; he had been out of touch with conditions in Judah, and it may be that his brother Hanani had grown up with him in the east, and had been equally shocked to find the state of things when he actually visited Jerusalem. He and his companions had perhaps come back to Susa with a petition to the king, and made use of their palace backstairs contact to get a hearing. They are not complaining about some recent disaster: the wall of Jerusalem was broken down by the Edomites in 587 BCE, and had not been rebuilt since. The inhabitants are in poverty and demoralized in the face of this continuing desolation.

Williamson and others suppose a recent destructive attack on the city; but while the razing of the walls in 587 (Ps. 137.7) and their rebuilding by Nehemiah are deeply chiselled in the Jewish soul, there is no mention of any earlier rebuilding of the walls in Ezra 1–6 or elsewhere, nor any mention here of an assault on the Temple, an inevitable target for raiders. Hanani means that the inhabitants are in dire straits and without hope because the ruin of 587 still stares them in the face. For hesitations over the destructiveness of the Edomites, see John Bartlett's *Edom* (1989).

Nehemiah had reacted as Ezra was later to do (Ezra 9.3; 10.6; Ps. 137.1), sitting on the ground, weeping, and mourning for certain days; and then fasting and praying. It was more than three months before he made his appeal to the king, so he was biding his time for a good opportunity. He gives the gist of his prayer in a full six-verse version, adapted for his Jerusalem audience with its reference to the king as 'this man'. He begins with a confession, like other postexilic leaders, and uses a series of rounded phrases from Deuteronomy, like a seventeenth-century Puritan praying in the language of the King James Version; Nehemiah had been brought up on Deuteronomy, and uses its wording again in speeches at 4.14, 4.20 and 13.25. Moses had not foretold the rebuilding of the wall, but he had foretold the Return (Deut. 30.4; Neh. 1.9); and it is for this that the cupbearer prays. He must gain permission to lead an *aliya* himself, with suitable conditions; if he can *gain mercy in the sight of this man*, he should be able to refortify the city and open the way for a widespread *gathering* of *outcasts*.

Mowinckel, Blenkinsopp and many commentators excise Nehemiah's prayer, 1.5-11a, as an insertion by the Chronicler; it is defended by Kellermann, *Nehemia*, pp. 9-11 and Williamson, *Ezra, Nehemiah*, pp. 167-68, and I refer the reader to the discussion there. Nehemiah's praying, which is important for Ps. 120.1, comes in any case in Neh. 1.4, 2.4. But I would add to Williamson's defence two considerations: (1) a confession of sin was normal at the beginning of the autumn festival (Pss. 42, 43, 44 in the Korah series; Ps. 50 in the Asaph series; Ps. 90 in Book IV); (2) whereas Nehemiah's Prayer is a mosaic of Deuteronomic phrases, that is not true of the Chronicler's prayers more generally (1 Chron. 29.10-19; 2 Chron. 20.5-12; Ezra 9.6-15); and whereas they may contain echoes of P-material, there is nothing of that here.

When he finishes, the cantor chants Psalm 120. His position is a little ambiguous. As Nehemiah's official psalmist he identifies himself with his leader: he was among his leader's close companions; when Nehemiah was distressed, he was distressed; it is a grief to him as to his leader to be living among Kedarites, and so on. But he is also distinct from Nehemiah, and in Psalm 121 he both speaks in his own name and addresses the Governor. He begins, *In my distress I called unto the LORD, And he answered me.* Nehemiah was indeed distressed at the report, sitting on the earth, mourning for days and fasting. He had prayed the long prayer just cited, and the LORD had answered him graciously and in full, with the king's decree. But the exiled party looks back over a tumultuous six months since that happily granted petition; nor are they by any means out of the wood. Powerful enemies are scheming against them still, men who have shown themselves consistently untrustworthy, *lying lips, a deceitful tongue*; and especially have they shown themselves so in the recent weeks described in Nehemiah 6. It is from these that leader and people need still to be delivered.

The Hebrew implies that prayer and answer in v. 1 were in the past, and most critics resist Gunkel's wish to emend. Kraus takes v. 2 as quoting this earlier prayer, and Seybold makes the rest of the psalm such a quotation; but the text gives the impression of seeking deliverance in a second, more urgent peril. Verse 2b: literally, *a tongue [that is] deceit*, like *I am peace* in v. 7; a modification of Ps. 52.6.

The speaker is not a private individual, or he would not be able to think in terms of vv. 3-4. He considers what punishment *he*, that is Yahweh, *will give* to the owner of this *deceitful tongue*; following the standard formula, 'Yahweh do so to X and more also...' (2 Sam. 3.9; Hos. 9.14); and the answer is a military one, *sharp arrows of the mighty* (cf. v. 7 *they are for war*), and even less pleasantly, *coals of juniper*. The *mighty*, גבור, is the particularly strong archer, who can fire his arrows right through a shield to inflict a painful wound. The *coals of juniper* are the red-hot charcoal that the defenders will drop on any assailants: they imply a fortified Jerusalem, and an effective response to siege-workers and battering-ram operators (cf. Judg. 9.53; 2 Sam. 11.21). The speaker sees himself (like other psalmists in Book V, as we shall see) as a new David, God's appointed agent betrayed and abused by men. The deceitful tongue is addressed also in Ps. 52.5; God will destroy its owner for ever in 52.6, and a גבור is mentioned in 52.2.

Most critics have seen the psalm as coming from a private individual, whether as a lament (Kirkpatrick, Gunkel), or a thanksgiving (Weiser, Kraus, Seybold, Allen); Eaton takes the speaker as a national representative (*Kingship*, pp. 82-83). The individual approach reduces the arrows–champion–coals–war theme to a vacuous metaphor. Kirkpatrick tells us that juniper (רתם) was still used by Arabs in his day for making charcoal, and that it retained its heat for a long time; the psalmist means it, and something nasty, but he is not thinking of a private torture chamber. The individual thanksgiving interpretation (with quoted prayer) is particularly weak. Religious commentators like Allen seem quite content if their psalmist has received an assurance from the priest (sometimes with an oracle) that his prayer has been heard; one might think that the wretched man, at death's door with sickness, falsely accused and subject to ordeal (Weiser), hounded by wealthy landlords, among other things, would like actually to be well, free and out of debt. The Nehemiah setting invests the whole with a reality testified in the Nehemiah Testimony.

The riddle of the psalm comes in v. 5, for Meshech is in the far north from Jerusalem, while Kedar is away in the east, in north Arabia, and it is not possible for a single person (*I*) to *sojourn among* both at the same time. But these two places are not mentioned at random. Meshech had been the name for a tribe in east Turkey in Assyrian times, on the waters of the upper Halys (cf. Ezek. 38.1-3; Gen. 10.2), but in Persian times they are found further east, on the Upper Euphrates.[1] Now the two leading enemies facing the new community were 'Sanballat the Horonite...and Geshem the Arabian'. Geshem the Arabian was in fact the king of Kedar; an inscription from the eastern Delta dated before 400 BCE is by 'Qainu bar Geshem, King of Kedar'.[2] The Kedarites were at this time settled widely over south Palestine, and even into Egypt,[3] and Geshem is involved because Nehemiah was acting within his *medinta*.

Sanballat's place of origin has been obscure. There is no place called Horon known to us, and the suggestion that he came from Beth-horon is improbable: 'Sanballat the Horonite' is a repeated phrase in the Nehemiah Testimony (2.10, 19, 13.28), and is intended to be in some way pejorative, like the other foreign leaders' identifications, Tobiah the Ammonite and Geshem the Arabian. It would be no discredit to Sanballat if he were born in a village in Israel. On the other hand the same consonants, החרני, could be vocalized as 'the Haranite', and it would be discreditable in the ears of a Judahite congregation if he were from a distant foreign city. It would be the more so in that Haran was the centre of the worship of the moon god, Sin, and Sin- is the first, theophoric element in the name Sanballat. Haran is a

---

1.   So H. Guthe, *Bibelatlas*, maps 5, 7. Kirkpatrick refers to inscriptions of the Mushki from the Assyrian period, and Herodotus knows of the Moschoi (3.94), without giving an exact location.

2.   E. Stern, 'The Persian Empire and the Political and Social History of Palestine in the Persian period', in W.D. Davies and L. Finkelstein (eds.), *Cambridge History of Judaism* (2 vols.; Cambridge: Cambridge University Press, 1984–89), I, p. 75. Stern identifies this Geshem with Nehemiah's opponent.

3.   Stern, 'The Persian Empire', p. 81. Cf. Isa. 42.11, 'the villages that Kedar doth inhabit'.

principal city in the bend of the Upper Euphrates; and it might well be that Sanballat had some of his co-provincials among his retinue, or mountain mercenaries from nearby. So we may think of Nehemiah saying, *Woe is me that I sojourn in Meshech, That I dwell among the tents of Kedar!*, as Juvenal laments, 'Syrus in Tiberim defluxit Orontes' (*Sat.* 3.62). A modern Frenchman, returning after many years to Marseilles, might say, 'I had no idea I should be living in Algiers!'.

Two solutions are canvassed for the Meshech/Kedar problem. One may emend, with Gunkel, to מַשָּׂא, a district also in north Arabia, mentioned alongside Kedar in Gen. 25.14; or one may say that they are symbols of barbarism, like Tartars and Philistines (Anderson), or Turks and infidels (Weiser), or Mongols and Vandals (Jacquet). The former is unacceptable and the latter deceptive. Men are spoken of in English as Philistines and vandals, and women as Tartars; these words have been adopted into the language as symbols, and in the Book of Common Prayer Turks and infidels means non-Christian Muslims more generally, in the same way. There is no sign that Meshech and Kedar functioned in this way in Hebrew; if the terms were symbolic, it would be more like an Englishman saying, 'Woe is me that I live among the Matabele and the Mohawk', which would leave the hearer bewildered. Seybold appeals to 1 Chron. 1.17 where Meshech is a son of Shem while in the parallel Gen. 10.23 the name is Mash son of Aram; the inference that Meshech was the name of an Aramaean tribe, and so close to Kedar, is far-fetched.

There is an Upper and a Lower Beth-horon in Ephraim (Josh. 16.3, 5). The only other candidate for 'the Horonite' is Horonaim in Moab (Isa. 15.5; Jer. 48.3); but then we should have expected 'the Moabite', like 'Tobiah the Ammonite'. The proposal of an original הַחֹרְנִי was made by S. Feigin in 1926 ('Etymological Notes'). It is a believable speculation that Sanballat's family were among the remote foreigners imported to Samaria by the Assyrians after 722, and that they had made good and been appointed to act officially for the Persian government.

Nehemiah's cantor had been in Jerusalem for only about four months, but with the daily tensions and the sleepless nights he might well feel, *My soul hath long had her dwelling With him that hateth peace.* שׂוֹנֵא is singular, and there is one principal enemy who hates peace, and that is Sanballat. *I am peace*, says the cantor elliptically, *But when I speak, they are for war*, לַמִּלְחָמָה. His words are close to the events which the Nehemiah Testimonies record of Sanballat. Nehemiah wished to build the wall in peace, but the Samarian Governor and his friends plotted together to fight (לְהִלָּחֵם) against Jerusalem (Neh. 4.2 [8]); and the precautions which were required even after the defences were complete (7.1-5a) show that the danger was still perceived as real during the festival.

PSALM 121

Nehemiah 1.11b–2.9

1.[11]Now I was cupbearer to the king. 2.[1]And it came to pass in the month Nisan, in the twentieth year of Artaxerxes the king, when wine was before him, that I took up the wine, and gave it unto the king. Now I had not been *beforetime* sad in his presence. [2]And the king said unto me, Why is thy countenance sad, seeing thou art not sick? this is nothing else but sorrow of heart. [3]And I said unto the king, Let the king live for ever: why should not my countenance be sad, when the city, the place of my fathers' sepulchres, lieth waste, and the gates thereof are consumed with fire? [4]Then the king said unto me, For what dost thou make request? So I prayed to the God of heaven. [5]And I said unto the king, If it please the king, and if thy servant have found favour in thy sight, that thou wouldest send me unto Judah, unto the city of my fathers' sepulchres, that I may build it. [6]And the king said unto me (the queen also sitting by him), For how long shall thy journey be? and when wilt thou return? So it pleased the king to send me; and I set him a time. [7]Moreover I said unto the king, If it please the king, let letters be given me to the governors beyond the river, that they let me pass through, till I come unto Judah;[8] and a letter unto Asaph, the keeper of the king's park, that he may give me timber to make beams for the gates for the castle which appertaineth unto the house, and for the wall of the city, and for the house that I shall enter into.[9] Then I came to the governors beyond the river, and gave them the king's letters. Now the king had sent with me captains of the army and horsemen.

The verses describe Nehemiah's petition to the king, and its granting, through the grace of 'the God of heaven'; and his subsequent journey to Jerusalem, protected from all dangers by a military escort, again under the good hand of God upon him (2.18). The narrative finishes at 2.9: the reaction of Sanballat and Tobiah in 2.10 introduces Nehemiah's need to prospect by night in 2.11. The formula, *And when X and Y heard of it...*, opens further paragraphs at 2.19, 4.1, 6.1, 16. Moved by his leader's tale, the cantor confesses his own faith. Where is his own help to come from? Nehemiah had told of the providential blessings he had enjoyed from the God of heaven; and that means, in plainer speech, *the LORD which made heaven and earth.*

A Song for the Ascents (למעלות)

1   I will lift up mine eyes unto the mountains:
     From whence shall my help come?
2   My help *cometh* from the LORD,
     Which made heaven and earth.
3   He will not suffer thy foot to be moved:
     He that keepeth thee will not slumber.
4   Behold, he that keepeth Israel
     Shall neither slumber not sleep.
5   The LORD is thy keeper:
     The LORD is thy shade upon thy right hand.
6   The sun shall not smite thee by day,
     Nor the moon by night.
7   The LORD shall keep thee from all evil;
     He shall keep thy soul.
8   The LORD shall keep thy going out and thy coming in,
     From this time forth and for evermore.

In the opening verse of both Psalms 121 and 123 the psalmist *lifts up his eyes*, now *to the mountains*, then to God 'sitting in the heavens'; and 125 similarly proclaims, 'As the mountains are round about Jerusalem, So the LORD is round about his people' (v. 2). The mountains are symbols of Yahweh's defence of his people and their city, and that is why the psalmist will lift up his eyes to them.

The realization that the Songs are a single block of writing commends the interpretation of one of the group by others. Otherwise critics find the mountains a problem. Most take them as hostile: either (Gunkel, Mowinckel) as the site of sanctuaries of alien gods, with whom Yahweh is contrasted; or as the abode of brigands (Weiser, Kraus, Anderson, Jacquet [with pitiful tale of the fate of an Anglican bishop and his daughter]). J.T. Willis, 'Psalm 121.1b', takes the question as rhetorical, following the thought of idolatrous shrines. Delitzsch and Dahood lift up their eyes to the heavenly mountain; Eaton thinks, more plausibly, of Yahweh's expected theophany coming over the Mount of Olives (*Kingship*, p. 83).

In the first two verses the cantor speaks for himself, and in intention for all the faithful present; but he is conscious (as is the reader of the Nehemiah Testimony today) that Nehemiah is a leader of rare decisiveness and wisdom, and that the whole enterprise depends on his continuance at the helm. All societies are dependent on the leadership qualities of the few, but in an ancient community like Israel this awareness was enhanced by the religious sense; it was the LORD who had sent Nehemiah, and if the LORD was behind the *aliya*, as he had promised in Deuteronomy 30, he would *keep* Nehemiah *from all evil.* Hence the change at v. 3 to the second person: indeed the LORD's keeping of Nehemiah is set in parallel with his keeping of Israel—*He that keepeth thee will not slumber. Behold, he that keepeth Israel Shall neither slumber nor sleep.* The experiences of Nehemiah 6 are in the psalmist's mind. Sanballat and Geshem had tried to lure him to the plain of Ono, 'they thought to do me mischief' (רעה, 6.2); and there were threats to slay him (6.10): the psalmist responds, *The LORD shall keep thee from all evil* (רע): *He shall keep thy soul/life* (121.7).

The change of person from *I* to *Thou* in v. 3 is the Gordian knot of most exegeses. The standard interpretation sees the setting as a *dialogue*: a father and his son going up to Jerusalem for the pilgrim festival (Seybold), or a priest blessing a pilgrim going back home from the feast (Gunkel, Mowinckel, Weiser, Kraus, Anderson, Allen), or a group of pilgrims encouraging one another *en route* (Kirkpatrick, Jacquet). But two considerations make this unconvincing. First, how is it imagined that such a dialogue could be put into regular use? Did the priest say to the pilgrim, 'Will you please read the first two verses on the card?', like a modern vicar at a baptism service? Mowinckel (*Psalmenstudien,* II, p. 170; V, pp. 47-50) imagines two choirs, one lay, one of priests; Jacquet presupposes a good deal of edifying committal to memory. Secondly, Eaton notes the *weight* of the language: this is the God who *made heaven and earth*, who *keepeth Israel* and will protect the 'pilgrim' *from this time forth for evermore*. Surely such language is not suited to an individual pilgrim: Allen is right to speak of 'scandalous presumption' (though he excuses it)— but it is also scandalous unrealism. Pilgrims no doubt often met the same fate as Anglican bishops.

Eaton and Dahood are more persuasive in seeing the *Thou* as a national leader, for Eaton the king. But even here the dialogue proposal raises difficulties; a single speaker, the leader of a Levitical choir, is speaking with some prophetic licence to a leader whose situation we know quite well.

The story of the caravan's coming produces the feel of a journey in the psalm. The LORD *will not suffer thy foot to be moved*—to slip on the ill-made treacherous paths of the Persian empire. *The LORD is thy shade on thy right hand*: robber bands note the strength of the escort of horsemen and infantry God has provided through Artaxerxes. *The sun shall not smite thee by day, Nor the moon by night*: Nehemiah was travelling in the early summer, when sunstroke would indeed be a peril; and the ancients noted the monthly cycles of some mental and physical illnesses, and ascribed them superstitiously to the moon. *The LORD shall keep thy going out and thy coming in*: each day's travelling has been blessed with Yahweh's protection, from the first step out of the tent to the last step in. But the psalm is not a thanks-giving but a promise. God has watched over leader and expedition in their long journey, and he will continue his providential care per-manently, *From this time forth for evermore.*

The journey motif is widely noted (e.g. by Weiser), and is asso-ciated with the supposed travel of individual pilgrims.

PSALM 122

Nehemiah 2.10-18

[10]And when Sanballat the Horonite, and Tobiah the servant, the Ammonite, heard of it, it grieved them exceedingly, for that there was come a man to seek the welfare of the children of Israel. [11]So I came to Jerusalem, and was there three days. [12]And I arose in the night, I and some few men with me; neither told I any man what my God put into my heart to do for Jerusalem: neither was there any beast with me, save the beast that I rode upon. [13]And I went out by night by the valley gate, even towards the dragon's well, and to the dung gate, and viewed the walls of Jerusalem, which were broken down, and the gates thereof were consumed with fire. [14]Then I went on to the fountain gate and to the king's pool: but there was no place for the beast that was under me to pass. [15]Then went I up in the night by the brook, and viewed the wall; and I turned back, and entered by the valley gate, and so returned. [16]And the deputies knew not whither I went, or what I did; neither had I as yet told it to the Jews, nor to the priests, nor to the nobles, nor to the deputies, nor to the rest that did the work. [17]Then said I unto them, Ye see the evil case that we are in, how Jerusalem lieth waste, and the gates thereof are burned with fire: come and let us build up the wall of Jerusalem, that we be no more a reproach. [18]And I told them of the hand of my God which was good upon me; as also of the king's words that he had spoken unto me. And they said, Let us rise up and build. So they strengthened their hands for the good *work*.

Nehemiah continues his tale, first the secret nocturnal inspection, then the good spirit of the public meeting; we may leave aside the interesting problems of Jerusalem topography. Sanballat ('the Haranite') is likely to have been concerned as governor of the Samaria *medinta*, hitherto including Jerusalem. Tobiah was 'allied' to the Jerusalem high priesthood (13.4-7), and is also spoken of contemptuously, first as 'the servant' (perhaps a play on his title as 'the king's servant'), and secondly as 'the Ammonite', and so barred from the Temple (Deut. 23.3-5: Neh. 13.1-3); his name suggests that he was (at least half) Jewish. It is their hostility that imposes the need for secrecy. Nehemiah had told of the ruined walls and charred remnants of the old city gates, and the story brings joy to the cantor as he contrasts that picture with the

A Song of the Ascents (המעלות); of David.

1 I was glad when they said unto me,
  We will go (נלך) unto the house of the LORD.

2 Our feet are standing (RV text)
  Within thy gates, O Jerusalem;

3 Jerusalem, that art builded
  As a city that is compact together:

4 Whither the tribes go up, even the tribes of Jah,
  For a testimony unto Israel,
  To give thanks unto the name of the LORD.

5 For there were set thrones for judgement,
  The thrones of the house of David.

6 Pray for the peace of Jerusalem: (RV text)
  May they prosper that love thee!

7 Peace be within thy walls,
  And prosperity within thy palaces.

8 For my brethren and companions' sakes,
  I will now speak peace upon thee (בך).

9 For the sake of the house of the LORD our God
  I will seek thy good.

achievement of the last months. It had begun with Hanani's coming to Susa, and the decision to make *aliya*: *I was glad when they said unto me, We will go unto the house of the LORD.* Having spent all our lives in the east, we were now to see the LORD's famous Temple. We made the long journey, and arrived; and now *Our feet have been standing Within thy gates, O Jerusalem.* The holy city, so long spoken of in the *golah*, is now addressed in an apostrophe of three verses.

The gates that had been burned with fire are now remade and standing (Neh. 7.1-3), a protection against any enemy's sudden attack. But above all Jerusalem has been (re)*builded As a city that is joined up together.* הבנויה does not necessarily imply a *re*building, though it may; but שחברה־לה יחדו does seem to imply this. חבר means to 'unite', 'join together', and is used, for instance, of coupling the curtains of the tabernacle together with clasps of brass (Exod. 26.11, 36.18); in the pual, as here, the two shoulder-pieces of the ephod are 'joined together' (Exod. 28.7, 39.4). So is Jerusalem *joined up together for itself*: the stones that had been scattered over the hillsides have been manhandled back into position, and the breaches filled. There is a limited perimeter complete round the Ophel, the more easterly of the hills of Zion, the area prospected in Nehemiah's moonlit ride. The defences had been completed three weeks before (Neh. 6.15), and the celebratory procession will follow at the close of the festival (Neh. 12.27-43). The psalmist's tone of triumphant *thanks unto the name of the LORD* is not difficult to understand.[1]

What these gates and walls symbolize so graphically is the resumption of Israel's (practical) independence. Hitherto, for many years, Jews have had to take their disputes to foreign courts—Sanballat's in Samaria for the northern villages, under the dubious influence of Tobiah, Geshem's for the southern ones. But now a Jew, Nehemiah, has been appointed Tirshatha (Neh. 8.9), and Judah is to be a separate *medinta*, as it was briefly under Sheshbazzar and Zerubbabel. So God's law will be the law of the land, as it was when *the thrones for judgement were set, The thrones of the house of David.* At first David (2 Sam. 15.1-6), and later Solomon (1 Kgs 3.16-28), presided alone; but in time the royal family shared the duties of judging the community between them (Jer. 21.11-12), and there were *thrones of the house of David* set up for the purpose. Now once more the psalmist delights to see the population streaming into the city, and going, when necessary, to Nehemiah for rulings (Neh. 5, 13). It is only a rump of Judahites and Benjaminites, so he does not like to say 'the tribes of Israel', as in pre-exilic times; so he calls them, with a conscious archaism, 'the tribes of Jah'. Such a *going up* to the festival, and to the national courts of judgment, was a *testimony* (עדות) *unto Israel*: the term is often used, as in Ps. 81.5, of a festal ordinance intended to symbolize the nation's unity under Yahweh.

The cantor calls on the crowds to pray for Yahweh's protection for their renewed city, with a series of word-plays: שאלו שלום ירושלם; שלום, שלוה, שלום, ישליו, all echoing the supposed 'peace–prosperity' etymology of Jeru*salem*. But the call to prayer is not vacuous piety. 'I am peace', the psalmist had said in 120.7, 'But when I speak they are for war'; and so had Sanballat and his crew shown themselves in Nehemiah 4 and 6. Nor can there be שלום without prosperity: good harvests, and an end to debt, and to the enslavement of Jew by Jew, and ordered trade, and normality. So all who care for her are to call down *peace on Jerusalem: peace within thy walls, And prosperity within thy towers.* חילך and ארמנותיך were a pair in Ps. 48.14, and as

1.   R.R. Marrs, 'Psalm 122, 3.4: A New Reading', *Bib* 68 (1987), pp. 106-109, writes, 'The significance of הבנויה is unclear... the significance of the construction of Jerusalem is inconsequential...'. So the New Reading becomes a new writing of the psalm.

there אַרְמְן means a tower built into the wall rather than RV's 'palace', of which there were not too many standing in 445 BCE.

In a few days the faithful will have gone back to their villages, and Jerusalem will be left almost a ghost town: 'the city was wide and large: but the people were few therein, and the houses were not builded' (Neh. 7.4). The citizens of this hopeful *civitas Dei* will be a few hundreds: those who have come up from Susa with Nehemiah, *my brethren*, and the old inhabitants and any new settlers (Neh. 11.1-2), *my companions.* In Neh. 4.17 the governor's mobile reserve consists of his 'brethren', his 'servants', and 'the men of the guard which followed me': it is likely that these are the members of his expedition, and comprise his (extended) family, their staff and the Persian escort. Finally the psalmist takes up his leader's aspiration. Neh. 2.10, Sanballat and Tobiah were grieved 'that there was come a man to seek the good (לבקש טבה ל) of the children of Israel': Ps. 122.9, *For the sake of the house of the LORD our God, I will seek thy good* (אבקשה טוב לך). Between them, they will see the place back on its feet.

The annual pilgrim feasts were occasions of joy (Isa. 30.29), especially Tabernacles, *the* feast of Yahweh; and almost all commentators understand 122 as a psalm of joy at such an annual festival: whether by an individual or by a choir (Mowinckel, *Psalmenstudien,* V, pp. 35-36); whether on arrival at the city (Jacquet); or in a procession of worship (Allen); or on departure (Delitzsch). Earlier commentators (Delitzsch, Kirkpatrick, Gunkel, Mowinckel), gave the psalm a late date: the Aramaizing -שׁ is used twice, and the periphrastic עמדות היו recalls a common use in Nehemiah (Kirkpatrick). More modern critics (Eaton, Weiser, Kraus, Anderson) take ישׁבו in v. 5 as a present, *There are set the thrones of judgement,* and ascribe the psalm to the royal period. All cite Isa. 2.3, Jer. 31.6 and Mic. 4.2, where it is said, 'Come ye, and let us go up to the mountain of the LORD, to the house of the God of Jacob', words which recall 122.1b.

There are, however, problems with this interpretation. First, the texts in Isaiah 2 and Micah 4 refer not to Israelites going on חג, but to foreign peoples going up to Jerusalem for the first time; and Jeremiah 31 speaks similarly of Ephraimites. So the situation is in some ways more like the long journey from Susa, and these prophecies may have influenced the psalmist's phrasing. There is an uncomfortableness over the חג view at this point. Gunkel takes it that a group of Diaspora Jews has decided to make the long and dangerous pilgrimage together; hence the announcement, *We will be going...,* and the joy in having done so. But the Law laid down from early times that all Jews were to make the חג three times a year; and for most critics, who assume local pilgrims, the announcement seems unnecessary and the joy exaggerated. The result is, in many commentaries, a feeling of unreal piety; and the question is left unanswered how the song/poem of a group of lay pilgrims found its way into the Bible.

PSALM 123

Nehemiah 2.19-20, 3.33-38

2.[19]But when Sanballat the Horonite, and Tobiah the servant, the Ammonite, and Geshem the Arabian, heard it, they laughed us to scorn, and despised us, and said, What is this thing that ye do? will ye rebel against the king? [20]Then answered I them, and said unto them, The God of heaven, he will prosper us; therefore we his servants will arise and build: but ye have no portion, nor right, nor memorial, in Jerusalem. []

3.[33]But it came to pass that when Sanballat heard that we builded the wall, he was wroth, and took great indignation, and mocked the Jews. [34]And he spake before his brethren, and the army of Samaria, and said, What do these feeble Jews? will they fortify themselves? will they sacrifice? will they make an end in a day? will they revive the stones out of the heaps of rubbish, seeing they are burned?

[35]Now Tobiah the Ammonite was by him, and he said, Even that which they build, if a jackal go up, he shall break down their stone wall. [36]Hear, O our God, for we are despised: and turn back their reproach upon their own head, and give them up to spoiling in a land of captivity: [37]And cover not their iniquity, and let not their sin be blotted out from before thee: for they have provoked *thee* to anger before the builders. [38]So we built the wall; and all the wall was joined together unto half *the height* thereof: for the people had a mind to work.

The section begins with ...סנבלט וישמע, like 2.10, and it recommences similarly at 3.33; the two subsections are held together by the theme of the enemies' laughing to scorn (לעג, 2.19, 3.33) and despising (בוז, 2.19, 3.36) the building. It ends with an imprecation (3.36-37), and a note of progress, like 6.14, 15-16. It is generally agreed that the lists of builders in 3.1-32 are a later insertion, so placed in the light of 2.20 and 3.34-38.[1] The sequence 2.20–3.33 is quite smooth: there is no need for a further note that the building had in fact begun.

Like the previous Songs, Psalm 123 has the cantor speaking in the first person singular; but, as in 122.2, it soon becomes clear that he

1.   See discussion in Kellermann, *Nehemia*, pp. 14-17.

A Song of the Ascents (המעלות)

1 Unto thee do I lift up mine eyes,
   O thou that sittest in the heavens.
2 Behold, as the eyes of servants *look* unto the hand of their master,
   As the eyes of a maiden unto the hand of her mistress;
   So our eyes *look* unto the LORD our God,
   Until he have mercy upon us.
3 Have mercy upon us, O LORD, have mercy upon us:
   For we are exceedingly filled with contempt.
4 Our soul is exceedingly filled
   With the scorning of those that are at ease,
   And with the contempt of the proud.

is spokesman for the community. The opening is similar to 121 as he *lifts up his eyes* (now נשאתי); there to the mountains as symbols of Yahweh's encompassing defence, here to 'the God of heaven' enthroned above. Nehemiah had spoken of 'the hand of my God which was good upon me' (2.18), and this combination of *eyes* and *hand* suggests the following image. Servants wait quietly, and watch the sign from their master's hand that will tell them that they may go to eat or sleep, and it is the same for the maid and her mistress; and so is it with us. The LORD's hand has been much in evidence in the *aliya* from Susa, but enemies remain, to north and east and south: we look for further signs of the hand of divine mercy.

With the additional י- on הישבי, compare the series of similar forms in Psalms 113, 114 (pp. 162, 165). Gunkel notes that there are a number of male servants present, but only a single maidservant, which he takes to be normal in a wealthy home; but girls were cheaper, and might be at harder work in the kitchen. There is an all-male staff awaiting the master in Lk. 12.35. Gunkel rightly says that the master's and mistress's hand signal refreshment, as in Lk. 17.8, rather than command or punishment. He cites Ps. 104.27 and Ecclus 30.30.

But the relation to the governor's testimony is most plain in its common theme of the scorn and contempt of the opposition. The three malcontents 'laughed us to scorn, and despised us' (Neh. 2.19, וילעגו לנו ויבזו עלינו); Sanballat laughed the Jews to scorn (3.33, וילעג על), with his mockery of their feeble building and rebellious aspirations; Tobiah also made contemptuous comments about a jackal knocking the wall down.

Nehemiah had called on God to listen, 'for we are despised' (3.36, היינו בוזה). It is this which draws so similar a cry from the psalmist.

We are exceedingly filled with contempt (בוז), *Our soul is exceedingly filled With the scorning* (הלעג) *of those that are at ease, And the contempt* (הבוז) *of the proud.* While we have been working our hearts out, and going sleepless, these fatcats have *been at ease*, and look down on our work *in their pride.* Perhaps the LORD will *have mercy on us*, and serve them out as he served us out, as the governor said. The psalmist was not disappointed: while Nehemiah was around, there were twelve years of firm government, and peace upon Israel.

The link with Nehemiah 2–3 is quite striking, and suggested, in much the form outlined, by Kirkpatrick; a context in Nehemiah's time is asserted by Jacquet, and considered by Rogerson and McKay, and by Allen. Gunkel also assigns the psalm to the Persian period, but sees it as an individual lament, with the speaker drawing in the thought of other pious Jews: the theme of contempt by the proud is common in communal laments. Kraus similarly says that the speaker makes himself the spokesman of a religious group distressed by mockery of Israel's God, such as is found in Psalms 42 and 115. Mowinckel, *Psalmenstudien,* I, p. 164 and II, p. 133, notes the abrupt move from the quiet opening to the passionate prayer of the last two verses.

Gunkel and Kraus go beyond the text: there is no reference to mockery of Yahweh—'Where is your God?', and so on—but only of scorn and contempt for the community. It is also easier for a public psalm chanted by the national choir at a festival to find a place in the collection of Songs, rather than an individual's cry from the heart. In addition it is perilous to interpret a psalm out of its setting in the Psalter: all commentators note the connection with 121 (*I [will] lift up mine eyes*), and several note the phrase רבת...לה נפשו, which is common to 120.6 and 123.4, and which suggested to Delitzsch a common authorship. 120, 121 and 123 are part of a collection belonging together, and ought not to be treated in isolation. Also the continued serial correspondence with the Nehemiah Testimony is impressive.

Sponsors of the 'religious group' theory do not always explain how psalms like 122 and 123 came first to be composed for group use and then found a place in the Psalter. Jacquet, on 122, does his best to recapture the atmosphere, supposing a party of pilgrims arriving for the feast: he writes, 'the group abandons itself first to *its admiration* at the spectacle of the magnificent City rebuilt by Nehemiah [*sic*]; then it expresses *its piety, its fervent attachment…* The Pilgrim *steps back*, moved' (*Psaumes*, III, pp. 427, 429; my translation, Jacquet's stress).

Allen says similarly, 'A pilgrim, come to worship in Jerusalem at one of the festivals, captures in song his joyful fascination with the scene…' (*Psalms 101– 150*, p. 158). Jacquet and Allen do not feel responsible for explaining how their pilgrim's song/poem has become part of the canon of Scripture. Did he, or a friend, write it down? Did they teach it to the group? Did they use it again the next year? Did they happen to know a priest who was impressed, and asked for a copy? How did one get a song of joyful fascination included in the Bible? It is easy to reply that we do not know; but some explanation is needed if a case is to be made for private effusions becoming public liturgy. On my hypothesis (and on the much criticized theory of Mowinckel), Psalms 122 and 123 were public liturgies from the start. One might then think that both the governor's testimonies and his cantor's responses were preserved in the Temple archive, and that there would be a public demand for a repetition at Tabernacles, 444, and in subsequent years; rather as the Cenotaph ceremony is repeated in Britain each year in November, and congregations sing 'O God, our help in ages past'.

PSALM 124

Nehemiah 4.1-17

But it came to pass, that when Sanballat, and Tobiah, and the Arabians, and the Ammonites, and the Ashdodites, heard that healing went up upon the walls of Jerusalem, *and* that the breaches began to be stopped, then they were very wroth, ²and they conspired all of them together to come and fight against Jerusalem, and to cause confusion therein. ³But we made our prayer unto our God, and set a watch against them day and night, because of them. ⁴And Judah said, The strength of the bearers of burdens is decayed, and there is much rubbish; so that we are not able to build the wall. ⁵And our adversaries said, They shall not know, neither see, till we come into the midst of them, and slay them, and cause the work to cease. ⁶And it came to pass, that when the Jews that dwelt by them came, they said unto us ten times, From all places whence ye shall return, *they will* be upon us. ⁷Therefore set I in the lowest parts of the space behind the wall, in the open places, I even set the people after their families with their swords, their spears, and their bows. ⁸And I looked, and rose up, and said unto the nobles, and to the deputies, Be not ye afraid of them: remember the Lord, which is great and terrible, and fight for your brethren, your sons and your daughters, your wives and your houses. ⁹And it came to pass, when our enemies heard that it was known unto us, and God had brought their counsel to nought, that we returned all of us unto the wall, every one unto his work. ¹⁰And it came to pass from that time forth, that half of my servants wrought in the work, and half of them held the spears, the shields, the bows, and the coats of mail; and the rulers were behind all the house of Judah that builded the wall. ¹¹And they that bare burdens laded themselves, every one of them with one of his hands wrought in the work, and with the other held his weapon; ¹²And the builders, every one had his sword girded by his side, and so builded. And he that sounded the trumpet was by me. ¹³And I said unto the nobles, and to the deputies, and to the rest of the people, The work is great and large, and we are separated upon the wall, one far from another: ¹⁴in what place soever ye hear the sound of the trumpet, resort ye thither unto us; our God shall fight for us. ¹⁵So we wrought in the work: and half of them held the spears from the rising of the morning till the stars appeared. ¹⁶Likewise at the same time said I unto the people, Let every one with his servant lodge within Jerusalem, that in the night they may be a guard to us, and may labour in the day. ¹⁷So neither I, nor my brethren, nor my servants, nor the men of the guard which followed me, none of us put off our clothes, every one *went with* his weapon *to* the water.

A Song of the Ascents (המעלות)

1 If it had not been the LORD who was on our side,
  Let Israel now say,
2 If it had not been the LORD who was on our side,
  When men rose up against us:
3 Then they had swallowed us up alive,
  When their wrath was kindled against us:
4 Then the waters had overwhelmed us,
  The stream had gone over our soul:
5 Then the proud waters had gone over our soul.
6 Blessed be the LORD,
  Who hath not given us as a prey unto their teeth:
7 Our soul is escaped as a bird out of the snare of the fowlers:
  The snare is broken, and we are escaped.
8 Our help is in the name of the LORD,
  Who made heaven and earth.

The unit is rather longer than those hitherto, but it is printed as a single paragraph in RV, and is treated as a unit in the commentaries, being the narrative of a single enterprise. It opens with the familiar 'But [it came to pass that] when X and Y heard...' (2.10, 19, 3.33): the next verse, 5.1, begins a different incident.

Nehemiah was as religious a general as Oliver Cromwell, and with more reason, for his defence force was so weak. In the hour of crisis 'we made our prayer unto our God' (Neh. 4.3), and the leader's pep-talk began, 'Be not ye afraid of them: remember the Lord, which is great and terrible' (4.8). He could promise his men, 'Our God shall fight for us' (לנו, 4.14), and when the wall was finished, it was clear that 'this work was wrought of our God' (6.16). It was therefore entirely natural for the cantor to open his psalm, *If the LORD had not been on our side* (לנו), *Let Israel now say, If the LORD had not been on our side, When men rose up against us, Then they had swallowed us up alive*. Sanballat and Tobiah, and their Arabian, Ammonite and Ashdodite levies, had risen up against Israel, and had been 'very wroth' (יחר מאד); as the psalmist says, *their wrath was kindled against us* (בחרות אפם לנו). Judah had said, 'The strength of the bearers of burdens is decayed' (Neh. 4.4), but Israel may now say something more happy. It had seemed all too likely that the enemy would come upon them suddenly and slay them, as they planned in secret (Neh. 4.2, 5), and that they should *swallow us up alive*. But 'God had brought their counsel to nought' (Neh. 4.9), by revealing their plots; with him *on our side, The snare is broken, and we are escaped.*

The psalm text fits the Nehemiah story well. Kirkpatrick says, 'The Psalm then may be regarded as a thanksgiving for the deliverance recorded in Neh. iv.7-23 [Heb. 1–17], the whole of which passage should be studied in connexion with it' (*The Book of Psalms*, p. 744); and Kirkpatrick did not add that the *scorn/contempt* theme of Psalm 123 fitted the *preceding* unit of Nehemiah. But a general scepsis with precise historical contexts has overshadowed the twentieth century, and even when Nehemiah is considered (Anderson, Jacquet), there are other possibilities—the Exodus (Eaton), the Return, or any of many crises.

However, the strongly Aramaizing language, noted by Delitzsch and many, sites the psalm after the Exile. אֲזַי ,לוּלֵי, -שֶׁ for אָז (here alone in the Old Testament, but found in Murabba'at, and in Aramaic inscriptions), the final ה on נַחְלָה (*Milel* according to Delitzsch, Aramaic emphatic according to Seybold, *Die Wallfahrtspsalmen*, p. 40), זֵידוֹנִים (also a hapax), formed like גֵּאיוֹנִים in 123.4: all mark the psalm as late. The liveliness of the thanksgiving bespeaks a recent and surprising deliverance, and Nehemiah's will be one of few such in the post-exile century. Kirkpatrick is right to note the numerous points in common with Nehemiah 4; and the series of correspondences between the Songs and the Nehemiah Testimony seem to confirm his conclusion.

The ascription to David is lacking in three Hebrew MSS, in LXX[A] and other versions; it is a late guess, inferred perhaps from the similar threat of drowning in the Davidic Psalms 18 and 69.

As elsewhere in the Songs (servants and handmaiden, vine and olive branches) the psalmist finds two related images for his theme. Israel had inherited creation myths in which God triumphed over a water-monster, Leviathan (Ps. 74) or Rahab (Ps. 89); and in both these psalms such monsters symbolize the powers of chaos still active in enemy armies. So here the enemy all but *swallowed us up alive*, we were almost *given as a prey unto their teeth*; as Gunkel says, it takes a monster to swallow one down, skin, hair and all. But the monsters were *water*-monsters, threatening to flood the land: but for God, *the waters had overwhelmed us, The stream had gone over our soul, Then the proud waters had gone over our soul.* שְׁטָפוּנוּ, *overwhelmed us*, recalls Isaiah's prophecy of the king of Assyria's coming like a flood in Isa. 8.7-8, and the pride of the waves is stayed in Job 38.11. The theme of creation is present to the psalmist's mind, for he ends his poem, *Our help is in the name of the LORD, Who made heaven and earth*; indeed the theme is in his head all through the sequence, for the same words recur in 121.2 and 134.3.

Creation was a theme of the autumn festival, which I am arguing to have been the setting for the Songs; but our psalmist is more at ease with homely images—the servants in their master's dining room, vine and olive branches, grass on the rooftop. So here the language of prey and teeth suggests the more familiar sight of a fowler's trap: the bird, drawn by a bait, lands on the wooden base and brings the net over its head. No doubt many an ancient Papageno so plied his trade, and a passer-by might see the pitiful winged creature trying in vain to escape; but now and then its endeavours, and the limitations of work-manship, might give it deliverance. So here have we been marvel-lously delivered: *Our soul is escaped as a bird out of the snare of the fowlers;* Sanballat's *snare is broken, and we are escaped.*

The psalm is generally categorized as a communal thanksgiving, which indeed it is (*Let Israel now say*); but this then raises problems for some, as the category is rare. Allen, following Crüsemann, postulates a group thanksgiving of a personal kind which has been adapted by v. 1 to national use. But this seems unnecessarily com-plicated, and depends on the classification of other psalms (94, 118) as individual; for the latter see pp. 182-91. Mowinckel, *Psalmenstudien,* II, pp. 5, 131, 175-76, notes the autumn festal themes in the psalm—creation, the threat of water chaos, the gathering of enemies and their frustration by divine grace.

PSALM 125

Nehemiah 5.1-19

Then there arose a great cry of the people and of their wives against their brethren the Jews. [2]For there were that said, We, our sons and our daughters, are many: but let us get corn, that we may eat and live. [3]Some also there were that said, We are mortgaging our fields, and our vineyards, and our houses: let us get corn, because of the dearth. [4]There were also that said, We have borrowed money for the king's tribute *upon* our fields and our vineyards. [5]Yet now our flesh is as the flesh of our brethren, our children as their children; and, lo, we bring into bondage our sons and our daughters to be servants, and some of our daughters are brought into bondage *already*: neither is it in our power to help it; for other men have our fields and our vineyards. [6]And I was very angry when I heard their cry and these words. [7]Then I consulted with myself, and contended with the nobles and with the deputies, and said unto them, Ye exact usury, every one of his brother. And I held a great assembly against them. [8]And I said unto them, We, after our ability, have redeemed our brethren the Jews, which were sold unto the heathen; and would ye even sell your brethren, and should they be sold unto us? Then held they their peace, and found never a word. [9]Also I said, The thing that ye do is not good: ought ye not to walk in the fear of our God, because of the reproach of the heathen our enemies? [10]And I likewise, my brethren and my servants, do lend them money and corn on usury. I pray you, Let us leave off this usury. [11]Restore, I pray you, to them even this day, their fields, their vineyards, their oliveyards, and their houses, also the hundredth part of the money, and of the corn, the wine, and the oil, that ye exact of them. [12]Then said they, We will restore them, and will require nothing of them; so will we do, even as thou sayest. Then I called the priests, and took an oath of them, that they should do according to this promise. [13]Also I shook out my lap, and said, So God shake out every man from his house, and from his labour, that performeth not this promise; even thus be he shaken out, and emptied. And all the congregation said, Amen, and praised the Lord. And the people did according to this promise. [14]Moreover from the time that I was appointed to be their governor in the land of Judah, from the twentieth year even unto the two and thirtieth year of Artaxerxes the king, *that is,* twelve years, I and my brethren have not eaten the bread of the governor. [15]But the former governors that were before me laid burdens upon the people, and took of them bread and wine, at the rate of forty shekels of silver; yea, even their servants lorded over the people. But so did not I, because of the fear of God. [16]Yea, also I continued in the work of this wall, neither bought we any land: and all my servants were gathered thither unto the work. [17]Moreover there were at my table of the Jews and the deputies an hundred and fifty men, beside those that came unto us from among the heathen that were round about us. [18]Now that which was prepared for one day was one ox and six choice sheep; also fowls were prepared for me, and once in ten days store of all sorts of wine: yea, for all this I demanded not the bread of the governor, because the bondage was heavy upon this people. [19]Remember unto me, O my God, for good, all that I have done for this people.

Psalm 125

A Song of the Ascents (המעלות).

1   They that trust in the LORD
Are as mount Zion, which cannot be moved, but abideth for ever.

2   As the mountains are round about Jerusalem,
So the LORD is round about his people,
From this time forth and for evermore.

3   For the sceptre of wickedness shall not rest upon the lot of the righteous;
That the righteous put not forth their hands unto iniquity.

4   Do good, O LORD, unto those that be good,
And to them that are upright in their hearts.

5   But as for such as turn aside unto their crooked ways,
The LORD shall lead them forth with the workers of iniquity.
Peace be upon Israel.

The Nehemiah story is again a rather long unit, compared with the opening ones; but it is a single story, a continuous paragraph in RV, and it closes with a short prayer (5.19), like 6.14 or the four prayers in ch. 13. However there is a revealing detail in 5.14: the narrator looks back on the events from a vantage point (at least) twelve years later, and speaks defensively of his large subsidies contributed over this period to the public good. It would seem likely therefore that the original narrative in ch. 5, told soon after the event, consisted of vv. 1-13, perhaps with the closing prayer in v. 19. This tale could be repeated at the annual festival during Nehemiah's governorship, with suitable additions; and at the end of his time it was expanded with vv. 14-18, an account of his persevering generosity. In this way we should have a much shorter original story, more in line with 1.1-11a; and an easier understanding of how the Nehemiah Testimony came to suffer so many later expansions.

The situation underlying the psalm is a little more complex than with the earlier Songs. There is a heathen power threatening the liberty of God's *people*, *Israel*, spoken of as *the sceptre of wickedness*.

The people exercising this sceptre are *the workers of iniquity* of v. 5. The sceptre of wickedness is not being exercised at the moment—it is not said that it *shall not rest upon the lot of the righteous for ever*, or that it *shall rest no longer*—but it is felt as a potent menace. *The lot* (גורל) *of the righteous* is the Land of Israel, distributed by Joshua by lot in Josh. 14-19, and for the moment *the righteous*, that is God-fearing Israelites, are holding on to the sceptre for all they are worth.

These God-fearing Israelites are spoken of in various ways. They are *the righteous* in v. 3, *the good* in v. 4, and *they that trust in the LORD* in v. 1. However, they are not quite identifiable with the LORD's *people* (v. 2), *Israel* (v. 5); for there are also some rather less God-fearing Israelites around. The psalmist is conscious that the threat of foreign domination, or the godless ways associated with it, may entice *the righteous* to *put forth their hands unto iniquity* (v. 3). In that case they would of course be *righteous* no more; and in fact some of them are righteous no more, but *turn aside unto their crooked ways* (המטים עקלקלותם, *bend their crookednesses*), and their fate will be to end up with the heathen *workers of iniquity*. *The LORD will* in fact *make them to go* (יוליכם) *with* the latter; that is, they will be expelled from the community of Israel, and have to live among the heathen.

This contrast of the *straight* (ישרים) with the *crooked* explains the emphasis in v. 1, and the connection of vv. 1-2 with vv. 3-5. *They that trust in the LORD* are having difficulty in holding the line. The less godly are a power in the land, and may get their way. It needs therefore to be stressed that the good are resolute: they are *as mount Zion, which cannot be moved, but abideth for ever.* The contrast is expressed verbally: the faithful are like mount Zion which cannot be *moved* (לא־ימוט); the unfaithful are those who *move* (המתים) crooked-nesses. For good measure it can be added that God is the same. If the righteous are *as mount Zion, the LORD is round about his people*, defending them, *as the mountains are round about Jerusalem.* As usual in the Songs, Israel and Jerusalem are pretty closely identified.

It will be seen that this situation of the psalm is that of Nehemiah 5. Jerusalem/Israel is independent, but only just: Sanballat and Geshem and their allies are waiting armed somewhere behind Mount Scopus, or the Mount of Olives, hoping for their chance. Before Nehemiah arrived they ruled *the lot of the righteous* with *the sceptre of wicked-ness*: the psalmist feels a loathing for their neglect of God's Torah such as an Iranian mullah feels for the American Satan beloved of the

Shah before the Islamic Revolution. Such a loathing is sustained and deepened by the fact that *wickedness* may be reintroduced at any time; if *they that trust in the LORD* relax their resolution and *are moved*.

Unfortunately not all Israelites are *upright in their hearts*. A fair number of the wealthy, החרים והסגנים, had paid no attention to God's Torah, but had *put forth their hands unto iniquity*: they had lent money so that the poor could pay their taxes and feed their families, and they had charged usury and enslaved the children of the bankrupt. Nehemiah's indignation at such godless cruelty had been natural, and effective. He had summoned an assembly, shamed the sinners, and extracted an oath of partial restitution. But the psalmist is well aware that this may not be the end of the matter: such people may well *bend their crookednesses* again. Some of them are allied with Tobiah, and have been in correspondence with him (Neh. 6); if a crisis should arise and the chips be down, these people may well side with the enemy; in which case we still do not need to worry. *The LORD shall lead them forth*, Tobiah and his friends, *with the workers of iniquity*, Sanballat and Geshem; and with *the LORD round about his people*, there will still be *peace upon Israel*.

Nehemiah prayed that God would remember unto him for good (לטובה) all that he had done for this people. His psalmist prays, *Do good, O LORD, unto those that be good* (היטיבה לטובים).

Kirkpatrick and Jacquet again set the psalm against a Nehemiah background, the former stressing the links with Nehemiah 6, the latter citing Neh. 5.9; other commentators are reluctant to give a historical setting. Delitzsch notes late Hebraisms: ישרים בלבותם for ישרי־לב, the article in פעלי לא האון, למען for פן. Seybold, *Die Wallfahrtspsalmen*, p. 40, adds עולתה as an Aramaic emphatic. Generally critics see the *sceptre of wickedness* as that of an occupying power, though this is not said in v. 3, and the opposite is implied in v. 5a. Kraus specifies what is suggested by many—that the occupying power is Persia; but the feeling towards the Persian empire is generally rather positive in the Old Testament. Allen cites Neh. 9.36-37 as an exception to this. While the situation presupposed by the psalm fits Nehemiah 5–6 well, there could be other similar relationships in other contexts. It is its placing between 124 and 126 that suggests the Nehemiah 5 background so forcibly. The debate whether 125 is a psalm of confidence or a communal lament seems vapid in face of a real and complex historical setting.

PSALM 126

Nehemiah 6.1-14

Now it came to pass, when it was reported to Sanballat and Tobiah, and to Geshem the Arabian, and to the rest of our enemies, that I had builded the wall, and that there was no breach left therein; (though even unto that time I had not set up the doors in the gates); ²that Sanballat and Geshem sent unto me, saying, Come let us meet together in *one of* the villages in the plain of Ono. But they thought to do me mischief. ³And I sent messengers unto them, saying, I am doing a great work, so that I cannot come down: why should the work cease, while I leave it, and come down to you? ⁴And they sent unto me four times after this sort; and I answered them after the same manner. ⁵Then sent Sanballat his servant unto me in like manner with an open letter in his hand; ⁶wherein was written, It is reported among the nations, and Gashmu saith it, that thou and the Jews think to rebel; for which cause thou buildest the wall: and thou wouldest be their king, according to these words. ⁷And thou also hast appointed prophets to preach of thee at Jerusalem, saying, There is a king in Judah: and now shall it be reported to the king according to these words. Come now therefore, and let us take counsel together. ⁸Then I sent unto him, saying, There are no such things done as thou sayest, but thou feignest them out of thine own heart. ⁹For they all would have made us afraid, saying, Their hands shall be weakened from the work, that it be not done. But now, *O God,* strengthen thou my hands. ¹⁰And I went unto the house of Shemaiah the son of Delaiah the son of Mehetabel, who was shut up; And he said, Let us meet together in the house of God, within the temple, and let us shut the doors of the temple: for they will come to slay thee; yea, in the night will they come to slay thee. ¹¹And I said, should such a man as I flee? and who is there, that, being such as I, would go into the temple to save his life? I will not go in. ¹²And I discerned, and, lo, God had not sent him: but he pronounced this prophecy against me: and Tobiah and Sanballat had hired him. ¹³For this cause was he hired, that I should be afraid, and do so, and sin, and that they might have matter for an evil report, that they might reproach me. ¹⁴Remember, O my God, Tobiah and Sanballat according to these their works, and also the prophetess Noadiah, and the rest of the prophets, that would have put me in fear.

The Nehemiah passage opens with the familiar, 'Now it came to pass that when it was heard (נשמע) to Sanballat...' (cf. 2.10, 19; 3.33; 4.1), and it closes with the first of the governor's imprecations (cf. 13.29).

A Song of the Ascents (המעלות)
1   When the LORD turned again the fortunes (שׁיבת) of Zion,
    We were like unto them that dream.
2   Then was our mouth filled with laughter,
    And our tongue with singing:
    Then said they among the nations,
    The LORD hath done great things for them.
3   The LORD hath done great things for us;
    Whereof we are glad.
4   Turn again our fortunes, O LORD,
    As the streams in the South.
5   They that sow in tears shall reap in joy.
6   Though he goeth on his way weeping, bearing the measure of seed;
    He shall come again with joy, bringing his sheaves *with him.*

It comprises two little incidents, both organized by Sanballat and Tobiah with the aim of discrediting Nehemiah. They are driven to this because the wall is now continuous, and all that remains is to make and set the wooden gates in their place. We shall hear in the next verses the official statement that the wall was complete (6.15), and that 'all the heathen that were about us saw, and were much cast down in their own eyes: for they perceived that this work was wrought of our God' (6.16).

The Revised Version renders v. 9b as a prayer; but the English *O God* is lacking in Hebrew, nor is the verb *strengthen* used elsewhere of God. Blenkinsopp takes חזק as an infinitive absolute, and renders, *But I strengthened my resolve the more*, following LXX, Syriac and Vulgate. He takes 6.1-14 as a single unit.

It is this unlooked for achievement which inspires the paean of joy in Psalm 126. After so long, after nearly a century and a half, *the LORD* has *turned the fortunes of Zion.* In 587 BCE it was said of Jerusalem, 'Raze it, raze it, Even to the foundations thereof' (137.7); and now David's city of Zion is encircled by a wall once more, largely of the same stones. בשׁוב יהוה את־שׁיבת ציון means 'When Yahweh turned the turning point of Zion', and is not related to שׁבית, 'captivity', as it is taken in RV. The vivid simile beautifully describes the elation produced by the sight; *We were like unto them that dream,* so happy we could not believe it was real (cf. Isa. 29.7-8; Acts 12.9). The religious psalmist gives all the credit to the divine providence; we might ascribe something to the resolution of governor and people. *Possunt quia posse videntur.*

Many commentators place the psalm after 538 BCE (Delitzsch, Eaton, Kraus, Rogerson and McKay, Allen), noting the joy of the returning exiles in Ezra 3 and the disappointments of Isaiah 59, Haggai 2 and Ezra 4–5. For Kirkpatrick these matters lie in the past, and the present situation is that of Nehemiah and Ezra (taken to be contemporary). The *dreaming*, the *laughter*, the *singing*, the *gladness*, the *joy*, are so immediate that Kirkpatrick is to be preferred: something dramatic has just happened, which has caused *the nations* to say, *The LORD hath done great things for them*. It is more likely that neighbouring peoples were impressed by the refortification of Zion than by the rebuilding of the Temple; indeed Nehemiah says they were (6.16).

Allen notes the occurrence of שיבת in an eighth-century inscription from Seiphire, meaning 'the restoration [of my father's house]'.

The nation's fortunes have been reversed over a few months, from foreign rule and exploitation to independence and the Law of God, from abject weakness to a fortress of strength. The psalmist catches the change of the people's mood that goes with this amazing reversal: *Then was our mouth filled with laughter, And our tongue with singing*. Mowinckel recalls the atmosphere in Norwegian churches on the Sunday after 8 May 1945; if Norwegians were so moved, what may we expect from what Gunkel calls 'the hot-blooded Hebrew'? With joy too comes pride. *Then said they among the nations, The LORD hath done great things for them*. For a people that has been so much despised (123.3-4), and which has heard so many jeers, 'Where is now thy God?' (42.4, 115.2), it is no light matter to know that they are once more respected. This intoxicating thought is taken up by Nehemiah himself in the following recital, at 6.16.

The great stone edifice evokes joy and pride, but not complacency. Too much hangs on the personality of the governor, who could be a target for assassins, or be demoralized by the fear of them (6.1-14); and the possibility of a sudden attack has receded but not disappeared (7.1-3). So although *the LORD has turned again the fortunes of Zion* with the coming of the new *aliya*, we still need to pray, *Turn again our fortunes, O LORD*. We need decent harvests (126.5-6), and houses to be built (127.1-2), and children to live in them (127.3-5, 128.3-4), and above all peace upon Israel (128.6); and forgiveness for our sins (130), and in time a horn to spring forth unto David (132). The long period of desolation we have suffered is *like the wadis in the Negeb*, dried up and barren through the insistent summer; but as Yahweh suddenly sends his blessing in the autumn rains, and turns them to flowing streams banked with flowers and verdure, so may he *turn again our fortunes*.

Gunkel followed Duhm in understanding the whole psalm as referring to the future. Verse 4a was almost identical to v. 1a, and such similar wording must refer to the same matter; and since v. 4 was a prayer for the future, vv. 1-3 should be taken in the same way, their perfects being prophetic. But most commentators have taken vv. 1-3 as referring to the past, and the rest to the future; as Eaton says, Gunkel's view strains the Hebrew (הגדיל). Both sides appeal to Psalm 85, where שבת שבות יעקב (v. 2) is followed by שובנו (v. 5); but the opening of the psalm is best understood with Eaton as an appeal for a turn of fortune (v. 5) in the light of God's having forgiven Israel and turned its fortunes in the past (vv. 2-4: so Goulder, *Korah*, pp. 102-108). Dahood and Jacquet take the whole psalm as referring to the past, the former with a Phoenician form of the perfect for MT's imperative שובה in v. 4.

It was the custom in Egypt, and perhaps widely in the ancient Near East, to weep when sowing—a survival of the sympathetic magic whereby the gods might be prevailed upon to send heavenly tears of rain. Certainly Israel has *gone on his way weeping* since the days of Nebuchadnezzar; but in a manner of speaking he has been *bearing the measure of seed* which has now borne fruit in today's harvest of success. The wall was completed on 25 Elul (Neh. 6.15), three weeks before Tabernacles; so its celebration coincided with the Harvest Festival (Neh. 12.27-43; Neh. 8). Hence the imagery of vv. 5-6: *They that sow in tears shall reap in joy.* The *sheaves* which are now being *brought* in with such *rejoicing* are a powerful symbol of a broader divine blessing. The seed sown in grief for the fallen city, and in the endurance of poverty, and in the disappointments of generations, have now become a harvest of happiness and hope. So did the tear-soaked seed of the Holocaust issue in the proud, defiant and triumphant Israel of 1948.

Egyptian sowing customs are associated with the death of Osiris; the discovery of the Ras Shamra myth texts has confirmed the existence of a similar dying and rising god in Syria. Weiser suggests that traces of such Canaanite religion have survived in Israelite life, but there is no clear evidence for such a practice in Israel outside this text, and Kraus notes that G. Dalman (*Arbeit und Sitte*, III, 43-44) denies it in more modern times. Kraus and others propose a 'prophetic speaker' for vv. 5-6, with an old proverb underlying it; but psalms are better attributed to a single speaker. The psalmist often assumes authority to speak blessing for his community (121.3-8, 122.6-8, 125.5b, 128.4-6).

משך, earlier taken to mean a *trail* of seed (Amos 9.13, BDB), is usually understood to mean a *leather bag* (KB). Perhaps we should suspect a play on words. Blenkinsopp thinks that Nehemiah's prayers to be remembered 'for good' (לטובה) carry a pun on the name Tobiah. In 120.5 the psalmist grieved that he must sojourn in משך; maybe the tears of the משך seed-time are now over with the gladness of an Israelite harvest-home.

PSALM 127

Nehemiah 6.15–7.5a

6.[15]So the wall was finished in the twenty-fifth *day* of *the month* Elul, in fifty and two days. [16]And it came to pass, when all our enemies heard *thereof*, that all the heathen that were about us saw, and were much cast down in their own eyes: for they perceived that this work was wrought of our God. [17]Moreover in those days the nobles of Judah sent many letters unto Tobiah, and *the letters* of Tobiah came unto them. [18]For there were many in Judah sworn unto him, because he was the son in law of Shechaniah the son of Arah; and his son Jehohanan had taken the daughter of Meshullam the son of Berechiah to wife. [19]Also they spake of his good deeds before me, and reported my words to him. *And* Tobiah sent letters to put me in fear.

7.[1]Now it came to pass, when the wall was built, and I had set up the doors, and the porters and the singers and the Levites were appointed, [2]that I gave my brother Hanani, and Hananiah the governor of the castle, charge over Jerusalem: for he was a faithful man, and feared God above many. [3]And I said unto them, Let not the gates of Jerusalem be opened until the sun be hot: and while they stand *on guard*, let them shut the doors, and bar ye them: and appoint watches of the inhabitants of Jerusalem, every one in his watch, and every one *to be* over against his house. [4]Now the city was wide and large: but the people were few therein, and the houses were not builded. [5]And my God put into my heart to gather together the nobles, and the deputies, and the people.

Nehemiah 6.1-14 closes satisfyingly with Nehemiah's prayer (6.14), and the new episode opens, first with a statement of the wall's completion (6.15), and then with the now familiar gambit, 'And it came to pass, when all our enemies heard...' (6.16; cf. 2.10, 19, 3.33, 4.1, 6.1). Kellermann, Williamson and Blenkinsopp all draw a line at the end of ch. 6, but this is to ignore the *form* (in the technical, German sense) of a Nehemiah episode. Each of the sections of the Nehemiah Testimony has described a minor crisis, and the way in which the governor responded to it. Nehemiah 6.15-19 fails to conform to this form: Tobiah's correspondence with the nobles constitutes a threat to security, which Nehemiah needs to counter by precautions over the gates. But he cannot have peace with a disloyal nobility and a

A Song of the Ascents (המעלות): of Solomon.
1   Except the LORD build the house,
     They labour in vain that build it:
     Except the LORD keep the city,
     The watchman waketh but in vain.
2   It is vain for you that ye rise up early, and so late take rest,
     And eat the bread of toil:
     For so he giveth unto his beloved sleep (RV text).
3   Lo, children are an heritage of the LORD:
     And the fruit of the womb is *his* reward.
4   As arrows in the hand of a mighty man,
     So are the children of youth.
5   Happy is the man that hath his quiver full of them:
     They shall not be ashamed,
     When they speak with their enemies in the gate.

skeleton population of the city; so he calls a public meeting of the nobles (החרים), the deputies and the people, to plan an increase in the number of inhabitants. In this way 6.15–7.5a can be seen as a coherent unit, following the form found regularly through the book, and of a more normal length. It begins with the news of the wall's completion, it develops with Tobiah's plots with the nobles, and it ends with Nehemiah's barring the gates and calling an assembly. So there will be no more secret correspondence in the dark, and the upper classes are included in making plans for the city's future. The section also closes with the climax of a divine initiative, 'my God put into my heart to gather the nobles...'.

It is agreed that the Nehemiah Testimony broke off at 7.5a, with the great list of those returning (= Ezra 2); it is not so clear at which word it ceased, and Williamson ends it with להתיחש, 'that they might be reckoned by genealogy'. But the repopulating according to Neh. 11.1-2 was organized by lot, not by families, which form the structure of 7.6-72. Nehemiah did not call the meeting to make a census, but to gain public support for some repopulation policy, and especially the support of the wavering upper class; he needed tact as well as firmness, and his democratic instincts were his community's salvation.

Williamson also suggests that the vague and common 'in those days' (v. 17) masks the fact that Tobiah's plotting may have taken place much later, and that the story has been inserted here because of its similarity to 6.1-9 and 6.10-14. But the Nehemiah Testimony has hitherto followed a chronological sequence, and it would be most easily understandable if Tobiah's attempts to subvert Nehemiah were taken before he became an established, successful and popular governor.

Psalm 127 makes a felicitous response to these events. Nehemiah
has been building a wall, and he is about to rebuild a good number of
houses; but there are enemies without with friends within, and the
whole enterprise might come to disaster in a moment. *Except the
LORD build the house, they labour in vain that build it.* The governor
has completed the wall, and set the gates in place, and put Temple staff
to guard them, and his brother to be in command, and watches from
the inhabitants for each length of the fortifications by their own home;
but a sudden attack on a dark night and all could be lost like Troy.
Except the LORD keep the city, The watchman waketh but in vain.

Jews under Nehemiah went to bed late if at all, and rose betimes;
they built, but also must harvest their crops; their return from their
fields was often so small that they defaulted on their debts, and had
begun to sell their children in order to eat. Yet all these expedients
might be useless unless Yahweh gave them his blessing. *It is vain for
you that ye rise up early, and so late sit down* to a meal, *And eat the
bread of toil: so he gives his favourites sleep.* Those whom the LORD
loves he blesses with their daily bread, and their nightly sleep also:
take no anxious thought for the morrow, what ye shall eat; for the
morrow shall take care of itself.

A setting for Psalm 127 in Nehemiah's time is hinted by Delitzsch, and asserted
by Kirkpatrick, with repeated citations of Neh. 7.1-4; but Gunkel categorized it as a
pair of brief Wisdom psalms (vv. 1-2, 3-5), and smiled that there should still be
those speculating on a historical setting. Weiser, Keet and Seybold are among those
who follow Gunkel in splitting the psalm: most critics have thought this unnecessary,
but have accepted the Wisdom label—Mowinckel, *The Psalms in Israel's Worship*,
II, p. 114, tries to explain how such a wisdom psalm became part of the autumnal
liturgy. However not many of the standard Wisdom themes come in the psalm (cf.
Allen): there is no requirement of the righteous, nor contrast with the wicked, for
example. With so many echoes of Neh. 7.1-5, one does not have to argue for the
unity of the psalm. In two articles, 'House/City' (1986) and 'Sleep... Security'
(1995), D.E. Fleming argues that the *house* is the Temple and the *city* Jerusalem,
and the psalm is a unity.

The ascription to Solomon is absent from the LXX, and is a late guess: *the LORD
built the house* in Solomon's time, and he was named Yahweh's *beloved*, יְדִידְיָהּ, in
2 Sam. 12.25. The Hebrew of v. 2c is rather loose. כֵּן, 'so', is unclear; perhaps a
gesture is implied, the hands raised in prayer, as (with a different gesture), 'The
LORD do *so* to me, and more also...'; but we do better not to accept LXX's כִּי or אָכֵן,
which is an attempt to make the text easier. שֵׁנָא, 'sleep', is naturally the object of
giveth, and makes good sense: you do not need to worry and stay up all night—God
will look after you and give you your rest as well. RVmg gives 'in sleep', which is a

strain linguistically. For numerous proposals to understand the words see Keet and Allen: J.A. Emerton's 1974 article is worthy of mention, rendering שנא as 'great honour'. Suggested links with the children in v. 3 are mistaken; children are often conceived in bed, but not in sleep.

The future strength of Jerusalem will indeed be its people, and their number depends in the long run on children, not imported adults. But here too we are totally in Yahweh's hands: *Lo, children are an heritage from the LORD*, a gift, a legacy undeserved from heaven. Sons and daughters, *the fruit of the womb*, are a windfall, *a reward*. Israelites thought that children conceived when the father was young, *the children of youth*, grew up the most strongly, as Jacob called Reuben 'the beginning of my strength' (Gen. 49.3); and it might well be that older children did do better, before their mothers were exhausted. The psalmist has an image of war in his mind. Such sons are *as arrows in the hand of a warrior*. He has one or two of them *in his hand* ready to shoot, as well as a *quiver full of them*. There will not be any insults or rudeness when such a man and his family *speak with their enemies in the gate*.

The gate of a town was the site of much intercourse: legal, as in Ruth 4, social, as in Prov. 31.31, commercial, as in Neh. 13.15-22, political, as in Neh. 6.5-8. Many think that the image here is social: a man's enemies will be careful how they speak when they eye his escort of well-built sons. But Fleming notes that the combination *enemies/gate* is always elsewhere in a military context (Gen. 22.17; Deut. 28.55, 57; 1 Kgs 8.37: 'Sleep...Security', 442); and the underlying reality is political. Sanballat can dare to send an envoy with an open letter to be read aloud to Nehemiah in the gate, like Sennacherib's Rabshakeh of old. Enemy governors will not be so bold when Judah is populous and armed; when there are *sabras* by the hundred thousand, and missiles as well as watercourses in the Negeb.

Many commentators think of a legal dispute *in the gate*, with accusers as *enemies*; but one is reluctant to think that just causes could be overturned by the menacing presence of a large family of bullies. Israelite judges were sworn to administer justice, and we have the impression that social pressure and bribery were a greater threat than physical force. D.J. Estes, 'Like Arrows' (1991), sees children as long-range offensive weapons giving their father social immortality: perhaps a bit aggressive as an interpretation, but closer to the realities of the 440s.

PSALM 128

Nehemiah 11.1-2, 7.26-33

11 ¹And the princes of the people dwelt in Jerusalem: the rest of the people also cast lots, to bring one of ten to dwell in Jerusalem the holy city, and nine parts in the *other* cities. ²And the people blessed all the men that willingly offered themselves to dwell in Jerusalem...

7 ²⁶The men of Beth-lehem and Netophah, 188. ²⁷The men of Anathoth, 128. ²⁸The men of Beth-azmaveth, 42. ²⁹The men of Kiriath-jearim, Chephirah and Beeroth, 743. ³⁰The men of Ramah and Geba, 621. ³¹The men of Michmash, 122. ³²The men of Beth-el and Ai, 123. ³³The men of the other Nebo, 52.

The continuous Nehemiah Testimony runs out at 7.5a. The wall has been built, and the designs of enemies frustrated; but the problem of defence, with so small a population, has been left hanging. The Nehemiah Testimony must have continued with some account of the Governor's measures for repopulation; and many critics attribute Neh. 11.1-2 to the 'first person narrative', for its commonsense policy and plain speaking seem in character.

However, 11.1-2 is a fair way ahead, and the long list of names and numbers in 7.6-72 is what actually comes next, and this list is not unitary. It purports to be a catalogue of those who returned with Zerubbabel, Jeshua, Nehemiah, Azariah, Mordecai and others, and is, with minor variations, the same as the list in Ezra 2. But it is divided into sections, the first group being of lay families (7.8-38), and the second of Temple personnel (7.39-59). The lay families are in three subsections, the first of which gives the sons (בני) of certain families, the second the men (אנשי) of certain towns, and the third the sons (בני) of other towns. It is the second of these which I have isolated above. The use of אנשי marks them off from the other units, and the figures are noticeably smaller, none of them reaching four figures, or indeed half of that except where two or three places are taken together. Nor, remarkably, is Jerusalem one of the places mentioned, supposedly as a site of settlement.

A Song of the Ascents (המעלות).

1 Blessed is every one that feareth the LORD,
  That walketh in his ways.

2 For thou shalt eat the labour of thine hands:
  Happy shalt thou be, and it shall be well with thee.

3 Thy wife shall be as the fruitful vine, in the innermost parts of thine house:
  Thy children like olive plants about thy table.

4 Behold, thus shall the man be blessed
  That feareth the LORD.

5 May the LORD bless thee (יברכך) out of Zion;
  That thou see (וראה) the good of Jerusalem all the days of thy life.

6 Yea, that thou see (וראה) thy children's children;
  And peace upon Israel.

It seems plausible therefore that this little section was originally a list of the contingents which Nehemiah brought *from* their villages to begin the repopulation of Jerusalem. They were marked down as אנשי, *men of* such a town, in the same way that Neh. 11.2 says that the people blessed all האנשים who volunteered to move to Jerusalem. They were to settle (לשבת) in the city, that is to live there permanently; so we have to think of them bringing their families with them—we may compare Mt. 14.21, which glosses Mark's 'five thousand men' with 'besides women and children'. There could be no permanent defence without new young people coming on, quite apart from the social perils of a community with too few women. We may think therefore, on the basis of the figures in Neh. 7.26-33, of a transfer of about 2000 men, a considerable defence force, with their womenfolk and children. The towns mentioned are all within eight miles of Jerusalem, mostly on the north side; and no town would lose more than about 350 men out of some 3500, on the 10 per cent ratio given. It is all believable. In 12.27-43 Nehemiah gathers singers for his celebration from much the same area, 'the circuit round about Jerusalem, and from the villages of the Netophathites; also from Beth-gilgal, and out of the fields of Geba and Azmaveth'.

When the Chronicler came to write his Ezra–Nehemiah, he took the three *aliyot* to be roughly contemporary. Nehemiah's achievement had been the building of the walls, and now that that was complete on 25 Elul (Neh. 6.15), the next event must be New Year five or six days later, and Tabernacles to follow, celebrated (of course) in the manner prescribed in the Holiness Code (Lev. 23). So he does not want a list of Nehemiah's new settlers, but a catalogue of the whole *golah*, some

50,000 immigrants, on the scale of the great tribal totals in Numbers 26; headed by a symbolic leadership of 12 (Neh. 7.7). The Nehemiah 7 list, those who gathered for the renewed worship in Nehemiah 8, is duplicated with the list in Ezra 2, those who set out from Babylon; and this is in conscious parallel with Numbers, which gives a catalogue of those at Sinai in Numbers 1–4—leaders, lay tribes, priests and Levites—and a second after the 40 years' wandering in Numbers 26. So Nehemiah's little אנשי-list is incorporated into the בני-lists from elsewhere, and his two introductory verses are held over. The Chroniclers wanted an impressive autumn festival: all Israel with their 12 leaders and ordered phratries (Neh. 7), New Year and Tabernacles (Neh. 8), a prolonged confession of sin (Neh. 9), and a covenant to be faithful, properly sealed (Neh. 10). Only then might there be leisure for Nehemiah's resettlement scheme (11.1-2).

Nehemiah 11.1-2 are assigned to the Nehemiah Testimony by Blenkinsopp, and (as a later revised form) by Mowinckel (*Nehemia*, pp. 14, 30); but are denied by Kellermann (*Nehemia*, p. 43), and Williamson, on three grounds: (1) there is no 'I' in the narrative, the standard sign of the Nehemiah Testimony; (2) in 7.5 Nehemiah settled the people by families, not as here by lot; and (3) there are several expressions not typical of the Nehemiah Testimony—שאר for *the rest* in place of the usual יתר (2.16; 4.8, 13, 6.1, 14); שרים, 'princes', for the normal חרים, סגנים; the unique עיר קדש for Jerusalem. But none of these considerations is weighty. There are many passages of two verses in the Nehemiah Testimony (e.g. 4.1-6, 5.1-5) without an 'I', and 11.1-2 is a fragment of a narrative that might well be without an 'I' which once was there, as Mowinckel suggested. The supposed census made by Nehemiah on a genealogical basis is a speculation, depending entirely on the editorial decision to include להתיחש at 7.5a in the Nehemiah Testimony; and I have argued against this above.

The five passages using יתר all have the word following a list of leaders: 'the nobles and the deputies and the rest of the [people]' (2.16, 4.8, 13), Sanballat, Tobiah, Geshem 'and the rest of our enemies' (6.1), 'the prophetess Noadiah and the rest of the prophets' (6.14). In 11.1 there is a contrast: the princes were living in Jerusalem, whereas the *remainder* (שאר) of the people cast lots who should come. יתר is used in a slightly pejorative sense, whereas שאר is neutral. Similarly the חרים וסגנים are rather undependable. They are not made privy to Nehemiah's plans (2.16), they need encouraging (4.8), they have been taking usury (5.7), they correspond with Tobiah (6.17). The שרים on the other hand are worthy people, who take part in the thanksgiving procession in 12.31-32. It is true that they turn out to be the same as the סגנים in 12.40. The distinction is probably comparable to that between barons (bad) and nobles (good) in mediaeval England. Jerusalem is called 'the holy city' in 11.1 because those who were to live there had to consecrate themselves (מתנדבים) to live according to *torah*, and not in the assimilated practices of 'the cities'—see below, pp. 72-73.

So 'the people blessed (ויברכו) all the men that willingly offered themselves to dwell in Jerusalem'; and what kind of a blessing might they have made if not in the terms of Psalm 128? *Happy is every one...* (אשרי, v. 1); *Happy shalt thou be* (אשרי, v. 2); *thus shall the man be blessed* (יברך, v. 4); *The LORD bless thee* (יברכך, v. 5). Such blessings are expressly on the community living in Jerusalem: *The LORD bless thee out of Zion, That thou see the good of Jerusalem all the days of thy life...And peace upon Israel* (vv. 5-6).

Nehemiah's initiative was double-edged. His transfer of 2000 men meant that Jerusalem had a fighting defence force. No longer could raiding parties of Kedarites or Edomites expect to seize Jewish crops with impunity: *thou shalt eat the labour of thine hands; Happy shalt thou be, and it shall be well with thee*. At the same time the walls would enable the young people to rear large families in security, and so provide safeguard for the future: *Thy wife shall be as the fruitful vine, in the innermost parts of thine house; Thy children like the olive plants, round about thy table* (v. 3); *Yea, that thou see thy children's children* (v. 6).

These blessings are called on the head of כל־ירא יהוה, *every one that feareth the LORD* (v. 1), *the man that feareth the LORD* (v. 4). This apparently innocent expression is significant. We find a repeated distinction made in the period of the Return, on which I comment at greater length below (pp. 170-74, 184-91). In Ps. 115.9-11 the people are called on to trust in Yahweh under three heads: Israel, the house of Aaron, 'ye that fear the LORD'. In Ps. 118.2-4 the people are to say, That his mercy endureth for ever, under the same three heads, Israel, the house of Aaron, they that fear the LORD. In Ps. 135.19-20, a little later, Israel is to bless Yahweh under four heads: house of Israel, house of Aaron, house of Levi, 'ye that fear the LORD'. This repeated, surprising distinction needs an explanation.

The Chronicler thought that Israel was coterminous with the *golah*, and no doubt many of the *golah* thought the same. The educated upper class was deported in 597/587, and they successfully fought the fight for national identity on the banks of the Euphrates, refining the *torah* traditions as they went. Those left behind were peasants whose aspirations were largely concerned with survival, and who were ignorant of any refinements of *torah* developed in the east; so it would be unsurprising if the returning exiles despised them as the עם הארץ. We find signs of this in the Passover celebration in Ezra 6.19-22: those involved are 'the children of the captivity'/'the children of Israel which were come again out of the captivity', the priests and Levites 'who purified themselves as one; all were pure', and 'all such as had separated themselves unto them from the filthiness of the heathen of the land, to seek the LORD'. As in the three psalms cited above, there are three groups: 'the house of Israel', that is *observing* Jews, the *golah*; 'the house of Aaron', the priesthood, including a number of non-*golah* priests who 'purified themselves as one', to raise their purity level to that of the *golah*-priests; and 'those who feared the LORD', any local lay people who 'separated themselves to them from all the filthiness of the heathen of the land'. Seeking the LORD and fearing the LORD are the same thing.

Nehemiah had only a limited *aliya* with him, according to 5.17 a hundred and fifty; he could not bring 2000 men into Jerusalem without drawing on local people who were contaminated with all the filthiness of the heathen. But he must not desecrate the city where the Temple stood, or he would truly have built in vain. He therefore stressed (11.1) that the new settlers were 'to dwell in Jerusalem *the holy city*', and ch. 13 shows him insisting that its standards of holiness be observed. They had been selected by lot, but they also 'willingly offered themselves (מתנדבים) to dwell in Jerusalem' (11.2)—that is, they accepted the call, and the demand implied to live by the full *torah*. 'The people blessed them all': they said *Happy is everyone that feareth the LORD, That walketh in his ways... Behold, thus shall the man be blessed that feareth the LORD.*

Psalm 128 is generally seen as a blessing on Israel as a whole, by priests at the autumn festival, whether as the pilgrims arrive (Kraus), or as they go home (Anderson). Eaton stresses the suitability of the fertility theme for a harvest feast. Gunkel, and many, give a postexilic date; Kirkpatrick specifies the time of Nehemiah, to encourage family life in the newly walled city. My only disagreement with all this is over the priests, who did not have a monopoly of blessing (Neh. 11.2)—the cantor of Psalm 128 is almost certainly a (Korahite) Levite (133.3); and over the technical meaning of *he that feareth the LORD.*

A more serious divergence is over the classification given by Gunkel, and those who follow him, to Psalm 128: a Wisdom psalm. The label is ironic for an interpretation that reduces the text to an assertion of self-evident stupidity; for it is obviously untrue that all God-fearing people are happy, or harvest a due reward for their labours, or raise large families. Although religious theory might triumph over experience in the pious circles that produced Psalm 1, the ordinary Israelite had to live with reality; nor were there lacking intelligent men like the authors of Job and Qoheleth to point up the folly of such theologizing. It must come therefore as a relief to many a reader to find that Psalm 128 is sensible. The author speaks for the community in welcoming those who have volunteered to leave their homes and move to the holy city; to give up their lax life, and *walk in the ways of the LORD*. The blessing it pronounces on them is the blessing of Neh. 11.2, a hopeful prayer that better times may lie ahead through their dedication: security for the farms, fruitfulness in the homes, and *the good of Jerusalem all the days of their life.*

PSALM 129

Nehemiah 13.4-14

[4]And [before this,] Eliashib the priest, who was appointed over the chamber of the house of our God, being allied unto Tobiah, [5]had prepared for him a great chamber, where aforetime they laid the meal offerings, the frankincense, and the vessels, and the tithes of the corn, the wine, and the oil, which were given by commandment to the Levites, and the singers, and the porters; and the heave offerings for the priests. [[6]But in all this *time* I was not in Jerusalem: for in the two and thirtieth year of Artaxerxes king of Babylon I went unto the king, and after certain days asked I leave of the king: [7]And I came to Jerusalem, and understood of the evil that Eliashib had done in preparing him a chamber in the courts of the house of God.] [8]And it grieved me sore: therefore I cast forth all the household stuff of Tobiah out of the chamber. [9]Then I commanded, and they cleansed the chambers: and thither brought I again the vessels of the house of God, with the meal offerings and the frankincense. [10]And I perceived that the portions of the Levites had not been given them; so that the Levites and the singers, that did the work, were fled every one to his field. [11]Then contended I with the deputies, and said, Why is the house of God forsaken? And I gathered them together, and set them in their place. [12]Then brought all Judah the tithe of the corn and the wine and the oil unto the treasuries. [13]And I made treasurers over the treasuries, Shelemiah the priest, and Zadok the scribe, and of the Levites, Pedaiah: and next to them was Hanan, the son of Zaccur, the son of Mattaniah: for they were counted faithful, and their business was to distribute unto their brethren. [14]Remember me, O my God, concerning this, and wipe not out my kindnesses that I have done for the house of my God, and for the observances thereof.

The passage presents difficulties, expounded by Mowinckel, *Nehemia*, pp. 35-37, and Kellermann, *Nehemia*, pp. 48-51. (1) Eliashib is said to have made the room available to Tobiah 'before this', לפני מזה, that is, before autumn, 445 BCE. It is difficult to believe that Nehemiah was unaware of this act of desecration, and had failed to notice that the Levites had gone back to their farms because they were not being paid; for according to 13.6 it had been going on for 12 years (till 'the two and thirtieth year of Artaxerxes king of Babylon')! (2) Nehemiah himself always speaks of 'the king' (1.11, and often), 'Artaxerxes

A Song of the Ascents (המעלות).
1　Much have they afflicted me from my youth up,
　　Let Israel now say:
2　Much have they afflicted me from my youth up,
　　Yet they have not prevailed against me.
3　The plowers plowed upon my back;
　　They made long their furrows.
4　The LORD is righteous:
　　He hath cut asunder the cords of the wicked.
5　Let them be ashamed and turned backward,
　　All they that hate Zion.
6　Let them be as the grass upon the housetops,
　　Which withereth afore it be plucked up:
7　Wherewith the reaper filleth not his hand,
　　Nor he that bindeth sheaves his bosom.
8　Neither do they which go by say,
　　The blessing of the LORD be upon you,
　　We bless you in the name of the LORD.

the king' (2.1). As Artaxerxes was king of Persia, it is a mistake to speak of him as 'king of Babylon', and this is an improbable mistake in the mouth of a high courtier: it is likely to be a careless carry-over from Ezra 5.13, where Cyrus is said to be king of Babylon, as Nebuchadnezzar was before him (5.12).

It looks therefore as if 13.6-7, or parts of those verses, were a later gloss. One of the Chroniclers thought Nehemiah must have been out of Jerusalem when the evil was done, and Neh. 5.14 told him that his term as Governor had been twelve years. Added to the date in 1.1, 2.1, that gave the thirty-second year of the reign; so he had probably gone back to 'Babylon' to have his position renewed, and come back thereafter. It is of course a curiosity that no event worth recording took place in Nehemiah's first governorship after the dedication of the walls. In other words, Nehemiah's second term is a fiction, a false inference made many years later.

So the Nehemiah Testimony was interrupted by the Chronicler at Neh. 7.5a, and this was followed by some fragments which we have in 11.1-2 and 7.26-33; but there remained a considerable block of first-person material available to him, the dedication of the walls in 12.27-43, and four incidents in our Nehemiah 13, each of which closes with a 'Remember' prayer like those in 3.36-37, 5.19 and 6.14. The Chronicler had followed the Nehemiah Testimony description of the wall-building in full detail, and he had crowned that with a chapter of liturgical celebration (Neh. 8); so naturally he decided to take the dedication procession next, in Nehemiah 12. The remaining incidents could be left over in a kind of postscript in ch. 13; and in time this arrangement invited the gloss of the second governorship in 13.6-7. His arrangement of the incidents is determined by his need to complete the liturgical description that he has begun in Nehemiah 8, and tells us nothing about the order of incidents in the Nehemiah Testimony. In fact 13.4-31 stood before 12.27-43 in the Nehemiah Testimony, and when the Chronicler rearranged them he signified that he had done so by beginning 13.4 ולפני מזה, 'However, before this...': the events in 13.4-31 had preceded the dedication procession at Tabernacles.

Kellermann (*Nehemia*, p. 48), is in two minds about לפני מזה, 'before this'; but he inclines to thinking that the gloss in 13.6-7 is post-Chronicler. In that case the Chronicler has probably inserted 'before this' as he does other vague temporal links, such as 'in those days'; and would so testify that in the Nehemiah Testimony the events of 13.4-31 stood before the dedication in 12.27-43. Kellermann and Mowinckel vary a little in the amount of vv. 6-7 that they ascribe to the gloss; but the total omission of them leaves a smooth carry-over from v. 5 to v. 8. Williamson and Blenkinsopp retain vv. 6-7, but their responses do not meet the objection about 'the king of Babylon'; Williamson (*Ezra, Nehemia*, p. 381), however, thinks that 'before this' is editorial.

The store-hall incident must have taken place shortly before Tabernacles in 445 BCE. It was at the autumn festival that people were to bring their tithes of corn, wine and oil: the new wine (תירוש) and the oil were not ready till autumn (Deut. 16.13), and it was then that tithes were to be brought to the Temple (Deut. 12.6, 11). It is unbelievable that Nehemiah allowed the Levites to be unpaid and the Temple unstaffed for any considerable period; once the second-Governorship theory is seen to be based on a misunderstanding, the autumn festival in question is likely to be the first at which he presided, that is, 445. Tobiah had been in correspondence with the סגנים, the Jerusalem leadership, in Elul (6.17-19), and the significance of this passage has been left in the air; it is now, once the repopulation scheme has been settled, that matters come to a head. Eliashib, one of the leaders (perhaps the same Eliashib the high priest of 13.28—see pp. 319-22), had let him have the use of the store-hall in the Temple; since people were not bringing their tithes in, the space was free. To Nehemiah this was religious apostasy as well as political treachery. He threw out Tobiah's furniture and belongings so that he should no longer be operating from the centre of Israelite life; he cleansed the chambers from 'the filthiness of the heathen'; he set the סנים in their place, and had the hall used for its proper purpose, the storing and distribution of the Temple staff's income, and other sacred items. There is no doubting Nehemiah's *mens conscia recti*. He was performing acts of חסד for the house of his God, and Eliashib and Tobiah were God's enemies, whom he would no doubt 'remember' in due course.

Williamson reduces Eliashib to a caretaker; but it is noticeable that he is said to be 'appointed over the chamber of the house of our God', בית־אלהינו בלשכת נתון—'the chamber', singular. Ezra similarly takes possession of 'the chamber of Jehohanan the son of Eliashib' after his successful mass meeting in Ezra 10.6. Every government has an administrative centre which an incoming ruler takes over, a White House or a 10 Downing Street: Judah was ruled from the high priest's לשכה in the Temple, and Nehemiah was displacing Tobiah, none too soon. Naturally Eliashib also had the disposal of other Temple facilities: he had let Tobiah have 'a great chamber', and Nehemiah cleansed 'the chambers' (v. 9).

Psalm 129 is a dual response to this narrative: it both gives thanks for the deliverance that God has brought to pass for Israel, culminating in the present *aliya*, and it cries shame and confusion on its opponents, *All they which hate Zion*. The psalmist is the spokesman for the nation, and he begins as he did in 124, 'If it had not been the LORD who was on our side, *Let Israel now say…*', and repeating the opening clause. The deliverance is still at work with the cleansing of the Temple, but this time the thought goes back to earlier deliverances also: *Much have they afflicted me from my youth, Let Israel now say; Much have they afflicted me from my youth, But they have not prevailed against me*. Right from the beginning, from Israel's youth in Egypt (Hos. 2.3, 15, etc.), there had been affliction, but the people had always survived; and they had survived a further, and dreadful affliction in the Exile. They had been slaves in Egypt, and sometimes perhaps in Babylon too; and few slaves escape the taskmaster's whip— *The plowers plowed upon my back; They made long their furrows*. It was no doubt common then, as later, to tie a slave's hands together, perhaps round a pillar, before administering the lash; but *Yahweh the faithful*, צדיק יהוה, who never fails to keep his covenanted promise, *has cut asunder the cords of the wicked*. We are free, and will suffer no more.

129.1 רבת, 'much', is an Aramaism also occurring at 120.6, *for a long time*: Allen follows RV text in rendering here *Many a time*. *Verse* 2: גם meaning 'yet', compare Ezek. 16.28, Eccl. 6.7. *Verse* 3: Israel's sufferings in the Exile were symbolized as a flogging in Isa. 50.6, 'I gave my back to the smiters', and perhaps in the obscure Isa. 51.23. Anderson and Allen see the *long furrows* as the weals of the lash on Israel's *back*. Delitzsch, and many, cite Mic. 3.12, 'Therefore shall Zion for your sake be a ploughed field'; but this had not actually happened, and the representative *Let Israel now say* requires a more personal *affliction*. *Verse* 4: Delitzsch, Kraus and others understand עבות as a strap on the forehead of the ox pulling the yoke (Gunkel and Kraus have the ox being whipped as well). But Israel is compared to a man, not an ox, and the *cord* should be a part of the whipping metaphor. Wellington tied the wrists of his soldiers to the triangle in similar circumstances.

In the face of such grace it is terrible to find traitors in Israel's midst, *who hate Zion*. Eliashib, one to whom was entrusted the care of God's house, had desecrated the place, sequestering its rooms to an evil-minded foreigner to whom he was related by an impure marriage. Tobiah was bent on his own advancement, and was one of the three main enemies of the present Governor. These men were not friends to Zion, to the purity of Temple worship that would enable Israel once more to flourish under God's blessing: in fact they *hate Zion*.

Weiser and Anderson see *the haters of Zion* as political and religious enemies from within the community; whereas Kraus, Eaton and Allen see the traditional *Völkersturm* of conspiring nations. But the latter picture is hard to fit in with the domestic blessing scene of v. 8, which rather suggests the ostracism of those who had belonged to the community. The faithful Kirkpatrick sites the psalm in Nehemiah's time, with Sanballat and Tobiah exceedingly grieved that there was come a man to seek the good of Jerusalem (Neh. 2.10).

The psalmist pronounces upon them the mildest of maledictions: that they should *be ashamed*, and that they should not flourish. The similarity of words יְבֹשׁוּ/יֵבֹשׁ, *be ashamed/wither*, leads from the one thought to the other. The priest and the Ammonite are to be *as the grass upon the housetops*, green in the rain-time, but without root-space, *which withereth afore it be plucked up*. The contrast is drawn with the happiness of reaping, so much in mind in Elul and Tishri, as the first line of *reapers* take the standing corn in their *hand*, and the second *fill their bosom* with the stalks until there are enough to *bind* them together. We hear their glad interchange in Ruth 2.4, where Boaz says to the reapers, '*The LORD be* with *you*', and they reply '*The*

LORD bless thee'. No such cries of blessing from *them which go by* are to crown the wiles of those who *hate Zion*; they will be ostracized.

The two uses of -שֶׁ in vv. 6, 7 and of קדמת in v. 6 are Aramaisms which, with v. 1, suggest a late date. The force of שלף in v. 6 is unclear. The normal 'draw out' suggests to Delitzsch that the plant withers before the grass seed is drawn out of its sheath; Driver, 'Studies in the Vocabulary of the Old Testament' (1930), derived it from a different root meaning to form a stalk. The sheaf-binder's חצן, the capacious fold of his robe, is the same as that which Nehemiah shakes out symbolically at 5.13; the same symbolism, exclusion from God's blessing, is involved here. Van der Wal, 'Structure' (1988), takes the psalm down to v. 8b as a summons of the priests to sing a song to Yahweh, with v. 8c as their benediction, comparing Psalm 134; but the reading of 134 is also doubtful.

PSALM 130

Nehemiah 13.15-22

13 [15]In those days saw I in Judah some treading the winepresses on the sabbath, and bringing in heaps of corn, and lading asses *therewith*; as also wine, grapes and figs, and all manner of burdens, which they brought into Jerusalem on the sabbath day: and I testified *against them* in the day wherein they sold victuals. [16]There dwelt men of Tyre also therein, which brought in fish, and all manner of ware, and sold on the sabbath unto the children of Judah, and in Jerusalem. [17]Then I contended with the nobles of Judah, and said unto them, What evil thing is this that ye do, and profane the sabbath day? [18]Did not your fathers thus, and did not our God bring all this evil upon us, and upon this city? yet ye bring more wrath upon us by profaning the sabbath.

[19]And it came to pass that when the gates of Jerusalem began to be dark before the sabbath, I commanded that the doors should be shut, and commanded that they should not be opened till after the sabbath: and some of my servants set I over the gates, that there should no burden be brought in on the sabbath day. [20]So the merchants and sellers of all kinds of ware lodged without Jerusalem once or twice. [21]Then I testified against them, and said unto them, Why lodge ye before the wall? if ye do so again, I will lay hands on you. From that time forth came they no more on the sabbath. [22]And I commanded the Levites that they should purify themselves, and that they should come and keep the gates, to sanctify the sabbath day. Remember unto me, O my God, this also, and spare me according to the greatness of thy mercy.

Nehemiah 13.4-14 closed with a 'Remember'-prayer, and so does 13.15-22; we have two neat recitals, one on the restoration of Temple premises to their proper use, one on the restoration of sabbath observance, each completed with an appeal to God for the restorer. But there is a difference of tone between the two prayers. 13.14 asked God not to wipe out Nehemiah's acts of charity for the Temple and its worship: 13.22 asks God to spare him according to the greatness of his mercy.

A Song of the Ascents (המעלות).
1   Out of the depths have I cried unto thee, O LORD.
2   Lord, hear my voice:
     Let thine ears be attentive
     To the voice of my supplications.
3   If thou, Jah, shouldest mark iniquities,
     O Lord, who shall stand?
4   But there is forgiveness with thee,
     That thou mayest be feared.
5   I wait for the LORD, my soul doth wait,
     And in his word do I hope.
6   My soul *looketh* for the Lord,
     More than watchmen *look* for the morning;
     Yea, more than watchmen for the morning.
7   O Israel, hope in the LORD;
     For with the LORD there is mercy,
     And with him is plenteous redemption.
8   And he shall redeem Israel
     From all his iniquities.

With Eliashib there had been a single Israelite renegade whom the Governor had properly disgraced, and he can pray to have his credit confirmed in the book of life. With the sabbath-breaking the whole community is involved, and Nehemiah can pray only to be spared in God's great mercy (חסד).

The difference is made clear in the Governor's words in 13.18: 'Did not your fathers thus, and did not our God bring all this evil upon us, and upon this city? yet ye bring more wrath upon Israel by profaning the sabbath'. By flagrant defiance of the divine Law, the community deserves, and invites, further retribution: its only hope is that God will spare them in his mercy.

The Nehemiah Testimony places the controversy 'in those days' (v. 15), and this should probably be taken literally: that is, it happened in the same weeks as the temple-hall incident, before Tabernacles, 445 BCE. Then all Judah brought the tithe of new wine and oil into the treasuries (13.12), the produce of the autumn: now Nehemiah sees some treading winepresses, which yield the תירוש, and others lading asses with grapes and figs, all the produce of September (13.15). The walls are complete and the gates can be shut, so the date is past 25 Elul (6.15); but it is not easily believable that the sellers should wait a year (still less twelve years) before turning an honest copper on the sabbath day.

Per contra, it is all too likely that lax ways have become endemic over six generations of acute poverty and Gentile penetration; and that Nehemiah had felt scandalized by them before, and was now in a position to take action. So the most plausible setting for the sabbath incidents is immediately after the hanging of the gates: two or three sabbaths are mentioned (13.20-21), and there were three or four between 25 Elul and the end of Tabernacles.

Psalm 130 also marks a sharp change of tone in the Songs series. Hitherto the dominant feeling has been of thankful optimism. There have been enemies without who are for war (120), who despise Israel (123); and there have been sinners within who have made their ways crooked (125), and who hate Zion (129).

But over the first ten Songs the psalmist has looked back on the success of his coming (122), and on the community's deliverance (124, 126, 129); and he has looked forward to blessing, and peace, and prosperity, and children, without any breast-beating. It is only with 130 that his confidence ebbs: something has happened which drives him to his knees to beg for a hearing, and for forgiveness, and redemption from iniquities, and for mercy (הַחֶסֶד).

The similar change of tone in the Nehemiah Testimony provides us with an explanation. Judah has much to thank God for at its Tabernacles, and may remember gratefully God's blessing over so many perils; but it must also remember the hideous danger into which it has betrayed itself by profaning the sabbath.

No doubt this arose in part from the introduction of so many new inhabitants from the outlying towns, who had drifted over a century and a half into the godless ways of the Gentiles. But Nehemiah holds the 'nobles' (חֹרִי) of Judah responsible, and as usual they are found to have been lax in oversight, if not conniving at law-breaking. The evil that has been done is an act of the community, requiring 'contending' at a public meeting; and the only hope is that God *shall redeem Israel From all his iniquities* (130.8).

Psalm 130.1-2. It was a tradition in the psalms for pleas *in extremis* to be spoken of as *Out of the [watery] depths*. Psalm 69 opens, 'Save me, O God: For the waters are come in unto my soul' (v. 2), and prays, 'Deliver me out of the mire, and let me not sink' (v. 15); and much of Psalm 88 has the speaker 'laid in the lowest pit, In dark places, in the deeps' (v. 7). It is likely that these words reflect some ritual of early times, when a priest or other national representative was committed for the night to the symbolic underworld (Goulder, *Korah*, pp. 202-205 and *David*, pp. 220-21); but by Nehemiah's time such rites have become a metaphor, like being on the rack, or carrying one's cross. The urgency of appeal for a hearing is again similar to 88.2-3, 'Let my prayer enter into thy presence; Incline thine ear unto my cry: For my soul is full of troubles, And my life draweth nigh unto the grave'; and the self-humiliating Psalm 102.

The cantor's situation, pleading for the forgiveness of the community's sin, introduces a new atmosphere in which God is addressed three times as אדני, 'our master'; we are his slaves and can only put forward to him our *supplications*, תחנוני. He uses the late Hebrew קשבות, *attentive*, also found only in (the parallel) 2 Chron. 6.40, 7.15, and (the same root) in Neh. 1.6, 11.

The Chronicler is adapting Solomon's Prayer of 1 Kings 8 with Ps. 130.2 and several verses of Psalm 132. The uses in Nehemiah 1 suggested to Kirkpatrick that Psalm 130 came from Nehemiah's time, and perhaps from the man himself. The frequent use of אדני is found also in Psalm 86, another psalm beseeching forgiveness; but it is difficult to date 86, and so to suggest in which direction dependence is to be seen.

Psalm 130.3-4. But what is the cantor to say in the face of such sinning with a high hand? Two frail arguments come to mind. First, we are but flesh, easily led astray: *If thou, Jah, shouldest mark iniquities, O Lord, who shall stand?* Such an approach made 130 one of Luther's favourite psalms, a *Pauline* psalm; though had he been a headmaster, he might have seen through it.

Secondly, the quality of mercy is not strained, it is the attribute of God himself: *But there is forgiveness with thee, That thou mayest be feared.* There is judgment with God too, vengeance is his, and he will repay: but Portia's rhetoric inclines to leave these other attributes in silence. God has been, since Sinai, a God who forgives iniquity; and it is this that makes him the object of such reverent worship.

סליחה, *forgiveness*, comes elsewhere in the Old Testament only at Neh. 9.17 and Dan. 9.9, and so testifies to the psalm's postexilic date. The archaizing יה in v. 3 may recall the use of the term in Exod. 15.2, Ps. 77.12 and other passages where Yahweh delivered his people.

Psalm 130.5-8. Although the psalmist is dependent solely on the Lord's *forgiveness* of *iniquities* and his *mercy*, his normal serenity has not deserted him: he *waits for the LORD*, and *hopes in his word*. *Yahweh's word* is likely to be his famous pronouncement of Exod. 34.6-7, '*Yahweh, Yahweh,* a God full of compassion...*plenteous* (רב) in *mercy* (חסד) and truth; keeping *mercy* for thousands, forgiving *iniquity* (עון)'.

'Waiting for the LORD' means confidently expecting that God will turn up trumps as he has so many times over the last year: there will be no more long furrows. One may be as confident as the Levites watching for the dawn; and our eyes are as firmly fixed on him as theirs are. The Targum understood them to be watching so as to offer the dawn sacrifice at the appropriate moment; though we might also think of them on Nehemiah's towers, watching for the end of the night of peril.

Verses 7-8 leave no doubt that the *iniquities* are committed by the community, *Israel*; it is not implied in v. 3 that they are the work of the individual singer. Nor has the psalmist really any doubt that things will be all right. God's *word* is his bond; he has covenanted with us, and *he shall redeem Israel from all his iniquities.* Nehemiah also prayed at 13.22 to be spared 'according to the *plenteousness of thy mercy*' (כרב חסך).

Kirkpatrick and Eaton see the psalmist as the nation's representative, as is surely right, and Eaton stresses the appropriateness of an element of atonement in the autumn festival. For form critics Psalm 130 is a puzzle, for the first six verses read to them like an Individual Lament, and vv. 7-8 are different. Gunkel's readers may be surprised to learn that the psalmist is penitent on his deathbed, 'in Not und Tod'; but that he was too modest to mention the fact!

Kraus hesitates between an individual penitent who in vv. 7-8 takes up a word of warning and of promise from the liturgy, and one who has recovered from his trials and addresses his song of thanksgiving to the congregation.

Allen has an earlier Individual Lament, vv. 1-6, adapted for two groups of voices, the second, vv. 7-8, speaking with confidence; F. Sedlmeier, similarly, 'Bei dir' (1992), sees vv. 1-6 as a personal experience of forgiveness, as in Isa. 59.2, later adapted for public use. R.R. Marrs, 'A Cry' (1988) analyses the repetitive structure and argues for the psalm's coherence. It is a relief to be away from such dilemmas and speculations.

Kraus also, as often, sees an oracle behind *the LORD's word*; and others cite Psalm 119, or the prophetic tradition, especially in Deutero-Isaiah. But the wording is close to the classic statement of Exodus 34, which every Israelite must have known by heart. More interestingly Kraus suggests that 130 was a night psalm, in view of vv. 5-6. God is often thought of as sending help 'in the morning', and 77, 88 and 90, three psalms similar to 130, seem to be written for night use. 134 is certainly a night-psalm, for it addresses 'ye servants of the LORD, Which by night stand in the house of the LORD'. 'By night' is the plural בלילות, so presumably several of the songs were night-psalms.

PSALM 131

Nehemiah 13.23-29

13 [23]In those days also saw I the Jews that had married women of Ashdod, of Ammon *and* of Moab: [24]and their children spake half in the speech of Ashdod, and could not speak in the Jews' language, but according to the language of each people. [25]And I contended with them, and reviled them, and smote certain of them, and plucked out their hair, and made them swear by God, *saying*, Ye shall not give your daughters unto their sons, nor take their daughters for your sons, or for yourselves. [26]Did not Solomon king of Israel sin by these things? yet among many nations was there no king like him, and he was beloved of his God, and God made him king over all Israel: nevertheless even him did strange women cause to sin. [27]Shall we then hearken unto you to do all this great evil, to trespass against our God, in marrying strange women? [28]And one of the sons of Joiada, the son of Eliashib the high priest, was son in law to Sanballat the Horonite: therefore I chased him from me. [29]Remember them, O my God, for the defilings of the priesthood, and the covenant of the priesthood, and of the Levites.

Nehemiah 13.22-29 follows the two similar disciplinary actions in the first part of the chapter, and like them concludes with a 'Remember' prayer—this time of a more imprecatory kind, like 6.14. The action is again dated 'In those days', and as with 13.15 it may be that the phrase is meant literally. Down to 7.5a the Nehemiah Testimony follows a straightforward chronological sequence, and I have suggested reasons for thinking that this was the case throughout, the order being only slightly amended (with the advancement of the Dedication procession) by the Chronicler.

The controversy over the Gentile marriages will then also have blown up in early Tishri. Over four months in Judah Nehemiah cannot have failed to notice the presence of a fair number of 'strange' wives, and children talking gibberish. He knew this was against the Law (v. 25: Deut. 7.3), and *a fortiori* for a priest; and that it was a 'trespass against our God', which, like the sabbath-breaking, would

A Song of the Ascents (המעלות); of David.
1   LORD, my heart is not haughty, nor mine eyes lofty;
     Neither do I walk in great matters,
     Or in things too wonderful for me.
2   Surely I have stilled and quieted my soul;
     Like a weaned child with his mother,
     My soul is with me like a weaned child.
3   O Israel, hope in the LORD
     From this time forth and for evermore.

surely incur his wrath and retribution. So he was not at all likely to have waited a year and more before taking action; especially where the offence was at the hands of the leading priestly family, and in an alliance with his arch-enemy, Sanballat.

Reforming governors make themselves popular when they successfully defy outsiders, raise the community's morale, increase security and restore national aspirations; but they chance their arm when they repeatedly weaken the current oligarchy, and in particular challenge the priesthood. The oppressive nobles may not have been too popular in Judah, but priests are dangerous enemies. Nehemiah had already risked offence by overriding Eliashib's arrangements in the Temple; he was certain to have caused powerful resentment by driving the high priest's grandson into exile. Besides there will have been other influential Jews scandalized to hear that their relations had been beaten, and had had their beards painfully pulled out. After so much apparent arrogance, he will have been wise to go humbly with his God, at least in public.

Psalm 131 is too brief to yield any certainty as to its original context; but we may say at least that it plausibly fits the Nehemiah situation. The psalmist speaks for his leader and himself, to deny any arrogance: *LORD, my heart is not haughty.* Still less is he ambitious for higher honours, the crown perhaps, as had been slanderously alleged (Neh. 6.7): *nor [are] my eyes lofty.* He had, as Governor, to insist on the divine Law being observed, but he had no intention to interfere in the conduct of religion in the Temple: that would be to *walk in great matters, in things too wonderful for him.*

Some of the phrasing is traditional. The heart of man is *haughty* (יגבה) at Prov. 18.12, and there is a generation with *lofty eyes* (עיניו רמו) at Prov. 30.13.

Nehemiah was a passionate man. It was his emotional drive that brought him from being a comfortable courtier in the capital to take a position of doubtful authority in a distant and poverty-stricken province; to sleepless nights, and constant 'contending', and intrigues against his life. It was no wonder that under so much pressure his patience had given way; that he should have ordered such violence in face of miscegenation, causing popular outrage without and spiritual upheaval within. His passion is now spent, and in the confidence of just judgment serenity returns. He feels *like a weaned child with its mother*. The passionate crying is over, the blind fury at the denial of milk that is no longer available: like the weaned child, he has *stilled and quieted his soul*. Anyone whose heart has thumped through scenes of violence and anger will know the sense of a divided self as repose returns. The rage subsides into normality, and the *soul* feels as if it were *upon one* (עלי) *as a weaned child*. Plato's charioteer has resumed control of his horses.

Psalm 131 closes on the same note as 130; with the same words, *O Israel, hope in the LORD*. But to *hope* is not vacuously to take the view that glad times are just around the corner; it is to trust in Yahweh by keeping the laws he has laid down, especially on central issues like marriage, whose neglect will destroy the people's integrity. Only obedience can yield a genuine *hope in the LORD*: optimism without submission was the recipe of the false prophets.

With its intensely personal opening, and its national appeal in v. 3, Psalm 131 poses the same problem to the interpreter as 130. Kirkpatrick saw it as an individual's renunciation of prophetic hopes of miraculous blessing, with a general pious appeal to close. Gunkel placed vv. 1-2 as a psalm of confidence, with v. 3 perhaps added when it was used liturgically. Seybold (*Die Wallfahrtspsalmen*, p. 37), thought the first two verses were written by a woman. But the general trend has been to follow Gunkel—as have Weiser, Kraus, Keet, Anderson and Allen. Either the first two verses were an individual thanksgiving left in the Temple archive, and later applied liturgically with v. 3 (Allen); or a צדיק, a member of a devout brotherhood that relied solely on Yahweh for everything, expressed his loyalty and trust in vv. 1-2, and appealed during worship to Israel generally to follow his example (Kraus).

Two different settings for a three-verse psalm seem excessive; and we may doubt whether Kraus's צדיקים groups ever existed, or whether, if they did, Israelites more generally would have put up with their priggish appeals during worship. Eaton holds the psalm together more plausibly with a national representative as speaker. Leaders cannot go wrong by denying that they are *haughty*; but presumably they do *walk in great matters* and *lift up their eyes*, since that is a leader's calling. We have to fit these denials in with the moving simile of the weaned child, which implies a return to stillness and peace of heart after a passage of violence and anger. It is not so easy to imagine a scenario where these features are combined: how fortunate we are to have them all implied in Neh. 13.23-29!

PSALM 132

Nehemiah 13.30-31

13 [30]Thus cleansed I them from every thing strange, and appointed wards for the priests and for the Levites, every one in his work; [31]and for the wood offering, at times appointed, and for the first-fruits. Remember me, O my God, for good.

The brief final note is puzzling. RV's *Thus* represents ו, 'and'. *Every thing strange* takes up Nehemiah's action against those who had married strange women (13.26): but 13.23 specified 'women of Ashdod, of Ammon, *and* of Moab', and we have heard only about the families which spoke the language of Ashdod. The *wards*, משמרות (NRSV, 'duties'), *of the priests and Levites* are a new matter, as are the *wood offering* and the *first-fruits*: hence the translation *Thus* is not very suitable.

It is noticeable that three of these four matters are dealt with in the verses between the Dedication procession (Neh. 12.27-43) and the Nehemiah Testimony passage in Neh. 13.4-31. In 12.44 'men were appointed over the chambers for the treasures, for the heave offerings, *for the first-fruits*, and for the tithes'. In 12.45 the priests and the Levites *performed the service* (וישמרו משמרת) of their God'. In 13.1-3 it is found written that 'an *Ammonite or Moabite* should not enter into the assembly of God for ever'.

While we cannot know what changes may have been made to this text, the present paragraph seems too short and inconsequential, and it is surprising to find its topics dealt with in the non-Nehemiah Testimony verses preceding. It may be that, as the Chronicler meant to end his work with the Dedication, he felt he should add a few lines providing for the Temple service for which he cared so much, transferring the content of the fourth paragraph of Nehemiah 13. When his successors came to append these four paragraphs, they might well then note that the content of the last episode had already been given, and avoid its duplication.

A Song of the Ascents (המעלות)
1   LORD, remember for David
    All his affliction;
2   How he sware unto the LORD,
    And vowed unto the Mighty One of Jacob:
3   Surely I will not come into the tent of my house,
    Nor go up into the couch of my bed;
4   I will not give sleep to mine eyes,
    Or slumber to mine eyelids;
5   Until I find out a place for the LORD,
    Tabernacles for the Mighty One of Jacob.
6   Lo, we heard of it in Ephrathah (RV text):
    We found it in the field of the wood (RV text).
7   We will go into his tabernacles;
    We will worship at his footstool.
8   Arise, O LORD, into thy resting place;
    Thou, and the ark of thy strength.
9   Let thy priests be clothed with righteousness;
    And let thy saints shout for joy.
10 For thy servant David's sake
    Turn not away the face of thine anointed.
11 The LORD hath sworn unto David in truth;
    He will not turn from it:
    Of the fruit of thy body will I set upon thy throne.
12 If thy children will keep my covenant
    And my testimony that I shall teach them,
    Their children also shall sit upon thy throne for evermore.
13 For the LORD hath chosen Zion;
    He hath desired it for his habitation.
14 This is my resting place for ever:
    Here will I dwell; for I have desired it.
15 I will surely bless her provision:
    I will satisfy her poor with bread.
16 Her priests also will I clothe with salvation:
    And her saints shall shout aloud for joy.
17 There will I make a horn to spring forth for David:
    I have prepared a lamp for mine anointed.
18 His enemies will I clothe with shame:
    But upon himself shall his crown flourish.

Mowinckel saw Psalm 132 as a drama accompanying the ark on its annual procession to the Jerusalem Temple. He interpreted it in line with the account in 2 Samuel 6 of David's original procession with the ark, and other texts. The drama was performed annually, at Yahweh's

Thronbesteigungsfest, and he describes the ritual in two long passages in his *Psalmenstudien* (II, 110-18; III, pp. 32-33). The psalm was self-evidently divided between various voices (Kraus gave vv. 1-5 to the King, v. 6 to a choir, vv. 7-10 to the priests, vv. 11-18 to a cultic prophet), and a choir repeated certain verses as was necessary. When the first verses had been recited, the procession set forth—or rather danced forth, since dancing is described in 2 Samuel 6, and brings experience of the divine to the participants. The company was led by a choir and by women with timbrels, as in Psalm 68. After six paces, as with David, there was a halt and sacrifice was offered. According to 1 Chron. 13.3 Saul had neglected the ark, so David is pictured as ignorant of its whereabouts, and 'his men' then appear (in dramatic form) with the news that it is found. Prayer is offered for the current king, as David's descendant, to inherit the merits of his progenitor; and a cultic prophet then produces a poetic version of 2 Samuel 7, in which God promised David's line the throne in perpetuity. The psalm naturally belonged in the monarchic period.

This striking reconstruction was accepted by Gunkel (with suitable hesitation about the nature of the festival); and with two such pipers in Kristiania and Halle it is no surprise that the children followed the Davidic dance. Of later commentators only Rogerson and McKay, Deissler and Jacquet took seriously the possibility that 132 was a post-exilic psalm; and Wellhausen and Kirkpatrick, who had thought so, were usually forgotten. However, for all its brilliance, Mowinckel's hypothesis is heavily flawed: the problem has been to find another one which is any better.

(1) The drama theory is both speculative and implausible. That there was a festal procession in the royal period is very likely, from Psalm 24: but the dialogue there is not a drama, but a challenge and response at the Temple gates. There is no evidence at all that the detail of 2 Samuel 6 was repeated year after year. 1 Chron. 13.3 does say that 'we sought not unto [the ark] in the days of Saul', but does not at all imply that its whereabouts were unknown: quite the contrary. The theory that cultic prophets delivered oracles of blessing in the middle of psalms is dear to Mowinckel, but it is based on readings (and rewritings) of Psalms 81 and 85 which I have argued elsewhere to be untenable (Goulder, *Asaph*, pp. 152-54; *idem, Korah*, pp. 108-11). The notion that a psalm was divided between a series of different speakers (as opposed to a chorus as in 136, or the dialogue of 24) is

fanciful; there is no evidence of such a practice in later use of this or any other psalm.

(2) David gathers the people to bring up the ark in 2 Samuel 6, and God promises him the throne for ever in 2 Samuel 7, but in neither case is there any oath. In Psalm 132 David *sware unto the LORD*, and *the LORD hath sworn unto David in truth*. The need to beef up God's promises with oaths is elsewhere a feature of the Exile (Ps. 89.4), or of the postexilic period (Ps. 110.4: p. 144); the repetition and development of the 2 Samuel 7 promise in vv. 11-12 recalls the more extensive similar development in 89.20-38, suggesting that such reinforced appeals belong when the institution is threatened or suspended.

(3) It is not only 1 Chron. 13.3 that shows an absence of the theme of searching for and finding the ark: it is nowhere in the tradition. Psalm 132 has introduced this theme with the greatest emphasis: David swears that he will not rest till he has found it, and a home for it, and it is found immediately he has finished speaking. There must be some explanation offered for this novel feature, over which Mowinckel has cast a smokescreen.

Porter, 'Psalm 132' (1954), p. 171, suggests briefly that Yahweh was thought to have been sought in a myth, as Anat sought Baal in the Ugaritic myth, or Marduk was sought at Babylon.

(4) Ephrathah was a village in Benjamin, where traditionally Rachel died giving birth to Benjamin (Gen. 35.16), and was buried (1 Sam. 10.2). David's father Jesse came from there (1 Sam. 17.12); but he later settled in Bethlehem. When David's line were established as kings of Judah, it was thought unsuitable for the royal dynasty to come from Benjamin: so the fiction was introduced that Ephrathah was another name for Bethlehem (Gen. 35.19, 'Ephrath [the same is Bethlehem]'; Mic. 5.2, 'Bethlehem Ephrathah', etc.). A similar problem arose from the fact that Kiriath-Jearim, where the ark was laid up, was in Benjamin. The Chronicler has produced a fictitious genealogy in which Ephrath is a wife of Caleb (1 Chron. 2.19), and Ephrathah-Caleb is a district in Judah (2.24), and Ephrathah is the grandmother of Kiriath-Jearim (2.50). We thus have a three-phase history of the name: first it is a town in Benjamin, then it becomes another name for Bethlehem, finally it is turned into a district in north Judah including Kiriath-Jearim. Delitzsch saw that the puzzle of the parallel of *Ephrathah* with *the field of Jaar* in v. 6 could be resolved

by invoking the third phase, and this has been taken up by many later critics; he did not stress the corollary that a late date is implied.

(5) In 2 Samuel 6 the ark is thought of as charged with infinite divine power. Yahweh is in it or upon it, and for Uzzah to touch it is to incur instant death; and similar force is implied in all the early legends in 1 Samuel. Eventually the ark is domesticated as one of the furnishings of the Temple. Yahweh is enthroned on the central wings of the two seraphim in Isaiah 6, and by the time of 1 Chron. 28.2 the ark of the covenant of the LORD has become 'the footstool of our God'; the same verse speaks of the Temple as 'a house of מנוחה' for the ark, and so is an interpretation of Ps. 132.7. It is often thought therefore that *the ark of thy strength* in v. 8 and *thy footstool* in v. 7 are identical; and if so, the concept of the ark as footstool belongs in the postexilic period.

(6) Verse 17 twice implies that there has been an intermission in the Davidic line. *I will make a horn to spring forth* (אצמיח) *unto David* recalls Jeremiah's prophecy, *I will make a shoot to spring forth unto David* (אצמיח לדוד צמח, 33.15). The same image of the shoot, צמח, is repeated in Jer. 23.5 and in Zech. 3.8 and 6.12, and symbolizes the new shoot springing from a bud after a tree has been felled (cf. Isa. 11.1, which itself may be a late gloss). An even closer parallel is in Ezek. 29.21, 'I will *make a horn to spring forth* unto the house of Israel' (אצמיח קרן ל-): the prophet promises a new beginning for the Davidic monarchy after the intermission of the Exile—as here, a new horn sprouting from the brow of a bull.

The second colon reinforces this: *I have prepared* (ערכתי) *a lamp for mine anointed*. In 1 Kgs 11.36 God gives the tribe of Judah to Rehoboam 'that David my servant may have a lamp alway before me in Jerusalem'; that is, David's light will continue to shine in his descendant. In 1 Kgs 15.4 Abijam has behaved badly: 'Nevertheless for David's sake did the LORD his God give him a lamp in Jerusalem, to set up his son after him'. In 132.17 God has *prepared/set in order a lamp*, that is, he has a Davidide in waiting. This is in line also with 132.18, *upon himself shall his crown shine* (יציץ). Zech. 6.11-13 had spoken of a diadem of silver and gold on the head of the man whose name is Shoot (צמח); the association of thought might be natural in the fifth century. This argument has long been familiar to those who have doubted a monarchy date for the psalm.

Other arguments have been deployed in favour of a late date, especially from the similarity of the Davidic ideology to that of the Deuteronomic historian. But these are ably countered by A. Laato, 'Psalm 132' (1992), and I do not advance them here. Laato dates the psalm to Solomon's reign.

The cumulative force of these points must make a postexilic date likely; but it does not solve the problem of the apparent ('self-evident') dramatic dialogue. I should like therefore to make a different suggestion. The starting place should be point (3) above. The psalmist has elaborated the 2 Samuel 6 tradition with notable emphasis. He has put into David's mouth a speech not found there, and underlined it with an oath and a vow; David undertakes not to sleep again until his vow is accomplished, a potentially formidable commitment; he must *find* (אמצא) *place/ tabernacles for Yahweh*; and he is released from his vow when *we heard of it in Ephrathah, We found it* (מצאנוה) *in the field of the wood*. The latter sentence makes plain the ambiguous phrasing of the former. Verse 5, *Until I find out a place for the LORD, Tabernacles for the Mighty One of Jacob*, leads us to think that David was trying to find a *site* for the ark, that is, the Temple site; but v. 6 makes it clear that what was found was *the present, temporary site* for the ark, in Kiriath Jearim. The (feminine) *it* that *we found* (מצאנוה) refers to the last feminine noun in v. 5, משכנות; there was in fact a single *tabernacle for the Mighty One of Jacob*, so v. 6 uses the singular suffix ה־. The widely canvassed suggestion that the *it* is the ark is forced: the ark has not been mentioned, and anyhow it is almost always masculine. So משכנות לאביר יעקב/מקום ליהוה should be taken as hyphenated: what David was trying to *find* was some place-for-Yahweh, some tabernacle-for-the-Mighty-One where the ark had landed up. In 2 Sam. 6.17 מקום is used for a temporary *place* for Yahweh (a tent), and משכנות had been used for the shrine [at Dan] in Ps. 43.3. So we have a further surprising emphasis in 132: why should the psalmist stress David's problem in *finding* the ark's temporary home, which is not referred to in 2 Samuel 6 or 1 Chronicles 13?

Now the community of the Return was beset by the problem of the lost furnishings of the old Temple. Fortunately (in the Chronicler's view) Nebuchadnezzar had kept all the vessels from the Jerusalem temple, and Cyrus brought them forth by the hand of Mithredath the treasurer, and numbered them unto Sheshbazzar, 5400 vessels of gold and silver (Ezra 1.7-11). Huge amounts of gold, silver and precious vessels are loaded on Ezra by Artaxerxes (Ezra 7.15-19) for the

Temple's requirements, and are duly handed over to the priesthood (8.26-30, 33-34). The altar could be rebuilt on its old foundation, and cedars could be bought from Lebanon, as in Solomon's time (3.1-7). But the ark was gone. It was the centrepiece of David's and Solomon's Temple (1 Chron. 13-16; 2 Chron. 6.41; 8.11), and it was no more.

But in the imagination of Israel it was not no more. The Chronicler is our only major authority for three centuries; but when the mist clears in the second century, we hear of a writing in which Jeremiah the prophet 'being warned of God, commanded that the tabernacle and the ark should follow with him... and he found a cavernous chamber in the rock, and there he brought in the tabernacle, and the ark, and the altar of incense; and he made fast the door... saying, Yea, and the place shall be unknown until God gather the people together again, and mercy come' (2 Macc. 2.4-8). So Jeremiah hid both the ark and its tabernacle. Now the same opening chapters of 2 Maccabees tell how *Nehemiah* found the fire which had been hidden in a well in the time of the Exile, and how it engulfed the sacrifices: 'Nehemiah offered sacrifices, after that he had builded both the temple and the altar... Nehemiah, having received a charge from the king of Persia, sent in quest of the fire the descendants of the priests that hid it... Nehemiah commanded to pour on great stones the water that was left... Nehemiah and they that were with him purified the sacrifice' (2 Macc. 1.18-36). Nehemiah is remembered as having looked for some of the holy things which had, in legend, been hidden before the fall of the Temple; the historian cannot say that he found the ark, and he does not want to say that he failed to find the ark, but he did seek and find the holy fire.

We cannot tell how early these traditions are; but we can say that something like them seems to be implied by Psalm 132. Its summoning of the ark to its final home is prefaced by a novel elaboration of the old story, in which the ark is lost; and this is the predicament described in the Maccabaean legend. David finds the ark, which is the situation which Nehemiah's community wishes to be theirs. The fact that it is associated with Nehemiah in 2 Maccabees 1 can hardly be an accident.

Some of the points argued here are also made by H. Kruse in 'Psalm CXXXII' (1983); and he also concludes that the psalm comes from Nehemiah's time.

Psalm 132.1-5. The speaker throughout is the psalmist, Nehemiah's cantor. *LORD, remember for David All...* recalls Neh. 5.19, '*Remember for* me, O my God, for good *all* that I have done...', compare 13.14, 22, 29, 31. עֲנוֹתוֹ are 'his self-deprivations', not his broader troubles, the effects of his own sin: 1 Chron. 22.14 interprets as David's expenditure. *The Mighty One of Jacob* was a phrase from Jacob's Blessing (Gen. 49.24), taken up in more recent times (Isa. 49.26, 60.16) to symbolize God's power to reinstate his people: compare v. 8, *the ark of thy strength*.

Psalm 132 is a carefully balanced psalm. David's swearing to the LORD in v. 2 balances the LORD's swearing to David in v. 11, and David's *tent* (אֹהֶל)—in fact his palace—is introduced as a counter to the LORD's *tabernacles*, מִשְׁכְּנוֹת. David himself conducts the ark to a mere tent (אֹהֶל) in 2 Sam. 6.17, but it is spoken of more grandiosely as *tabernacles, dwelling-places* in the plural as in Pss. 43.3, 84.2.

Gunkel suggests that the idea of not going to his home to sleep came from David's dialogue with Uriah in 2 Sam. 12.10-11; but it is sleep which David gives up here, not just his comfortable bed (still less, as is sometimes said, relations with his wives). The point of the vow is expressed somewhat clumsily: we might have expected הַמָּקוֹם לַיהוה, *the* place for Yahweh where the cows had brought the ark from Philistia, but the psalmist has left it vague, without the article—there must be *a place for Yahweh* somewhere, David thought.

Verse 4: שְׁנָת is described by Delitzsch as 'aramaizing' (cf. GKC 80g).

Psalm 132.6-10. David's speech, which began after his vowing *unto the Mighty One of Jacob*, ends with the same words: the *we* following is the community of Israel, seen as continuous through history. The psalmists of the Songs look back on afflictions 'from my youth up', from the days in Egypt; and the weals from the taskmasters' whips, whether there or in Babylon, are spoken of as plowers making long their furrows 'on my back'. So here it was *we*, in David's time, Israel may now say, who *heard of [the ark-site] in Ephrathah*, who *found it in the wood-country*. The psalmist's *we* is especially suitable because the hope is that the community will find the tabernacle and ark once more.

Gunkel thought that Ephrathah was the same as Bethlehem, and that David's men heard while there that the ark was at Kiriath-Jearim. This can hardly be right. The parallelism sets *Ephrathah* with *the fields of the wood/Jaar*, so Ephrathah should be the place where the ark was; nor is there any obvious reason for mentioning the obscure Ephrathah instead of the well-known Bethlehem if they were the same. Also David is in Jerusalem, not Bethlehem, after 2 Samuel 5; and there must be a reason for *the fields of the wood/Jaar* rather than Kiriath-Jearim. Delitzsch's solution is clearly preferable for *Ephrathah* (see above); it has become a name for northern Judah. Kiriath-Jearim in Benjamin is a similar embarrassment, and has been changed to Baale-Judah even in 2 Sam. 6.2, so as to bring the ark's temporary abode within Judahite territory. קרית means 'town' and יערים means 'woods', but in 1 Sam. 7.1 the ark comes not to the town itself but to the house of Abinadab on the hill: so the psalmist avoids the problem with a circumlocution, שדי־יער, *the woodland country*.

With v. 7 the psalmist announces his intention of going, perhaps processing, to the Temple: the next and final piece from the Nehemiah Testimony will describe Nehemiah's Dedication procession to that place of worship. *Thy footstool* need not mean the ark, for the same expression comes in Ps. 99.5, where it is probably too early to carry that meaning. But the community does wish with full heart that it could escort the ark the next day as David did. Somewhere in the surrounding wooded countryside it lies waiting. In days of old the ark had set forward under divine impulse, and Moses had said, 'Arise, O LORD' (Num. 10.35). The psalmist says the same magical words now, in the hope that the *LORD and the ark of his strength* will take a similar initiative. If so, then he *will* be able to *worship at his footstool* in the fullest sense. Each evening the ark came to rest (נָחֹה, Num. 10.36) in the desert, giving Israel its sought for resting place (מנוחה, 10.33); and Israel's desire now is that it will settle in its final resting-place (מנוחה).

Nehemiah's last act before his celebration had been to make proper provision for the priesthood. The faithless son of the high priest had been banished, the priests' duties had been set out, and their income from first-fruits, and so on, guaranteed, with a full supply of wood for the sacrifices (Neh. 13.30-31). All that is now needed is their sanctity: *Let thy priests be clothed with righteousness*. The cantor need not have worried about *thy saints*, that is the covenanted people, *shouting for joy*: Neh. 12.27 describes their coming 'with gladness, both with thanksgivings and with singing, with cymbals, psalteries and with harps', and the priests and Levites purify themselves in v. 30 for good measure.

But all this concern with David was not accidental; and though it would be very nice to have the ark, there was an even more important side to David's life. He had been so faithful a king that God had pro-mised the kingdom to his descendants also; and just as the ark was lurking somewhere in the countryside, so somewhere among the wor-shippers was one of David's line who might be *thine anointed.* So the prayers end with the greatest petition of all, *For thy servant David's sake, Turn not away the face of thine anointed.* Two generations before it had looked as if Zerubbabel might have been the one, and a crown had been made for him (Zech. 6.9-14); but the LORD had turned away his face, refused him, and the crown had been worn by his high priest. Now once more hope was springing eternal.

Psalm 132.11-18. The psalmist has now completed the first part of his petition, and moves on to the second part, different in form but similar in purpose. By recalling God's covenant with David through Nathan in 2 Samuel 7, he is but turning the screws on the Almighty: the Lord not only promised a Messiah, he swore there would be one. That is right, is it not? Well, then, how about it? The indirect appeal has the additional advantage of reassuring the doubters among the *saints*: this is coming, you know, for we have it on the divine oath. The cultic prophet so often summoned to speak the words is otiose: every Israelite knew the story in 2 Samuel 7, still more every Levite cantor. It is true that God did in the past *turn away the face* (תשב פני) of Zerubbabel; but he will never *turn* (ישוב) *from* his oath.

A friendly gloss has been placed on the content of Nathan's promise too. God said that David's house would rule the kingdom in perpetu-ity; one (Solomon) would come forth from his loins to succeed him, and others thereafter. When he (Solomon) committed iniquity (as he did), God would punish him (by dividing the kingdom between Reho-boam and Jeroboam). There was nothing about *If thy children will keep my covenant...Their children also shall sit upon my throne for evermore*: that has been glossed for the present situation. The com-munity is conscious of a much higher aspiration to faithful obedience than in the monarchy, and trusts that the converse of Nathan's promise of punishment may come true.

The syntax of אמת is disputed, but RV's *in truth* may be accepted: the word is probably due to 2 Sam. 7.28, 'thy words are *truth*'.

The *For* at the beginning of v. 13 is also a significant gloss. The Davidic covenant of 2 Samuel 7 is not said to be in any way dependent on the capture of Zion; but here God has sworn to David *because* (כי) *the LORD hath chosen Zion.* This in fact shows the psalmist's situation. The only part of the old ideology which is in place is the Temple, secure in a fortified Zion (vv. 13-14): *the LORD hath chosen...he hath desired...This is my resting place...Here will I dwell.* Everything else is a hope: the promised Davidic king (vv. 11-12, *If thy children will keep...Their children also shall sit...*; vv. 17-18); peace and plenty (v. 15, *I will abundantly bless... I will satisfy...*); a devout priesthood and laity (v. 16). The situation is that of the other Songs, in the days of Nehemiah.

The repeated אוה, *desire*, is similarly an advance on Ps. 68.17's חמד, *delight*, or 78.68's אהב.

The thought of Psalm 132 is not so different from that of the other Songs. The promise of *blessing on the provision of bread for the poor* is in line with 122.7, 'Peace be within thy walls, And prosperity within thy towers', and 128.2, 'For thou shalt eat the labour of thy hands'. *David,* and his *children's children* who will *sit upon his throne* are in line with 122.5, 'For there were set thrones for judgment, The thrones of the house of David'. David is the great archetype for the Chronicler, the hero of 1 Chron. 10-29; and he features in Nehemiah 12, vv. 36, 37(×2), 45 and 46. Hope in the Lord is the keynote of 130.7 and 131.3. *Zion,* and God's *resting place* there, are the centre of thought throughout the Songs: 'the house of the Lord' is mentioned at 122.9 and 134.1, and is implied in 133.2.

What is not mentioned elsewhere is the ark and the promised king; and 132 differs from the other Songs in length, and in the absence of step-parallels and similes. The last two elements may be due to a different poet among the Levites; but the main differences can be explained from the situation. All the Songs hitherto have been responses to Nehemiah's testimonies of his achievements, but with Neh. 13.31 these are at an end. All that remains is the great procession to the Temple, planned as the climax of the festival (Neh. 12.27-43). As the doubled column mounts the walls and goes with music to the Temple courts where it will unite, the thought naturally turns to the first such procession, led by King David and described in 2 Samuel 6. So many things are the same: the priests, the Levites, the music, the

popular joy, the arrival at the Temple, the sacrifices. But two things
are not the same: there will be no ark, and no David. But who knows?
All things are possible with God. Perhaps the *LORD* will *arise* and
come with *the ark of his strength* from where Jeremiah hid both ark
and tabernacle. And—surely soon—he *will not turn from his oath*, but
will *cause a horn to spring forth unto David, the lamp* which he has
prepared for his Anointed.

PSALM 133

Nehemiah 12.27-43

12 [27]And at the dedication of the wall of Jerusalem they sought the Levites out of all their places, to bring them to Jerusalem, to keep the dedication with gladness, both with thanksgiving and with singing, with cymbals, psalteries and with harps. [28]And the sons of the singers gathered themselves together, both out of the Circuit round about Jerusalem, and from the villages of the Netophathites; [29]also from Beth-gilgal, and out of the fields of Geba and Azmaveth: for the singers had builded them villages round about Jerusalem. [30]And the priests and the Levites purified themselves; and they purified the people, and the gates, and the wall. [31]Then I brought up the princes of Judah upon the wall, and appointed two great companies that gave thanks and went in procession; *whereof one went* on the right hand upon the wall toward the dung gate... [37]and by the fountain gate, and straight before them, they went up by the stairs of the city of David, at the going up of the wall, above the house of David, even unto the water gate eastward. [38]And the other company of them that gave thanks went to meet them, and I after them, with half of the people, upon the wall, above the tower of the furnaces, even unto the broad wall; [39]and above the gate of Ephraim, and by the old gate, and by the fish gate, and the tower of Hananel, even unto the sheep gate: and they stood still in the gate of the guard. [40]So stood the two companies of them that gave thanks in the house of God, and I, and the half of the deputies with me... [43]And they offered great sacrifices that day, and rejoiced; for God had made them rejoice with great joy; and the women also and the children rejoiced: so that the joy of Jerusalem was heard even afar off.

It is certain that the Nehemiah Testimony included an account of the dedication procession, because of the 'I' elements; but the account has been interrupted with lists of names. Verses 32-36 give prominence to Ezra (vv. 33, 36) as Nehemiah's supposed partner in the enterprise, and so leader of the anti-clockwise column; vv. 42-43 give a balancing series of names. Very likely some of the names are historical, but they were not part of the Nehemiah Testimony, as may be seen from v. 37, which follows on from v. 31. Some critics are suspicious of anything mentioning Levites, as an interest of the Chronicler, and other matters; but the Nehemiah Testimony will have given a worthy account of this, the climax of Nehemiah's endeavours, and (as I have argued)

A Song of the Ascents (המעלות); of David.
1   Behold, how good and how pleasant it is
     For brethren to dwell together in unity!
2   It is like the precious oil upon the head,
     That ran down upon the beard,
     Even Aaron's beard;
     That came down upon the collar of his garments;
3   Like the dew of Hermon,
     That cometh down upon the mountains of Zion:
     For there the LORD commanded the blessing,
     Even life for evermore.

its final instalment. Matters which have found echoes elsewhere include: the men of Netophah, Azmaveth and Geba in 7.26-33; the priests purifying of the themselves, as in Ps. 132.9, 16; the people's rejoicing, as in the same verses; and שדות גבע, *the fields of Geba,* recalling שדי־יער, *the fields of the wood* in 132.6.

In 12.37 the right-hand column go up 'by the stairs of the city', על־מעלות עיר, and it has been suggested that the Songs of המעלות might have been sung as they went, and been named accordingly. But the stairs were only a brief section of the procession, nor would it be suitable to name the Songs after the route of only half the celebrants.

Nehemiah's procession is symbolic. It compasses the city, like processions in Psalms 48 and 87 in earlier times; but it does so *on* the walls, now rebuilt, whereas they went round outside, and it does so in two columns, where they (presumably) went in one. The two companies meet at the Temple, and so symbolize the unity of the people. Israel needs to be drawn together: the Governor and the princes, who have so often been at loggerheads; the Levites who have supported Nehemiah and the priests, whose leaders have been connected with Tobiah and Sanballat; the newly inducted citizens from the villages and those who had lived in Jerusalem before. For the moment at least all can join in the 'thanksgiving and gladness' at what has been achieved. The cantor hits the note with v. 1, *Behold, how good and how pleasant it is For brethren to dwell together in unity!* His *Behold!* points to the cheering crowds mingling in the Temple court, with the raucous background of music and chanting. These *brethren,* fellow Jews from Diaspora and from Palestine, from the Circuit and from the city, are now to *dwell together* (שבת גם־יחד), and they certainly look as if they are enjoying it.

Gunkel, following a suggestion of Rauh, interpreted the *brethren dwelling together* as of married brothers continuing to live under one roof after their father's death, in line with Deut. 25.5. But, as Eaton notes, even if the psalm were based on a wisdom saying with this as its point, the psalm is not about this: it is concerned with God's blessing *there*, in *Zion*. It is doubtful, however, whether Eaton's own interpretation is adequate, that the psalm is a part of the annual autumn festal liturgy: fellow Jews do indeed rejoice together at such festivals, but they do not *dwell together* (שבת). Kirkpatrick makes this objection, and refers v. 1 to Nehemiah's repopulation of Jerusalem in Neh. 11.1-2.

The scene before the psalmist is an evident sign of *the LORD's blessing:* the long threatened collapse of the Jewish community will never happen. *The LORD has commanded Life for evermore* for his people, and here is the beginning of an eternal future. The singer's imagination moves to two similes, both images of divinely bestowed life. The first—perhaps occurring to him because the high priest was being reconsecrated for the year in the liturgy—is of the oil of consecration that Moses poured over Aaron's head (we have the tradition in Lev. 8.12). Jewish tradition says that the oil was lost with the Exile, and that thereafter consecration was done by robing the high priest: if so, there is here a further instance of the Songs psalmist's nostalgia. Just as he looked back to the thrones of the house of David in 122.5, and to the missing ark in 132.3-6, so now he speaks of the precious oil (שמן הטוב) poured out over the head of Aaron.

The word which links the images is יָרֶד, which comes three times. God's blessing comes down on Israel, and it comes down liberally: *like the precious oil… which came down on Aaron's beard, That came down upon the collar of his garments.* It was not a film on an archbishop's finger anointing a modern monarch or invalid: it was a bowlful of holy oil, covering Aaron's head, and running right down his beard, and over the open neck of his ephod. God gives generously, and grudges not; and the sacramental oil which transformed the all-too-human Aaron of Exodus 32 into the archetypal priest of Leviticus 8 was not given by measure.

Allen notes that elsewhere the Hebrew for *garments* is מדים, not מדות as here; he translates 'over his body', since מדות often means 'stature, measure'. This would give an even more generous volume of oil, but it is doubtful whether על־פי can mean 'over', rather than 'according to'. Delitzsch and others have thought that the second יָרֶד(ש) referred to Aaron's long beard going down, rather than the oil; but this is contrary to the poet's regular repetitive parallelism. There has been a variety of views about the force of the simile: Delitzsch thinks of the many spices mixed in the sacred oil (Exod. 30.22-38) that symbolize the unity of Israel; Kirkpatrick of the names of the tribes of Israel on the high priest's breastplate over which the oil runs; NEB of the fragrance of the oil; Kraus of its freshness. But none of these aspects is indicated by the text. Eaton is better with a stress on the command of life for Israel in v. 3; this seems to be indicated by the repeated ירד.

Gunkel, Kraus, Seybold and others regard the Aaron element as a gloss by Temple tradents; but speculative emendations need a stronger set of arguments than metrical irregularity, and a supposed origin in secular simplicity.

A second image which occurs to the psalmist is that of the dew: the long summer in Judah yields dry nights and rainless days, and the return of the dew, *coming down* in autumn *on the hills of Zion*, is the welcome sign of the renewal of *life*. The surprising element in the image is that it is *the dew of Hermon* which is said to *come down upon the hills of Zion*; for beyond question *the dew of Hermon* comes down on Hermon, not on Zion, 150 miles to the south. Appeals to occasional strong north winds, or to a supposed current expression, *the dew of Hermon*, meaning a very heavy dew, seem optimistic.

We may rather think of the psalmists' own history. They had in earlier times been priests in the great northern sanctuaries: the Asaphites at Bethel, the sons of Korah at Dan. When their holy places had fallen into Assyrian hands in the 720s, many of these had taken refuge in Jerusalem (Goulder, *Korah*, ch. 3; *Asaph*, chs. 14–15), and their festal psalmodies had been taken over and adapted for Jerusalem use—42–49, 84–85, 87–89, the psalms of the sons of Korah; 50, 73–83, the psalms of Asaph. As they were of levitical descent, the Dan priesthood had accepted the title Levites; and had not only sung their old psalms, but had taken the lead with new ones as required. They had by the fifth century fully concurred in the ideology of their adopted city. *The dew of Hermon*, the mountain on whose spur Dan stood, had *come down upon the hills of Zion*, surrounding Jerusalem. It was *There* that *the LORD commanded the blessing*. The theme was one which went back half a millennium: a psalmist in David's time asked Hermon, the 'mountain of Bashan', 'Why look ye askance, ye high mountains, At the mountain [Zion] which God hath desired for his abode? Yea, the LORD will dwell *in it* for ever' (68.16-17; Goulder, *David*, pp. 202-204).

Gunkel emended ציון to עיון, a place a bit closer to Mount Hermon; but this, and similarly motivated changes to the MT, should be resisted.

PSALM 134

A Song of the Ascents (המעלות).
1   Behold, bless ye the LORD, all ye servants of the LORD,
    Which by night stand in the house of the LORD.
2   Lift up your hands in holiness,
    And bless the LORD.
3   The LORD bless thee out of Zion;
    Even he that made heaven and earth.

The psalmist closes his series of Songs with a double commission, first
to the Temple staff and secondly to the Governor. Nehemiah's Testimonies are at an end, and his cantor's responses to them; but the festal
sequence needs to be finished off as ordinary daily life begins. Two
things will be necessary to maintain the blessing which the LORD
commanded in 133.3: the constant outpouring of worship by the
Levites (and priests), the *servants of the LORD*, and the equally constant outpouring of the divine blessing on the Governor, on whose
judgment and resolution so much must continue to depend.

Critics have been divided on who the *servants of the LORD* are:
some, like Kraus and Rogerson and McKay, seeing them as the people
at large, while others, like Delitzsch and Mowinckel, take them to be
priests and Levites. Allen says that עבדים is never used of cultic
officials, although the verb, and the noun עבודה are standard words
for worship. But עֶבֶד יהוה is used of high officials, especially the king,
or the patriarchs, or the prophets (BDB *s.v.*; cf. Eaton, *Kingship*,
pp. 149-50). There would be no space in *the house of the LORD* for
the people at large, nor would they be permitted access. Especially
would this be true *by night*, when later tradition described in detail
the duties of the Levites and priests keeping the gates, preparing for
the dawn, and so on (see Delitzsch, *ad loc.*). 1 Chron. 9.33 speaks of
Levites in the Temple who 'were employed in their work day and
night'. העמדים, 'standing', is a word used for standing to minister: in
Deut. 10.8 and 18.5, 7, for example. A relevant passage cited by

Kirkpatrick is Neh. 12.44, 'For Judah rejoiced for the priests and for the Levites that stood' (העמדים).

Gunkel wished to excise the opening הנה as being metrically superfluous; perhaps the word had been introduced in error from 133.1. But this seems unnecessary: the cantor is calling to his fellow Levites to be about their business. קדש is usually rendered with RVtext as 'to the sanctuary', but the absence of a preposition is clumsy. RVmg gives 'in holiness', which would correspond with the high state of purity described in Nehemiah 12.

Most commentators have seen v. 3 as addressed to Israel as a whole: the suffix is in the singular, *The LORD bless thee*, but the very same two words with singular suffix open the Aaronic blessing in Num. 6.24. This would then involve a change of speaker at v. 3, what Gunkel calls a little liturgy (so also Auffret, 'Literary Structure', pp. 87–89 [1989]): the people have called on the priests and Levites to bless the LORD in vv. 1-2, and the priests respond in v. 3. Such dividing of the text, without any indication or evidence from later usage, is uncomfortable and unnecessary. The same words, 'The LORD bless thee out of Zion' are addressed to an individual Israelite at 128.5, and 121 is best seen as addressed to a single person, Nehemiah. When so much of the Songs cycle has been centred on Nehemiah, it is unlikely that he should be omitted from the final psalm. His endeavours have shown throughout that he has the great power of Yahweh behind him, the Mighty One of Jacob whose ark is the ark of his strength; and he will need that same blessing in the future, from the God *who made heaven and earth*. The Israel to which he has brought new life has a world destiny.

The phrase *who made heaven and earth* is often said to be part of a special Zion theology, and related to Gen. 14.22, where אל עליון, the creator of heaven and earth was the God of Salem. But this is doubtful: the Melchizedek passage is likely to be a late intrusion with Salem originally a holy place near Shechem (Goulder, *Asaph*, pp. 86-88). But it may be that the autumn festival was in part a celebration of creation as Mowinckel thought (*Psalms in Israel's Worship,* I, pp. 140-46 and *passim*), especially at the end of the feast, cf. Psalms 89 and 104.

Isaiah 30.29 speaks of a song 'as in the night when a holy feast is kept... when one goeth with a pipe to come into the mountain of the LORD'; and *m. Suk.* 5.1-4 describe the night-time celebrations at the opening of Tabernacles. Mowinckel (*Psalmenstudien,* V, pp. 46-47), infers from this that 134 belongs on the night of 15 Tishri; but the plural, בלילות, seems to imply that the Levites' night-time prayers were not performed on a single occasion, but over a period. This is the more significant because in 130 the psalmist's soul looked for the LORD 'More than watchmen *look* for the morning; *Yea, more than* watchmen for the morning', and Kraus suggested that this was an indication of a night-time psalm.

Mowinckel thought the plural was intensive, 'in the depth of night', and others have suggested 'in the night-watches'; but both these proposals seem strained.

This then raises the question of the way in which we may think that the Nehemiah Testimonies and their accompanying psalms were used. The gathering of the tribes to Jerusalem in 122.4, and the procession in 132, as well as other details, have suggested to many scholars that the occasion of the Songs was the autumn festival, Tabernacles. Until the coming of the H and P codes to Jerusalem, Tabernacles was a seven-day feast (Deut. 16.13-15); it was only with Ezra's coming that an eight-day celebration became the rule (Neh. 8.18; Lev. 23.39; Num. 29). But already before the Exile it had become usual to sing a psalm both in the morning and in the evening during a festival: 'It is a good thing... To shew forth thy lovingkindness in the morning, And thy faithfulness every night' (92.2-3). Tabernacles would then require 15 psalms if there were to be one at each service ($7 \times 2 + 1$): beginning from evening on the 15 Tishri and closing at evening on 21 Tishri. It would be necessary to run from evening to evening if the full seven days were to be covered, in the same way that Yom Kippur involves a fast 'from evening to evening' (Lev. 23.32), or sabbath requires three services, and three meals (evening, morning, evening).

Now there are 15 Songs of the Ascents, 120–134; and if they were used one apiece at the 15 services during Tabernacles, 120 would be the psalm for the evening of the fifteenth, and all the even-numbered psalms would be used for the evening services, and the odd-numbered ones in the morning. This would then coincide with the two night psalms just mentioned. 130 would be the psalm for sundown at 19th/ 20th and 134 for sundown on 21st/22nd. We might also think 132 suited for evening use with the Davidic vow, 'I will not give sleep to mine eyes, Or slumber to mine eyelids...' 132 would in any case fall for the evening of 20th/21st, and so would open the final, climactic day of the festival, the day on which in 445 BCE the dedication procession was held. The hypothesis I am proposing is that the Nehemiah Testimonies were delivered one apiece at each of 14 services through the seven days of Tabernacles in 445, with Psalms 120–133 as responses to them; and that 134 was a final psalm to complete the week, and to set Israel on its way for the year.

Not only is this a rather plausible idea in itself: it is borne out by what looks like parallel use elsewhere in the Psalter. Book IV consists of 17 psalms, the number which would be needed for the fuller eight-day celebration that came in from Ezra's time; and 105 and 106 are a pair of postexilic psalms that may well have been added to a pre-exilic collection (see further pp. 193-94). Now, a noticeable feature of the Book IV psalms is their propensity for alternation. Three psalms begin יהוה מלך, 'The LORD reigneth', 93, 97, 99; and 95.3 declares that 'The LORD is...a great King'. Two psalms (96 and 98) begin, 'O sing unto the LORD a new song', and these two psalms both end with three verses calling on the sea to roar and on nature at large to rejoice 'Before the LORD, for he cometh to judge the earth. He shall judge the world with righteousness, And the peoples with his truth/equity' (96.11-13; 98.7-9). Psalm 94, like 96 and 98, promises judgment on the wicked; and 100, like 96 and 98, calls on all peoples to join in the worship of Yahweh. There seems thus to be a double sequence of alternating psalms: the odd numbers celebrate Yahweh's kingship, the even-numbered ones call on the Gentile nations to join in his worship at the coming judgment.

The psalms in Book IV are numbered 90–106, and we should therefore have the same mnemonic as with the Songs: if they were a festal sequence, evening and morning, the even-numbered psalms would have to fall in the evening and the odd numbers in the morning. This time we have three probable morning psalms, 95, 97 and 101. Psalm 95, the *Venite*, has been used as a morning psalm in churches from early times: its challenge, 'Today, if ye will hear his voice, Harden not your heart', seems more appropriate in the morning, when there is time for such resolutions (95.7). Psalm 97.11 says, 'Light is sown for the righteous', and 101.8 says, 'Morning by morning will I destroy all the wicked of the land'. There are two probable evening psalms, the even-numbered 90 and 102: 'O satisfy us in the morning with thy mercy' (90.15) suggests that the plea is made the evening before; 'My days are as a shadow that declineth' (102.12) would be suitable for an evening lament. None of these texts gives the confidence of 134.1, but they are such indications as we have. Psalm 91 contains references to both day and night.

> I expounded this hypothesis in an early article, 'The Fourth Book of the Psalter' (1975), and it is criticized by Gerald H. Wilson, 'Pitfalls and Promise' (1993), 45-46: I am one of the pitfalls. Wilson accuses me of (1) circular argument (I had adduced Mowinckel's nine themes of the Autumn Festival as evidence that Book IV comprised liturgical psalms); (2) of making the *assumption* (Wilson's italics) that there was alternation in the Book's psalms; (3) of straining the evidence of the psalms' timing—eleven of them give me no support, two (91, 94) are against me, only four (90, 97, 101, 102) give me any help. But the *concentration* of Mowinckel's themes is not irrelevant (and most of the psalms are agreed to be hymns, national laments or royal psalms, and so liturgical); the alternation is not assumed but plainly evidenced; and Wilson does not explain why he thinks 91 and 94 to be 'clearly' against the theory (94.1, 'shine forth'?—but in 50.2 this refers to God's coming with lightning for judgment).

A third group with a similar alternation is the opening series, Psalms 2–8. Here 3.6 has, 'I laid me down and slept; I awaked; for the LORD sustaineth me', a suitable morning text. Psalm 4.5 has, 'Commune with your own heart upon your bed, and be still', and 4.9, 'In peace will I both lay me down and sleep: For thou, LORD, alone makest me dwell in safety': Psalm 4 is a Compline psalm, like 134. Psalm 5.4 runs, 'O LORD, in the morning shalt thou hear my voice: In the morning will I order *my prayer* unto thee, and will keep watch'. Psalm 6.7 says, 'Every night make I my bed to swim; I water my couch with my tears'. In Ps. 8.4 the singer considers 'the heavens, the work of thy fingers, The moon and the stars which thou hast ordained'; he does not consider the sun. Once more the even numbers go with the evening psalms, it seems, and vice versa; though here there is no collection of 15 or 17. These are not the only collections in the Psalter, however, that suggest an evening–morning alternation: we shall find two further such groups in 105–118 and 135–150.

It may be convenient then to set out the whole schema which I am proposing for the Songs and for the Nehemiah testimonies. The Songs were a response to the testimonies, and were chanted in the Temple area through Tabernacles, 445 BCE, and in the years following:

Date	Nehemiah	Topic	Psalm
E 15	1.1-11	Lament at Jerusalem's plight	120
M 15	2.1-9	Artaxerxes: journey from Susa	121
E 16	2.10-18	Arrival at Jerusalem, seeking good	122
M 16	2.19-20, 3.33-38	Contempt and scorn	123
E 17	4.1-17	God frustrates planned attack	124
M 17	5.1-13 (19)	Usurers and enslavers capitulate	125
E 18	6.1-14	Wall completed despite plots	126
M 18	6.15–7.5a	Gates guarded, houses to build	127
E 19	11.1-2, 7.26-33	Repopulation	128
M 19	13.4-14	Tobiah and Eliashib discountenanced	129
E 20	13.15-22	Sabbath-breaking	130 E
M 20	13.23-29	Mixed marriages forbidden	131
E 21	13.30-31	Priesthood cleansed and provided for	132
M 21	12.27-43	Dedication procession	133
E 22			134 E

(E stands for evening; M stands for morning)

It may be suitable to end this first part of the book with some comments on the type of argument which I have used here. There are many tables of this kind in scholarly literature, for example proposals of chiasmus, or suggestions of parallels between New Testament epistles and Graeco-Roman rhetoric. It is difficult for such schemes to convince. Where a text is thought to be chiastic, it is often in the exegete's discretion how to divide the passage, and even where to start or to finish it. A well-known instance from the Psalter is for Psalms 15–24:[1]

Liturgy at the Temple Gates	15						24
Individual Psalm of Confidence		16				23	
Individual Lament			17		22		
Royal Thanksgiving				18	20–21		
Creation Hymn/Torah Psalm				19			

This initially attractive schema stirs the reader's suspicions on several grounds. How have Psalms 20 and 21 become combined into a single unit? What is so special about Psalm 19 that it should be the centre of such a structure? Who singled out Psalms 15–24 out of Book I as in

---

1. The scheme was proposed by P. Auffret, *La Sagesse a bâti sa maison: Etude de structures littéraires dans l'Ancien Testament* (OBO, 49; Freibourg/Göttingen: Universitätsverlag/Vandenhoeck & Ruprecht, 1982), pp. 407-38; it is approved by M. Millard, *Die Komposition des Psalters*, pp. 1–25 (24).

some way a unit? Why should anyone wish to arrange psalms chiastic-
ally anyhow? So even if the scheme *were* in the mind of some ancient
editor, there is little prospect of its finding general agreement today.
The same would be true of the application of rhetorical subsections to
a Pauline epistle. We have no given subsections of the epistle: the
exegete has a free hand, and he may also categorize them as he will.

My argument is free from these objections. Both my texts are
complete in the Hebrew biblical corpus: the Nehemiah Testimony is
the whole first-person Nehemiah 'Memoir', as agreed by the scholarly
community; the psalms are 'The Songs of the Ascents' as written into
the headings of Psalms 120–134 and no others. I have no discretion
over the division of either corpus. The psalms are the 15 Songs in the
manuscripts; the Nehemiah sections are defined by the recurrent for-
mulas, the opening 'Now when X and Y heard...', the closing
'Remember...' prayers, or similar markers. The same divisions, with
minimal differences, are to be found in the standard discussions cited.
The order of the Songs is given: the order of the Nehemiah Testimony
is as given down to ch. 12; the only alteration is the displacement of
13.4-31, for which I have given a number of arguments.

The language of the Songs is marked throughout with late
Hebrew/Aramaizing forms such as might be expected from the fifth
century. Their centre of gravity is Jerusalem/Zion, which are mentioned in almost every psalm, and there is joy in its being built as a
city that is joined together (122.3), in its walls and towers (122.7),
with an awareness that it will need to be watched over (127.1). In all
this it is well suited to the time of Nehemiah, who rebuilt the walls
and towers and joined them and set watches over them. The Songs are
marked by a spirit of courage, hope and triumph, allied to a strong
desire for peace, which is not common in the Psalter, but which finds
a clear echo in the Nehemiah Testimony. The notoriously difficult
120.5, 'Woe is me, that I sojourn in Meshech, That I dwell among the
tents of Kedar', is resolvable on the basis that Nehemiah had come to
live among followers of Sanballat from Haran in Meshech, and
Geshem the Arabian, king of Kedar.

For a scheme of this kind to convince, it must fulfil two requirements: every one of the fifteen psalms must be a suitable response to
the Nehemiah Testimony episode aligned with it; and a sufficient
number must correspond with the given episode in some rare or
striking matter. Here we may claim the latter status for 122 (the

brothers' urging to go to Jerusalem, the joy in arriving, the intention 'to seek the good' of the people); of 123 (contempt and scorn of the proud); of 124 (divine deliverance from enemy plots); of 126 (the turning of Israel's fortunes to the amazement of the nations); of 127 (the building of houses and keeping of the city, with the need for children); of 128 (repopulation); and of 132 (David's procession with the ark as foreshadowing the dedication procession). I have offered justifications for each of the other Songs. I find it difficult to think that so much common material has been aligned by accident.

Part II

PSALMS 107–119 AND THE RECONSECRATION OF THE TEMPLE

Whereas the middle section of Book V was a self-proclaimed unity, the Songs of Ascents, its first section appears to be a heterogeneous jumble. There are, it is true, a series of Hallelujahs, either at the beginning (111, 112, 113) or at the end (113, 115, 116, 117) of some of these psalms; and in Jewish tradition 113–118 are linked together as the Passover Hallel. But the basis of even these connections is unclear, and the remaining psalms appear dissociated. Psalm 107 is often thought to be a thanksgiving of those returning from exile; or perhaps a collection of personal thanksgivings. Psalm 108 is a compound of sections from two much earlier psalms, 57.8-12 and 60.8-14, which speak of God as אלהים. Psalm 109 is a protracted curse for false accusation. Psalm 110 is a blessing on the national leader in war. Psalm 114 is a Passover hymn, perhaps of great antiquity. Psalm 119 is *sui generis*, 176 verses set in alphabetic octets in praise of the Law. It is understandable that no discussion has usually been thought necessary on the order of these psalms.

But someone has set the psalms in this order, and that someone was closer to their composition than we are; indeed, since all of them show signs of being written after the Exile, and the order must have been fixed before their translation in the LXX, the interval is much shorter than for Books II and III. We should not therefore easily adopt a counsel of despair and accept their apparent heterogeneity at face value; and we have a suggestion to hand from the Songs of the Ascents. If 120–134 were the celebration psalmody for Nehemiah's achievement in re-establishing Jerusalem as a city, perhaps 107–119 were the celebration psalmody for another such achievement. Fourth-century Jews remembered two such triumphs: the first Return, which ended with the rebuilding of the Temple and a celebratory Passover (Ezra 1–6); and the coming of Ezra with the amplified Law (Ezra 7–10, Neh. 8–10). At least 107 gives encouragement to explore such a possibility.

Psalm 107 is, we may think, a communal thanksgiving for the Return. It is heavily indebted to Second Isaiah, whose prophecies of the Return are frequently echoed, and sometimes cited verbatim. It sets out four images, all of them drawn from Second Isaiah—wandering in the desert, imprisonment, sickness and storm at sea—which represent the just punishment for Israel's sins. But in each case trial is followed by a triumphant refrain: 'Then they cried unto the LORD in their trouble, And he delivered them out of their distresses... Let them praise the LORD for his goodness, And for his wonderful works to the children of men!' These four symbolic scenes are followed by some more general comments on God's reversal of punishment and blessing, also drawn from Second Isaiah. The psalmist draws also on other Scriptures, notably the book of Job.

This view of 107 is by no means agreed: there is a central cleavage among commentators, with a variety of individual conclusions. Older critics, such as Delitzsch and Kirkpatrick, accepted the psalm as a straightforward celebration of the Return; and this is the view of some more recent scholars, such as Jacquet. But the four groups are not represented either as suffering the Exile directly, or as returning from it, and most modern commentators think of them as four representative groups whom Yahweh has delivered from trouble, and for whom thanks is being offered in the Temple. For a review of the variety of opinion see Beyerlin, *Werden und Wesen*, pp. 1-6.

Eaton sees 107 as a single psalm celebrating God's power to deliver from all kinds of trouble. But vv. 2-3 seem to imply the Return, and 33-43 do not fit smoothly on to the four-group section with its refrains. Hence most twentieth-century writers—Mowinckel (*Psalmenstudien*, I, pp. 173-74, *Psalms in Israel's Worship*, II, p. 42), Kraus, Dahood, Allen, and (more hesitantly) Rogerson and McKay and Anderson, suggest an older psalm with four groups in peril which was later adapted as a thanksgiving for the Return in the Temple. Gunkel has an appealing picture of a more individual kind: so many Jews came from the Diaspora with their own thanksgivings that time ran out, and the priests composed a General Thanksgiving which covered all or most topics in vv. 1-32. A hymn, vv. 33-43, was later appended on the reversal of fates, like Hannah's Song—a suggestion taken up by Kraus also. An even more complex development is suggested by W. Beyerlin, who has devoted a whole book to the psalm: the shipwreck section, vv. 23-32, was a later expansion, as well as vv. 2-3, 33-43.

The offering of personal thanksgivings by individuals in a *Dankfestliturgie* is an unevidenced (and implausible) hypothesis; and Gunkel's position is weakened by having to postulate two psalms combined. Kraus's two-stage composition is unlikely because of the pervasiveness of Second Isaiah references, which are as influential in vv. 2-3, 33-43 as in the main block; and the same objection applies to Beyerlin—see below, pp. 120, 124, 127.

Psalm 107.1-9

1   O give thanks unto the LORD; for he is good:
For his mercy *endureth* for ever.

2   Let the redeemed of the LORD say *so,*
Whom he hath redeemed from the hand of the adversary;

3   And gathered them out of the lands,
From the east and from the west,
From the north and from the sea.

4   They wandered in the wilderness in a desert way;
They found no city of habitation.

5   Hungry and thirsty,
Their soul fainted in them.

6   Then they cried unto the LORD in their trouble,
And he delivered them out of their distresses.

7   He led them also by a straight way,
That they might go to a city of habitation.

8   Let them praise (יודו) the LORD for his goodness,
And for his wonderful works to the children of men!

9   For he satisfieth the longing soul,
And the hungry soul he filleth with good.

Ezra 1–3 gives an account (of a problematic kind, see pp. 197-98) of the first Return. In ch. 3 Jeshua, Zerubbabel and others rebuild the altar and relay the Temple foundations: 'they set the priests in their apparel with trumpets, and the Levites the sons of Asaph with cymbals, to praise the LORD, after the order of David king of Israel. And they sang one to another in praising and *giving thanks unto the LORD,* [saying] *For he is good, for his mercy* [endureth] *for ever* toward Israel' (3.10-11). Very likely most of the events of Ezra 1–3 owe much to the imagination of the years; but it is entirely plausible that 107.1 has retained its original context in the popular memory. This was the wording with which the returning exiles of the sixth century gave thanks for Yahweh's eternal חסד. In v. 2 they are the redeemed of the LORD, and in v. 3 gathered from the points of the compass: 'redeem' is a frequent verb in Second Isaiah, and Isa. 62.12 says, 'They shall be called...*the redeemed of the LORD*...Sought out'. We have similar reference to the Return in the prophecies of Jeremiah: 'Behold, I will *gather them from* all *the lands*' (32.37); 'Yet again shall be heard in this place...the voice of joy...*Give thanks to the LORD* of hosts, *for* the LORD *is good, for his mercy* [endureth] *for ever*' (33.11). The same words open Psalm 136, and provide its refrain, leading up to vv. 23-24, 'Who remembered us in our low estate...And delivered us from our adversaries'. The context is steadily the Return and Restoration.

It is often observed that, despite the division between Books IV and V, 107 is closely related to 105 and 106. Psalm 105 also begins '*O give thanks unto the LORD*', and recounts Yahweh's mercies from Abraham to the Exodus. Psalm 106 opens 'Praise the Lord. *O give thanks unto the LORD; for he is good: For his mercy* [endureth] *for ever*', and recalls the sad tale of national rebellions from Egypt to the Exile. Psalm 107 then completes the trio with the redemption from Babylon, rather like the two Books of Chronicles and Ezra–Nehemiah. There are a number of echoes of the language of the earlier psalms, especially 106: '[God would] scatter them in *the lands*' (v. 27); 'Nevertheless he regarded *their distress*, When he heard their cry' (v. 44); 'Save us, O LORD our God, *And gather* us *from* among the nations, *To give thanks* unto thy holy name' (v. 47). Here too the thanks are for the gathering.

Hebrew and Greek alike give three points of the compass and 'the sea' as the places from which the exiles have returned; and since there are four groups described, and the fourth go down to the sea in ships, we may think a correlation is intended. Those from the east have come across the desert from Babylon, perhaps on the highway proclaimed by Second Isaiah. It is unlikely that the two middle groups are intended to correspond with west and north; though it might be thought that those from the west (of Judah) have returned from Egypt, known to the Deuteronomists as 'the house of bondage', and symbolized here as a prison. Second Isaiah twice speaks of the return as coming from the north (Isa. 43.6, 49.12); and at 43.5-6 he specifies east, west, north and Teman as the places from which Israel will be *gathered*. But 49.12 has, 'Lo, these shall come from far: and lo, these *from the north and from the sea* (מים)'; so the psalmist has included the exiles who went to Asia Minor, Cyprus and such places overseas. South of Judah there are deserts, and Edomites; not many Jews will have settled there.

For the exiles from Babylon Second Isaiah had foreseen a majestic highway built for God's, and his people's, progress (35.8, 40.3-4, 42.10-12, 49.10-12, 51.9-10); but reality, as the psalmist knows, was not so simple. He sees the party losing its way in the ill-marked steppe, like the caravans in Job 6.18-20, 'wandering' (תעו) as in Isa. 35.8; the

ישׁימון recalls Ps. 106.14, where the Israelites wandered for forty years. They can find no place of human habitation, and are out of food and water; but at their prayer these needs are supplied as in Isa. 49.10, 'They shall not *hunger* nor *thirst*'. Isaiah 42.16 prophesied, 'I will lead the blind by a *way* they do not know', and Ezra 8.21 prays for *a straight way* (דרך ישׁרה) from Babylon to Jerusalem. So the description of the passage of the eastern exiles is framed in terms of Deutero-Isaianic prophecy.

Verse 2. צר מיד is taken as 'from the clutch of adversity' by Kirkpatrick and Gunkel, cf. v. 6; but יד suggests a personal adversary, as the Babylonians had been, and the combination always has this meaning elsewhere in the Old Testament (Beyerlin, *Werden und Wesen*, p. 69). *Verse 3.* MT and versions have מים, apart from some Latin MSS: Gunkel follows these and the Targum with the suggestion of מימן, 'from the south'. But Isa. 49.12 supports 'from the sea', as does the fourth group in vv. 23-32. Beyerlin, *Werden und Wesen*, pp. 67-69, cuts vv. 2-3 from his original psalm, despite the echoes of Second and Third Isaiah which they have in common with the rest of Psalm 107.

Verse 4. MT links דרך with 'desert', as in RV above; LXX Syr link it attractively with עיר. Here and in v. 7 the עיר מושׁב is a settlement in the wilderness, where fellow humans might save the travellers from death; at v. 36 it is a town of their own. *Verses 5-7*: The imperfects stress the repetition of the troubles. *Verse 8.* Delitzsch and Eaton take לבני אדם with יודו, rendering 'Let them declare his goodness to Yahweh, and his wonderful works to the children of men'; but Allen prefers the RV construction, following Ps. 36.8.

Psalm 107.10-16

10   Sitting (ישׁבי) in darkness and in the shadow of death,
Being bound in affliction and iron;

11   Because they rebelled against the words of God,
And contemned the counsel of the Most High:

12   Therefore he brought down their heart with labour;
They fell down and there was none to help.

13   Then they cried unto the LORD in their trouble,
And he saved them out of their distresses.

14   He brought them out of darkness and the shadow of death,
And brake their bands in sunder.

15   Let them praise (יודו) the LORD for his goodness,
And for his wonderful works to the children of men!

16   For he hath broken the gates of brass,
And cut the bars of iron in sunder.

A second image which Second Isaiah uses for the Exile is imprison-ment: 42.7, 'to bring out the *prisoners* from the dungeon, and *them that sit in darkness* out of the prison house' (אָסִיר...יֹשְׁבֵי חֹשֶׁךְ); 49.9, 'saying to the *prisoners* (אֲסִירִים), Go forth, and to them that are in *darkness*, Shew yourselves'. חֹשֶׁךְ is paralleled with צַלְמָוֶת in Isa. 9.1. Thus the opening of the second section of the Psalm is drawn from Second Isaiah; and so is the closing v. 16, which is taken almost word for word from Isa. 45.2, 'I will *break in pieces the doors of brass, and cut in sunder the bars of iron*' (דַּלְתוֹת נְחוּשָׁה אֲשַׁבֵּר וּבְרִיחֵי בַרְזֶל אֲגַדֵּעַ). So the prisoner of v. 10 is *bound* in misery and *iron* from Second Isaiah; the combination of fetters with *affliction* is probably due to Job 36.8. Israel's rebelling is carried over from Ps.106.43, 'they *were rebellious* in their *counsel*'; the consequent oppression by their enemies is in 106.42, their distress and cry in 106.44, and their deliverance in 106.45-46. Jerusalem *fell down* (כָּשְׁלָה) because of her sins at Isa. 3.5, and *falling down* was a peril for even the young in Isa. 40.30 (כָּשׁוֹל יִכָּשֵׁלוּ): there was *none to help* also in Isa. 63.5.

Second Isaiah does not represent the Babylonian Exile as a time of slave-labour, nor does any other text. The psalmist has filled this in from his own imagination, but behind it may well be the national tradition of having been slaves in Egypt in Exodus; there had been a house of bondage (עֲבָדָה), and they had been ground down by hard labour; and Second Isaiah saw the Return as a new Exodus. We know from Jeremiah that many Jews fled to Egypt after 587 BCE (Jer. 42–44), and it may be that when the psalmist says that the redeemed were gathered 'from the west', which does not mean 'the sea', he is thinking of Egypt. This must remain a speculation, as there are no linguistic reminiscences of Exodus, but it is an attractive one.

Delitzsch notes the psalmist's fondness for word-play: אָמְרוּ/הֵמִירוּ (v. 11). The refrain verses, 13 and 15 vary slightly from vv. 6 and 8.

Psalm 107.17-23

17 Fools, because of the way of their transgression,
   And because of their iniquities, they are afflicted.
18 Their soul abhorreth all manner of meat:
   And they draw near unto the gates of death.
20 Then they cry unto the LORD in their trouble,
   And he saveth them out of their distresses.

21   He sendeth his word and healeth them,
      And delivereth *them* from their pits.
22   Let them praise (יודו) the LORD for his goodness,
      And for his wonderful works to the children of men!
23   And let them offer the sacrifices of thanksgiving,
      And declare his works with singing.

Fools because of the way of their transgression is an echo of Isa. 35.8, which prophesies that 'an highway shall be there and a *way…* *fools* shall not err [therein]': אוילים, 'fools', is a rare word, and the combination with דרך in v. 17 is contorted. The Exile is interpreted as God's *afflicting* (ענה) Israel (Isa. 60.14, 64.11), and such *affliction of the soul* is understood as going without food in Isa. 58.3, 5. The image of sickness is present in Second Isaiah—God's servant 'has borne our sickness' (Isa. 53.4)—but it is more pervasive in earlier parts of the prophecy, which will have been a seamless robe to the psalmist. The folly *of the fools* consists in their *transgression* of the divine will, like the sick Hezekiah in Isa. 38.17, or the bruised and suppurating body politic of Isa. 1.1-6. As the king turned his face to the wall in Isa. 38.2 and was consigned to *the gates of* Sheol in 38.10, so do the psalmist's fools refuse food and draw near the gates of death. The picture may also owe something to Job 33.20, 22, 'his life abhorred bread…Yea, his *soul draweth near* unto the *pit*'. Job's *pit* (שחת) and Hezekiah's consuming *pit* (שחת בלי, Isa. 38.17) probably stand behind 107.19's 'their pits' (משחיתותם). God *sent his word* as in Isa. 55.11, 'so shall my *word* be that goeth forth out of my mouth; it shall not return unto me void…', one of the few texts where the divine word is hypostatized; and it *healed them*, as God intended in Isa. 6.9 that Israel should turn and be *healed*.

The cry in trouble, the deliverance and the summons to thanksgiving in vv. 19, 21 follow the pattern of vv. 6, 8; 13, 15; but v. 22 makes the scene clearer. The context is liturgical. The psalm is to be followed by a sacrifice, as 'the sacrifice of thanksgiving' is offered (ויזבחו זבחי תודה); and God's wonderful works are to be recited (ויספרו) with singing (ברנה). There are further details in v. 32. The praise is to be given 'in the assembly of the people' (בקהל־עם), 'in the seat of the elders' (במושב זקנים). It recalls the context which I have proposed for the Songs of Ascents, with Nehemiah leading a procession of the senior burghers to the Temple: there is thanksgiving and singing (Neh. 12.27), and great sacrifices and rejoicing (12.43), and the recital of Nehemiah's own achievements. We have the same atmosphere in Ezra 3: Jeshua and Zerubbabel, newly returned from Babylon, rebuild the altar and offer burnt offerings upon it (3.1-3); they keep the feast of Tabernacles (3.4); six months later they lay the foundation of the Temple with the Asaphites singing thanks to the Lord 'for he is good, for his mercy [endureth] for ever to Israel' (3.10-11).

A difficulty in translating Psalm 107 is its liking for the imperfect, with or without וֹ; hitherto RV has preferred the English past tense, from v. 17 the present. The ambivalence arises from the psalm's double reference: these images stand for past events, the Exile and the Return; but also for regular events as the images are played out in the lives of individuals.

Psalm 107.23-32

23 They that go down to the sea in ships,
   That do business in great waters;
24 These see the works of the LORD,
   And his wonders in the deep.
25 For he commandeth, and raiseth the stormy wind,
   Which lifteth up the waves thereof.
26 They mount up to the heaven, they go down again to the depths;
   Their soul melteth away because of trouble.
27 They reel to and fro, and stagger like a drunken man,
   All their wisdom is swallowed up.
28 Then they cry unto the LORD in their trouble,
   And he bringeth them out of their distresses.
29 He maketh the storm a calm,
   So that the waves thereof are still.
30 Then are they glad because they be quiet;
   So he bringeth them unto the haven of their desire.
31 Let them praise the LORD for his goodness,
   And for his wondrous works to the children of men!
32 Let them exalt him also in the assembly of the people,
   And praise him in the seat of the elders.

Isa. 49.12 spoke of the exiles being gathered *from the sea* (מִיָּם). Isa. 42.10 calls, 'Sing unto the LORD...ye that *go down to the sea*', as 107.23 speaks of יֹרְדֵי הַיָּם, *they that go down to the sea*. Isa. 54.11 addressed Zion as 'O thou afflicted, *tossed with tempest*': the Hebrew is סֹעֲרָה, like the storm סְעָרָה in Ps. 107.25. So a fourth Deutero-Isaianic image of the Exile underlies the fourth section of the psalm. The Return is here seen as like a merchant vessel caught in the storm. God speaks (ויאמר) as in 105.31, 34, and the wind rises. The sailors go up and down, and their wisdom is swallowed up, as the counsel of the Egyptians *was swallowed up* (בלע) in Isa. 19.3; they stagger like a drunken man as the earth *staggers like a drunken man* (נוע תנוע כשכור) in Isa. 24.20. But other passages may have been influential also. God silences the roaring of the waves in Ps. 65.8; in Job 12.24-25 he makes the leaders wander in a pathless waste, grope in the dark, and *stagger like a drunken man*; in Jon. 1.11 the sea *is made quiet* (שתק). So the psalmist's spirited description of the storm is determined for much of the way by scriptural, and especially Isaianic phrasing; the whole image of exile as a storm is dependent on Isa. 54.11, and the return of some exiles from Asia, Syria and Cyprus by sea seemed prophesied in Isa. 42.10 and 49.12.

In the MT vv. 21-26 and v. 40 are marked with an inverted nun, a symbol of hesitation over the text. These symbols have been a mystery. Doubt over v. 40 seems explicable: the princes have arrived in the psalm surprisingly, and many exegetes find the syntax of vv. 39f. difficult. We may think that an editor missed the echo of Isa. 54.11 and found the storm scene out of place for so un-nautical a people as the Jews; so he 'bracketed' vv. 21-30, with v. 31 identical to v. 21, but only six of his nuns survived. Jacquet thinks that the section has been expanded by an editor, but his expansions do not tally with the nuns either. There is no satisfactory solution.

Beyerlin, *Werden und Wesen*, pp. 20-21, exaggerates when he says that the 'strophe' has 'absolutely no contact with prophetic material': Isa. 42.10, 49.12 and 54.11 are obvious links with Second Isaiah, and the others which I have cited are noteworthy. There is less nautical matter in Second Isaiah, which is why there are more parallels with other Psalms, Jonah, and so on. Beyerlin's texts from Proverbs (23.34; 30.19; 31.14), with the corollary of a wisdom connection, are remote.

Psalm 107.33-43

33   He turneth rivers into a wilderness,
      And watersprings into a thirsty ground;
34   A fruitful land into a salt desert,
      For the wickedness of them that dwell therein.
35   He turneth the wilderness into a pool of water,
      And a dry land into watersprings.
36   And there he maketh the hungry to dwell,
      That they may prepare a city of habitation;
37   And sow fields, and plant vineyards,
      And get them fruits of increase.

38   He blesseth them also, so that they are multiplied greatly:
      And he suffereth not their cattle to decrease.
39   Again, they are minished and bowed down,
      Through oppression, trouble, and sorrow.
40   He poureth contempt upon princes,
      And causeth them to wander in the waste, where there is no way.
41   Yet setteth he the needy on high from affliction.
      And maketh *him* families like a flock.
42   The upright shall see it, and be glad;
      And all iniquity shall stop her mouth.
43   Whoso is wise shall give heed to these things,
      And they shall consider the mercies of the LORD.

The influence of Second Isaiah continues. In Isa. 50.2 God says, 'Behold, at my rebuke I dry up the sea, I *make the rivers a wilderness*' (נהרות אשים מדבר), and he dries up the pools at 42.15; the fruitful land which becomes a salt desert reminds us of the cities of the plain in Genesis 19. The *thirsty ground*, צמאון, comes in Isa. 35.7. Verse 35 virtually repeats Isa. 41.18b, 'I will make the *wilderness into a pool of water*' (אשים מדבר לאגם מים); a *leitmotif* of Second Isaiah (35.7; 43.19-20). Second Isaiah promised the building of new homes for the returning exiles, and the need for expansion (49.19, 54.1-3); the psalmist's *city of habitation* answers Isaiah's prophecy, 'thou shalt make the desolate cities to be *inhabited*' (יושיבו ערים נשמות, 54.3). The blessing and multiplying recalls texts in Genesis (12.2; 17.20).

But reality is not allowed to escape: all was far from smooth at the Return (v. 39). Even so, comfort was to be taken from the book of Job: '*he poureth contempt on princes*' (שופך בוז על־נדיבים, 12.21), '*and causeth them to wander in the waste, where there is no way*' (ויתעם בתהו לא־דרך, 12.24). So the 'princes' suffer the same fate as the Israelites in v. 4. In Job 21.11, as in v. 41, the blessed 'send forth their little ones *like a flock*' (כצאן); in Job 22.19 'the righteous *shall see and rejoice*' (יראו צדיקים וישמחו), and in Job 5.16 '*iniquity stoppeth her mouth*' (ועלתה קפצה פיה). The psalmist ends on the same note as the prophecy of Hosea: '*Whoso is wise* shall give heed to *these things;* and he shall *understand*' (מי חכם ויבן אלה נבון, Hos. 14.10). His poem ends where it began, with *the mercies of the Lord.*

Gunkel and others reverse vv. 39 and 40, with appeals to the further inverted nun; but the Return context makes the less optimistic tone natural, and the somewhat awkward v. 40 is to be explained by its being taken over from Job 12.

In the above interpretation I have swum against the century's tide; but for three good reasons.

(1) The four groups in vv. 4-32 are to be explained as four traditional images of Israel in exile: the psalm has merely used a little imagination to fill them out, often with the aid of other biblical passages. The alternative explanation, offered in its starkest form by Gunkel (but others are little different), is implausible. If we are to think of four groups of sufferers for whose deliverance the psalm might be a composite thanksgiving, the selection is curious. Of all those attending a festival in Jerusalem, few surely will have got lost in the desert. Hardly any will have been released from prison: Israel did not run a prison system with penitentiaries like St Quentin. In the pre-exilic period (posited by many critics for the earlier version) Israelites did not often go to sea. One would have expected those who have escaped the slavery, debt and false accusations so often invoked by commentators, which must at least have been common troubles, like sickness.

(2) The individualistic picture evoked in these interpretations is the child of Protestant piety, and lacks evidence in Old Testament Israel. We do hear of Paul paying the costs of certain Christians who had made vows in Acts 21, and of his ill-starred visit to the Temple; but anything in the nature of a *Dankfest* for private individuals in earlier times is a speculation. What we hear about is a round of pilgrim feasts at which the whole people gave thanks for national blessings; and what is more, we hear about such in Ezra 3.

(3) Kraus says 'In reference to the reception of the psalm in circles of the post-exilic community, it is likely that the desert wandering could have been transferred to the journey of those returning from Mesopotamia' (*Psalmen*, II, p. 738, my translation, with references to Second Isaiah, cf. p. 739). But the Second Isaiah references are ubiquitous, and embedded in the text. Jacquet is surely justified in saying, 'Finally, is it the result of sheer chance that the poem uses, from one end to the other, *the same images* which Isaiah used to describe the Return from the Exile?' (*Les Psaumes*, III, p. 161, my translation, Jacquet's stress). Psalm 107 is clearly a thanksgiving for the Return, by one very familiar with Second Isaiah.

This leaves us then with the question of the date. It is natural to think of the late sixth century, the period of the first Return, when there must have been a deep spirit of thankfulness for divine deliverance through Cyrus; such joy is described in Ezra 3. The Deutero-Isaianic prophecies were then comparatively recent, and must have seemed vivid testimonies to God's infallible purposes. The only hesitation arises from Psalm 107's use of Job in the later verses; for the linguistic connections are too close, too numerous and too clustered (cf. Job 12.21, 24; 21–22) to be accidental, and the smooth contexts in Job contrast with their occasional awkwardness in Psalm 107 (especially v. 40). But dates for Job in the fifth and fourth centuries are but speculations. The disaster of 70 CE produced a volume of varied reaction from *2 Baruch* and *4 Ezra* to Josephus; and we may think that the earlier catastrophe issued not only in the *Vergeltungsdogma* of the Deuteronomistic History, but also a protest of a more radical stamp in Job, including the expansion in Job 32–37.

Beyerlin, *Werden und Wesen*, pp. 13-18, carefully notes the contacts with Second Isaiah and Job, which he argues convincingly to be sources for Psalm 107 and not vice versa; and he stresses that the Job passages are often from additions to the book, including the Elihu chapters. This leads him to date the psalm late in the third century, with links to the wisdom poetry of Ben Sira; and to take vv. 2-3 accordingly as a late gloss. It seems easier to suspect the supposed late date of Job, and to follow the suggestions of Second Isaiah's omnipresent symbolism of the Return.

PSALM 108

1   A Song, a Psalm of David.
2   My heart is fixed, O God;
      I will sing, yea, I will sing praises, even with my glory.
3   Awake, psaltery and harp;
      I will awake the dawn.
4   I will give thanks unto thee, O LORD, among the peoples:
      And I will sing praises unto thee among the nations.
5   For thy mercy is great above the heavens,
      And thy truth reacheth unto the skies.
6   Be thou exalted, O God, above the heavens:
      And thy glory above all the earth.
7   That thy beloved may be delivered,
      Save with thy right hand, and answer me.
8   God hath spoken in his holiness; I will exult:
      I will divide Shechem, and mete out the valley of Succoth.
9   Gilead is mine; Manasseh is mine;
      Ephraim also is the defence of my head;
      Judah is my lawgiver.
10   Moab is my washpot;
      Unto Edom will I cast my shoe:
      Over Philistia will I shout.
11   Who will bring me into the fenced city?
      Who will lead me unto Edom?
12   Wilt not thou, O God, which hast cast us off,
      And goest not forth, O God, with our hosts?
13   Give us help against the adversary:
      For vain is the salvation of man.
14   Through God we shall do valiantly:
      For it is he that shall tread down our adversaries.

Psalm 108 is, by common consent, a combination of parts of two older psalms, 57.8-12 and 60.7-14. These two psalms form part of the 'Prayers of David' (72.20), which normally use אלהים for God, whereas Book V uses יהוה overwhelmingly. Out of the nine uses of אלהים in the Book, six occur in this psalm. It is also commonly said that the main part of 108 is the section from Psalm 60. The opening of 60 ran, 'O God, thou hast cast us off, thou hast broken us down: Thou hast been angry...', whereas 60.7-14 are optimistic, indeed triumphant in tone. It seems easy therefore to explain why the author of 108 should have substituted the confident verses at the end of Psalm 57 for this depressing introduction.

Dahood thinks the two sections of Psalm 108 could have been independent units incorporated both here and in 57 and 60; other critics are agreed that 108 has drawn on the two Prayers of David. For an account of the original context of 57 and 60 , see my *Prayers of David*, pp. 116-23, 141-51. Gunkel, and most critics, take the passage from 60 as the primary focus of 108—as indeed its greater length and specificity imply. Tournay, 'Psaumes 57, 60 et 108' (1989) also sees 57 and 60 as the originals: 108 is the work of postexilic Levites prophesying the fall of paganism—a view not far from my own, but lacking focus.

It remains to seek a plausible explanation of why the author should have had such an interest in the second part of Psalm 60. Kirkpatrick suggests that the enmity felt towards Edom was powerful after 587 BCE, and that the psalm might have been reused in the period of the Restoration; Jacquet and Allen make a similar comment. But 108 takes the passage over not with the Edom verses but with the oracle against Shechem and Succoth, and it is this which needs to be explained.

Both Kirkpatrick and Delitzsch also notice that the opening verses link on to 107. The refrain of 107 began, 'Let them give thanks to the Lord' (יודו ליהוה), and 108.4 begins, 'I will *give thanks unto* thee, O *Lord*' (יהוה...אודך); here 57's אדני has been replaced by יהוה, whereas the six אלהים's have been untouched. The object of gratitude in 107.1 was Yahweh's mercy (חסד), and it is the same in 108.5 (חסדך). So we may think that the same context is possible. The ebullient tone of the two psalms is similar.

Psalm 107 suggested a setting such as we find in Ezra 3: the high spirit of thankfulness at the fulfilment of Second Isaiah's prophecies of the Return, the sacrifices of thanksgiving offered on the lately rebuilt Temple altar, the Asaphite choir singing antiphonally the very words of 107.1, the gathering of the entire community for the festival. Furthermore the Chronicler notes that the music was performed 'after the order of David king of Israel', so the Psalms of David are in mind. However, the community's hopes of rebuilding the Temple are soon to be frustrated: for there is pretended support, and then outright opposition, from the inhabitants of Samaria and the rest of the country (Ezra 4). Samaria is especially singled out in 4.10 and 17. But Samaria was not yet built in the days of David king of Israel: he had announced an oracle of God against Shechem, the older city so close to it.

We have thus a believable explanation for the order, as well as for the selection of the psalm sections. With Psalm 107 Judah rejoices at the return of her exiles, and celebrates with songs and with sacrifices of thanksgiving. The joy continues into 108: the national spokesman, the Asaphite choirmaster, takes up 107's call to give thanks to Yahweh for his mercy. There lies to hand *A Song, a Psalm of David*, culled from the old David collection, 51–72. The words of 57.8-12 are particularly apposite: *My heart is fixed...I will sing, I will sing praises...psaltery and harp.* Only the old *Awake, my glory* seems obscure and is amended to *even with my glory*, that is the human image of the divine Glory of v. 6: if the speaker is to *awake the dawn*, his glory is presumably awake already. His praises are sung *among the peoples*: the returned exiles are conscious of their international standing. *God* is *exalted* not only *to* (עַד) *the heavens* as in Psalm 57, but *above* (מֵעַל) them, as in the following verse עַל־שָׁמַיִם.

After this happy proem comes the theme of the moment. As Shechem fell under divine judgment in David's time in Psalm 60, so now will the same fate lie in store for Samaria, its latter-day successor. *Thy beloved ones*, once David's loyal followers, are now seen as the Judahite remnant; they need to *be delivered* from their powerful neighbours, and an *answer* given to the speaker's prayer. The text of Psalm 60 is understood as an oracle, *spoken* by *God in his holiness*, that is as an oath. He swore to *divide Shechem and to mete out the valley of* her ally *Succoth*. Although Judah consists in little more than the city ruins and the villages for 20 miles around, the whole land is God's. *Gilead is* his, on the east bank of Jordan, *Manasseh* on the west: *Ephraim*, centre of old Israel, is his helmet, *Judah* his מְחֹקֵק—the word meant 'general' in the days of Psalm 60, but it may well mean RV's *lawgiver* in Psalm 108. God has nothing but contempt for Israel's other neighbours. *Moab*, with its Dead Sea, is just his *washpot*; he *will cast his shoe unto Edom*, the symbol of his possession of the land of that country. Only the third stich needs amending: in David's time the Cherethites, Pelethites and Gittites of *Philistia* were the king's private army, and could be called on to *Shout for me!*; but those days are gone, old mercenaries are modern enemies, and the text is changed to *Over Philistia will I shout.* The closing verses promised an expedition to punish Edom, and Psalm 108 is happy to retain this prospect of sweet revenge. Only Psalm 60's *ramparted city* (מצור) needs improving to *fenced city* (מבצר): the eyes of the psalmist 108 are set on Bozrah, the nearest Edomite stronghold (בצרה).

Most commentators are content to leave the context open. Mowinckel, in *Psalmenstudien,* III, pp. 65-73, suggested that the original context in 60 went back to David's campaign against Edom, and that 108 marked the resumption of such hostilities by Joram in the ninth century; but he is silent on this matter in *Psalm in Israel's Worship*, II, p. 59. Rogerson and McKay see the psalm as the prayer of an Israelite leader before dawn, in preparation for a battle; Edom is taken to be a poetic expression for Israel's enemies generally.

PSALM 109

Psalm 109 is the most shocking psalm in the Psalter, the pure vitriol of distilled hatred. The speaker repeatedly speaks of himself as *accused* (vv. 4, 20, 29), and wishes an *accuser* on his enemies (v. 6), who are sometimes thought of as a group (vv. 2-5, 13, 15, 20-29), and sometimes as a single person (vv. 6-19). He offered them *love*—friendliness—and they have given him *hatred* in return (vv. 3, 5), with *the mouth of deceit* and *a lying tongue*, all kinds of slander and false allegation (v. 2). He *shewed no mercy*, but *persecuted the poor and needy man* to death (v. 16), and *cursed* him (vv. 18, 28). They make him *a reproach*, a laughingstock, and *shake their head* at him (v. 25). The speaker feels himself to be in acute danger, and powerless. He fasts, and is wasting away (vv. 23-24), but his resource is in fact to turn himself into a living *prayer* (v. 4 תפלה ואני), if prayer is the word. He speaks of his enemies' curses, but it is hard to imagine anything more comprehensive or pitiless than his own offering. Such futile imaginings are the last weapon of the desperate.

The speaker's own position is not too clear. He speaks of himself as *poor and needy* (vv. 16, 22), but in v. 4 he showed *love* to his opponents, which suggests that he had seen himself on a parity with them; nor perhaps would they trouble to *accuse* him and tell lies against him unless he had something which they wanted. They have clearly appealed to some higher authority against him, but his position is not hopeless because the higher authority may go against them (v. 6). He feels that he can depend on God because God has promised him his חסד, and God's *name*, his reputation, is at stake (v. 21). He looks forward to giving *great thanks to the Lord* in public *among the multitude*, presumably at a national festival (v. 30).

This unclarity has left a longstanding division in the interpretation of the psalm. A majority of exegetes have seen the speaker as an individual: one of the pious 'poor' falsely accused by the godless 'rich', and in peril of his life; his health wasted away under the magic force of their evil words. A smaller number of commentators has taken him to be a national representative: falsely accused to a suzerain power, he sees the enemy as preparing to attack him militarily, and laying down a barrage of lying curses to weaken him. The balance of the evidence seems to favour the latter view, though in a slightly amended form.

Kirkpatrick, Gunkel, Schmidt, *Das Gebet des Angeklagten im Alten Testament*, Mowinckel in *Psalmenstudien*, V, pp. 94-96, Kraus, Weiser, Dahood, Rogerson and McKay, Anderson, Jacquet and Allen all take the individual view. Delitzsch thought the psalm went back to David, and wondered if the enemy was Doeg. Olshausen favoured Alcimus in Maccabaean times. Mowinckel's pupil Birkeland persuaded him to a representative understanding in *Die Feinde des Individuums* (1933), and in *Psalms in Israel's Worship*, I, p. 219, and elsewhere he sees a national context. So also Eaton, both in his commentary and in *Kingship*, p. 81.

(1) The speaker sees himself as having a special relationship with God. He is 'the God of my praise' (v. 1), 'Yahweh my Lord' (v. 21), 'Yahweh my God' (v. 26). He has covenanted his חסד to him (vv. 21, 26), and undertaken to deliver him (vv. 21, 26, 31). God's reputation is involved in keeping this covenant: 'for thy name's sake' (v. 21). Language of this personal kind was proper for Israel's leadership; it is used by kings and by Moses, and occasionally by prophets. The speaker here describes himself as 'thy servant', a term often used of David. God undertook to bless the house of David in perpetuity (2 Sam. 7); but he gave no undertaking to deliver every ordinary Israelite from sickness or oppressors. It is surprising that scholars have so easily believed this 'democratized' understanding of חסד. Israelites must have been ill a lot, and died in their forties; the slavery laws, or Nehemiah 5, or many other texts, show that many of them were ruined and expropriated by the better off. How could any plebeian Israelite have supposed that God's reputation was at stake by whether he emerged from trouble or not? It was otherwise for the king: 'A thousand shall fall at thy side, And ten thousand at thy right hand; *But* it shall not come nigh thee' (91.7).

(2) The speaker says that when all has turned out well, *I will give great thanks unto the LORD with my mouth; Yea, I will praise him among the multitude* (v. 30). How are we to imagine this scene? Great numbers of pious Israelites have gathered for a *Dankfest*? One after another they take their turn to give great thanks for their particular deliverance, like converts giving testimony at an evangelical meeting?

Where is the evidence for such an implausible occasion? But we know that all Israel used to gather for the three great pilgrimage festivals, or at least in practice for 'the Feast', Tabernacles. Many psalms suggest that the king, or other leading figure 'declared God's wonderful works unto a generation to come' (Ps. 71.14-24, for instance: cf. Eaton, *Kingship*, pp. 182-95). We can well see an Israelite leader leading the thanksgiving for God's promised deliverance: indeed the אודה and the חסד recall Ps. 107.1 and its refrain, and 108.4-5. Thanksgiving for national mercies is a theme of all three opening psalms of the Book.

(3) There is a question over why such a psalm was preserved. Allen says optimistically, 'The psalm was presumably put to prolonged use in the context of the religious court and as a prayer to be recited by victims of legal persecution generally' (*Psalms 101–150*, p. 78). One hesitates to think that the priesthood encouraged the use of such vitriolic superstition, which is (as Gunkel notes) quite alien to normal Israelite spirituality. The parallels cited, like Psalms 55, 58, 69, or Jeremiah 17–18, are misleading. The three psalms are in the name of David, who was understood to be Yahweh's anointed suffering from the attacks of wicked men like Absalom and Ahitophel; Jeremiah was a prophet delivering the word of the Lord, and opposed by faithless people in high places. Psalm 109 is more easily understood in such a national context: it is full of reminiscences of Davidic psalms (especially 35, 37, 69), and its editors have seen it as a *Psalm of David*. Public enemies, with one particular figure at their head, have Israel's leader in trouble, with false accusations to a 'suzerain'. Once the crisis is over, the 'prayer' which has been so effective, is retained against another such moment of peril.

(4) The weakness of Eaton's scenario is the lack of a specific and plausible 'suzerain'. But the context suggested by Psalms 107 and 108 supplies this. Ezra 4 describes a false offer of cooperation in building the Temple by 'the adversaries of Judah and Benjamin' (4.1-2). When this was declined they wrote *an accusation* (שׂטנה) to the Persian king (4.6), alleging that Jerusalem had been a rebellious city in the past, and that if the city is rebuilt it will again refuse tribute (4.11-16). The king sustained the objection and ordered building to halt (4.17-22); and work on the Temple was then suspended for the rest of Cyrus's reign, and until the second year of Darius, two decades (4.23-24).

The author of Ezra 4 is in a chronological muddle, and represents the correspondence as with King Ahasuerus, who *succeeded* Darius. But the folk memory is undoubtedly correct. The first Return, remembered as led by 'Sheshbazzar', had been early in Cyrus's reign. Haggai and Zechariah alike speak of the building of the Temple in Darius's reign; and there is repeated suggestion that the work has been delayed, and of an intermission between the foundation and the completion (Zech. 4.8, 8.9). In Zech. 3.1-2 the Accuser (השטן) stands at Joshua's right hand to accuse him before the angel of the Lord; and the Lord says, 'The Lord rebuke you, Accuser!' The prophet's vision of heaven reflects the reality on earth—Israel's leadership is being *accused* to authority, and Yahweh is justifying it. Ps. 109.6 echoes the language of Zech. 3.1, 'let *an accuser stand at his right hand*'.

C.L. and E.M. Meyers (*Haggai–Zechariah 1–8*, pp. 184-85), interpret the vision as the reflection of an earthly accusation to the Persian king by the Public Prosecutor. 'The Lord that hath chosen Jerusalem' (3.2) suggests that he argued for the permanent ruin of the city. Joshua's filthy garments, and his investiture, suggest that he argued for the permanent abolition of the priesthood. They do not make a direct relation with Psalm 109, but say, 'The best analogy to usage in a legal context is Ps. 109.6'. The first of the Meyers's Prosecutor's suggested arguments would fit well with Ezra 4.8-16. Their suggestion about the priesthood is less convincing: more likely there was a personal attack on Joshua on the grounds that he was not of the high-priestly order of Eleazar–Phinehas.

We thus have a setting made to measure the psalm. The high hopes of the returned exiles (Ps. 107), threatened by the hostility of Samaria/ Shechem (Ps. 108), have now been frustrated, it appears permanently. The local governor, Bishlam (or whatever his name may have been), and his advisers (Mithredath, Tabeel, perhaps; Ezra 4.7), have written to warn Cyrus of the aspirations of the renewed community; the king has authorized them to suspend any building, and they have enforced his ruling. The details emerge from the text.

Psalm 109.1-5

1   For the Chief Musician. A Psalm of David.
      Hold not thy peace, O God of my praise:
2   For the mouth of the wicked and the mouth of deceit have
      they opened against me.
3   They compassed me about also with words of hatred,
      And fought against me without a cause.

4   For my love they are my accusers (יִשְׂטְנוּנִי):
     But I *give myself unto* prayer.
5   And they have laid upon me evil for good,
     And hatred for my love.

When the exiles returned to Palestine, they knew their position to be weak, so they approached the Governor Beyond the River, or his local representative, with friendly, perhaps naive, overtures (*my love*, vv. 4, 5). The more wary Nehemiah, three generations later, kept his intentions to himself and did his planning by night; he provoked the same armed hostility, but was prepared for it. The Samaritans' offer to assist in the building (Ezra 4.1-2) probably reflects a requirement by the governor that he supervise and limit any building. When Joshua and Zerubbabel declined, he delated them to Cyrus (*they are my accusers*). No doubt he despatched Bishlam, or whoever his leading informant was, to the royal court (*the mouth of the wicked man and the mouth of deceit have they opened against me, words of hatred*). The king stood by his officials and ordered the suspension of operations; which they enforced with arms (*fought against me*, יִלְחָמוּנִי, v. 3).

The psalmist is driven to his ultimate resource (*But I* [am] *prayer*, וַאֲנִי תְפִלָּה, if that is the right text). As *Chief Musician* he can speak in the name of the people; and he is in a position to draw on the rich vocabulary of complaint to God in his Davidic repertory: his psalm is a pastiche on *a Psalm of David*, as was well understood by his editor. '*Hold not thy peace*' comes in Ps. 35.22: God is spoken of as '*my praise*' at the opening of one of Jeremiah's imprecations (Jer. 17.14). David's enemies *loved evil* rather than *good, deceit* and *a tongue of lies* in Ps. 52.5-6; they *reward evil for good* in 35.12 again, and there are *deceitful words without cause* in 35.19-20, with an encircling crowd in 35.15-16. There is an imprecation in 35.4-8, and the speaker *fasts* and *prays* in 35.13 as in 109.24, though with more charity. In 69.5 come those who '*hate me without a cause*', and curses follow in 69.23-29. The curious *But I* [am] *prayer* (וַאֲנִי תְפִלָּה, v. 4) is probably due to 69.14, '*But as for me, my prayer is unto thee*' (וַאֲנִי תְפִלָּתִי לְךָ): the later psalmist has read this as 'But I, my prayer, am to thee', and has understood the prayer as his full self in action. The opening of 109 is much indebted to 35 and 69.

There are many hesitations over the text, רֶשַׁע, for רָשָׁע, niphal for qal פָּתְחוּ in v. 2; emendations of וַאֲנִי תְפִלָּה in v. 4. But good sense is available for the first (see above), where the versions support MT, and the qal is the harder reading in the second. Gunkel says the third is impossible, but other commentators adduce 110.3, 'Thy youth [are] dew', or 120.7, 'I [am] peace', as possible parallels. Kraus interprets *Hold not thy peace* as a request for a [positive] oracle from the priest, but I think God is thought of as making his voice felt rather in the dire events of vv. 6-19.

Kraus and Weiser, Jacquet and Allen also advocate a longstanding suggestion that the imprecations are not the psalmist's curses, but those of his enemies which he cites, as Hezekiah laid the Rabshakeh's letter on the altar. The principal evidence for this is the change from plural to singular in these verses (though most MSS have the plural in vv. 13, 15, taken by Allen to refer to the victim's family). But, as Allen himself notes, there is a problem in that then v. 16 has the psalmist persecuting 'the poor and needy', whereas in v. 22 he claims to be 'poor and needy' himself: hence, whereas Kraus and Weiser attribute vv. 6-19 to the citation, Jacquet and Allen limit it to vv. 6-15.

Psalm 109.6-20

6   Set thou a wicked man over him:
    And let an accuser stand at his right hand.
7   When he is judged, let him come forth guilty:
    And let his prayer become sin.
8   Let his days be few:
    And let another take his office.
9   Let his children be fatherless,
    And his wife a widow.
10 Let his children be vagabonds, and beg:
    And let them scavenge (ודרשו) from their desolate places.
11 Let the extortioner snare all that he hath;
    And let strangers make spoil of his labour.
12 Let there be none to continue mercy unto him;
    Neither let there be any to have pity on his fatherless children.
13 Let his posterity be cut off;
    In the generation following let their name be blotted out.
14 Let the iniquity of his fathers be remembered with the LORD;
    And let not the sin of his mother be blotted out.
15 Let them be before the LORD continually,
    That he may cut off the memory of them from the earth.
16 Because that he remembered not to shew mercy,
    But persecuted the poor and needy man,
    And the broken in heart, to slay *them*.
17 Yea, he loved cursing, and it came unto him;
    And he delighted not in blessing, and it was far from him.
18 He clothed himself also with cursing as with his garment;
    And it came into his inward parts like water,
    And like oil into his bones.

19   Let it be unto him as the raiment wherewith he covereth himself,
       And for the girdle wherewith he is girded continually.
20   This is the reward of mine accusers (שֹׂטְנַי) from the LORD,
       And of them that speak evil against my soul.

The *accusers* of Israel's leader (v. 20), are headed by a particular informer (vv. 6-19), who attracts all the desperate bitterness of the powerless. He is in fact an official, liable to lose his *office* (פְּקֻדָּה has this meaning normally, rather than 'property'; cf. v. 6, הַפְקֵד, 'appoint'). He is a senior official gone to Susa with his false accusations, and the hope is that he will have an equally corrupt judge to enquire into him (*a wicked man over him*), with a prosecutor (*accuser*) *standing at his right hand*. *When judgement is given*, it may then be expected that he will *come forth guilty*, God treating *his prayer* as so much *sin*. He should then be executed shortly afterwards (*Let his days be few*), and *his office* go to a better man.

Both Psalms 35 and 69 contained imprecations on the speaker's enemies, but they were limited to blindness, fever, discomfiture in battle and removal from the book of life, in the latter, more severe psalm. The extension here to the family of the wicked is due to 37. Psalm 37.25 suggests the seed of the wicked begging for bread, and in 37.28, 38 they are cut off; in 37.14, 32 the wicked seeks *to slay* the righteous, who are referred to in the former verse as *the poor and needy* (עָנִי וְאֶבְיוֹן, cf. 35.10). It is this which has influenced the development of 109.9-13, coupled, no doubt, with all too common experience. The father executed, widow and children are reduced to beggary; their home is pulled down, and they *scavenge* (דָּרַשׁ) what they can *from their ruins*; but the confiscated estate is now in the hands of *strangers*, who *snare* every penny they can, like the enemies in 38.13. There was to have been a *posterity* (אַחֲרִית) to the man of peace in 37.37, but the accuser's is to be cut off in v. 13. Whereas God *continued his kindness* to those who know him in 36.10, there is to be no such *kindness continued* to the accuser's family—they are to die in the gutter, and that will be the final end of him. As in 34.16 the face of the LORD is against them that do evil, *To cut off the remembrance of them from the earth*.

Thus the psalmist has drawn his primary inspiration from the bleak series of David psalms, 34–37 (and there is similar thought and language to the end of Book I). Verses 16-19 return to the accuser's own iniquity. The Israelite leader, Joshua ben Jozadak as we may think

(Zech. 3.1), is spoken of as *poor and needy* like David (35.10; 37.14; 40.18): the community was indeed desperately poor, and in dire need of defence. They were also *broken in heart* (cf. 34.19) by the trials of the Exile; and it is quite likely that the threat of *slaying* the leader is to be taken literally, in view of what was plotted against Nehemiah (Neh. 6), as well as being a standard feature of Psalms 34–41. The *cursing* is the psalmist's interpretation of the accuser's delation, backed up no doubt by the latter's prayers; what is קללה for the enemy is תפלה for the psalmist. The cursing is seen as a magical force—Gunkel says, like Nessus's shirt—which is worn by the accuser and seeps into his being like water or oil; perhaps the image owes something to Ps. 73.6, 'Violence covereth them as a garment'. It is a girdle which he cannot take off, *wherewith he is girded continually;* the intolerable shirt of flame which human power cannot remove. *This is the reward* of the accusers (now in the plural); the *lex talionis* applies to them, exactly as it does (once more) in 35.4-8. They *speak evil against my soul*: no doubt they are urging the king to have Joshua and other leaders executed, and the same fate should await them.

Verse 8. מעטים, plural, is found elsewhere only in Eccl. 5.1, and is seen by Delitzsch as a sign that the psalm is postexilic. Most commentators see פקדתו as 'his office' (cf. LXX ἐπισκοπήν); not only is the verb הפקד used in v. 6 to mean 'appoint', but the disposal of his property is dealt with in v. 11. *Verse 10.* RVmg has *let them seek [their bread] far from their desolate places.* This is strained and obscure: the demolition of the homes of the disapproved is an age-old punishment, still beloved of the government of Israel, and gives an easy sense both to מחרבותיהם and to the 'seeking', that is, scavenging. It was going in postexilic times (Ezra 6.11; Dan. 3.29).

Psalm 109.21-31

21 But deal thou with me, O GOD the Lord, for thy name's sake:
Because thy mercy is good deliver thou me,
22 For I am poor and needy,
And my heart is wounded within me.
23 I am gone like the shadow when it is stretched out:
I am tossed up and down like the locust.
24 My knees totter through fasting;
And my flesh faileth of fatness.
25 I am become also a reproach unto them:
When they see me, they shake their head.

26   Help me, O LORD my God;
     O save me, according to thy mercy:
27   That they may know that this is thy hand;
     That thou, LORD, hast done it.
28   Let them curse, but bless thou:
     They have arisen (קָמוּ), and they shall be ashamed,
     but thy servant shall rejoice.
29   My accusers (שׂוֹטְנִי) shall be clothed with dishonour,
     And they shall cover themselves with their own shame as with a mantle.
30   I will give great thanks unto the LORD with my mouth,
     Yea, I will praise him among the multitude.
31   For he shall stand at the right hand of the poor and needy,
     To save him from them that judge his soul.

In its final section the psalm does become a prayer, turning to God,
יהוה׳ אדני. ואתה has promised to *deliver* his people, so his *name* is at
stake; but his חסד *is good*, that is dependable, so all will be well. The
psalmist has been *fasting*, as no doubt have been many others in view
of the crisis, by which their *heart has been pierced within* them. He is
thin *as a shadow when it is stretched out*, as light as *the locust* which
can be *tossed* down from the trees; his *knees totter*, and all his healthy
fatness has vanished. Such abstinence was undertaken to move God to
action; as was the (imagined) scene of the Samaritan authorities
gloating and *shaking their head* at the *sight* of the miserable Judahites.
If only *Yahweh* will *help* and *save* us in accordance with his חסד, they
will *know that this is* his *hand*: they may carry on *cursing*, but as
Yahweh *blesses* us, *they will be covered with shame*. But the psalm
ends on a happy note. *Thy servant shall rejoice*—the successor of
King David, who so often spoke of himself so. He, or the psalmist
speaking in his name, *will give great thanks to Yahweh, praising him
among the multitude* who come to the festival. God did in fact *stand at
his right hand and save him from* the Samaritan accusers, and from
the Persian court who were called on to *judge his soul*, and condemn
him to be executed. We actually have the *great thanks* and *praise*
(אהללנו) that he composed to celebrate the deliverance in Psalms 111–
118 (הללויה).

The psalmist is still much influenced by his Davidic models. Ps.
69.17 prays, 'Answer me, *O Lord; for thy mercy is good*'. Ps. 55.5
has '*My heart is sore pained within me*'. 102.12 has 'My days are *like
a shadow that is stretched out*'. David afflicted his soul with *fasting* in
35.13 and 69.10, and in 69.11 this became his *reproach*; in 22.7-8 also

he was a *reproach* of men, and all who *saw* him *shook the head* at him. In 35.26 he prays, '*Let them be ashamed... Let them be clothed with shame and dishonour*', and we have almost the same wording in 71.13. This is then contrasted with the *rejoicing* of the loyal in 35.27, and David's promise to *praise* God for his righteousness all the day long in 35.28; and there are similar vows in 22.25 and 71.22-24.

Verse 23. כנמותו is not quite the same as 102.12 נמני: *according to its lengthening.* *Verse 28.* MT has קמו, *they have arisen,* LXX assumes the easier קמי, *they that arise against me.* The Ezra 4 setting makes sense of MT: the Samaritan accusers *have arisen* against Judah, *and they shall be ashamed. Verse 30.* The אודה recalls the refrain of Psalm 107, and 108.4. For all its hideous difference, Psalm 109 is part of a sequence. Indeed we may think the author has written all three psalms (and more): he draws on many details of the Davidic laments in 109, as he drew more directly on the Davidic 57 and 60 in 108; and he uses the same technique to incorporate many texts and themes from Deutero-Isaiah in Psalm 107.

The consistent recurrence of these earlier 'Davidic' lament echoes seems to confirm the exegesis above. The author is soaked in the Davidic psalter, and sees himself as the successor of Davidic poets of old. This is a Psalm of David, and he is the מנצח reciting it in the name of the current *servant of Yahweh*. He has taken Psalm 35 in particular as his model, but filled in details from similar psalms, 34–41, 69–71, 22, and others. But the older psalmists really did trust in Yahweh's *mercy*: they fasted when their enemies were in trouble, and they limited their imprecations to the shaming, confounding and death of the national enemies. The present situation is more desperate. Not only is Judah in a state of most parlous weakness, and her leader in the hands of Persian kings infinitely more powerful than him; but Yahweh had shown in 587 BCE that his חסד did not exclude the massacring of the national leadership and the loss of independence. So as the Samaritan *accusers* plead the case against Joshua *to slay him*, there is less faith and hope in Yahweh, and much less charity. The fasting is entirely self-regarding, the imprecations are comprehensive and pitiless, the wild imaginings of the panic-stricken. But such anxiety was not necessary: this time all was to be well.

PSALM 110

Psalm 110 has been understood in a number of settings, from the reign of David to late Maccabaean times. The late nineteenth century saw conservatives like Delitzsch and Kirkpatrick defending the Davidic position, while the priest–king combination in v. 4 was a magnet to Maccabaean radicals like Duhm. The present century has seen a strong reaction in favour of a monarchic dating, with a good number of critics still thinking of David. The second-century proposals are no longer in vogue, partly because of a general inclination to see the LXX and the Qumran fragments as evidence that the Psalter was virtually fixed by the third century, partly from the confessed absence of prophecy in the Maccabaean period. But a number of scholars have adduced Zech. 6.9-14 as a relevant text, where the high priest Joshua is saluted as 'the Branch' (צמח), and is to be crowned with a double crown as king and priest; and this suggestion is not liable to either of the objections to Simon Maccabaeus and his successors.

Almost all commentators since Gunkel have accepted his classification of 110 as a royal psalm. Some (Eaton, Rogerson and McKay) have been content to leave the identity of the original king open, but many, in the light of v. 4, incline to David. Mowinckel, *Psalmenstudien,* III, pp. 88-93, regarded a Davidic date as almost certain, but in *Psalms in Israel's Worship,* I, p. 153 he opted for Solomon; Kraus speaks of the earliest times. Booij, 'Ps CX' (1991) argues (with several textual conjectures) that Melchizedek was a Canaanite king, and so the date must be early, before Canaanite connections became disreputable.For a more detailed account of (numerous) more specific proposals see Allen, *Psalms 101–150,* pp. 83-86.

A minority of scholars has preferred a postexilic date. Some of these have taken an eschatological/messianic interpretation, including Rehm, *Der königliche Messias,* pp. 329-31, with an eye to Zech. 3.8; while Schreiner, 'Psalm 110', has revived the nineteenth-century interest in Zech. 6.9-15. He thinks the psalm was an earlier royal psalm rewritten at the time of this passage's redaction. The following factors are relevant to the issue:

(1) Psalm 110 opens with an oracle addressed by Yahweh to 'my lord'; the latter is commonly envisioned as the king, for whom אדני is a common address in the Davidic histories; he is to rule over his enemies, who will be his footstool after widespread slaughter. There is a second oracle in v. 4b. This recalls another royal psalm of unquestioned early date, Psalm 2, where there are royal oracles in vv. 6 and 7-9; with similar threats of divine anger on the kings of the earth, and a similar view of the centrality of Zion.

These points do not carry the argument, however. We have seen in 108–109 evidence of a late sixth-century psalmist's familiarity with the Davidic Psalter, and his powers of pastiche. We have here a third *Psalm for David*, and an imitation of Psalm 2 is as likely as an early companion-piece. The language in fact favours this alternative. David is normally spoken of in 2 Samuel as אדני המלך, and this fuller title might have been expected if the psalm were composed for any Judaean king. אדני on its own would be a suitable term for any highly respected figure: the Hittite elders use it of Abraham in Gen. 23.6. The opening word נאם similarly raises questions. There are a number of royal psalms isolated by Gunkel, and more by other critics, but none of them uses נאם, which comes only once elsewhere in the Psalter, in the ironic 36.2, where Transgression is the oracle-giver. There as here נאם is the first word, a rarity, but found also in 2 Sam. 23.1, David's 'oracle'; Num. 24.3-4, 15-16, Balaam's 'oracles'; Isa. 56.8, Zech. 12.1, 'oracle of Yahweh'. Perhaps the psalmist is influenced by the very common use of the word in the prophets, and he may be imitating his familiar psalm cycle in the 30s.

(2) In v. 4 the 'lord' is given a second oracle under Yahweh's oath: he is a priest for ever after the order of Melchizedek. It is widely noted that in early times David acts as both king and priest: he wears the priestly ephod, conducts the ark, offers the sacrifices, makes his sons priests, and so on. Only in later times does it come to be felt that sacrifice is for priests only, and Uzziah is stricken with leprosy when he offers incense in 2 Chronicles 26. Priests were under special divine protection, so the king was happy to have this additional guarantee. Further, appeal is made to Gen. 14.18-22, where Melchizedek was both king of Salem and also priest of אל עליון. The king of Jerusalem in Joshua 10 is called Adoni-zedek, and this led to the conclusion that the god worshipped in Canaanite Jebus was אל עליון, with an association to a god Zedek; and that Zadok had been priest–king of the place.

The oracle would then be divine confirmation that David has succeeded to the joint authority in perpetuity.

Earlier commentators had suggested that the (Maccabaean) psalmist had read Genesis 14, but Gunkel derided such simplicity, and the Melchizedek tradition was generally held to be ancient. The theory that Zadok was priest–king of 'Salem' was repeated so often that it became a fact: sometimes in H.H. Rowley's version, where Psalm 110 is a liturgical dialogue, and David addresses v. 4 to Zadok, more usually with the king taking over the 'old Jebusite' dual authority. Similar comments are made by Claus Westermann on the passage (*Genesis*, II, pp. 182-208), in an apparently contradictory analysis. He says that 14.18-20 'very probably arose in the time of David' (p. 192), and legitimated the [Salem] cult. At the same time it is an episode in the Abraham story, and cannot have existed independently of that story (p. 203, referring to J.A. Emerton, *VT* 21). But 14.18-20 have been inserted into 14.12-17, 21-24, the tale of Abraham's defeat of the Mesopotamian kings which 'can only derive from a late, indeed post-exilic, period' (p. 192). The natural conclusion of these premisses is that the Melchizedek story is postexilic also. The Jerusalem cult needed to be legitimated not only in David's time, but also to sixth-century hearers of the Genesis traditions, which seem to justify worship at Shechem, Bethel, Hebron and Beersheba, but not Jerusalem.

This sparkling hypothesis is laced with difficulties. In the first place, why does God swear, and why is it thought necessary to say that he does not go back on his word? In the earlier promises to the fathers in Genesis, God's word is sufficient (Gen. 12.1-3, 13.14-17, 15.4-5, 13-16, 18.10, 28.13-15, etc.); it is not till the later 22.16 that the promise is confirmed with an oath. Similarly the covenant with the house of David is merely a promise in 2 Sam. 7.4-16. It becomes an oath in Ps. 89.4, 36 after the disaster of 597 BCE, and again in 132.11 in Nehemiah's time; we may note the parallel phrasing of the latter, '*The Lord hath sworn* unto David in truth; He will not turn from it'. It is the uncomfortable experience of Yahweh's having apparently *failed* to keep his covenanted word that leads to the insistence on his oath and its irreversibility.

Then there is the strangeness of the context in v. 4. On the Davidic/ royal hypothesis the king is saluted as also being priest. We should have expected then something like, 'Thou art a priest for ever after the order of Melchizedek: Thy offerings shall be acceptable in my sight. I will hearken to thy prayers; and thou shalt teach my people Torah'. But the text in fact continues with a promise that the Lord will fill the place with dead bodies and strike through the head over a wide land. Such is not commonly the vocation of the clergy. The context therefore suggests just the opposite of the royal theory: the 'lord' is in fact a priest, who is being called to a special vocation as secular leader of the nation, including leadership in war—like Archbishop Makarios of Cyprus, or Pope Julius II, or Simon Maccabaeus, or Joshua ben Jozadak.

Finally there is the problem of Melchizedek. The theory of a second-millennium Canaanite priest–king of Jerusalem is a tissue of speculations. There is no evidence for Jerusalem being called Salem in the royal period, nor any pre-exilic evidence of the existence of Melchizedek. We first hear of Salem in Ps. 76.3, a psalm of Asaph, composed for worship in (northern) Israel. Salem is the name of a town near Shechem, where Jacob is said to have built an altar to אל אלהי־ישראל (Gen. 33.18-20). The Asaph psalms refer to God frequently as אל (×19), and once as אל עליון (78.35: also in parallel 73.11, cf. 78.17). When the Asaph psalms were transferred to Jerusalem after 722, Salem was retained in the genial belief that Salem = (Jeru)salem. Gen. 14.18-20 (22) is widely believed to be a late insertion into the Abraham saga. It portrays Abraham as paying tithes to the (Jeru)salem priesthood, who otherwise do not enjoy a high profile in the book of Genesis, and as being blessed by them. The priest is named as Melchi-zedek as a suitable ancestor of the first Jerusalem high priest, Zadok; and the name suggests his kingship also (מלך), since he must take the initiative in supporting Abraham. Also the story is likely to have arisen during the Exile, when priests were the natural leaders of a leaderless people.

For a discussion of Salem and its possible identification with Jerusalem, see Emerton, 'The Site of Salem...' (1990), and my response in *Asaph*, pp. 86-89.

We may think then that Joshua ben Jozadak has a better claim to be thought of as the 'lord' of Psalm 110 than David or any of his royal successors. He was a priest, the high priest, Zechariah tells us (6.11). He had been active in plans to build the Temple (6.13), and had been accused to higher authority for his pains (3.1-2). At first he was associated with Zerubbabel of the Davidic line (ch. 4); but in time Zerubbabel fades out, and Joshua alone is hailed as the Branch (3.8, 6.12), the righteous צמח for David foretold by Jeremiah (Jer. 23.5). A crown is to be set on Joshua's head (6.11), and he is to sit on Yahweh's throne and rule—'and he shall be a priest upon his throne'

(6.13). So will he build the Temple. Zechariah does not mention filling the place with dead bodies, but we may think of an explanation for this.

So Joshua seems a plausible candidate to be the 'lord' of Psalm 110: he was a priest who was hailed as David's successor and given royal honour; he belongs in the same context I have inferred for 107–109; and the evidence comes from contemporary sources, Haggai and (especially) Zechariah. This raises a further point. Zechariah is spoken of (1.1) as the son of Berechiah the son of Iddo. Now all these three names are associated with the Asaphite guild of psalmists. A Zechariah of the sons of Asaph takes a lead in Hezekiah's reformation (2 Chron. 29.13), and another is the leading Levite in Nehemiah's procession (Neh. 12.35). Berechiah is said to be the father of Asaph in 1 Chron. 6.24 (39) and 15.17; and Iddo is not only mentioned in the main Asaph genealogy (1 Chron. 6.6 [21]), but is spoken of as the seer (2 Chron. 12.15) and the prophet (2 Chron. 13.22) who composed a form of the national history. We may infer therefore that the sixth-century prophet Zechariah is likely to have been of the Asaphite clan; and since the Asaphites are said to have been the only singers at the time of the Return (Ezra 2.41), the 110th psalmist probably came from the same circle.

Psalm 110

1   A Psalm of David.
     The LORD said unto my lord, Sit thou at my right hand,
     Until I make thine enemies thy footstool.
2   The LORD shall stretch the rod of thy strength out of Zion:
     Rule thou in the midst of thine enemies.
3   The people are freewill offerings in the day of thy army:
     In holy attire from the womb of the morning,
     Thy youth are to thee as the dew.
4   The LORD hath sworn, and will not repent,
     Thou art a priest for ever after the manner of Melchizedek.
5   The Lord at thy right hand
     Hath stricken through kings in the day of his wrath.
6   He shall judge among the nations,
     The places are filled with dead bodies;
     He hath stricken through the head over a wide land.
7   He shall drink of the brook in the way:
     Therefore shall he lift up the head.

In Nehemiah's time the assertion of Judah's independence roused hostility and the threat of violence from its jealous neighbours: the official Persian governor, Sanballat, was aided by Ammonites, Arabs and Ashdodites, who sent armed levies 'to fight against Jerusalem' (להלחם, Neh. 4.2 [8]). Similar violence was undertaken, with more success, against Gedaliah, an earlier Judahite leader, by Ishmael ben Nethaniah, with backing from the Ammonites (Jer. 40.13-16). It is therefore unlikely that Zerubbabel, Joshua and the other leaders of the Return would have been able to sponsor a national renaissance without armed resistance; and indeed Psalm 109 tells us not only that there was opposition in the form of accusation to higher authority, but that it included violence—'they *fought against* me without a cause' (וילחמוני, 109.3).

In these circumstances the new leadership would have been lucky to avoid a fight. Gedaliah had been murdered through insufficient wariness (Jer. 40.13–41.3), and Nehemiah avoided both battles and assassination by wisdom and vigilance (Neh. 4, 6); but 109.3 suggests that it came to blows. It is easy then to connect this with the otherwise surprising elevation of Joshua to secular authority, as the successor of David, in Zechariah 6. The use of royal language—the 'Branch', crown, throne—must have risked alarming and provoking the Persian authorities: but if the community were actually attacked, *fought against*, there would be little option but to choose a commander and respond. The sudden disappearance of Zerubbabel from the scene could be explained by the same hypothesis. Zech. 4.1-10 speaks as if Zerubbabel were the destined national leader, alongside Joshua as the second anointed one of 4.11-14; and 6.11, 14 has suggested to many critics that an earlier form of the text assumed the same double leadership. But the present form of 6.9-14, like 3.1-5, attributes the leadership to Joshua alone. There is nothing like a national crisis for forcing the leadership issue. We cannot tell if Zerubbabel lost support by indecisiveness, or bad policy, or poor generalship, or if he was killed in battle: but it is easy to think that a moment of high peril made it clear that Joshua was the man to lead the people. Mr Amery spoke in God's name in the House of Commons in June 1940, and caused Mr Churchill to replace Mr Chamberlain as Prime Minister of Britain; and we may think that the same office fell to Zechariah ben Berechiah in Judah in 517 BCE, to promote Joshua in place of Zerubbabel.

Verses 1-2. The psalmist then follows the lead of the prophet. Joshua is to be installed in an office which has all the trappings of Davidic kingship, but to which it would be impolitic to give the name of king (cf. Neh. 6.6). He is escorted to a throne on the *right hand* of Yahweh's altar, and enthroned, and presented with the *sceptre: Sit thou at my right hand!* The words are proclaimed as a divine *oracle*, נאם יהוה, like so many prophecies (not least from Zechariah); and the psalm as a whole is framed on the model of an old Davidic enthronement psalm, Psalm 2, whose theme is not less military and vindictive. Yahweh's calling for Joshua is to *put his enemies as the footstool of his feet*, like his illustrious eponym who bade his lieutenants put their feet on the necks of the conquered Canaanite kings (Josh. 10.24); and Yahweh *put* all things under David's *feet* (Ps. 8.7). As Yahweh set his king upon his holy hill of *Zion* (Ps. 2.6), so now will he *stretch forth the sceptre of* Joshua's military *power out of Zion*; and no earthly army can resist this magic symbol. His projected activities are as general, not as archbishop. His *enemies*—Samaritans, and very likely Ammonites, Edomites and Philistines—*compass him about* (109.3), but he is to *rule in the midst of them* (רדה בקרב). One is reminded of the 1967 Israel–Arab War, when attacks on three fronts provoked a national crisis, and an archaeologist turned out to be a successful general.

Kraus offers three parallels for אדני as an address to the king: but of these 1 Kgs 1.13 has *My lord the King*, and 1 Sam. 26.18 uses *My lord* alone to avoid repetition. 1 Sam. 22.12 is the only clear instance, but again *The King* has been used twice in 22.11. אדני is used as a term of respect to others than the king in 1 Sam. 1.15, 26, 1 Kgs 18.7 and elsewhere. True parallels for נאם יהוה at the beginning of an oracle are limited to Ps. 36.2, Isa. 56.8 and Zech. 12.1, so the phrase is likely to be late. It is noticeable that Psalm 110 speaks of God throughout as יהוה or אדני, never as עליון אל, as might have been expected if David were being invested with ancient Jebusite authority. The king is 'the man of [Yahweh's] right hand' in Ps. 80.18; but in Israelite tradition the king has no man at his right hand—the place is reserved for Bathsheba (1 Kgs 2.19) and Jezebel (Ps. 45.10), who stands (Goulder, *Korah*, p. 134).

Verse 3. The following lines also recall the spirit of those innocent days: the zeal, the enthusiasm, the dedication of young people, girls as well as men from many countries, flocking to enlist for the defence of the infant state of Israel. As the psalmist puts it poetically, *The people are freewill offerings* (נדבת). This was the thought of the returning exiles in Ezra 1, 'everyone whose spirit God had stirred', who brought up with them *the freewill offering* (הנדבה) of the Babylon Jewish community (1.4); and Ezra 8.28 says that the exiles as well as the silver and gold are a נדבה to Yahweh. The verb התנדב is used in a more straightforward sense of *enlisting* in Judg. 5.2,9. They come *in the day of thy army* (חילך): 2 Chron. 26.13 speaks of a חיל צבא of some three hundred thousand men, and we may think similarly of *the day of* Joshua's חיל. For the raising of an ancient army one had, like Lars Porsenna, to name a trysting day. Often the result was disappointing ('Shame on the false Etruscan Who lingers in his home'); but not now. *Thy youth*, the young men from the villages of Judah, *are to thee dew from the womb of the dawn*; as Milton would say, thick as autumnal leaves that strew the brooks in Vallombrosa. Dew was to the Israelites a divine gift, a mysterious blessing there on every plant in the morning when there had been no rain in the night; the sudden enrolment of the *youth* of Judah in their unlooked for thousands was a similar marvel from heaven. They have come too *in holy attire*. Ancient Semitic warriors consecrated themselves for battle in their gold and silver bangles no less than with swords and shields (Judg. 8.24; Ps. 68.13-14), and let their hair grow long (Ps. 68.22). A proud man was ben Jozadak upon the trysting day.

The MT, as translated by RVmg, makes excellent sense in the context I have suggested: the many suggestions for changing the vowels (and some consonants) are a mistake. נדבת has the two parallels in Ezra 1.8, 8.28, and in the latter the exiles are said to be holy as well as the precious metal נדבה. יום חילך can mean 'the day of your mobilization' without strain. הדרי/ת־קדש means holy garments for angels in Ps. 29.2, but for ordinary human worshippers at Ps. 96.9; the Targumic (and Syriac) reading הררי־קדש may be due to Ps. 2.6 הר־קדשי. ילדתיך is the only instance of the word to mean *thy young men*: in Eccl.11.9-10 it means *thy youth*. The Greek (and not uncommon other) pointing ילדתיך has been influenced by the same form in Ps. 2.7; with so much in common with Psalm 2 we must suspect that 110 has repointed the word. Mowinckel, *Psalmenstudien,* III, pp. 88-93, accepts *I begat you* as the original meaning, with birth from the Dawn goddess: but this seems implausible, and requires a switch into the divine first person for which there is no introduction.

Verse 4. For half a millennium Judah had been led in war by kings, the line of David; and the Return had brought the expectation that Zerubbabel of that line would continue the tradition. But when, for whatever reason, Zerubbabel was no longer available, his priestly colleague Joshua had stepped into the breach; and his success was the evident sign of divine approval. But how could such an innovation be legitimated? The legend of a priest–king of Salem, Melchizedek, in the days of Abraham, came happily to mind. Salem was thought to be identical with Jerusalem, and so it appeared that in the days of yore, from which the best precedents come, God's city was ruled by one who *combined* the royal with the priestly office. Furthermore his very name, Melchi*zedek*, מלכי־צדק, seemed to foreshadow the present need; for Joshua was the son of Jeho*zadak*, י׳הוצדק, and the descent must have run through *Zadok*, צדוק, David's priest. The psalmist feels confident therefore that he may deliver a second oracle, *Thou art a priest for ever after the manner of Melchizedek*—that is, king as well as priest. The designation is said to be *for ever*; like the promise to David in Ps. 21.5 of 'length of days *for ever and ever*'. Like other post-Exile oracles (Ps. 89.4, 36; 132.11), the word is confirmed by both oath and guarantee of permanence: *The Lord hath sworn, and will not repent*. Those who have broken their word once must be required to swear thereafter.

Modern commentators often date Genesis 14 'late': Abraham has become an inter-national general able to defeat an alliance of Mesopotamian kings, the very enemies who had deported the king of Judah in chains in 587 BCE. The Melchizedek verses, 14.18-22, are widely seen as an insertion into the narrative, that is, later still; with Abraham paying tithes and Melchizedek blessing him, we seem to have a legitimation for the ascendancy of the (Jeru)Salem priesthood. But then both the dating and the fit with Joshua seem too good to be true: we must think that the story came into circula-tion during the Return, and was put about to justify his double position as priest and king. For the surprising final י- on דברתי see note in Allen, *Psalms 101–150*, p. 81.

Verses 5-7. The authority of a *priest after the manner of Melchizedek* is to act as king in addition; Joshua is not king because he is not of the line of David, but he is a Melchizedek-type priest, able to lead the army. He has already in fact won one battle: *The Lord at thy right hand Hath struck through* (מחץ) *kings in the day of his wrath.* Even if the text did not tell us so, we might have inferred such a past victory, for the psalmist could hardly have dared to voice his oracle without such a clear sign from heaven. The description of the enemy as *kings*, and the mention of Yahweh's *wrath*, are indebted to Psalm 2 again: 'The *kings* of the earth set themselves...be wise, O ye kings...For *his wrath* may soon be kindled' (2.2, 10, 12).

Further victories may now be expected, as Yahweh *judges among the nations* and the place *is filled with dead bodies. He hath struck through* (מחץ) *the head over a wide land.* The constricting fear of national annihilation, suddenly removed by an amazing triumph in the field, issues in exuberant confidence and uninhibited blood-lust. Yahweh has shown his hand at last: *vae victis!* We are back in 1967 once more. The Egyptian army has been *struck through over a broad front* in Sinai, and the desert is *filled with corpses.* Let the Syrian army beware which has crossed the border into Galilee, and the ill-advised Palestinians!

Joshua might not be called 'king', but he could be honoured by all the appurtenances of kingship. Verse 1 spoke of his *sitting* on a royal-type throne, v. 2 of *the rod of his strength*, his sceptre. His priesthood after the manner of Melchizedek probably implies an anointing. But a central rite in the coronation of the kings at Jerusalem had always been their drinking from the sacred spring. Adonijah had had himself made king at the spring En-Rogel (1 Kgs 1.9); but David sent Zadok and Nathan to make Solomon king at the spring Gihon (1 Kgs 1.33-40). There they are to anoint him and blow the trumpet; and it is likely that all the kings of Judah thereafter followed this tradition. Hence the final line for Joshua: *He shall drink of the brook in the way.* Gihon rose by the road into Jerusalem from the south. Any ruler consecrated by such a draught of holy water might depend on Yahweh's permanent blessing: *Therefore shall he lift up the head.*

Psalm 110 is followed by a series of Hallelujah psalms: 111, 112 and 113 open with הללו יה; 113 also closes with it, as do 115, 116, 117, and 118. Only 114 is without it (though a transfer from 114.1 to 113.9 is often suspected). There is a second noticeable feature of these psalms. Psalms 111 and 112 are a pair of alphabetical psalms, each consisting of a neat series of 22 cola, half-verses each beginning with the ordered letters of the Hebrew alphabet. After these comes the 'Hallel' group of psalms, 113–118, traditionally used at Jewish festivals, back into the BCE period. These in turn are followed by the great alphabetical psalm, 119, with 22 stanzas of eight verses apiece following the sequence of the Hebrew alphabet; and after these come the Songs of Ascents.

It looks therefore as if the alphabetic psalms, 111, 112 and 119, form a kind of frame to the festal psalms, 113–118. With their constricting formal pattern and their marked Torah spirituality, the alphabetic psalms stand apart from the festal psalms, and are often thought to be among the latest in the Psalter; but caution is needed here, as there are features linking them to their predecessors. 111 and 112 are a pair in that they share many thoughts and expressions; and they also have features in common with Psalm 1, another late psalm. Furthermore the הללו יה that opens 111 and 112 cannot be part of the original psalms because it does not begin with an א, and so lies outside the psalms' structure. We may think therefore of 111 and 112 as a preface to 113–118, coming from the same school as the authors of 1 and 119 (if not the same person), whose work has for some reason been used to extend the festal series, 113–118; I postpone discussion of what such a reason might be to pp. 208-209. The הללויהs that open Psalms 111 and 112 have been placed there to ease their position before 113, though they are not unsuitable (especially before 111).

Psalm 111 is more directly a praise of God; 112 a reflection on the blessings attending his faithful service. The distinction raises an interesting question for form critics. Gunkel assigns 111 to the category of a Hymn, while 112 (אשרי..., טוב...) is a Wisdom psalm. Yet, as Gunkel himself argues, 111 and 112 share the same form and the same vocabulary (and probably one author). If 111 is a hymn, presumably for liturgical use, how are we to think of the use of 112? Most critics have opted for a liturgical use for 111, though Allen (*Psalms 101–150*, p. 90), lists some exceptions.

Psalm 111

1		Hallelujah.
	א	I will give thanks unto the LORD with my whole heart,
	ב	In the council of the upright and in the congregation.
2	ג	The works of the LORD are great,
	ד	Sought out of all them that have pleasure therein.
3	ה	His work is honour and majesty:
	ו	And his righteousness endureth for ever.
4	ז	He hath made his wonderful works to be remembered:
	ח	The LORD is gracious and full of compassion.
5	ט	He hath given meat (RVtext) unto them that fear him:
	י	He will ever be mindful of his covenant.
6	כ	He hath showed his people the power of his works,
	ל	In giving them the heritage of the nations.
7	מ	The works of his hands are truth and judgement:
	נ	All his precepts are sure.
8	ס	They are established for ever and ever,
	ע	They are made in truth and uprightness.
9	פ	He hath sent redemption unto his people;
	צ	He hath commanded his covenant for ever:
	ק	Holy and reverend is his name.
10	ר	The fear of the LORD is the beginning of wisdom;
	ש	Good success (שכל) have all they that do them:
	ת	His praise endureth for ever.

Even if we have to do with a later psalmist, the fit of the theme is good. Psalm 111 begins אודה, *I will give thanks*: the same word which has dominated the opening psalms in Book V—107.8, 15, 21, 31; 108.4; 109.30. These are psalms of thanksgiving for the Return, and 111 is the same. The LXX prefixes to 112 the heading τῆς ἐπιστροφῆς Ἀγγαίου καὶ Ζαχαρίου, and the Syro-Hexaplar does the same for 111 (Kirkpatrick). *The council of the upright* and *the congregation* are not to be distinguished: the speaker of 111 is the high priest's cantor, who will lead the nation (*congregation*) in thanks for his deliverances through history. Since they are at Yahweh's festival, they may be taken to be יְשָׁרִים, 'upright', a national סוֹד like that spoken of in Ezek. 13.9, סוֹד עַמִי.

A rather different picture is drawn by Kraus: 'It was normal that at the great annual feasts those giving thanks stepped forward in the Temple forecourt and gathered a circle of listeners around them'. The evidence for this 'normal' procedure is said to be Ps. 22.23, 'In the midst of the congregation will I praise thee', which is open to exactly the same questions. Kraus denies that the עֵדָה was an *ecclesiola in ecclesia*, but what is the difference between his 'circle of listeners' and an *ecclesiola?* Did the national liturgy leave space for such private initiatives? How many such pious testimonies are to be thought of, and were they simultaneous or serial? Did Levites stand by and ask for a copy for the Temple psalm archive?

The works of Yahweh extend from the Exodus to the present day. They are *great* and *miraculous* (נִפְלָאֹת): *He hath sent redemption unto his people*, redeeming them first from Egypt and now from Babylon. *He hath made his wonderful works to be remembered*, especially perhaps at Passover, which was a formal remembrance of the Exodus (Exod. 12.14). *He hath given meat unto them that fear him*: every Israelite knows the story of the manna and the quails in the desert, but in recent times ordinary life has been disrupted (e.g. Neh. 5), and despite these troubles, and endemic peril of drought, war, locusts, and other things, the community has never starved. As he promised at Sinai, *Yahweh is gracious and full of compassion*, and he has remained *mindful of his covenant* to be Israel's God. He not only provided the food in the wilderness; more impressively still, *He hath shewed his people the power of his works, In giving them the heritage of the nations*. Israel took over the land in the days of the settlement: and a core of this land still remains in their hands to this day.

From v. 7 the thought moves to Yahweh's covenant at Sinai, with its *sure precepts, established for ever, and made* (by Yahweh) *in truth and uprightness*. The terror of Exodus 19–20 is reflected in that *his name is holy and terrible* (נוֹרָא). Already in v. 4b Exod. 34.6 is echoed, 'Yahweh, a God *full of compassion and gracious*'; and 34.10-11 continues, 'Behold, I make a *covenant*...I will *do marvels*...and all the people among which thou art shall see *the work of the Lord*', in driving out the Canaanites, as in vv. 5-6. The thought concludes with the success (שֵׂכֶל) that will attend the people who observe this covenant; a topic to be filled out in 112. *The fear of Yahweh is the beginning*, or perhaps with Gunkel, the better part, *of wisdom*, of a life of contentment and blessing.

Verse 1. הללויה suitably invites the assembled עדה to join in celebrating the great national deliverances of past and recent past. It is much easier to envisage the occasion as led by the high priest as a part of the public liturgy, rather than by a private charismatic individual (Weiser, Kraus). עדת צדיקים at Ps. 1.5, and צדיקים at 33.1, may be taken in the same sense of the whole community. *Verse 2b.* דרושים, 'to be marked, learned and inwardly digested'. *Verse 4a.* זכר probably a *public* memorial is involved; cf. Allen 'proclaimed'. חנון ורחום: the order is reversed from Exod. 34.6 for the sake of the initial ח. *Verse 5.* טרף, usually 'prey', is used more generally for food in later texts: Mal. 3.10, Job 24.5, Prov. 31.15—here for the initial ט. *Verse 8.* וְיָשָׁר is justified by Delitzsch as *recte* ('uprightly'), but almost all other critics follow the easier וְיוֹשֵׁר of a few MSS, and the Versions. *Verse 10.* עשׂיהם can refer to פקודיו in v. 7; they are the subject of v. 8, and constitute the *covenant* of v. 9.

Mowinckel is perhaps a little hard in saying that acrostic psalms are 'not poetry, only metric prose', and 'almost never achieve such luxuries as an ordered arrangement or a continuous thread of thought' (*Psalmenstudien*, V, pp. 123-25); Psalm 111 does proceed from the Exodus via the desert feeding to the settlement, with scattered references to Sinai. On the other hand Allen's exposition of a structure that is formal (acrostic), historical, strophic and chiastic, seems a little optimistic. I should settle for Gunkel's 'modest art'.

Psalm 112

1		Hallelujah.
	א	Blessed is the man that feareth the LORD,
	ב	That delighteth greatly in his commandments.
2	ג	His seed shall be mighty upon earth:
	ד	The generation of the upright shall be blessed.
3	ה	Wealth and riches are in his house:
	ו	And his righteousness endureth for ever.
4	ז	Unto the upright there ariseth light in the darkness:
	ח	*He is* gracious and full of compassion, and righteous.
5	ט	Well is it with the man that dealeth graciously and lendeth;
	י	He shall guide his affairs (יכלכל דבריו) in judgement.
6	כ	For he shall never be moved;
	ל	The righteous shall be had in everlasting remembrance.
7	מ	He shall not be afraid of evil tidings:
	נ	His heart is fixed, trusting in the LORD.
8	ס	His heart is established, he shall not be afraid,
	ע	Until he see *his desire* upon his adversaries.
9	פ	He hath dispersed, he hath given to the needy;
	צ	His righteousness endureth for ever:
	ק	His horn shall be exalted with honour.

10   ר   The wicked shall see it, and be grieved;
       שׁ   He shall gnash with his teeth, and melt away:
       ת   The desire of the wicked shall perish.

Psalm 112 is the *verso* of 111: the character of Yahweh, set out in 111, is mirrored in the character of his follower, and the blessings of the God are the fortune of his worshipper. Thus *'Blessed is the man that feareth the LORD'* (v. 1a) takes up *'The fear of the LORD* is the beginning of wisdom' (111.10). *That delighteth greatly in his commandments* (v. 1b) echoes 'Sought out of all them *that delight* therein' (111.2). *His* (the worshipper's) *righteousness endureth for ever* (v. 3b) is identical with *'his* (Yahweh's) *righteousness endureth for ever'* (111.3). The upright is *gracious and full of compassion, and righteous* (v. 4b), as *'Yahweh is gracious and full of compassion'* (111.4). *The righteous shall be had in everlasting remembrance* (v. 6b), as Yahweh's works shall *be remembered* (111.4). *His heart is established* (סמוּךְ, v. 8, *grounded*), as Yahweh's precepts were *established* (סמוכים, 111.8). Hesitations over the boldness of some of these parallels are misplaced: the theme of Psalm 112 is that Yahweh's faithful are his reflection, both in their disposition and in their blessedness.

This then leads back to the question of the use of the psalm. Mowinckel (*Psalms in Israel's Worship*, II, p. 52) speaks of 'learned, private psalmography', and Allen thinks of an author for 112 who has drawn on the phraseology of 111; but most exegetes see the two psalms as a pair. The glorification of the upright in Psalm 112 is merely an extension of the praise of Yahweh in 111, and just as a hymn like 89 (2-3, 6-19) can include the cry, 'Blessed (אשׁרי) is the people that knows the תרועה' (89.16), so 112 is a kind of indirect praise of Yahweh, and is not unsuitably prefaced with הללו יה. Thanks to Yahweh, his follower will prosper and need fear no trouble, and his family will continue after him: it is Yahweh's righteousness and grace which are to be seen in his life. So just as Psalm 111 is a hymn, proclaimed by the national spokesman to the assembled people, so 112 may be seen as a kind of hymn also. *Hymns Ancient and Modern* includes not only 'Praise to the holiest', but also 'How bright those glorious spirits shine'.

There is, happily, no question here of a circle of poor and oppressed but faithful Israelites: *the man that feareth the Lord* has done all right. His children are *mighty upon earth,* and are successful (*blessed*). *Wealth and riches are in his house.* In any trouble (*darkness*) *there ariseth light* for him, and *he shall not be afraid of evil tidings* because he knows that Yahweh is sure to bail him out soon, and that he will shortly have the satisfaction of *seeing his desire upon his enemies*. The parallel with Psalm 111 however means that it is a mistake to see him as a kind of Job before the storm, a member of the upper middle class. What is being described is the destiny of the normal Israelite. God's people *delight in his commandments*; their *righteousness endureth for ever*, and they are *gracious and full of compassion*, like Yahweh himself. They *lend*, and *disperse*, and *give to needy* fellow-Israelites. Their *heart is fixed, trusting in the LORD* because he has shown himself to be *mindful of his covenant* (111.5). He has brought them back from Exile as he brought them out of Egypt, and their *seed shall be mighty upon earth*. They will be prosperous and happy, and their enemies, Samaritans, Ammonites and such, *the wicked, shall be grieved and shall gnash with their teeth*. The psalm is not, as so often thought, a statement of an individual *Vergeltungsdogma*, the laughable theory that the religious are always successful. It is a statement of the faith that God will be true to his promise and bless his obedient community. It may be that this faith was equally misplaced, but at least we may respect it.

I noted that Psalm 109 was in many details a restatement of themes (and phrases) from psalms in the 30s, especially 33–37; and it is striking that 112 draws similarly on 37. Most obviously 111 and 112 are, like 37, acrostic psalms running accurately through the Hebrew alphabet (37 adopting the less constricting pattern of two lines per letter). The theme of 112 is that of 37. The *righteous, upright* man (37.37) *trusts in the LORD* (37.3, 5), he acts with *righteousness and judgement* (37.6), he *delights in* Yahweh's ways (37.23), the law of his God is in his heart (37.31), he is *gracious* and *giving* (37.21), he deals *graciously and lends,* and *his seed is blessed* (37.26), he *inherits the land* (37.9, 18). *The wicked* plots against him, and *gnasheth* upon him with *his teeth* (37.12), but he *shall perish* (37.20), and the righteous shall *see it* when he is cut off (37.34). So much coincidence is not accidental: we seem to have the same mind at work as with 107–109, where there was a steady drawing on a fixed block of scriptural text—first Deutero-Isaiah, then particular sections of the Psalter. The adoption of the acrostic form is part of this adaptive writing, and its exigencies account for the loss of the red-blooded feelings of joy so apparent in Psalms 107, 108 and 110, and of hatred in 109. There is no reason to date 111 and 112 much after 500 BCE.

Verse 3. גבור, *a mighty warrior*, is there for the ג, and should not be amended (Kraus). *Verse 4.* The syntax is obscure, but RV gives the best sense: *the light* is the expectation of Yahweh's aid in *darkness*, and it is the *upright* man, not Yahweh, who is *gracious and compassionate. Verse 5.* RV has *He shall maintain his cause in judgement*, which may be right. Critics object that the righteous man should not be in court anyhow: but cf. 109, and also 37.33.

Sherwood, 'A Royal Psalm?' (1989), suggests that 112 represents the character of the just king, who brings light to his community, and who is to be imitated by the postexilic leadership; but the evidence for this is not too strong.

PSALM 113

1   Hallelujah.
      Praise, O ye servants of the LORD,
      Praise the name of the LORD.

2   Blessed be the name of the LORD
      From this time forth and for evermore.

3   From the rising of the sun unto the going down of the same
      The LORD's name is to be praised.

4   The LORD is high above all nations,
      And his glory above the heavens.

5   Who is like unto the LORD our God,
      That hath his seat on high,

6   That humbleth himself to regard
      The heavens and the earth?

7   He raiseth up the poor out of the dust,
      And lifteth up the needy from the dunghill;

8   That he may set him with princes,
      Even with the princes of his people.

9   He maketh the barren woman to keep house,
      And to be a joyful mother of children.
      Hallelujah.

Psalm 113 is, by common consent, a hymn; but the substance for which it praises God is controverted. Delitzsch saw it as written 'under the vivid impression of the deliverance from Babylon', and Kirkpatrick speaks of 'the gratitude of Israel for the restoration from the Captivity'. Gunkel however, followed by most modern critics, thinks this a mistake: 'That "the poor" is rather an individual, is evident from the contrast with "the princes of his people"'. On this occasion we may think that the older opinion is correct.

Among modern exegetes, Eaton and Anderson allow a secondary place to the Restoration view.

(1) Few psalms express a livelier sense of *joyful thanksgiving*. The psalm opens and closes with הללו יה: this probably implies an invitation

to the crowds to respond at the festival, as the preacher invites a modern black Pentecostal congregation. The *servants of Yahweh* are to praise his name; perhaps again the whole people, perhaps the professional choir, as at 134.1 and 135.1, since the praise of Yahweh seems to be their sole business. Yahweh's name comes seven times in the opening five verses, and the שם יהוה itself three times. It is to be praised both now, in the present liturgy, and permanently hereafter; and not only by Israel, but among the nations, *from the rising of the sun to its going down*. Such enthusiasm is best understood if the community has something important to be grateful for. The fact that the occasional poor boy makes good, and one or two childless women become pregnant, seems rather inadequate. The congregations imagined by Delitzsch and Kirkpatrick had something to enthuse over.

Most commentators take עבדי יהוה to mean the whole people; compare 34.23, or 135.1, where the same phrase becomes 'O house of Israel...' in vv. 19-20. Kraus imagines two choirs of priests singing vv. 1-4 and 5-9 antiphonally; but Allen and others divide the psalm after v. 3. *Verse 3.* The parallel in Mal. 1.11, 'from the rising of the sun...', suggests that Yahweh's praise is expected among the Gentiles, not just in the Diaspora: see Isaiah 60, Ps. 126.2. The concluding הללו יה is placed at the beginning of 114 by LXX; but the likely reason for such a transfer would be to provide a symmetrical beginning to 111–114, and it would therefore be the easier reading. The asymmetry is probably connected with liturgical use: according to *m. Pes.* 10.6, there was a break in the Hallel in first-century family usage, the house of Hillel after Psalm 114, the house of Shammai after 113.

(2) A *contrast* is drawn between *the LORD our God*, who is *high above all nations*, and the gods of the heathen, as in Psalm 115: *Who is like unto Yahweh...?* It is implied therefore that Yahweh achieves where other gods cannot penetrate. But we should not suppose the ancient Israelite to be so simple-minded as not to be aware that sometimes poor Ammonites and Arabs rose from the dunghill to authority, and that there were Babylonian women who conceived late in life. For the former, what about Job? But to the sixth-century psalmists, Yahweh alone was the God who had raised his people from misery to independence, and from barrenness to the rearing of large families.

Most commentators understand vv. 5b, 6a as a parenthesis, and take 6b with 5a— *Who is like unto the LORD our God* [...] *In heaven and on the earth?* Kraus even emends the text to place 6b immediately after 5a. But this leaves a weak end to 6a, *That humbleth himself to behold*, with no object. As Yahweh's glory is *above the heavens* in v.4b, he may reasonably be thought to *humble himself to regard*, that is, look down on, *the heavens* as well as *the earth*, as in RVmg.

(3) *The Song of the Sea*. The wording, *Who is like unto the* LORD *our God?*, recalls Exod. 15.11, '*Who is like unto* thee, o LORD, among the gods?' With so much careful echoing of earlier texts in our psalms, it is likely that the parallel is intended. The act for which God was shown to be incomparable in the Song of the Sea was the Exodus: the act for which he has now shown himself to be incomparable is the exodus from Babylon. The similar Deut. 3.24, 'For *what* god is there *in heaven or in earth* that can do according to thy works?', similarly refers to the Exodus complex.

(4) *Hannah's Song*. There is an unquestionable echo of another Scripture in vv. 7-9. *He raiseth up the poor out of the dust, And lifteth up the needy from the dunghill That he may set him with princes*, comes word for word (with two added terminal ḥireqs, v. i.) from the Song of Hannah, in 1 Sam. 2.8. The *barren woman* who becomes a mother will then be an echo of 1 Sam. 2.5, '*The barren woman* hath borne seven'; and very likely her being *joyful* (שמחה) stems from 1 Sam. 2.1, 'I *rejoice* (שמחתי) in thy salvation'.

Why should the psalmist draw in this way on Hannah's Song? Because it is the classic statement for the reversal of fates. Deutero-Isaiah had spoken of Zion as a *barren woman*: 'Sing, O *barren*, thou that didst not bear...for more are the children of the desolate than of the married wife' (Isa. 54.1-10), and already in this text lies the suggestion that the desolate and barren Hannah was to outstrip the established Peninnah. The depopulation of Jerusalem after 587 BCE naturally suggested the image of the childless woman/widow (Lam. 1; Isa. 66.7-8). Her poverty similarly suggested the life of the beggars, sleeping for warmth by the piles of ashes and dung: as Isaiah says again, 'Come down, and *sit in the dust*, O virgin daughter of Babylon; sit on the ground without a throne' (Isa. 47.1), 'Shake thyself *from the dust*: arise, *sit thee down*, O Jerusalem' (Isa. 52.2); or Lam. 4.5 speaks of the high-born 'embracing *dunghills*'. So the reverse movement, from dust to throne, in Hannah's Song, is a natural text to symbolize the Return. It is not the first time the Second Isaiah reversal theme appears in Book V: the same idea is in 107.37-43.

Willis, 'The Song of Hannah', interprets Psalm 113 as a victory hymn: it comes from Shiloh, where Hannah's Song is said to have its origin, and belongs in the

preexilic northern kingdom: while one may sympathize with his symbolic understanding of the poor and barren, the overall suggestion seems weakly supported.

There are five terminal י-'s in vv. 5-9: four of them with participles, המגביהי (5b),
המשפילי (6a), מקימי (7a) and מושיבי (9a), and one with an infinitive, להושיבי (8a). The
participles are not without parallel, for example, Deut. 33.16 and Zech. 11.17;
Delitzsch calls them *hireq compaginis*, and they are explained as ornamental by GKC
90m, and by Dahood as genitival following כ in v. 5a. The instance with the
infinitive is unparalleled (GKC 90n), and is usually understood to be an error for
להושיבו, 'That he may set him'; or perhaps as affected by מושיבי in 9a. Whatever the
explanation, these endings link 113 to 114, where v. 8 has similar ההפכי and also
מעינו־מים; and perhaps also to 110.5 דברתי.

(5) The Song of Hannah saw the exalted poor man as seated among
the princes (נדיבים)—naturally *Israelite* princes—and inheriting 'a
throne of glory'. In postexilic Israel נדיבים were few, and the psalmist
does not want to create the impression that Yahweh might exalt the
poor to sit among oppressive *foreign* princes; so he clarifies the point
by adding *Even with the princes of his people*. So Gunkel's conclusion
is hasty: vv. 7-8 are a transcription of 1 Sam. 2.8 with a defensive
gloss in the last half-verse. Poor man and barren woman are symbols
for exiled, and now returned, Israel: the symbols are carefully pan-
Israelite, which does not reduce them to descriptions of ordinary beggars and childless wives.

The Hebrew of v. 9 is not straightforward: Eaton translates, 'The barren one of
the household he establishes as a joyful mother of children'. The hiphil of ישׁב is used
for 'to take, establish' a wife in late texts Ezra 10.2, 14 and Neh. 13.23.

(6) It is perilous to ignore Jewish interpretative tradition. The late
Talmudic tractate *Sopherim* specifies the use of Psalms 113–118 for
use at the festivals (Tabernacles, Passover, Pentecost, Dedication), and
certain New Moons, understanding them to refer to the *Heilsgeschichte*
(18.2). The Targum of 113 reads, 'Who maketh the congregation of
Israel, which was like a barren woman mourning for the men of her
household, to be full of crowds, like a mother who rejoiceth over
sons'. *Sopherim* 18.2 prescribes a domestic use of Psalms 113 and 114
before the Passover meal, and 115–118 after it; and we appear to have
an echo of this in Mk 14.26, 'And when they had sung a hymn, they
went out unto the mount of Olives'. Whoever arranged Book V in
order, set 113 between 111 (with its twin 112) and 114, both hymns
of praise for the Exodus events. It looks therefore as if Jewish

understanding of 113 as praise for the Restoration goes back centuries into the BCE period, as far as our sources take us.

In view of these considerations, it seems that Psalm 113 should be understood as a hymn of praise for the Restoration.

PSALM 114

1   When Israel went forth out of Egypt,
    The house of Jacob from a people of strange language;
2   Judah became his sanctuary,
    Israel his dominion.
3   The sea saw it, and fled;
    Jordan was driven back.
4   The mountains skipped like rams,
    The little hills like young sheep.
5   What aileth thee, O thou sea, that thou fleest?
    Thou Jordan, that thou turnest back?
6   Ye mountains, that ye skip like rams;
    Ye little hills, like young sheep?
7   Tremble, thou earth, at the presence of the Lord,
    At the presence of the God of Jacob;
8   Which turned the rock into a pool of water,
    The flint into a fountain of waters.

Here the text is perspicuous: a hymn of praise for the 'works of Yah-weh'—the Exodus (vv. 1, 3a, 5a), the earthquake at Sinai (4, 6), the provision of water in the desert (8), the dryshod crossing of Jordan (3b, 5b), the Jerusalem Temple (2a) and the settlement of the land (2b).

Verse 1. As the Egyptians do not speak Hebrew, they are thought not able to talk properly (לעז). *Verse 2.* The 'his' has no apparent referent, and is sometimes held to support LXX's הללו יה at the beginning of 114. Other suggestions are that it is a carry-over from 113 (Kirkpatrick), or a deliberate raising of tension in preparation for v. 7 (Gunkel); but perhaps the referent is *the house of Jacob*, whose *sanctuary* was *Judah*, that is, Jerusalem, and his *dominions* (ממשלותיו, pl.) the land of *Israel*. Amos speaks of 'the sanctuaries of Israel' (מקדשי־ישראל, 7.9; cf. Isa. 16.12, Ezek. 28.18), and the *dominions* would be the long-divided northern and southern king-doms. *Verse 3.* Almost all commentators take Yahweh to be the unstated object of *saw*: see 77.17, where 'the waters saw thee, O God,...they were afraid' and the earth trembled (77.19), or the invading kings who saw [God] at 48.6. RV takes the waters to have seen the Exodus, as the syntax implies; but *the earth* does *tremble at the presence of its Lord* in v. 7. *Verse 7.* אלוה—*the earth* is thought of as less than God's people, which alone can speak of יהוה or אלהי־יעקב: God is its אדון, and (like

Job) it refers naturally to him as אלוה. *Verse 8.* For the terminations to ההפכי and למעינו, see below.

It is usually thought that the psalm is from after the Exile. Kraus and Weiser argued from the distinction between Judah (*his sanctuary*) and Israel (*his dominion*), for a date before 722 BCE; but there is a stronger case for a later setting. Kirkpatrick notes the pleonastic י- at the end of ההפכי, and the pleonastic ו- at the end of מעינו, both in v. 8, and therefore links 114 with 113. Gunkel notes that אגם־מים recurs in 107.35 and Isa. 41.18. There are also various evidences that the psalm is 'post-Deuteronomic'. The idea that *Judah* (i.e. Jerusalem) *became his sanctuary* is the most striking, since this implies the illegality of the old northern shrines; but we may also note that the Sinai tradition has been fused with the Exodus tradition; that Joshua's crossing of the Jordan has been developed as a parallel to Moses' crossing of the Red Sea, and accepted as an independent story; and that the same is true of the water from the rock, which now has two forms (cf. Exod. 17 and Num. 20).

Kraus disputes Gunkel's argument over v. 2: the psalm comes from Judah, which considered Jerusalem to be God's *sanctuary* from David's time, and [the land of] Israel as his dominion. But the Exodus story was not accepted in Jerusalem until the seventh century (Goulder, *Asaph*, Part II); and Gunkel's case is cumulative.

In a brilliant analysis Gunkel comments too on the *elaborations* to our Pentateuchal tradition. In Exod. 15.8 (and similarly in Exod. 14, Ps. 77.17) the waters pile up and stand up in a heap: here *the sea fled.* In Josh. 3.13, 16 the waters of Jordan are cut off, stand, and rise in one heap: here *Jordan is driven back*, and flows northwards. In Exod. 19.18 the whole of Mount Sinai quaked greatly: here it is not the single mountain but *the mountains* and *the little hills* beside—nor do they merely quake like a modern volcano, but *skip like lambs*. In Exodus 17 and Numbers 20, Moses strikes the rock, and water comes forth abundantly: here God *turns the rock into a pool of water,* and the rock is basalt (החלמיש), the hardest of known rocks. The whole world is expected now to *tremble at the presence of the Lord*, and nature is anthropomorphized—the poet *addresses* the sea, Jordan, the mountains, the hills, the earth. Why has he made these consistent changes? Because, says Gunkel, he lives in a period of national humiliation, when no miracles happen, so he feasts his imagination on the marvels of long ago, and paints in a little more colour than that already supplied by tradition.

Gunkel thought the hymn best suited to Passover, like many before him; and Kraus supported this, partly on the ground that the crossing of Jordan is also dated at Passover in Joshua 5. There are other suggestions in the field: Mowinckel, *Psalmenstudien,* II, pp. 54-55, *Psalms in Israel's Worship*, I, pp. 114-15, thought of the Enthronement Festival, that is, Tabernacles, and Weiser the festival of the Renewal of the Covenant. But Gunkel and Kraus can appeal not only to the Paschal associations of Exodus and Jordan, but also to the Jewish domestic tradition, which has for so many centuries linked the Hallel psalms with Passover.

Kraus, 'Gilgal', and *Worship in Israel*, pp. 152-65, argued persuasively that the various cultic elements in the Joshua 3–5 narrative were not later insertions but significant parts of an original cultic legend of the crossing of the Jordan: the original spring festival celebrating the entrance into the Land was thus at Gilgal, and later taken to Jerusalem, as is seen in Psalm 114. The Passover celebration at Josh. 5.10 strengthens the case for 114 as a Paschal hymn; but the echoes of the Red Sea crossing may be no older than the Deuteronomic historian.

The apparent Paschal associations of Psalm 114 raise the more general question of the setting of the whole psalm-series, 107–118. I have argued (mostly with support from other scholars) that all the psalms so far discussed are postexilic, and that most are hymns celebrating the Return. More specifically, Psalm 107 gave thanks for the Return in images drawn from Second Isaiah; 108 exulted in Israel's deliverance, with vilification of Shechem, adapting Psalms 60 and 57; 109 was an extended curse on the community's accuser(s); 110 celebrated the repelling of an armed attack with the aid of volunteers under the leadership of Joshua ben Jozadak; and 111 (and 112), 113 and 114 were Hallel hymns, praising God for his deliverances of old, and for those of more recent times. I have noted the way in which the earlier of these psalms echo the story in Ezra 1, 3–4: the Return under Sheshbazzar, the exiles' thanksgiving in the same words that open Psalm 107, the opposition from Samaria, the letter of accusation sent to the Persian king. Psalm 110 had a number of associations with Joshua, found in Zechariah 3–6.

Now the story in Ezra 1–6 ends in triumph. In ch. 6 Darius the king confirms Cyrus's order for the building of the Temple, and the latter is completed on 3 Adar (our February–March) in the sixth year of Darius (6.15). Its dedication is celebrated with joy, and with massive sacrifices (6.16-18); and this is followed a few weeks later by a celebration of Passover. 'And the children of the captivity kept the passover upon the fourteenth *day* of the first month'. Everyone cleansed themselves and 'they kept the feast of unleavened bread seven days with joy: for the Lord had made them joyful, and had turned the heart of the king of Assyria unto them, to strengthen their hands in the work of the house of God, the God of Israel' (6.19-22). So perhaps we have a setting for the joyful spirit of the Hallel psalms, and their repeated appeal to the deliverance of the Exodus, and even for the reference to *Judah his sanctuary*. I return to the suggestion in discussing the remaining psalms in the sequence.

There is no *Hallelujah* at the end of 114, whereas the phrase forms a conclusion to Psalms 113, 115, 116, 117. This will be due to the dominant Jewish domestic tradition (of Beth Hillel, *m. Pes.* 10.6), which had a break in the *Hallel* after 114. The *Hallelujah*s functioned as links between the members of the two series. The second series comprised 115–118: although Jewish tradition limits the whole to 113–118, the presence of *Hallelujah*s before 111 and 112 suggests that an earlier use included 110–114 as the first series. This would also give a more even balance between the two halves, and would account for Beth Shammai's division after 113 (also *m. Pes.* 10.6).

PSALM 115

Where there was unanimity over Psalm 114, there is diversity of opinion over 115. Delitzsch thought the psalm to be a prayer before a battle. Gunkel took it to be an assembly of fragments—two verses of communal lament, followed by six in hymnic tone, a warning, a blessing and a final hymnic passage—the whole being combined into a cultic liturgy, sung antiphonally. The antiphonal suggestion is already in Kirkpatrick, and is widely followed (Weiser, Eaton, Kraus, Dahood, Anderson, Jacquet, Allen), sometimes on the strength of the repetitions in vv. 9-11, sometimes with the people taking vv. 1-8, 16-18, while the priests speak vv. 9-15 (Eaton). Mowinckel, *Psalms in Israel's Worship*, II, p. 50, thought the psalm was the liturgy for a Day of Penance. Weiser thought it might be pre-exilic; but most critics take it to be from after the Exile. They also mostly see it as a plea for vindication in a time of national humiliation (v. 2). A better exegete, in my view, was Henry V, King of England, who had his chaplains sing the psalm after the victory of Agincourt, and 'commanded euerie man to kneele down on the ground at this verse, *Non nobis Domine*' (Holinshed's *Chronicle*, cited in Kirkpatrick, *The Book of Psalms*, III, p. 683). He is followed (with characteristic hesitation) by Rogerson and McKay. I shall argue that Psalm 115 is best read as a thanksgiving for the Return and Restoration, with the promise of further future blessing.

Psalm 115

1   Not unto us, O LORD, not unto us,
    But unto thy name give glory,
    For thy mercy, and for thy truth's sake.
2   Wherefore should the nations say,
    Where is now their God?
3   But our God is in the heavens:
    He hath done whatsoever he pleased.

4   Their idols are silver and gold,
     The work of men's hands.
5   They have mouths, but they speak not;
     Eyes have they, but they see not;
6   They have ears, but they hear not;
     Noses have they, but they smell not;
7   They have hands, but they handle not;
     Feet have they, but they walk not;
     Neither speak they through their throat.
8   They that make them shall be like unto them,
     Yea, every one that trusteth in them.
9   O Israel, trust thou in the LORD;
     He is their help and their shield.
10   O house of Aaron, trust ye in the LORD;
     He is their help and their shield.
11   Ye that fear the LORD, trust in the LORD;
     He is their help and their shield.
12   The LORD hath been mindful of us; he will bless *us*:
     He will bless the house of Israel;
     He will bless the house of Aaron.
13   He will bless them that fear the LORD,
     Both small and great.
14   The LORD increase you more and more,
     You and your children.
15   Blessed are ye of the LORD,
     Which made heaven and earth.
16   The heavens are the heavens of the LORD;
     But the earth hath he given to the children of men.
17   The dead praise not Jah,
     Neither any that go down into silence:
18   But we will bless the LORD
     From this time forth and for evermore.
     Hallelujah.

Verses 1-8. Like Psalm 113, 115 begins on a note of high joy, marked by repetition. Something marvellous has happened, but the credit is due *not unto us, O Lord, not unto us.* The situation is something for which to *give glory*, a triumph, which is due to *Yahweh for his* חסד, for his faithfulness to his covenantal promise, the חסד which endures for ever, and is claimed as the basis of the Return (Ezra 3.11, Ps. 107.1, 8, 15, 21, 31). This deliverance is a sufficient response to the standard Gentile mockery, *Where is now their God?* (79.10; 42.4, 11). The Gentile gods, especially those in Babylon, once so honoured and now seen to be so hollow, are nothing but *the work of men's hands*, without even human abilities: *our God*, on the other hand, *is in the heavens*, and *hath done whatsoever he pleased*—in this case restoring leadership and quasi-independence to his people.

Greek, Syriac and some Hebrew MSS take 114 and 115 as a single psalm, and this is defended by Lubszcyk, 'Einheit und heilsgeschichtliche Bedeutung'; but the two psalms seem very different, and their joining may be due to the absence of *Hallelujah* between them. Weiser suggests that the renunciation of foreign gods took place at an annual Renewal of the Covenant festival, cf. Josh. 24, and E. Luke, *CBQ* (1974) argues similarly; but the evidence is hardly enough for the conclusion. *Verse 7: their hands... their feet* are taken by Delitzsch and many as *casus pendens*; the subject of the verbs is the idols.

Verses 9-15. The central problem of 115 has been the triple division apparently implied by vv. 9-11, repeated in vv. 12-13, and in 118.2-4 (also in 135.19-20, with Levi). If *(the house of) Israel* means the whole people, and *the house of Aaron* the priesthood, who are *they that fear the LORD*? They can hardly be New Testament-style proselytes in the making; v. 14 following seems to be concerned with the natural expansion of the Jewish people alone.

Delitzsch accepted the 'God-fearers' as proselytes, and this was defended by Gunkel and Kraus, with reference to 1 Kgs 8.41 and Isa. 56.6 (and Jethro and Naaman). But from early times Israel had always aspired to have Gentiles come with gifts to Yahweh's Temple (Ps. 68.30-32; 47.9-10), and the Deuteronomic historian was not going to omit that from Solomon's consecration prayer (with the Queen of Sheba coming!). Third Isaiah has a similar vision in ch. 60. In view of this problem, most critics opt for a division into only two (Kirkpatrick and many; the proselyte position is most fully refuted by Joachim Becker, *Gottesfurcht*, pp. 156-60): 'Israel' means 'lay Israel' as opposed to the *priests, the house of Aaron*, and the whole together comprise *those that fear the LORD. Israel* is distinguished from *the priests and Levites* in Ezra 9.1, 10.25. But this has its problems. The third person in vv. 9b, 10b, 11b, *He is their help and their shield*, reads like a promise to three sections of those present: if *those that fear the LORD* means the whole people, we should have expected *our help and our shield*. Kirkpatrick, supported by Jacquet, also suggested that the 'God-fearers' were an inner circle, perhaps fervent Levites; but surely all Israel *feared the LORD*, and the term is used in New Testament times for those on the margin of the community.

Verses 9-11: the Versions read (ו)חטב as indicatives, perhaps to give better sense to the third persons, *their help, their shield.*

An answer is suggested by the description of the Paschal celebration in Ezra 6.19-21: And the children of the captivity kept the passover upon the fourteenth *day* of the first month. For the priests and the Levites had purified themselves as one; all of them were pure: and they killed the passover for all the children of the captivity, and for their brethren the priests, and for themselves. And the children of Israel, which were come again out of the captivity, and all such as had separated themselves unto them from the filthiness of the heathen of the land, to seek the LORD, the God of Israel, did eat, and kept the feast of unleavened bread seven days with joy.

The Passover is not eaten by 'all Israel' in the old sense of the whole people. The priests and Levites have purified themselves to a man, so they are all right; and they kill the paschal animals for 'the children of the captivity', for their fellow priests, and for themselves. No mention is made in 6.20 of the ordinary Israelites who had remained in the land. The reason for this becomes plain in 6.21. During the seventy years of the captivity the ordinary Israelite had given up the uneven struggle to maintain *kashrut*: he had sunk into 'the filthiness of the heathen of the land'. The only local people who were permitted to join in the Passover, therefore, were those who 'separated themselves unto them from the filthiness of the heathen of the land, to seek the LORD, the God of Israel'. We find similar horror at the assimilation of the local people in Ezra 9, and in Zechariah 5, the vision of the woman Wickedness in the Ephah; no doubt their laxity seemed the worse because purity rules had been tightened up in Babylonia.

The passage thus discriminates three groups: (1) 'the children of Israel, which were of the captivity'—these are 'pukka' Israelites, who have maintained their purity through the trials of the exile; (2) the priests [and Levites], who had 'purified themselves as one'—'all of them were pure', though the mention of 'their brethren the priests' suggests that some were purer than others; (3) 'all such as separated themselves to them', that is, a number who gave up 'the filthiness of the heathen' with suitable purification rituals, 'to seek the LORD, the God of Israel'. It is clear from the last phrase that the author sees only group (1) and the priests from the Exile in group (2) as Israel proper. Group (3) are only *seeking* the LORD, the God of Israel, and may be thought to be the same as the psalmist's *they that fear the LORD*. We then have an explanation for the surprising third persons, *He is their help and their shield*: Israel proper, the priests and the God-fearers are three sections of the celebrating community, and Yahweh is the promised defender of each. They are called on each to trust in Yahweh in vv. 9-11, and in 12-13 his blessing on each is pronounced, *both small and great*, the peasant and the landowner (Jer. 6.13, 16.6, rather than young and old).

The combination 'our *help and* our *shield*' comes in Ps. 33.20: the psalms in the 30s have often been a source for our psalmists. Cf. also Ps. 29.1-2, 'Give *unto the Lord the glory* due unto *his name*' with 115.1.

Not only is this triumphal reading of Psalm 115 suggested by the *giving of glory to Yahweh's name* and *not unto us*, and by the traditional use of the psalm at festivals: it seems to be confirmed by v.12a, *The LORD hath been mindful of us* (cf. v. 3b, *He hath done whatsoever he pleased*). This is interpreted by many as the indication of an oracle (by Weiser of a theophany). But Kirkpatrick is surely on sounder ground when he sees Yahweh's remembrance of his people as evidenced in the Return (cf. the ten *remembrance* texts used in the New Year liturgy, where *remember* means *act*). It is this which demonstrates Yahweh's חסד, and for which *glory is to be given to his Name*. The situation of the Restoration is happily reflected in these verses: the urgent need for a divine *help and shield* in face of enemy threats (cf. 110), and the longer-term need for blessing in the form of *increase more and more, you and your children* (113.9; Isa. 54.1-10; Neh. 7.1-5). Such blessing is in fact assured (v. 15): *the LORD made heaven and earth*, and he will enable us to be fruitful and multiply. A similar policy, and confidence, has been evident in modern Israel, since 1947.

Verses 16-18. The psalm ends with a triumphant הללו יה, like 113 and 116–118: probably this was the response of the entire people (cf. 44.9). This final cry should not be regarded as a later addition: v. 17a says *The dead praise not Jah*, and it is difficult to explain this aberrant form of Yahweh unless it means that they cannot join in the united cry, *Hallelu Jah!* The heavens belong to God; he has given man the earth. Generation after generation dies away, and can praise Jah no more; and after 587 BCE it looked to some as if that would be the end of his praises. But now he has re-established Israel on a permanent footing; and *we*, Israel, *will bless Jah From this time forth and for evermore.*

Suggestions of a 'change of voice' should be restricted to this final phrase. Ezra 3.10-11 says that the Levites, the sons of Asaph praised the LORD, 'And they sang one to another in praising and giving thanks unto the LORD, *saying*, For he is good, for his mercy *endureth* for ever toward Israel. And all the people shouted with a great shout'. They shouted הללו יה. Psalm 115, like 107 (and all these psalms), was sung by Asaphite Levites, who had inherited the responsibility over many generations (Goulder, *Asaph*); they might sing antiphonally when there was a refrain, as in vv. 9-11, which first suggested the antiphonal idea (in Delitzsch). The notion of a much more complex change of voices arises from Gunkel's breaking up of the psalm according to its different 'forms'. But (quite apart from Gunkel's mis-interpretation of the thrust of the whole) the change of form does not at all imply a different speaker; nor is any account made of the difficulties of teaching 'the people' to chant a fixed form of words over some ten verses (1-8, 16-18). Are we to think of the circulation of the text on papyrus to the heads of father's houses? Or of a mass choir practice for thousands? One wonders if Gunkel and Kraus have used their imaginations on such problems.

Another feature which recalls Psalm 107 is the debt the psalmist owes to Second Isaiah. 107 drew on the variety of images the prophet used for Zion's plight and recovery; 115 turns to other themes. Isaiah 48.9, 11: '*For my name's sake* I will defer mine anger, and for my *praise* will I refrain for thee...and my *glory* will I not give to another' (cf. v. 1). The mockery of heathen idols is a repeated motif of the prophet (40.18-20, 44.9-20, 46.6-7—cf. Ps. 115.4-7). Isa. 44.9, 'They that fashion a graven image are all of them confusion...their own witnesses see not nor know' (cf. v. 8). Isa. 49.14, 'But Zion said, Jehovah hath forsaken me, and the Lord hath forgotten me' (cf. v. 12, *The LORD hath been mindful of us*). Isa. 54 foretold Zion's marriage and motherhood to many children, as in v. 14. Isa. 45.18, 'For thus says *the LORD* that created *the heavens*; he is God: that formed *the earth* and made it': the contrast between Yahweh as creator of heaven and earth and the idols is basic to the prophecy, and evidence of his power to restore Zion, as in 115.3, 16-18.

We may also note the similarities to Psalm 113. '*Unto thy name* give the praise' recalls the triple appeal to Yahweh's *name* in 113.1-3. *The nations* and their *idols* contrasted with *our God in the heavens* echoes 113.4-5, '*The LORD* is high above all *nations*, And his glory *above the heavens*. Who is like unto *the LORD our God*?' His blessing of the people, and promise of *increase more and more, you and your children*, reminds us of 113.9, where the once barren wife becomes the joyful mother of *children*. Finally both psalms end with the triumphant הללו יה. Both psalms come from the same group of Asaphic composers, perhaps from the same hand.

The accumulated evidence seems handsomely to justify the Agincourt–Rogersonian interpretation. Psalm 115 is a hymn of thanksgiving for the Restoration, referred to in v. 12, *The LORD hath been mindful of us*, and hinted in vv. 1, 3b. It promises *help and defence* in the military perils of the late sixth century, and for the longer term *increase more and more* in population. It reflects the situation described in Ezra 6.19-21, where the Restoration Passover was celebrated by three groups—Israel proper, that is the returned exiles who were ritually pure; the priests, who had purified themselves to a man; and 'those who fear the LORD', those from the local Judahites who had separated themselves 'to them, to seek the LORD, the God of Israel'. The psalm was written to be part of the Passover liturgy, and it has remained a part of it ever since.

PSALM 116

Like Psalm 115, 116 carries a large majority of critics in a consensus. The psalm is an Individual Thanksgiving. The speaker has been in dire trouble, probably though not certainly sickness (v. 11 implies slandering enemies, and v. 16 mentions chains), and he is giving thanks to God for his recovery. He was on the point of death and cried for help, and his prayers were not in vain. He has come now to the Temple to pay the vows he made in his distress: these include a thanksgiving sacrifice and a libation of wine, and prayers in the presence of all God's people. However scholarly consensuses are rarely complete; and a minority view, represented by Birkeland and Eaton, sees the speaker as a national figure (to Eaton the king). The language used is echoed from other, royal psalms, like 18, and God is spoken of as 'our God'. The nation should be seen therefore as having undergone dire perils which nearly brought it to extinction, and its leader personally too: perhaps the *bonds* were literally on his wrists, or perhaps they were metaphorical. The setting for the psalm will be one of the great annual festivals, when the national leader offered sacrifices and prayers before the assembled people. It is a Communal Thanksgiving, or (despite its non-hymnic form) a hymn.

There are problems with both these interpretations. For the majority view, the idea of private thanksgivings at public festivals is just a speculation, and a rather implausible one. Allen offers a scenario:

> The people had gathered for a festival. Amidst the communal worship in the temple courts there were services in which individuals had opportunity to bring thank offerings and to accompany their sacrificial worship with words of testimony and praise for answered prayer. This psalm was composed for recitation in front of the congregation on such happy occasions (Allen, *Psalms 101–150*, p. 115).

Where is the evidence for such claims? It consists of statements in psalms like 116 and 22 in which the speaker undertakes a prayer of thanksgiving before the people: but whereas we know that national figures led worship at festivals, and gave thanks for national deliverances (as presupposed by Birkeland and Eaton), services for individuals are simply guesswork. Secondly, notice Allen's problem over the origin of the psalm. One might have thought that 116 was a cry from the heart: *I was in misery, and He helped me.* But if he takes this option, there is the embarrassment of how the psalm came to be in the psalter—'Excuse me, sir, that was a beautiful prayer you made: do you think we could have a copy for the Temple collection?' So he avoids that by making the psalm a hack job: it was composed [by the Levite staff] 'for recitation on such happy occasions'—'Berekiah, do you think you could do us a thanksgiving psalm suitable for recovery from sickness, childbirth, prison, libel, etc.? About 20 verses'.

There is a third problem for the Individual Thanksgiving view. As I have noted above, Jewish tradition, stretching back for many years into the BCE period, understood the Hallel psalms to be hymns of praise for national deliverances, and in particular for the deliverance from bondage in Egypt. In some cases (113, 114, 117) this understanding was clearly correct. Is it not rather surprising that the levitical authorities who presided over Israel's stock of hymns and national thanksgivings should have taken a piece designed and used for private services, and deliberately misapplied it?

On the other hand, Eaton is in difficulties over the language; for not only are there a number of Aramaisms in the psalm, which suggest a late date, but also the author seems to draw on and adapt earlier psalms, 18, 27, 28, 31, 56, not all of which may be so very early. It would seem better therefore to posit a setting similar to that of the other Hallel psalms, which also use a non-classical terminal ־ֹ, and also draw on psalms in Book I, and which have been classed together by Jewish tradition. The singer may be speaking in the name of Joshua ben Jozadak, offering sacrifice and prayer before the people at the Paschal festival, thanking God for his own, and Israel's, preservation from near-extinction. God had indeed *broken his bonds in sunder.*

Psalm 116

1   I love the LORD, because he hath heard
     The voice of (קוֹלִי) my supplications.
2   Because he hath inclined his ear unto me,
     Therefore will I call *upon him* as long as I live.

3   The cords of death compassed me,
     And the constrictions (מצרי) of Sheol found me:
     I found trouble and sorrow.
4   Then called I upon the name of the LORD;
     O LORD, I beseech thee, deliver my soul.
5   Gracious is the LORD, and righteous;
     Yea, our God is merciful.
6   The LORD preserveth the simple:
     I was brought low, and he saved me.
7   Return unto thy rest, O my soul;
     For the LORD hath dealt bountifully with thee.
8   For thou hast delivered my soul from death,
     Mine eyes from tears,
     And my feet from falling.
9   I will walk before the LORD
     In the lands of the living.
10   I had faith (האמנתי), for I will say (אדבר),
     I was greatly afflicted.
11   I said in my alarm,
     All men are a lie.
12   What shall I render unto the LORD
     For all his benefits toward me?
13   I will take the cup of salvation,
     And call upon the name of the LORD.
14   I will pay my vows unto the LORD,
     Yea, in the presence of all his people.
15   Precious in the sight of the LORD
     Is the death of his devoted ones (לחסידיו).
16   O LORD, truly I am thy servant:
     I am thy servant, the son of thine handmaid;
     Thou hast loosed my bonds.
17   I will offer to thee the sacrifice of thanksgiving,
     And will call upon the name of the LORD.
18   I will pay my vows unto the LORD,
     Yea, in the presence of all his people;
19   In the courts of the LORD's house,
     In the midst of thee, O Jerusalem.
     Hallelujah.

In Psalm 108 the sixth-century psalmist had adapted parts of two old
'royal' psalms, 57 and 60, both ascribed to David; and we have seen
how often, in other psalms in the series, phrases and catenas of
phrases have been taken over from these David collections and reused.
What better could he do? the Asaphite composer might feel. So now,

in celebration of the Return, and its sealing in the rebuilding of the Temple, he adapts some of the most relevant of the old psalms.

Verses 1-4. The first to come to mind is Psalm 18, understood by the Heading to be written 'on the day that the LORD delivered [David] from the hand of all his enemies' (18.1), a situation so like Israel's now: 'I care for thee (ארחמך), *O LORD...I will call upon the LORD... The cords of death compassed me...*The cords *of Sheol* were round about *me*' (18.2, 4-6). The catastrophe of 587 BCE had nearly seen the end of God's people, like David hunted by Saul and in peril from Achish. The singer, who has shared the trials of the Exile, speaks in the name of the community. He prefers the stronger *I have loved,* אהבתי, for 18's ארחמך, as in 31.24 and other psalms, and he uses the past to signify that his love was constant, even in trouble. Psalm 18.7 is grateful that God heard the prayer 'out of his temple', and there is a similar prayer which David offered in the Temple: '*Unto thee, O LORD, will I call...Hear the voice of my supplications,* when I cry unto thee, When I lift up my hands toward thy holy דביר' (28.1-2, cf. 6). The psalmist is thankful because *God hears the voice of his suppli-cations, in the courts of the LORD's house* (v. 19). The repeated *cords* (חבלי) of 18.6 seem clumsy, so he substitutes מצרי, *straitnesses*: the same rare word is used of the Exile in Lam. 1.3 in conjunction with 116's surprising repeated מצא, 'she *findeth* no rest: all her persecutors overtook her within the *straits* (מצרים)'. The *rest* comes in 116.7, 'Return unto thy *rest*, O my soul'. God *inclined his ear unto* David in 17.6, as in v. 2.

Verse 1. אהבתי has no object, as also have אקרא in v. 2 and האמנתי in v. 10; com-pare 114.3, 'The sea saw': God is understood as object in each case. שמע: God hears prayer regularly; there is no need to emend to ישמע from alleged dittography. קולי, as against 28.2, 6, קול construct: pleonastic י־ termination, see 113.5-9, 114.8. *Verse 3.* the slightly unsuitable מצרי and repeated use of מצא arise from the intrusion of language from Lam. 1.3. The metaphors of 18.5-6 were more apt.

Verses 5-9. A favourite text of the Hallel psalmists is Exod. 34.6, where *the LORD* declared himself *gracious, righteous and merciful*: we have had the same reference at 111.4 and 112.4. *Our God*, the God of Israel, brought us out of Egypt and proclaimed this to be his nature at Sinai; and he has been true to his word. Ps. 19.8 said that the Sinai law rejoiced *the simple* (פתי): *the LORD* undertook then to be Israel's God and to *preserve the simple* (פתאים)—*I was brought low* in Baby-lonia, *and he saved me.* As in Psalms 42 and 43, the psalmist addresses *his soul*: with the Restoration it may *return unto its rest* (Lam. 1.3, p. 178), *For the Lord hath dealt bountifully with* it. There will be peace in our time. Some more of David's words spring to mind, from Ps. 56.14, '*For thou hast delivered my soul from death.* Hast thou not delivered *my feet from falling?* That I may *walk in the* light *of the living'*. Ps. 57.8-12 had been drawn on in Psalm 108, and the words of 56 are found to be equally true in the present deliverance from a people's death, and its return to life among the nations. The singer adapts 'in the light of the living': 27.13 had '*in the land of the living'*, but the present theme is not of the survival of an individual, David—it is the survival of a people, Israel, *in the lands*, plural, *of the living*. This plural is hard to explain on the Individual Thanksgiving theory. Maybe the psalmist is drawing on earlier writings, but the genuineness of his feeling comes through strongly: it is like modern Israel in 1948.

Verse 7. מנוחיכי is explained as an Aramaism (GKC 901); but it may be related to other י־ terminations, as suggested by Kirkpatrick. For other Aramaisms see vv. 12, 19.

Verses 10-12. Psalm 27.13 ran in full, '[I had fainted] unless *I believed* to see the goodness of the LORD *in the land of the living'*; so our singer begins a new thought, *I believed*. He had faith all through the last months of tension; *for I will say, I was greatly afflicted.* He can now confess publicly how great has been the strain, as it became clear that Samaritan and other professions of help were double-talk: *I said in my alarm, All men are a lie.* Verse 11a is taken over from Ps. 31.23, *I said in my alarm,* and our psalmist knows Psalm 31 well— '*incline thine ear unto me* (31.3), pluck me out of the net (31.5), thou hast seen *my affliction* (31.8), let the lying lips be dumb (31.19), O love the LORD, all ye *his saints'* (31.24). But the psalmist is not making an idle cento from earlier poems: the situation of Psalm 116 is best interpreted from 108 and 109 and the narrative of Ezra 3–4. People had offered to help in the Temple-building, but then they had sent accusations to the royal court. So the psalmist's joy is real, as his fears were real—*I was greatly afflicted, I said in my alarm, All men are a lie.* It is the deliverance from these menaces which issues in the great religious response of v. 12, *What shall I render unto the LORD For all his benefits toward me?* He *believed* all along, and his faith has been justified.

Verses 13-19. The thing that the singer can *render unto the LORD* is the vows that he made in his distress (like King David: 'Thy *vows* are upon me, O God; *I will render thank offerings unto thee'*—56.13 again). The *rendering of vows,* and in particular *the sacrifice of thanksgiving* are promised in vv. 14, 17-19; but in addition there is the preliminary v. 13, *I will take the cup of salvation, And call upon the name of the LORD.* This is often taken to be a libation (Gunkel effectively invokes the parallel of a king of Byblos pictured in the action of such a raising of the cup); but Eaton points to 23.5 where the [royal] singer's *cup* overflows at his thanksgiving dinner—cf. also 16.6, where Yahweh is his *cup. I will take the cup of salvation* sounds as if the singer will drink [at least some of] it himself. Kirkpatrick parallels 'the cup of blessing' at the Paschal meal; and as the worshipper had his share of a *thank offering,* תודה, this comment may be very much to the point.

These offerings are made because the psalmist and his community have survived. *The death of his devoted ones,* the faithful partners in his covenant, *is a costly matter in Yahweh's eyes,* and he has not let us go. The singer is *Yahweh's servant,* a phrase often used of the king (Eaton, *Kingship,* 150), and Yahweh *has opened* [the lock] *for my chains.* The same word *chains, bonds,* מוסר־/רות is used as a symbol of the Captivity in Ps. 107.14 (cf. 107.10); perhaps literal shackles are in mind, as well as the metaphor. His great thanksgiving, and the offerings that go with it, are part of the public liturgy, and performed proudly, and with emphasis, *In the courts of the LORD's house, In the midst of thee, O Jerusalem. Hallelujah!* It is seventy years and more since God's people could thank him for the Passover, and for the new Passover, in God's own courts, and in his blessed city, Jerusalem. The apostrophe, addressing the city directly, is a final paean of joy: χαίρετε, νικῶμεν.

Verses 12, 19 contain Aramaizing forms like v. 7, בתוככי, תגמולוהי; and there is an embellished form מותה for מות in v. 15. See also קולי in v. 1.

Recent reliance on chiastic analyses has not produced agreement. Barré, 'Structure' (1990), argued that Psalm 116 was a symmetrical whole, while W.S. Prinsloo, 'Psalm 116' (1993), disputed the symmetry, while defending the unity of the psalm (against Gunkel). T. Booij, 'Psalm 116, 10-11' (1995) sees the strong personal language as evidence of an emotional crisis which the speaker has finally overcome: the current scepsis over any historical setting makes the psalm difficult to interpret, whereas the traditional Hallel context gives satisfactory sense.

PSALM 117

1   O praise the LORD, all ye nations;
      Laud him, all ye peoples.
2   For his mercy is great toward us;
      And the truth of the LORD *endureth* for ever.
      Hallelujah.

Psalm 116 began with echoes of 18; and 18 ended, 'Therefore will I give thanks unto thee, *O LORD*, among *the nations*…Great deliverance giveth he unto his king; and sheweth mercy (חסד) to his anointed'. But the psalmists had often called on the nations to praise Yahweh directly (47.2; 96.7-9; 98.4-6; 100.1), and that is what the singer does here. The ground of praise is once more Yahweh's *mercy toward us* in the deliverance from the Exile; as the Asaphites sang in Ezra 3.11, *'praising* and *giving thanks unto the LORD; for* he is good and *his mercy* [endureth] *for ever toward* Israel'. This text, and Exod. 34.6 which underlies it, have been the *leitmotif* of the whole psalm sequence since 107.1.

It is not surprising perhaps that the psalmist should call the Gentile nations to join in Yahweh's praise (cf. 126.2); or that the substance of their praises should be the stock expression of gratitude for the Restoration. It is less obvious why Psalm 117 should be so short; or, being so short, why it is a psalm in its own right—96, for example, includes a call to the nations in a psalm mainly addressed to Israel. This is a topic to which I return after considering 118.

PSALM 118

Psalm 118 is a paean of joy celebrating some great deliverance, and accompanied by a festal procession. The question is, Is the deliverance a national one from a historical peril, or from a recurrent one, expressed in a myth? Or could it even be a personal deliverance expressed in the language of an ancient ritual? Nineteenth-century commentators vied in specific proposals: Delitzsch thought it was written for the dedication of the rebuilt Temple, described in Ezra 6.16-18; Kirkpatrick for the thanksgiving for the completion of the Jerusalem walls at Tabernacles in 444 BCE; and there were the regular Maccabaean suggestions. But Mowinckel (followed by Johnson, *Sacral Kingship*, p. 126, Weiser, Eaton and Anderson) preferred a pre-exilic date, and a ritual centred on the king. He had suffered certain humiliations (vv. 5, 18), and the triumphal procession to the Temple gates, through them, and up to the altar, symbolizes his victory by divine power over the ever-surrounding enemy. A half-way elaboration of the mythical interpretation is offered by Gunkel and Kraus. A postexilic individual has by God's grace survived his trials, and offers public thanks, with a procession of his friends, using old monarchic ritual language. More recently Dahood and Allen have returned to a [less specific] historical view, and Jacquet even to Ezra 6: the psalm is a celebration of a national victory.

Mowinckel vacillated over the date. In *Psalmenstudien,* II, pp. 120-27, he accepted a postexilic date; in *Psalms in Israel's Worship,* I, p. 170, Psalm 118 is probably pre-exilic, but in II, p. 30 it 'has still preserved the earlier "royal I" style'.

Gunkel dismissed the old historical theories by cataloguing them: what credence could be given with so much disagreement? But this is not an argument: the Maccabaean proposals were absurd by 1930, but this is no reflection on the more sober suggestions. His own theory is, however, a severe strain on the imagination (cf. Eaton, *Kingship*, pp. 61-62): how many people cured of their illnesses brought processions of friends to the Temple at the festival, and why did they use adapted phrases from royal liturgies to describe imaginary Gentile enemies? Mowinckel's hypothesis (*Psalmenstudien,* II, pp. 120-28; *Psalms in Israel's Worship, passim*) is more credible, but it has a direct problem in the address to an enemy leader, *Thou didst thrust sore at me...*: this seems to require an actor to take the enemy's part (so Eaton). Also, the detail does not fit Tabernacles comfortably, even if Jewish tradition associates the psalm with this feast. *The righteous* are in *tents*, not booths as the Law required; and it remains a puzzle how festal branches (עבתים, cf. Lev. 23.40) were to be used to *bind the festal procession* together. More significantly, Psalm 118 has numerous connections with 115 and 116—the same triple division of the celebrants, use of the same earlier psalms 18 and 56, even the same groups of verses: so 118 comes from the same group of psalmists, even the same hand—and 115 and 116 were marked with strong indications of postexilic language.

It is not surprising therefore that there has been some reaction, with Dahood, Jacquet and Allen in favour of a straightforward military victory; but one may think that there are specific points in the text that favour Delitzsch's understanding. As the Lord said, ὁ παλαιὸς χρηστός ἐστιν.

Psalm 118.1-20

1 O give thanks unto the LORD; for he is good:
   For his mercy *endureth* for ever.
2 Let Israel now say,
   That his mercy *endureth* for ever.
3 Let the house of Aaron now say,
   That his mercy *endureth* for ever.
4 Let them now that fear the LORD say,
   That his mercy *endureth* for ever.
5 Out of the distress (המצר) I called upon Jah:
   Jah answered me *and set me* in a large place.
6 The LORD is on my side; I will not fear:
   What can man do unto me?
7 The LORD is on my side among them that help me:
   Therefore shall I look down on (אראה) them that hate me.
8 It is better to trust in the LORD
   Than to put confidence in man.

9   It is better to trust in the LORD
     Than to put confidence in princes.
10   All nations compassed me about:
     In the name of the LORD I will cut them off.
11   They compassed me about; yea, they compassed me about:
     In the name of the LORD I will cut them off.
12   They compassed me about like bees; they are quenched as the
     fire of thorns:
     In the name of the LORD I will cut them off.
13   Thou didst thrust sore at me that I might fall:
     But the LORD helped me.
14   Jah is my strength and song;
     And he is become my salvation.
15   The voice of rejoicing and salvation is in the tents of the righteous:
     The right hand of the LORD doeth valiantly.
16   The right hand of the LORD is exalted:
     The right hand of the LORD doeth valiantly.
17   I shall not die, but live,
     And declare the works of Jah.
18   Jah hath chastened me sore:
     But he hath not given me over unto death.
19   Open to me the gates of righteousness:
     I will enter into them, I will give thanks unto Jah.
20   This is the gate of the LORD;
     The righteous shall enter into it.

Verses 1-4. 118 is the climax of the psalm sequence 107–118. Psalm 107 opened with the same verse, *'O give thanks unto the LORD; for he is good: For his mercy* [endureth] *for ever'*; and these words both open our psalm (118.1) and close it (118.29). They were the chant of the Asaphite Levites at the founding of the second Temple (Ezra 3.11); and they have been a background to many passages in the series (107.8, 15, 21, 31, 108.3, 109.30, 111.1, 117.2). Yahweh's חסד, promised in Exodus 34, has now been enacted in the Restoration. The joy which this evokes, and which is described in Ezra 3.11-13 and 6.22, may be felt in the triumphant repetitions that are so marked a feature of the psalm.

Psalm 118 has much in common with other psalms in the group. It appeals to the same tripartite division of the celebrants as in 115.9-13 (see pp. 170-72). *Israel* is observant Israel; that is, 'all the children of the captivity', the returning faithful who have kept *kashrut*, including those refinements of Torah which had been developed over two generations in Babylonia. *The house of Aaron* are the priests, 'who had purified themselves as one: all of them were pure'. *They that fear the LORD* are 'all such as had separated themselves unto them from the filthiness of the land, to seek the LORD' (Ezra 6.20-21). The mass of ordinary Jews who do not meet these exacting standards are welcome to stand by and join in the shouting; but they should feel left out and uncomfortable until they have toed the party line. These celebrations are for *the righteous* (vv. 15, 20), those who are *kosher*, in good standing.

Verses 5-9. Further links with the preceding psalms are to be seen in the use of the same scriptural passages as 116. Psalm 116 opened with a restatement of the early verses of Psalm 18, '*The cords of death compassed me,* And the straitnesses (מצרי) *of Sheol found me*' (116.3; 18.5). 118.5 draws on 18.20, 'He brought me forth also into *a large place*', out of *the straitness,* המצר, the Exile and the trials consequent thereupon (the same rare word as in 116.3); and *Yahweh answered* him *with a large place.* In 18.18 the singer is delivered 'from *them that hate me*' (118.7); in 18.44-48 Yahweh is the אל who gives victory over *the nations* (118.10-12, 27). Psalm 56.10-14 ran, 'This I know, *that God is on my side...In God I have put my trust, I will not be afraid: What can man do unto me?... Thou hast delivered my soul from death, my feet from falling, That I may walk before God in the* light *of the living*'. Most of 56.13-14 reappeared as 116.8-9; and much of 56.10-11 reappears as 118.6. The latter is then expanded with the help of the adjacent 54.6, 9, in a way by now familiar: 'Behold, God *is my helper*: the Lord is *with* (ב) them that uphold my soul...mine eye hath *looked down on* (ראתה) mine enemies'. This provides the substance of v. 7. The repeated *doeth valiantly* of vv. 15-16 (עשה־חיל) similarly echoes Ps. 60.14, 'Through God we shall *do valiantly*'.

Allen renders v. 7a, *Yahweh is on my side as my helper,* taking בעזרי as *beth essentiae* with plural of majesty; but RV gives good sense, and a clear echo of 54.6.

The religious professions of vv. 8-9 correspond with the situation described in the first six chapters of Ezra. The returned exiles were offered help by *man,* by *princes,* but they turned it down, *trusting in the Lord rather than putting their confidence* in Samaritans and governors. As the latter proceeded to cause them much anxiety and trouble, this policy appeared fully justified.

Verses 10-16. Paranoiacs always think that they have enemies *compassing them about*; but it is well known that they are often right. The arrival of a stream of assertive, self-confident Jews from Babylon, with claims to quasi-independence and the building of a national Temple, will have been as popular with the local governor, and the Ammonites, Arabs, and others of the district, as the more modern *'aliyot* have proved: the tales of Ezra 3–5 and Nehemiah 2–6 bear this out. Psalm 110 spoke of the people as *freewill offerings in the day of* mobilization: '*thy youth are to thee dew from the womb of the morning*'. So the psalm sequence also bears witness to a threat from the neighbouring peoples, perhaps an attack. The Hebrew tenses, and the ambiguity of the root מוּל, prevent certainty over the event referred to. Perhaps אֲמִילַם should be rendered 'I will cut them off', with RV, a threatening future to boost self-confidence. Perhaps, more graphically, it should be 'I will circumcise them', as the Hasmonaeans were to do; or less colourfully, 'I will repel them'. Or it may be that an attack was made and blood shed, and we should render with a present, 'I cut them off, I repel them'. The aggressors are compared to *bees*, like the Amorites of old (Deut. 1.44), or *a fire of thorn* bush twigs *blown out* by the wind before it can heat the cooking pot (Ps. 58.10—one more echo of Pss. 54–60).

Dahood renders 'circumcise', though he takes an early date and thinks only of the Philistines; cf. BDB. KB justify LXX's ἠμυνάμην with an Arabic cognate. O. Becker, 'Psalm 118.12', translates קוֹצִים as (still glowing) cut off 'wick-ends'; but again the David-psalms are our guide. Psalm 58.10 says menacingly, 'Before your pots can feel [heat from] the thorns, He shall take them [the thorns] away with a whirlwind, the green and the burning alike': the wording of 118.12 is shorter and simpler, but the meaning is the same.

Verse 13 addresses the leader of *all* these *nations*: *Thou didst thrust sore at me that I might fall*: again our singer had a precedent in Psalm 52 for addressing the enemy leader. The present villain sounds like the Bishlam of Ezra 3, or the Tattenai of Ezra 5, or some similar character. They had delated the Israelite leaders to the Persian court, and this *thrust* had nearly made singer and people *fall*; but *Jah* was their *strength*. Verse 14 is in fact identical with Exod. 15.2, Moses' Song at the crossing of the sea: *Jah is my strength and my song/ defence, And he is become my salvation*. Nor is this an accidental echo. Exodus 15.6 ascribes the Egyptian debacle to *the right hand of*

Yahweh (118.15-16), and v. 21, *And art become my salvation*, again takes up Exod. 15.2; while v. 28, the penultimate verse, closely follows Exod. 15.2cd, 'This is *my God* (אלי), *and I will* praise him, My father's *God* and *I will exalt* him'. It is not an accident either that Yahweh is referred to five times in these verses as 'Jah' (vv. 5, 14, 17, 18, 19), or that he is אל (v. 27). The whole psalm is a celebration of a renewed Red Sea triumph, under the exalted right hand of Jah.

Verse 13. LXX gives a passive for thou didst thrust, and many prefer this; but it is an easier reading. *Verse* 14. Loewenstamm, 'The Lord is My Strength' (1969) defends RV's my song, but KB and many prefer my defence, for which there are Ugaritic parallels, and also names like Zimri, Zimriah. The aberrant form זמרת recurs in Exod. 15.2 and Isa. 12.2.

Verses 17-20. Both Targum and Talmud (*b. Pes.* 119a) say that 118 was chanted antiphonally, and many commentators suggest divisions between two choirs of Levites, the people, the priests, with sections at the beginning of the procession, the Temple gates and the altar. We do well to be sceptical of such proposals. The whole psalm is likely to have been sung at the gates, the newly constructed gates to the newly constructed Temple of the 510s—hence *the voice of rejoicing and salvation in the tents of the righteous*. There is no mention of any movement. *The righteous* are 'the children of the captivity', the priests, and those residents who have purified themselves and joined them (vv. 2-4); and they are mostly *in tents* because Jerusalem was still a pile of ruins. The *rejoicing and salvation* are the joy of the Temple dedication at Paschaltide described in Ezra 6.22.

Frost, 'Asseveration', maintained that v. 20 was spoken by the gatekeeper, *[Only] the righteous shall enter into it*, and that v. 21 was from an excluded worshipper who asserted his innocence by a statement of thanksgiving. Such divisions between different speakers are speculations.

The Temple gates were kept by Levites (1 Chron. 26), and the psalms were composed by Levites, successors to the sons of Korah and of Asaph. We should therefore see the speaker of Psalm 118 as a Levite, a singer of the sons of Asaph according to Ezra 2.41. The repulse of the *encompassing nations* is a clear sign of Jah's blessing. Neither the singer nor his people *will die*; *he will live and recite the works of Jah*. He will tell the festal crowd in the liturgy of the deliverance from Egypt, and the new deliverance which Jah has wrought.

Accepting the *Vergeltungsdogma* theodicy, like most of the generation of Second Isaiah, he recognizes that the Exile and later trials have been a *sore chastening* from Jah; *but He hath not given me over unto death.*

Now comes the moment of drama symbolizing the triumph of the Return: he calls, *Open to me the gates of righteousness; I will enter into them, I will give thanks unto Jah. This is the gate of the LORD; the righteous shall enter into it.* From monarchical times there had been such processions for the righteous through the Temple gates: Psalms 15 and 24 emphasize the moral sides of righteousness (as was all too important), but clean hands and not lifting up one's soul to an idol were conditions too. Now, with the expansion of purity laws, 'righteousness' is increasingly defined ritually, and Ezra 6.19-20 (with Ps. 115.9-13, 118.2-4) make it plain that צדיקם could be known at once from their ritual commitment. So the fellow Levites on the gate will open up when the psalm is done, and let the procession through *as far as the horns of the altar.*

Mowinckel, *Psalmenstudien*, II, p. 128, takes the procession to have come up the Kidron valley, and entered by the great East Gate into the Temple area. This is the route taken by half of Nehemiah's procession—but *along* the newly rebuilt walls—in the celebration of Neh. 12.27-43; and also by Solomon's new bride in Cant. 3.1-11, where she can be the cynosure of the eyes of all the 'daughters of Jerusalem'. He refers to the naming of gates of certain Babylonian temples, and perhaps the East Gate was then called שער־צדק; it was a double gate (Allen).

Psalm 118.21-29

21   I will give thanks unto thee, for thou hast answered me,
      And art become my salvation.
22   The stone which the builders rejected
      Is become the head of the corner.
23   This is from the LORD;
      It is marvellous in our eyes.
24   This is the day which the LORD hath made;
      We will rejoice and be glad in it.
25   Save now, we beseech thee, O LORD:
      O Lord, we beseech thee, send now prosperity.
26   Blessed be he that cometh in the name of the LORD:
      We have blessed you out of the house of the LORD.
27   The LORD is God, and he hath given us light:
      Bound the festal procession (אסרו־חג) with cords, as far as
      (אד) the horns of the altar.

28 Thou art my God, and I will give thanks unto thee:
   Thou art my God, I will exalt thee.
29 O give thanks unto the LORD; for he is good:
   For his mercy *endureth* for ever.

Verses 21-25. I will give thanks unto thee in v. 21 repeats the phrase from v. 19b: it is the same levitical speaker, with the same echo of Exod. 15.2 as in v. 14b, *And art become my salvation.* The visible sign of Yahweh's *exalted right hand* lies before the procession: the noble *gates*, and beyond them the new Temple. We should probably think of the East Gate as *the gate of the LORD*, with the procession coming northwards up the valley outside the city, as in Cant. 3.1-11. For decades the old Temple had lain in ruins, and poverty-stricken survivors of 587 BCE had used some of its elements to build their homes; but the bigger stones might be beyond their ability for convenient moving, and in any case might be buried under the rubble. Zechariah had prophesied to Zerubbabel that the great mountain of Zion should become a platform on which he should produce the headstone, הראשה את־האבן הוציא (Zech. 4.7), one of Solomon's grand ashlars recovered as the holy site was cleared. He had laid the foundation, and he should finish the building (4.9). Well, the building is now complete, whether at Zerubbabel's hands or Joshua's; and *The stone which the builders refused Is become the head of the corner* (אבן...היתה לראש פנה). We may think that the wretched inhabitants of exilic Jerusalem did not so much *reject* the great cornerstone as could not shift it: οὐ μὰν ἐκλελάθοντ' ἀλλ' οὐκ ἐδύναντ' ἐπίκεσθαι. But there it stands, the crown of God's house as of old, a manifest sign of his providence: *This is the LORD's doing; It is marvellous in our eyes.* Today is a day of triumph, under the hand of God: *This is the day which the LORD hath made* so splendid; *We will rejoice and be glad in it.*

Verse 22 is treated by many as a proverbial saying loosely related to the context: Israel is the stone hitherto rejected by the nations. Delitzsch, working from the Ezra 6 context, sees the relevance of Zechariah's prophecy to Zerubbabel of the *head stone.* The interpretation of האבן הראשה as a *reused* key-stone from the former Temple follows C.L. and E.M. Meyers, *Haggai–Zechariah*, I, pp. 246-47. They note the widespread reuse of sacred building materials on former sanctuary sites in the ancient Near East (Ellis, *Foundation Deposits in Ancient Mesopotamia*). As האבן הראשה in Zech. 4.7 is apparently the *coping-stone*, not the *foundation-stone*, it is possible that the similar phrase in v. 22 has the same meaning; פנה will then mean 'gable', not 'foundation cornerstone'.

Verses 25-29. The prudent poet knows that divine blessing does not always last. He has survived the malice of his neighbours: what is now needed is an annual growth in GDP of Chinese proportions—*Save now, we beseech thee, O Lord: O Lord, we beseech thee, send now prosperity.* We found the same aspiration with Nehemiah in Psalms 127–128, and it is looked for in the earlier *aliya.* But surely we may depend upon Yahweh if we keep his Law: *Blessed is he who comes* in procession *in the name of the LORD.* Indeed prayers have already been offered by the Temple staff in God's new house: *We have blessed you out of the house of the LORD.* After so many years we have come through the tunnel: *The LORD is God, and he hath given us light.*

Petuchowski, 'A Prayer for Rain', saw v. 25 as a contrast to the previous verses of thanksgiving; he noted its use in liturgies for Sukkot in Mishnah (*m. Suk.* 4.5) and Talmud (*b. Suk.* 25a), and suggested that it was designed there as a prayer for rain. But, as he concedes, use may vary from intention over half a millennium; and Israel's political position remained very weak even after the triumph of the Return. The repeated אנא is an Aramaism, also found at 116.4.

Hitherto the procession has advanced up the Kidron valley, the ruined city on its left, the open country on its right, without need of discipline. Now it is to pass through *the gates of righteousness,* into the holy (and constricted) Temple courts. The Levite organizers want it to be ordered and controlled, and to this end have corded off a pathway. The psalmist calls to his colleagues to contain the hundreds of jubilant marchers within these bounds: *Bound the festal procession with cords, as far as the horns of the altar.* They may go right up to the sacred altar where the daily sacrifice is offered, to its most holy part, its horns, towering above them. It is as the singer says in Ps. 26.6, 'I will wash mine hands in innocency; So will I compass thine altar, O LORD'. The procession will circle round behind the altar, like the faithful in Soviet Union days round the tomb of Lenin; and then back between the further cords, so that those following may sense the wonder for themselves. The speaker repeats the third time, *I will give thanks unto thee,* with a final echo of Exod. 15.2 (see above); and closes, as he began, with a restatement of the Exiles' chorus (Ezra 3.11, Ps. 106.1, 107.1, 118.1), *O give thanks unto the LORD; for he is good: For his mercy* [endureth] *for ever.*

Many critics translate עבתים as 'foliage, branches', and so on, with an eye to its use in Lev. 23.40 for the Tabernacles *lulab*. But עבת there is an adjective (עץ-עבת), and in all instances given in BDB עבתים is used as a noun meaning 'ropes, cords', in association with אסר, 'bind', in Judg. 15.13; 16.11-12; and אסר may mean 'confine' as well as 'tie up' (2 Kgs 17.4; Gen. 40.3, 5: *DCH* sub 2a). Hence the translation, 'Bound the procession with ropes', follows given meanings for the words, and gives good sense. For a complex reconstruction of supposed textual corruption see Meysing, 'Text-reconstruction'.

It is possible in this way to ascribe the whole psalm to a single voice; always an easier hypothesis than claims of a dialogue psalm, especially where 'the people' are given a sizable part. The singer was an Asaphite Levite (as in many other psalms), returned from the East (Ezra 2.41), and speaking both in his own name ('I') and for the community ('we'). The repetitions in vv. 1/29, 2-4, 10-12, 15-16, are an invitation to others to join in—first his fellow-Levites perhaps, later the whole assembly. It will be in such a way that Jewish tradition came to speak of the psalm as being chanted antiphonally.

A context in Ezra 6, following Delitzsch, may thus be seen to fit Psalm 118 well. (1) It explains the opening and final verse of thanksgiving in line with the exiles' chorus of Ezra 3.11. (2) The three groups celebrating in vv. 2-4 correspond with the ritually pure from the east, the priesthood, and those seeking purity, from Ezra 6.21-22. (3) These groupings, and the echoes of Psalms 18 and 56, link 118 with 115 and 116, postexilic thanksgiving hymns of similar origin. (4) The defeat of aggression from the surrounding communities fits with the hostility described in Ezra 4–5, and repelled in Psalm 110. (5) The repeated echoes of Exodus 15 would be well suited to the Paschal celebration of Ezra 6. (6) The 'chastening' theodicy, coupled with the renewed expectation of 'life', belongs comfortably with the Restoration. (7) The high note of joy and the detail of the procession of the righteous (so different from the bloodthirsty victory parade of Psalm 68) would be suitable for the happy atmosphere of the Second Temple dedication of Ezra 6.22.

PSALMS 107–118

The above analysis has suggested some conclusions. Psalms 107–118 are in some measure a unity. They can all be understood as psalms celebrating the Return, and the Restoration of Temple worship. They almost all share a technique of composition: they take phrases, and groups of phrases, from sacred literature, especially Deutero-Isaiah in 107, and the David psalms (in particular 27–37 and 56–60). There is a strong note of joy through the series, with the exception of 109, and many of them call on the people to respond in a cry of praise, הללו יה. A central text, Exod. 34.6, declaring God's חסד to Israel, is constantly in mind, and especially in the form ascribed to the returned exiles in Ezra 3.11. We are left then with the question, How are we to explain the concentration of these common elements?

In asking a similar question about the Songs of Ascents, I thought that an answer was suggested by the fact that 134 was a night-time psalm, and would make a suitable conclusion to a collection of 15 psalms: there is a description of Nehemiah's celebration of the building of the walls in Nehemiah 12, and the Songs might be the psalmody for a seven-day autumn festival, beginning and ending at sundown. I sought to support this proposal with evidence that 130 and 132 might be evening psalms; though here the basis of inference was flimsy. However, we might suitably attempt the same quest with 107–118. Here again we have some repeated apparent relation to the story of Ezra 1–6, which culminates in the celebration of the new Temple at Passover; and here again we find some, if limited, support in the texts. 108 is often thought to be a morning psalm, for the speaker says, 'I will awaken the dawn' (אעירה שחר, 108.2). Psalm 118 seems similarly to be designed for morning worship: 'This is the day which the LORD hath made; We will rejoice and be glad in it' (118.24). This is a special day, a feast day with procession and sacrifice to be performed in it, with a day-long spirit of celebration.

It is surprising, in the face of this statement of intention to spend the day ahead, that Gunkel thinks of torches when commenting on 118.27, 'Yahweh . . . hath given us light'. A more obvious reference would be the rising sun.

These are the only two psalms with any clear indication of the time of use; but another psalm makes use of morning imagery which is suggestive of timing. Psalm 110.3 says, 'Thy youth are to thee [as] the dew from the womb of the morning'. Perhaps the poet was just searching for an image that would reflect the mystery of divine blessing, and hit upon the dew; or perhaps it was also relevant that the volunteers came streaming in as the sun rose, in time for the expected battle. At all events the use of the figure makes the psalm especially apt for morning worship.

Three psalms out of a dozen, one of them uncertain, are no proof. But they are an encouragement to try a liturgical hypothesis. This time the morning psalms all fall on the even numbers (108, 110, 118); and since the group begins with 107, we should have a collection of 12 psalms (107–118) running evening–morning, as the Songs of Ascent and Book IV seemed to do. But there seems to be a difficulty with the number 12. There were 15 Songs of Ascents, enough for the full seven-day Tabernacles, evening to evening; and there were 17 psalms in Book IV, enough for the full revised eight-day Tabernacles, evening to evening. Psalms 107–118 seemed to be a psalmody suited to the Passover/Massot of Ezra 6: but Unleavened Bread lasts seven days, not six.

A solution to this problem is however not far to seek. When discussing Psalm 107, I noted that many commentators had drawn attention to similar phrasing in 105 and 106, and had suggested that these three psalms formed a trio. In particular their opening verses were similar:

105.1   O give thanks unto the LORD, call upon his name. . .
106.1   Hallelujah.
        O give thanks unto the LORD; for he is good:
        For his mercy [*endureth*] for ever.
107.1   O give thanks unto the LORD; for he is good:
        For his mercy [*endureth*] for ever.

With the same wording to open and to close Psalm 118, it may be thought possible that 105 and 106 originally opened a collection, 105–118. Psalm 105 gives thanks for the LORD's marvellous works from

Abraham to the Exodus, 106 from the Exodus to the Exile, 107 for the Return: the three psalms form a continuous whole, the *Heilsgeschichte*, with suitable penitence for Israel's rebellions. For the linguistic connections, see above, p. 119. Furthermore it is noticeable that the Exodus is the fulcrum between Psalms 105 and 106. Although there is brief reference to later matters, 105 reaches its climax with the Egyptian plagues (vv. 24-38), and ends 'And he brought forth his people with joy, *And* his chosen with singing' (105.43; Exod. 12, 15). Psalm 106 begins its narrative at v. 7, 'Our fathers understood not thy wonders in Egypt...But were rebellious at the sea, even at the Red Sea'. So the long recital would not be unsuitable to open a Passover celebration.

But if 105–118 were originally a collection, why should the first two psalms be broken off and attached to Book IV? Book IV comprises 17 psalms (90–106), and I have commented above, p. 109, on their quality of alternation (93, 95, 97, 99 stressing Yahweh's kingship, 96 and 98 having considerable elements in common), and on 92.2, 'To shew forth thy lovingkindness in the morning, And thy faithfulness every night'. It seemed plausible therefore to think of the Book as a collection of autumn festival psalms, when Yahweh's kingship and judgment were especially in mind. But 91 seems to be a blessing on the king, and in royal times Tabernacles was a seven-day festival (Deut. 16.15), and would require only 15 psalms (7 × 2 + 1) for an evening-to-evening celebration. But by the fourth century an eighth day had been added for 'a holy convocation' (Lev. 23.36 [Holiness Code]), and two extra psalms would be needed: Psalm 104, the Creation psalm, was the fifteenth psalm in the Book—what more natural than to append two psalms from the beginning of a later collection, 105–118, which carried the story from creation to modern times?

We have one or two small indications that 105–118 formed a sequence at the beginning of Book V. Psalms 105 and 106 are a pair of psalms, suitable for the evening and morning of the same day; and so are 111 and 112, the two alphabetic psalms, which would also fall to the same day. We should also have some explanation for the independent existence of the extremely short psalm 117. Why is it not tacked on to the end of 116 in the same way that the last verses of 18 are, when 18 is so clearly in the psalmist's mind for 116? Perhaps an extra psalm was needed to fill a liturgical lacuna.

But we have a much stronger indication that the liturgical hypothesis is on the right lines. Israel came out of Egypt on Passover night, that is 15 Nisan, but from Deuteronomic times Passover was assimilated to the established seven-day festival, Unleavened Bread (15–21 Nisan, Deut. 16.1-8). There has accordingly been a long-standing tendency to spread the events of the Exodus over the week. In modern Jewish worship Exod. 12.21-51 is read on the first day of Unleavened Bread (15th), Exod. 13.1-16 on the third (17th) and the Red Sea story, Exod. 13.17–15.26, including the Song of the Sea, on the seventh day (21st). This is an old tradition: the tractate Sopherim provides for Psalm 114 to be sung on the 21st.

Now we may trace this exegesis right back into the Book of Exodus. Israel was in Egypt on the night of 15th Nisan (Exod. 12.6-10), at Rameses, and they spent the night of 16th at Succoth (12.37). The night of 17th they camped at Etham, in the edge of the wilderness (13.20); but at 14.1 Yahweh turns them back and they camp before Pi-hahiroth for the night of 18th. While they are there, Pharaoh decides to send his army after them, and the angel of God frustrates their advance by moving the pillar of cloud to between the two forces (14.19). As it a pillar of *cloud*, it is implied that this took place by day, still on 18th. Moses then stretches out his hand and Yahweh sends a strong east wind all the night, that is the night of 19th (14.21). In the morning watch (still on 19th), Israel goes through on dry ground, and the Egyptians follow (14.24); and the LORD takes off their chariot wheels (14.25). Moses again stretches out his hand at Yahweh's command, and at dawn the sea is back to its normal depth (14.27), and the Egyptians dead to a man; 'dawn' implies another day, 20th. Exodus 15.1 begins 'Then sang Moses...', and the interpreter may, if he will, see the Israelite celebrations as on the last day of Massot, the 21st.

Now this exegesis to cover the whole festal week is only possible because the authors of the Exodus chapters have themselves been stretching the story out, no doubt in the same interest; and we may set out the narrative in parallel with the psalms hypothesis:

Nisan	Exodus Event	Evening/Morning Psalm	
15th	Out of Egypt (Rameses)	105	106
16th	Succoth	107	108
17th	Etham	109	110
18th	Pi-hahiroth	111	112
19th	Sea divided	113	114
20th	Egyptians drowned	115	116
21st	Song of the Sea	117	118

Such an arrangement explains a number of features of the psalm sequence. In particular it explains why 114 is placed where it is. It was on the night of 19th that Yahweh sent a strong east wind, and in the morning watch Israel went across on dry land: how suitable that on the morning of the 19th Nisan the returned Levites should sing, 'When Israel went forth out of Egypt, The house of Jacob from a people of strange language...The sea saw it and fled'! It was on the last day of the feast, 21st, that Moses and Israel celebrated with the Song: how suitable that on the morning of 21st Psalm 118 should be chanted—'Jah is my strength and my song/defence; And he is become my salvation...Thou art my God, and I will give thanks unto thee; Thou art my God I will exalt thee', and five uses of the form Jah! It was on the 20th that the Egyptian army was annihilated: how suitable that the psalms for 20th should be 115 and 116, thanksgivings for deliverance of which the former seemed natural on the field of Agincourt! With 105 and 106 dividing at the Exodus, and 107 a development of Second Isaiah's New Exodus theme, it is easy to see the whole sequence as a Paschal celebration, well fitted for the dedication week of Ezra 6. We may even note that Israel spent the night of 16th at Succoth, and that 108, the psalm adapted for 16th morning, included the line, 'I will...mete out the valley of Succoth'.

> For the above analysis I have made the assumption that the authors of the psalm sequence had the Exodus narrative in approximately our form, that is with the P elements already inserted into the older J narrative. I have argued (*Asaph*, 271-74, 340-41) that this process took place in Babylon in the sixth century, and the Asaphites could have brought the composite narrative with them. But if this were not so, the J form already contains movement towards filling the week up.

The liturgical theory may thus claim to have reached the status of plausibility; but it has still one more river to cross. There were 15 Songs of Ascents, and (I have argued) originally 15 psalms in Book IV, sufficient for a seven-day festival, evening to *evening*; and our present Book IV has 17 psalms, sufficient for an eight-day festival, evening to evening. Psalms 105–118 comprise only 14 psalms, sufficient for a seven-day Unleavened Bread festival, evening to *morning*. What about the final psalm to close the sequence? For this we shall need to consider Psalm 119, the spare psalm between 105–118 and the Songs of Ascents.

The Historicity of Ezra 1–6

The above analysis of Psalms 107–118 is in part dependent on the historicity of elements in Ezra 1–6. It is notorious that the most varied opinions have been held on this topic, from the total scepsis of C.C. Torrey to the comparative acceptance of more modern critics like H.G.M. Williamson and J. Blenkinsopp. I should myself incline to a middle position such as that defended by P.R. Ackroyd in *Exile and Restoration*; but it would go beyond the bounds of this book to discuss many vexed questions—the authenticity of the official letters, the apparent muddle over the Persian kings, whether the Chronicler is the author. The points that are significant for my analysis are four:

(1) *There was a major Return of exiles at the end of the sixth century* (Psalm 107). It is unimportant for us whether this was led by one Sheshbazzar. Such a Return is implied by the prophecies of Haggai and Zechariah, and by Ezra–Nehemiah's presupposition of the *golah* as the sole genuine Israel. The association of *O give thanks unto the LORD*...with the Return (Ezra 3.11-12) seems to be widely testified (106.1, 107.1, 118.1, 29, 136).

(2) *The project of rebuilding the Temple was held up by objections from Samaria* (Shechem, Psalm 108), including *accusations to the Persian authorities* (Psalm 109). The detail set out in letters in Ezra 4–6 is probably fiction, but the outline is plausible: Judah was part of the territory of Sanballat, governor in Samaria in the 440s, and governors do not normally see their territories diminished without appeal to higher authority. The vision of Joshua and the Accuser in Zechariah 3 seems to be a reflection of such a crisis. The prophets mention a number of other reasons for the delay—half-heartedness, greed, poverty, and so on—but then the prophets are concerned primarily to move the people to action.

(3) *The lead in the Rebuilding was taken by Joshua ben Jozadak the high priest* (after the order of Melchizedek, Psalm 110). His position, and his displacement of Zerubbabel, are suggested by references in Zechariah 1–6. The only element for which Zechariah does not give evidence is the mobilization and (probable) victory achieved by Joshua (Psalm 110): but it is remotely unlikely that Judah could have achieved semi-independence in the late sixth century without some armed opposition.

(4) *The Dedication of the rebuilt Temple took place at Passover* (Ezra 6.16-22: Psalms 113–118 as a Paschal Hallel). It is noticeable that Passover is seen by the Chronicler as a season for the reform and renewal of Temple worship: it had marked the reform of Josiah in 2 Kgs 23.21-23, and this is described at length in 2 Chron. 35.1-19. A similar extended description is provided of Hezekiah's similar reform, which is said to have been celebrated at Passover (2 Chron. 30, without sanction in 2 Kgs); and the Temple staff sanctify themselves as in Ezra 6.19-20. It is questionable, however, whether this should raise doubts over the historicity of the Ezra 6 celebration. The rebuilding of the Temple would find its most natural antitype in the original consecration by Solomon, which took place at Tabernacles (1 Kgs 8.2). Ezra 6.15 tells us that the rebuilding was finished on 3rd Adar, in the sixth year of Darius, and it is unlikely that so precise a date should be a fiction: Passover would be five weeks after that, and it would then be the obvious festival for the Dedication. We may think that the Paschal associations were kept alive by the Paschal psalmody; and it may be that the combination of Joshua's Passover and Josiah's Passover led the Chronicler to site Hezekiah's renewal at Passover.

It is difficult to escape the conclusion that critics' opinion of Ezra 1–6 is largely a function of their wider convictions. Thus Williamson, Blenkinsopp and Eric Meyers, 'From Zerubbabel to Nehemiah' (1987) may surprise by their defence of the genuineness of the Aramaic letters, the author's knowledge of the succession of Persian kings, and so on. Morton Smith, of a more sceptical turn of mind, has no hesitation in describing the letters as 'fakes', and reconstructs the history in series of imaginative possibilities; but he descries a historical base to the chapters not too different from my own hypothesis (*Palestinian Parties*, pp. 78-89). Gunneweg, 'Interpretation', Ackroyd, *Cambridge History of Judaism*, I, pp. 136-43, and Grabbe, *Judaism*, are similarly discriminating.

PSALM 119

Psalm 119 is a glorification of the Law: 176 verses praising the Law, in intention in every line (vv. 122 and 132 missed out); 22 stanzas of eight verses beginning with the same letter, the whole Hebrew alphabet being taken in sequence. This elaborate structure is itself a salute to the divine revelation, since the latter is spelt out in precisely these letters, and the number of books in the canon was often later reckoned at 22. There are further eight synonyms for the Law: תורה (×25), עדה (×22 pl. + עֵדוּת ×1), פקדים (×21), מצוה (×21 pl. + 1 collectively), חקים (×21 + חֻקּוֹת once), משפט (×19 pl. + 4 sing.), דבר (×20 sing. + 3 pl.), אמרה (×19); דרך is further a frequent, and ארח an occasional alternative. The psalmist does not always have the same eight in varying order in each stanza, but such is the general pattern. The divine name is used 22 times. Whatever other themes occupy the poet's mind, devotion to the Law is central.

There is indeed a second recurrent theme, the failure of *the proud/ wicked* to keep God's law, and their persecution of the psalmist; and this combination has raised the question of the setting and purpose of 119. Gunkel described it as a *Mischgedicht*; in the first place an individual lament (with its invariable 'I'), but also an individual thanksgiving with confessions of confidence, hymnic passages, wisdom sayings, and so on. But the fullest analysis has been made by Alfons Deissler in his *Psalm 119 [118] und seine Theologie* (1955). Deissler took the author to be a Wisdom teacher with a deep knowledge of Scripture, who put together an anthology of sayings and themes arranged round the alphabet. Scriptures used included Deuteronomy, Jeremiah, Ezekiel, Job and Proverbs, as well as the Psalms. The work was intended both as a prayer and as an instruction for his pupils; it was designed to evoke love for the God who had revealed himself in every word of Scripture, and it represented the common confession of teacher and class. By this means their ways in life would be set in true wisdom under God's guidance. We have a good general parallel to the psalm in the writing of Ben Sira, and may think of its setting as in a *beth-hammidrash* (Ecclus 51.23), perhaps in the late third century.

Deissler's general view has commended itself (Kraus, Anderson, Allen), even if his date has been felt to be too late. However, Wisdom schools are not so well attended as they were, and evidence for their existence disappears in earlier centuries. Nor is the description of 119 as an Anthology quite accurate. All the psalms from 107 to 118 have drawn on earlier scriptures, and 119 does the same; but the author resolutely (and repetitively) keeps his central theme in mind, and the impression of inconsequence should be ascribed in the first place to the constriction of his alphabetic format. Sometimes, as in the *teth*-stanza, there is evidence of an author's thread of thought: Yahweh's goodness in teaching the psalmist a lesson through his past affliction (vv. 65-72). Besides, there are many verses with no obvious scriptural source. Klaus Koch, in a famous review in *TLZ* (1958), and E. Lipinski in *RB* (1968), p. 349, were critical of Deissler's picture. The Deuteronomic language, and the absence of Priestly vocabulary, suggested a sixth century setting; and the contacts with Wisdom books like Job and Proverbs were marginal.

For critiques of the Wisdom school theory, see J.L. Crenshaw, 'Education in Ancient Israel', Stuart Weeks, *Early Israelite Wisdom*, pp. 133-56. Jon Levenson, 'The Sources of Torah' (1987) is sympathetic to Deissler, but stresses the psalmist's openness to new Torah, which implies an earlier date than Ezra–Nehemiah. He also notes the absence of any words for 'book', 'write', 'Moses', and so on, which we might have expected. Levenson is right to deny that תורה = Pentateuch, but perhaps expects rather much from his psalmist.

John Eaton offers a review of commentaries on Psalm 119 from Delitzsch on in *Psalms of the Way and the Kingdom*; as usual, full of perceptive insight. I agree with Eaton in deploring widespread emendation of the text in the quest for neatness; and he is clearly right in stressing that the psalm is primarily a prayer to God, not an instruction. Devotion to *torah* is not a theme of Proverbs. For date, he aligns 119 with Deuteronomy, and inclines to see it in the royal period; but the argument is stronger for Psalm 19, which is set in a group of royal psalms (18, 20, 21), than for 119. There is a welcome insistence on the positive piety of the psalm: God, not *torah*, is the centre of the psalmist's concern.

It is a controversial question whether the use of 'I' excludes cultic intention. Deissler himself thinks of the psalm as in part a prayer for a teacher leading the devotions of his pupils, and Mowinckel, Birkeland, Eaton and others have argued for 'I' often being a representative leader, perhaps the king. Our psalmist speaks a number of times as if he were representing a group of like-minded people, *them that fear thee* (vv. 63, 74, 79); he might be a senior Levite espousing the cause of the expanded Law brought from Babylon in the Return, and resisted (and despised) by the incumbent Judaean 'princes'. He certainly seems to see himself as a new Jeremiah (v. 23, cf. Jer. 36.1-2, 26; v. 84, cf. Jer. 15.15; v. 85, cf. Jer. 18.20, 22; v. 154, cf. Jer. 50.34), and this may influence his use of 'I'. Many more recent hymns have been written in the first person singular for liturgical use—'Just as I am...', 'Long my imprison'd spirit lay...' Lipinski thought that Beatitudes had originally been a liturgical formula (e.g. Pss. 84, 89), and 119.1-2 was an adaptation. The form of the psalm certainly does not exclude a liturgical purpose, and there are features that suggest it.

From biblical times Israel had a festival to celebrate the giving of the Law on Sinai, the feast of Pentecost; and it is Pentecost that offers the most plausible setting for Psalm 119. Aside from the first three verses, the whole psalm is addressed to God. Theories of private devotion ring of anachronism; nor is there any easy way to account for the psalm's preservation and use if it was composed for individual prayer. But we may easily think of Levites, with a long tradition of psalm-writing, feeling the need to dignify the Law festival with a Law-psalm. The מנצח might suitably lead the Temple celebration of שבעות with a sustained prayer, in his own person, but including his fellow God-fearers. He not only glorifies the Law, promising obedience even in face of persecution: he *has sworn*, נשבעתי, to keep it (v. 106), and praises God *seven times*, שבע, *in the day* (v. 164). Later tradition suggests a more detailed pattern of its intended use. Pentecost, a single day's feast, was celebrated in the early centuries of our era with an all-night vigil: the (mediaeval) Zohar says, 'Therefore the pious ones of old used not to sleep on this night [Pentecost], but they used to study the Torah and say, Let us acquire a holy inheritance for ourselves and our sons in two worlds' (Emor, 98a).

The association of the Law-giving with Pentecost is as old as the text of Exodus. In Exod. 19.1 the Israelites come into the wilderness of Sinai in the third month (Sivan), and there is a succession of days before the Law is given; for an analysis see my *Asaph*, pp. 290-93. Pentecost normally falls on 6 Sivan. For an account of early Jewish traditions see J. Potin, *La fête juive de la Pentecôte*. Unsurprisingly, *b. Sopherim* 18 prescribes Psalm 29 rather than 119 for liturgical use at the festival: Psalm 29 was understood as describing the Sinai theophany, and was considerably shorter than the alternative. The cabbalists read the beginning and end of each book in their Tiqqun for Pentecost: for the Psalter they recited Psalms 1, 19, 68, 119 and 150 (*Jewish Encyclopaedia*, 'Pentecost', IX, p. 583).

This is suggestive, despite the lacuna of so many centuries, for the original setting of Psalm 119. Verse 164 says, *Seven times in the day have I praised thee* (שבע ביום הללתיך); and there are references to worship virtually round the clock. Verse 55: *I have remembered thy name, O LORD, in the night*; v. 62, *At midnight I rise* (אקום) *to give thanks unto thee*; v. 147, *I prevented the dawning of the morning and cried*; v. 148, *Mine eyes prevented the night watches*. The last verse continues, *That I might meditate in thy word*, which is rather reminiscent of the Zohar passage.

The mention of *night watches* (אשמרות) is also suggestive. In Mk 13.35 the master of the house may come at any of four hours, late, midnight, cockcrow and dawn; followed (in Mk 15) by four day watches, the third hour, the sixth hour (noon), the ninth hour and evening, sundown; at Mk 6.48 Jesus walks on the Sea of Galilee 'about the fourth watch of the night', that is, between cockcrow and dawn. A four-part day is testified well back into Old Testament times. At Neh. 9.3 Israel 'read in the book of the law of the Lord their God a fourth part of the day, and *another* fourth part they confessed, and worshipped the LORD their God'. At Exod. 12.6 the paschal lambs are to be killed on 14 Nisan 'between the two evenings', which means between the ninth hour and sundown, since 14 Nisan ends at sundown, and it is then that they were in fact killed in Mishnaic times. The phrase 'between the two evenings' is frequent (Exod. 16.12; 29.39, 41; 30.8; Lev. 23.5; Num. 9.3, 5, 11; 28.4, 8).

We do not have so clear a picture of the divisions of the night, but the pattern we find in the Gospels is likely to be old. There are frequent references to midnight (Exod. 11.4, 12.29; Judg. 16.3; Ruth 3.8; Job 34.20), and Gideon's attack on the Midianites 'at the beginning of the middle watch' (Judg. 7.19) probably means 'soon after midnight', counting three night watches, late, midnight and cockcrow as in Mark 13. Israelites worked while it was light (Mt. 20.8), and ate with their families thereafter, 'at evening' (Lk. 24.29; Acts 20.7-8, 'many lamps'): so there were three אשמרות, first watch (Lam. 2.19, = 'late'), midnight, and morning watch (Exod. 14.24; 1 Sam. 11.11, = 'cockcrow'). Our psalmist has praised God seven times in the day, and these seven times include midnight, the night watches and dawn;

he *rises at midnight*, so he probably used seven of the eight breaks in the day for his devotion. We have a similar use of the watches through Maundy Thursday/Good Friday in the traditional Byzantine vigil: in Egeria's time (381 CE) the vigil began at sundown and ended at 3 pm.

De Vaux, *Ancient Israel*, p. 182, concludes that there were three night watches till Egyptian or Roman influences made it four; he implies three *four-hour* watches. But midnight is so frequently referred to that it surely marked the beginning of a watch, and that would leave one six-hour and two three-hour watches. It is easier to think that 'evening' marked the end of the day, and the night watches began 'late' (9 pm), at midnight and at cockcrow (3 am). For Egeria see Wilkinson, *Egeria's Travels*, pp. 134-38 (ch. 35). Beckwith, *Calendar and Chronology*, pp. 1-3, argues for a three-part day as well as a three-watch night: he claims baldly that Neh. 9.3 'does not apparently reflect a normal practice'. He follows de Vaux in ascribing the change to an eight-part day to Roman usage; but not only is there no evidence for this, but it is also implausible. Judaea had been under Roman direct rule for only 20 years when Jesus walked on the water, and occupied countries do not easily change their time divisions to match political changes.

Since there are 22 stanzas to the 119th Psalm, the author might be thought to take three stanzas to each watch; this would then leave the final stanza over as an epilogue for the closing watch of the day, first evening (3 pm). Such an arrangement would suit the structure of the psalm. Verses 1-24 would fall at evening, vv. 25-48 at first watch, vv. 49-72 at midnight: it is in this third trio that the night references come—*I have remembered thy name, O LORD, in the night* (v. 55), and more specifically, *At midnight I rise to give thanks unto thee* (v. 62). Verses 73-96 would then be taken at morning watch, and vv. 82-84 say, *Mine eyes fail for thy word... When wilt thou execute judgement?* As in 130.6 the psalmist's soul looks for the Lord more than watchmen for the morning, so do our singer's eyes strain after the fulfilment of God's promise, the judgment so often given at dawn in the ancient world. Verses 97-120 would fall at dawn: v. 97 says, *Oh how I love thy law! It is my meditation all the day*, and v. 105, *Thy word is a lamp unto my feet, And light unto my path*. Verses 105 and 130 are the only references to light in the psalm, and the section would be suitable for a dawn liturgy, where the sun appears as a lamp and a light for more physical walking; the same parallel is drawn in Psalm 19, with which 119 shows many affinities. Verses 121-44 would then follow at the third hour, and the seventh section of the liturgy would comprise vv. 145-68 at noon. It is here that the psalmist can look back on his day of meditation: *I prevented the dawning of the morning and cried* (v. 147, looking back to vv. 73-96); *Mine eyes prevented the night watches* (v. 148, thinking of the opening of it all, vv. 1-24). Thus all the night devotion is included from beginning to end; and at v. 164 he can say triumphantly, *Seven times in the day have I praised thee*. He has run the whole day round, and can complete his devotions with a series of prayers for the future, vv. 169-76, six of them opening with the feminine jussive ־ה.

So much temporal reference seems to support the hypothesis of a liturgical origin for Psalm 119; no doubt for Levites and other 'pious men of old', who 'by night stand in the house of the LORD' (134.1). But when are we to think of such a pattern of worship arising? The devotion to the Law persuaded Gunkel, and many others, to site the psalm very late, in the fourth century; but a number of features may incline us rather to the period of the Return.

(1) *The Alphabetical Form.* There are no alphabetical psalms among the old northern collections of the Sons of Korah and the Asaphites; nor in the Prayers of David (51–72). In Book I there is a rough alphabetic structure to 9 and 10, and a loose one to 37 (every two stichs, with a third for ה), and a tighter one to 25 and 34 (each of which has twenty-two verses starting with the letters in series, but closes with a non-alphabetic verse). In Book V Psalm 145 is similar, but omitting נ. The closest alphabetic parallels to Psalm 119 are 111 and 112, and Lamentations 3. Psalms 111 and 112 are composed on the extremely tight *hemi*-stich structure: they are ten-verse psalms with the succession of letters governing each half-verse, and both belong, I have argued above, to the period of Restoration. Lamentations 3 is still closer to Psalm 119: it has 66 verses, structured in triads running through the alphabet, just as Psalm 119 is structured in octets. The freshness of the picture of desolation and the depth of grief suggest a setting for the Lamentations poem soon after the disaster of 587 BCE. So a sixth-century setting for 119 seems plausible; we could understand that after Psalm 119 it was felt that the form had been given its ultimate expression.

(2) *Deuteronomic Language.* The language of 119 is so saturated with expressions common in the Deuteronomic paraenesis that it may be asked whether the two authors come from the same community, or are even the same person. 'And now, O Israel, hearken unto *the statutes* (חקים) and unto *the judgements* (משפטים), which I *teach* you,

for to *do them*... You shall not add unto *the word* (דבר) which I
command you...that ye may *keep the commandments* (מצות)...You
are alive every one of you this day. Behold, I have *taught you statutes
and judgements*, even as the LORD my God *commanded* me...And
what great nation is there, that hath *statutes and judgements* so *righteous* as all this *law* (תורה)?' (Deut. 4.1-8). דבר, מצוה, משפט, חק, תורה
(including the Ten דברים) are all common Deuteronomic expressions;
so is דרך (Deut. 5.33, 9.12, etc.), and to a lesser extent עדה (Deut.
4.45, 6.17, 20). The only words for the Law that are not found in
Deuteronomy are אמרה (apart from Deut. 33.9), and פקוד, which
occurs only in the Psalter and has been taken over from Ps. 19.9. The
centrality of *learning* (למד), and *keeping* (שמר) the law, and of doing
so *with one's whole heart* (Deut. 4.29, 6.5, etc.), are again Deuteronomic; and so is the *wisdom and understanding* that it brings (Deut.
4.6). The spirit of Psalm 119 is well expressed in Josh. 1.8, 'This
book of the law shall not depart out of thy mouth, but thou shalt meditate therein day and night, that thou mayest observe to do all that is
written therein'.

With so much in common, we may ask what differences are to be
found. Deuteronomy presents the hope that Israel may 'live and go in
and possess the land' (4.1), and frequently warns of the perils of
idolatry; neither of these emphases comes in Psalm 119. But perhaps
even this is not significant. Deuteronomy was a fictional document
looking forward to the Davidic–Solomonic empire, and accounting
for its collapse with the theory that this was the punishment for
strange worship. In the late 500s it was vain to expect a reoccupation
of the land (from the River to the Brook of Egypt); but the psalmist
may pray to 'live', or to 'be quickened', in a more spiritual sense
(vv. 25, 37, 40, 88, 107, 116, 144, 149, 154, 156, 159); it is God's
law and promises that give him *life* (50, 93). He is also frequently
distressed by the ways of the proud 'which are not after thy law', even
if these no longer involve the worship of Moloch. Another Deuteronomic word which is missing from 119 is ברית: but it may be that
modern biblical theologians have over-emphasized the importance of
the *covenant*.

We may also contrast the frequency of this Deuteronomic vocabulary with the comparative rarity of the standard terms of P or the
Holiness code. Thus we have only one instance of עֵדוּת, which is
common in Leviticus and Numbers; there are eight ק-verses, but none

of them opens with any form of קְדוֹשׁ, nor does this root come in the psalm; there is only one mention of sin (v. 11), and none of uncleanness, or the centrality of sacrifices as a means of contact with God. All this leaves us with the impression that Psalm 119 belongs after the D-paraenesis, but before the coming of the Priestly code—in other words between 520 and 400 BCE.

(3) *The Situation of the Psalmist.* Although his comments are so indirect, we may descry three elements in the background of 119. (a) The psalmist has suffered affliction, by which God has taught him a lesson. (b) The author is living in a community in which he and like-minded God-fearers are in tension with those in authority, who persecute them. (c) There is an ultimate authority, 'kings': *I will speak of thy testimonies before kings* (v. 46).

(a) *Before I was afflicted I went astray; But now I observe thy word* (v. 67); *It is good for me that I have been afflicted, That I might learn thy statutes* (v. 71); *in faithfulness thou hast afflicted me* (v. 75). The suggestion is of an affliction (עִנָּה, Deut. 8.2, 3, 16) which is now over, and which has had a good educational effect; the complex of ideas suggested to Kirkpatrick that the affliction of the Exile was in mind. Verses 69-70 speak of *the proud* and their lies, which may mean the persecutors of section (b); but *Their heart is as fat as grease* recalls the Gentile oppressors of 73.7. Here the speaker will have suffered *affliction* along with the rest of his people.

(b) In more than 30 verses reference is made to *the proud, the wicked, evil-doers*, and so on. These are influential Israelites who *reproach, deride and despise* the psalmist (vv. 22, 42, 51), *persecute* him (vv. 84, 86, 150, 157, 161), and are in fact *princes* who *sit and talk against* him (v. 23), and *have persecuted him without a cause* (v. 161). Their *cords have wrapped* him *round* (v. 61), they *forged a lie against* him (vv. 68, 86), they *dug pitfalls for* him (vv. 85, 110), they *had almost consumed him* (v. 87), and *waited for* him *to destroy* him (v. 95). The psalmist is much distressed by their apostasy: his *eyes run down with rivers of water Because they observe not thy law* (v. 136, cf. 139).

Our knowledge of the postexilic period is limited, but such evidence as we have suggests a change in the balance of power in the fifth century. When the first exiles returned with their amplified law-traditions, they were supported by only a minority of the resident population, spoken of as 'fearers of Yahweh' (יִרְאֵי יְהוָה, 112.1; 115.11, 13; 118.4;

cf. Ezra 6.21). The greater part of the residents did not 'separate themselves from the filthiness of the heathen of the land', and prophets like Haggai and Malachi are disappointed by the lack of a united devotion. Two generations later Nehemiah is opposed by the 'nobles and deputies' who lent on usury (Neh. 5.7), and by an old guard of priests with Gentile connections (Neh. 13); and it is easy to picture our psalmist among the harried minority in either of these contexts. But with the coming of Ezra the persecution seems rather to be the other way round; and the later biblical writings give the impression of a dominant *torah*-piety. The author of Psalm 119 speaks of his community as 'those that fear thee' (יראיך, vv. 63, 74, 79), and this would correspond happily with 'those who fear Yahweh' in Psalms 112, 115 and 118. The insistent persecution theme fits better in the earlier part of the postexilic period. The psalmist has taken on the mantle of Jeremiah, who was persecuted by princes who dug pits for him just before the Exile.

(c) The 'kings' of v. 46 could be the kings of Persia, of whom Cyrus spoke to Sheshbazzar, according to Ezra 1.8, and Artaxerxes to Nehemiah (Neh. 2.1-8) and Ezra (Ezra 7.6).

(4) In the same way that Psalm 107 drew on Deutero-Isaiah, and 108–118 on various psalms and other texts, so has 119 drawn on Psalm 19 as a principal source of inspiration. Psalm 19 sees a parallel between the heavens which declare the glory of God, and in particular the sun from whose heat nothing is hidden, and the law of Yahweh which enlightens the eyes. In the same way *thy word is a lamp unto my feet, And light unto my path* (v. 105); *The opening of thy words giveth light; It giveth understanding unto the simple* (v. 130, פתים), as 'the testimony of the LORD maketh wise the simple' in 19.8 (פתי). The psalm extols the תורה of the LORD, his עדות, his פקודים, מצוה and משפטים (vv. 8-10). 'More to be desired are they than gold, yea, than much fine gold' (19.11), just as *I love thy commandments Above gold, yea, above fine gold* (119.127, cf. 72). They are 'Sweeter also than honey and the honeycomb' (19.11), just as *How sweet are thy words unto my palate! [Yea, sweeter] than honey to my mouth!* (119.103). Psalm 19.14 prays that presumptuous sins 'have not dominion over me': 119.133 prays, *Let not any iniquity have dominion over me.* 19.12 says that in keeping the Law there is great reward (עקב); the same word, עקב, is used with the sense 'end' in 119.33, 112.

The dependence is of 119 on 19, which has only five of the eight synonyms for the Law, but including פקודים, which occurs only in the Psalter. Psalm 119 is extremely short of metaphors, but includes the gold and honey of 19. Many commentators divide 19 and ascribe all the parallels to '19B', but cf. Eaton, *Kingship, ad loc.*

The links with Psalm 19 are widely noted, but not their significance. It has been a feature of 107–118 that the wording took up phrases from earlier groups of psalms, especially Psalms 32–37. Now 116 opened with echoes of Psalm 18 ('The cords of death encompassed me, And the pains of Sheol...'); 117 echoed 18.51 by summoning the nations to the praise of Yahweh; and 118 had a reminiscence of 18.21, 'He brought me forth also into a large place'. It is not an accident therefore that Psalm 119 draws on 19. Indeed 18.23-25 run, 'For I have kept the ways of the LORD, And have not wickedly departed from my God. For all his judgements were before me, And I put not away his statutes from me. I was also perfect with him, And I kept myself from mine iniquity'. These words have provided the tone of Psalm 119 in general: we may think particularly of v. 30, *I have chosen the way of faithfulness: Thy judgements have I set [before me]*, or v. 102, *I have not turned aside from thy judgements; For thou hast taught me.* The parallel provides a good instance of 'democratization': the ancient protestation of a king's loyalty in Psalm 18 has become the profession of a leading Levite, and in intention of the whole community. But more significantly, the context shows that 119 was written by the same group that produced 116–118; indeed, we may think by the same hand.

Allen, *Psalms 101–150*, p. 141, argues for a later date, citing the following Aramaisms/late Hebraisms: כעל (v. 14), גרס (v. 20), תאב(ה) (vv. 20, 40, 174) קים (v. 28, 106), שוה (v. 30), טפש (v. 70), שבר (v. 116,166), יאב (v. 131), שלט (v. 133). But 13 such uses in 176 verses is not more common than similar later Hebrew in 107–118; and we may notice the absence of ־שׁ, which is a notable feature both of the fifth-century Ascents psalms, and of 135–150; and of the third-century Song of Songs and Ecclesiastes.

These considerations lead to the probable conclusion that Psalm 119 stems from the same period of Restoration as 105–118. These are psalms that have put the trials of the Exile behind them, and celebrate a new hope. The tight alphabetic form of 119 is a phenomenon of the sixth century, most closely paralleled in Lamentations 3. The thought and language of 119 is Deuteronomic and not influenced by the

Priestly or Holiness codes. It belongs in the late sixth century. The oppressed community of the devout think of themselves as 'fearers of Yahweh', like the devout of Psalms 112, 115 and 118, and Ezra 6. Finally, 119 draws on Psalm 19, and has echoes of 18.23-25; as 18 has been a clear influence on 116–118, and the earlier psalms in the series have reminiscences of contiguous psalms, it looks as if 119 is consciously the climax of a series.

There is a big difference between 119 and 105–118: the earlier psalms are concerned with the practicalities of the Restoration—accusations, military threats, the need for prosperity—whereas Psalm 119 is concerned with the *torah* of Yahweh. But then we have seen that this difference is a function of the liturgical season. At Passover it is proper to think of the Return as a new Exodus, and of Jah as our strength and salvation, and to recall the days when Israel came out of Egypt. At Pentecost the thoughts of the God-fearer concentrate on the Law, the commandments, the precepts and the rest, which were given on Sinai: then is the time to meditate on this revelation (as the Church of England once knew the third Sunday in Advent as Bible Sunday), studying it and drawing out new truths from it.

In this way there is an explanation for the arrangement of Book V. The community of the Return celebrated Passover (Ezra 6.19-22) with a sequence of fourteen psalms, 105–118, of which the odd numbers were used in the evening, and the even numbers in the morning (108, 110 and 118 displaying evidence of morning use). These psalms covered 15–21 Nisan, closing with 118 on the twenty-first morning, with its echoes of Exodus 15. But Passover was not felt to close on 21st. Even in the days of our psalmists, Israel's coming out of Egypt (114.1) was associated not just with the fleeing of the sea (114.3), but with the skipping of Sinai like a ram at the presence of the Lord (114.4, 6-7). With time the Paschal season was recognized as extending to Pentecost, with the counting of the Omer in traditional observance. So Psalm 119 marks the climax and close of the fifty-day Pentecost which began with Passover. It is a long psalm because it was designed to be used for a Pentecostal vigil, with three-stanza praises *seven times in the day*, beginning *before the night watches*, with *rising at midnight, preventing the dawning of the morning*, and *meditating on it all the day*. When it was done there was a break in the Psalter, marked by the first of the headings, *A Song of Ascents*. These provided a psalmody for the next festival, Tabernacles.

Part III

PSALMS 135–150 AND EZRA

PSALMS 135–150

I noted at the beginning of this book (pp. 13-17) the parallel between
Psalms 105–118 and 135–150:

105–106	Two Historical Psalms	135–136
107	A Psalm Celebrating the Return	137
108–110	Psalms for David	138–145
111–118	Hallelujah Psalms	146–150.

There seemed to be a relationship between the first of these two
psalm-series and the story of the Return in Ezra 1–6; and as the
second series can be shown to be later than the first, the suggestion
must be that it was formed on the model of the first. We might think
that there were a succession of *aliyot*, 'Ascents', of considerable
groups of exiles reaching Jerusalem in the century and a half after
Cyrus's conquest of Babylon; and that three of them have left their
stamp on the Fifth Book of the Psalter, with Psalms 105–119, 120–
134 and 135–150.

It is important that we allow the evidence of the psalm groups to
suggest their own setting in life, and not impose a hypothesis from
outside. The Songs of Ascents suggested a setting in Nehemiah's time,
and 105–119 contained enough elements to suggest a link with the
Passover celebrations of 516 BCE; but 135–150 contain fewer details
that might fit in with any later *aliya* of which we know. However it
would be disingenuous of me to pretend that I did not think such a fit
existed. The Book of Ezra–Nehemiah describes three Ascents: the first
under Sheshbazzar, Jeshua and Zerubbabel; one under Nehemiah; and
one under Ezra. If there was another major Ascent in the period, we
do not know of it. There is therefore some hesitant, provisional presumption that Psalms 135–150 may be in some way related to the
Return under Ezra. In the exegesis below I shall limit myself normally to speaking of the third Ascent, or such phrases. Where any
echoes of our Ezra narratives occur, I will naturally note them. But I
leave the problems of the historical Ezra over for discussion in an

Appendix, where I argue that 135–150 provide our best—indeed contemporary—evidence for Ezra's expedition.

It would be difficult to show that Psalms 135–150 were all written by the same psalmist, but there are many links between individual psalms which suggest that they come from the same group. For instance, no other psalms in the Psalter give clear echoes of the Genesis 1 creation story. Psalm 136.7-9, '[He] made great lights...The sun to rule by day...The moon and stars to rule by night' is familiar with the wording we have in Gen. 1.10; Psalm 148 calls upon all creation to join in the praise of the LORD, with phrasing close to Gen. 1.20-24; Psalm 150.1 similarly speaks of the firmament, רקיע, of God's power from Gen. 1.7. These three references make it likely that the psalmists who wrote them all belonged to a community which knew the P creation story. Psalm 135 has many phrases in common with 136. Psalms 140–143 again share a series of phrases, and are reckoned by Kirkpatrick, and many commentators, to belong together. Delitzsch links several of the Hallel psalms, 146–150, as being by the same hand.

There are some favourite passages in earlier Scriptures that are drawn on by several of the psalms. For instance, 33.1, 'Praise is comely', recurs with a different syntax in 147.1; 33.2 'Sing praises unto him with the psaltery of ten strings; Sing unto him a new song' comes in 144.9, and similar phrases in 149.1, 3 and 150.3; 33.6 speaks of the word of the Lord as the agent of creation, and the same comes in 147.15, 18; 33.7, 'He layeth up the deeps in storehouses', comes again in 135.7; 33.9, 'For he spake, and it was done; He commanded, and it stood fast', is taken up in 148.5-6; 33.17-18, 'An horse is a vain thing for safety; Neither shall he deliver any by his great power. Behold the eye of the LORD is upon them that fear him, Upon them that wait for his mercy', is drawn upon in 147.10-11. There are a number of texts which are 'favourites' for the psalm group, for instance Psalm 104 and Isaiah 61; we may note these as we come to them, but their combined impact is to bind the group together.

There are also some attitudes that are common to these psalms, and in some contrast to their predecessors. Psalms 105–106 combine joy in the wonderful acts of Yahweh with a strong sense of Israel's repeated guilt in disobedience; they are still dominated by the retribution theodicy. This has disappeared in Psalms 135–136, which are more concerned with God's promise of the full land of Israel, and a contempt for the gods of the heathen. On the whole, with the exception of 109–110, the earlier psalms in Book V are irenic, and the Nehemiah psalms are repeatedly anxious for the peace of Jerusalem; we may contrast the bitter vengefulness of 137.7-9 and 149.6-9. Whereas the threats in the first two series are threats to the community, those in Psalms 139–145 are threats to an individual, the community's leader, who is attacked, imprisoned, and on trial for his life. Psalms 145–150 think in terms of the kingdom of God, a concept not found in the earlier groups.

PSALM 135

1   Hallelujah.
    Praise ye the name of the LORD;
    Praise *him*, O ye servants of the LORD:
2   Ye that stand in the house of the LORD,
    In the courts of the house of our God.
3   Praise ye the LORD; for the LORD is good:
    Sing praises unto his name; for it is pleasant.
4   For Jah hath chosen Jacob unto himself,
    And Israel for his peculiar treasure.
5   For I know that the LORD is great,
    And that our Lord is above all gods.
6   Whatsoever the LORD pleased, that hath he done,
    In heaven and earth, in the seas and in all deeps.
7   He causeth the vapours to ascend from the ends of the earth;
    He maketh lightnings for the rain;
    He bringeth forth the wind out of his treasuries.
8   Who smote the firstborn of Egypt,
    Both of man and beast.
9   He sent signs and wonders into the midst of thee, O Egypt,
    Upon Pharaoh, and upon all his servants.
10 Who smote great nations,
    And slew mighty kings;
11 Sihon king of the Amorites,
    And Og the king of Bashan,
    And all the kingdoms of Canaan:
12 And gave their land for an heritage,
    An heritage unto Israel his people.
13 Thy name, O LORD, *endureth* for ever;
    Thy memorial, O LORD, throughout all generations.
14 For the LORD shall judge his people,
    And repent himself concerning his servants.
15 The idols of the nations are silver and gold,
    The work of men's hands.
16 They have mouths, but they speak not;
    Eyes have they, but they see not;

17   They have ears, but they hear not;
      Neither is there any breath in their mouths.
18   They that make them shall be like unto them;
      Yea, every one that trusteth in them.
19   O house of Israel, bless ye the LORD:
      O house of Aaron, bless ye the LORD:
20   O house of Levi, bless ye the LORD:
      Ye that fear the LORD, bless ye the LORD.
21   Blessed be the LORD out of Zion,
      Who dwelleth at Jerusalem.
      Hallelujah.

Like Psalm 106, 135 begins and ends with *Hallelujah*: the singer calls, and the massed congregation shouts back, as in a modern Pentecostal service. But 135 is strongly marked by the whole of the series 105–118. Psalm 113 began, '*Hallelujah. Praise, O ye servants of the LORD, Praise the name of the LORD*', as in 135.1. Psalm 116.19, '*In the courts of* the LORD's *house, In the midst of thee*, O *Jerusalem*' is divided between 135.2b and 9. 115.3, '[Our God] *hath done whatsoever he pleased*' comes in 135.6a. The whole sequence on heathen idols in 135.15-18 is nearly identical to 115.4-8; and the final appeal to the different groups to bless Yahweh follows 115.9-11 and 118.2-4. Our psalmist draws on many other texts in Scripture, but the 105–118 group is his primary model. He is also consciously following the Songs of Ascents, for 134.1-3, '*Behold, bless ye the LORD*, all *ye servants of the LORD*, Ye that *stand in the house of the LORD*... The *LORD* bless thee *out of Zion*' have shaped 135.(1-)2a and 21.

Other notable quotations are Jer. 10.13 in v. 7, 'he causeth the vapours to ascend from the ends of the earth; he maketh lightnings for the rain, and bringeth forth the wind out of his treasuries' (וַיּוֹצֵא in Jeremiah becomes מוֹצֵא for מוֹצִיא in 135); and Deut. 32.36 in v. 14, 'For the LORD shall judge his people, And repent himself for his servants'. There is no need to think of the psalmist as a text-grubber; he knows the Scriptures like the back of his hand, and finds divine words to express his own heartfelt sentiments.

Psalm 135.1-7. 135 is said by Delitzsch to be a mosaic of earlier texts, but the psalmist is the master of his pieces. The *servants of the LORD* (v. 1) are the whole gathered people, as in v. 14, massed in the Temple *courts*—not the Temple staff of Psalm 134. They are to *praise the name of the LORD* because *he is good*, he has done something for them. What he has done is to *choose Jacob unto himself, Israel for his*

peculiar treasure, as Moses put it in Deut. 7.6; and he has been faithful
to his choice. *For*, the psalmist confesses, *I know that the LORD is
great...above all gods*: we were deported to Babylon, but Yahweh has
shown himself greater than all their idols. *I know:* the Babylonian
captivity is a recent experience, and it is worth giving four verses to
the standard obloquy of powerless heathen images—the long-estab-
lished mockery of Bel and Nebo, first found in Deutero-Isaiah, but
still relevant for those who have lived under their shadow. *The LORD*,
by contrast, *has done whatsoever he pleased*, he has kept his promise
to us. He is the Lord of nature, *causing the clouds to ascend from*
nowhere, flashing forth his *lightnings* to give us *rain*, and *bringing the
winds out of his storehouses*; and he is the Lord of his people, for
whom also he will *do whatsoever he pleases*, and establish us once
more.

Verse 3. זמרו לשמו כי נעים divides critics: is it the *praise* (Delitzsch) or the *name*
(Eaton) which is pleasant? The same phrase without לשמו recurs in 147.1, suggesting
the former.

Almost all commentators date the psalm late (Jacquet even in the Greek period),
with its repeated ־ש (vv. 2, 8, 10), ־ל for the accusative (v. 11), והרג, ונתן for imperfects. It is unusual however to see the selection of historical references as significant;
Kraus, for example, asks why there is no reference to Sinai, and concludes
(following the then popular Short Credo hypothesis of von Rad) that Psalm 135 was
composed for Paschal celebrations. Allen sets it more suitably at Tabernacles, with
its praise of the lord of both nature and history; Weiser pointed to v. 7 as an indicator
of the autumn clouds, storms, rain and wind.

Psalm 135.8-14. The psalmist's heart is full of *praise* and *blessing*;
and it is not vacuous praise for events seven centuries back, now irrel-
evant. The heart of the psalm is v. 14: *For the LORD will vindicate his
people, And repent himself concerning*—better perhaps, *have compassion upon*—*his servants*. It follows Psalms 105–106 in giving a brief
outline of the *Heilsgeschichte*, but the selection of events is significant.
The LORD *smote the firstborn of Egypt*, and *sent signs and wonders
upon Pharaoh*; he released Israel from its slavery in Egypt, as now he
has released Israel from its deportation to Babylon. He *smote great
nations and slew mighty kings*; as our psalmists look forward to when
we shall bind their kings in chains, and their nobles with links of iron
(149.8). Then it was *Sihon king of the Amorites, And Og king of
Bashan, And all the kingdoms of Canaan*; now Jerusalem and Judah
are already semi-independent, and in time all the West Bank will be

filled with thriving settlements, and Transjordan too. The LORD *gave their land for an heritage, An heritage unto Israel his people.* The gifts and the calling of God are without repentance: so his *name* will be exalted *for ever*, and *remembered* in praise *from generation to generation*. It is the evident sign that he is acting on that promise now which has elicited the present hymn, and no lament. Yahweh is in process of *vindicating his people, And taking compassion* (יתנחם) *upon his servants.*

Psalm 135.15-18. The contrast with Psalms 105–106 is as important as the parallel. There a much fuller account was given of the Egyptian plagues and the Exodus (105.24-38, 106.7-12), and 105.44-45 was as here the climax with Israel taking possession of the lands of the nations. But Psalm 106 is largely given to explaining how this happy state of affairs was subverted: the LORD 'gave them into the hand of the nations: And they that hated them ruled over them' (v. 41), because of their continual rebellions. The psalm ends with a prayer that God will 'save us, and gather us from among the nations' (v. 47). Like 135, 106 is a hymn and not a lament; but it comes from the early period of Return, when the sins expounded by the historians lay heavy on the writer's conscience, and the gathering of the exiles lay mostly in the future. But life has moved on now. The gods of the heathen are not an ever present temptation, the cause of the divine wrath of 587 BCE, but the powerless idols of Babylon lampooned by the prophets. The psalmist *knows* from experience that the LORD is great, and that his gift of the Land of Israel is *for ever, throughout all generations*. The gathering has begun in earnest: vindication is at hand.

Psalm 115.6 has 'Noses (אף) have they, but they smell (יריחון) not': 135.17 amends to 'Neither (אף) is there any breath (רוח) in their mouths'—more pointfully, but with less gusto.

Psalm 135.19-21. In Psalm 115 the mockery of the idols (vv. 4-8) is followed by a triple appeal to trust in the LORD (vv. 9-11), to Israel, the house of Aaron, and 'ye that fear the LORD'; and in 118.2-4 the same three groups are called on to confess the permanence of his mercy. The Passover for which these psalms seemed to be composed (Ezra 6.14-22) was celebrated by (1) 'the children of Israel which were come again out of the captivity', (2) the priests and the Levites who had purified themselves as one, and (3) 'all such as had separated themselves unto them from the filthiness of the heathen of the land to seek the LORD'. So we had some explanation for the triple division. Psalm 135, with its eye on 115 as a model, repeats the triple division, though perhaps the last category is no longer so distinct; but adds a fourth, 'O house of Levi'. There were not many Levites (74) in the list of those returning in Ezra 2 (v. 40), and Mowinckel thought this historically plausible (*Ezra*, pp. 27-28): there was little enthusiasm to return to second-class citizenship in the Jerusalem Temple. So perhaps we should think with him that there were no Levites worth mentioning in 516, and that the Chroniclers have added them in later, from family loyalty; or perhaps the Levites were doing the singing in Psalms 115 and 118 (Ezra 3.10-11). But there were Levites in the later Return (Ezra 8.15-20, cf. Neh. 8), and they need their place by the time of Psalm 135.

PSALM 136

Psalm 136 is a kind of pair to 135: the first halves of its vv. 17-22 virtually repeat 135.10-12, and the structure of the psalm more generally is the same—praise/thanks for Yahweh's lordship over nature and history from the Exodus to the Settlement, and then to the Return. Both psalms are in fact celebrations of the end of the Exile, that 'the LORD who dwelleth at Jerusalem' *remembered us in our low estate, And hath delivered us from our adversaries.*

1   O give thanks unto the LORD; for he is good:
    For his mercy *endureth* for ever.
2   O give thanks unto the God of gods: For his mercy...
3   O give thanks unto the lord of lords: For his mercy...
4   To him who alone doeth great wonders: For his mercy...
5   To him that by understanding made the heavens: For his...
6   To him that spread forth the earth above the waters: For...
7   To him that made great lights: For his mercy...
8   The sun to rule by day: For his mercy...
9   The moon and stars to rule by night; For his mercy...
10 To him that smote Egypt in their firstborn: For his...
11 And brought out Israel from among them; For his mercy...
12 With a strong hand, and with a stretched out arm: For...
13 To him which divided the Red Sea in sunder: For his...
14 And made Israel to pass through the midst of it: For...
15 But shook off Pharaoh and his host in the Red Sea: For...
16 To him which led his people through the wilderness: For...
17 To him which smote great kings: For his mercy...
18 And slew famous kings: For his mercy...
19 Sihon king of the Amorites: For his mercy...
20 And Og king of Bashan: For his mercy...
21 And gave their land for an heritage: For his mercy...
22 Even an heritage unto Israel his servant: For his mercy...
23 Who remembered us in our low estate: For his mercy...
24 And hath delivered us from our adversaries: For his...
25 He giveth food to all flesh: For his mercy...
26 O give thanks unto the God of heaven:
    For his mercy *endureth* for ever.

Psalm 136 uses the same late Hebrew as 135: ‫שׁ‬־ (v. 23), ‫ל‬־ for the accusative (vv. 19-20), piled up articles, ‫שׁפל‬ (elsewhere only in Eccl.10.6), ‫פרק‬ (elsewhere only Lam. 5.8). Like Psalm 135, it draws widely on Deuteronomy: vv. 2-3 on Deut. 10.17; v. 12 on Deut. 4.34; v. 16 on Deut. 8.15; Sihon and Og on Deuteronomy 3; v. 22 on Deut. 32.36. It is also striking that v. 5 echoes Jer. 10.12, '*by his under-standing* hath he stretched out *the heavens*', where 135.7 took up the following verse, Jer. 10.13, '*he causeth the vapours to ascend...*' The same author has written both psalms. Psalm 136 slightly expands the themes of 135, and it much increases its element of participation. Where 135 merely began and ended with 'Hallelujah', in which the people could join, 136 provides for a regular chanted refrain; perhaps this was at first the response of choir to cantor, but in time we may think the whole congregation would be welcome to join in (135.19; 136.1-3 ‫הודו‬). The refrain is the slogan of the Return. At the laying of the Temple foundation stone the Asaphite Levites had sung 'one to another in *praising and giving thanks unto the LORD,* saying, *For he is good, for his mercy* endureth *for ever toward Israel*' (Ezra 3.10-11). Psalm 136.1 is virtually identical, and reproduces also the first verse of Psalm 106, its model as a thanksgiving for Israel's history.

Psalm 136.1-9. Having begun with the Exiles' chorus, the psalmist completes his first triplet with Yahweh's dominance over all the gods and lords of heathendom, the senseless idols of 135.15-18. He has come safely back from Babylon, and knows, as in 135.5, who is in charge of the pantheon. A second triplet, vv. 4-6, covers Yahweh's powers in creation: first that he *made the heavens* (Gen. 1.1) *by his understanding* (Jer. 10.12); and then that he *stretched out* (‫רקע‬, cf. Isa. 42.5) *the earth above the waters* (Ps. 24.2; Gen. 1.10). In a third triplet Yahweh *made great lights* (‫אורים‬), *the sun to rule* (‫ממשלת‬) *by day, the moon and the stars by night.* The language is close to Gen. 1.16, 'And God *made* the two *great lights* (‫מארת‬), the greater light *to rule* (‫ממשלת‬) the *day,* the lesser light *to rule* the *night:* [he made] the *stars* also'. The psalmist is less cautious than the P author of Genesis 1, in that he gives authority to the stars; but he clearly knows the Priestly account of creation, as do Psalms 148 and 150. His ‫אורים‬ are unique in the Old Testament, less prosaic than P's ‫מארת‬.

Psalm 136.10-22. The triplet form continues, with each triad of verses opening with ‫ל‬־ (vv. 4, 7, 10, 13, 16). The first and second take up the Exodus from Egypt (vv. 10-15; 135.8-9), the type of our recent exodus from Babylon, and God's leading of us through the desert (v. 16; 107.4-8). Then come the killing of the Canaanite kings, the victories over Sihon and Og, and the taking of the Land as a heritage. Here, vv. 17-22, the phrasing of 135.10-12 takes over, and the triplet scheme collapses, a sign that Psalm 136 is following 135 and not vice versa. This passage of Israel's history is cardinal to the community of the Return, now gaining in confidence and ambition. Did God say his people should inherit Jerusalem and a few villages and towns on the West Bank? Did he not say, 'Unto thy seed have I given this land, from the river of Egypt unto the great river, the River Euphrates'? That is why we keep hearing of Sihon king of the Amorites and Og the king of Bashan.

Psalm 136.23-26. The psalmist closes by bringing his story up to date. The LORD *remembered us in our low estate*, in our deportation and misery in Babylonia; he *hath delivered us from our enemies*, from the Babylonians whom he overthrew at the hand of Cyrus, and the Edomites and others, still a threat to our liberty. The psalm sequence will return to these *adversaries* in 137.7-9; but for now the thought is just of *thanks to the God of heaven* (Neh. 1.4, 2.4), who has brought the exiles home and re-established his people in his chosen city. *He giveth food to all flesh*, too: perhaps the psalmist has in mind the hunger of the desert passage (107.9), or some more recent national famine (Delitzsch).

Allen thinks that the *low estate* and the *deliverance from our adversaries* refer to ancient events in Egypt; but the psalmist mentions them *after* the Settlement. Other critics have suggested that the period of the Judges is in mind, but this would be unclear and not very pointful. It is better to see a reference to a recent deliverance (Kirkpatrick) in the same way that the similar 135.10-12 lead on to a current vindication (135.14), or the longer recital of Psalm 106 leads up the present situation in 106.46-47.

He giveth food to all flesh (v. 25) suggested to Weiser that Psalm 136 was intended for Tabernacles, which was especially the harvest festival; whereas Kraus and Anderson saw the Exodus and Settlement themes as indications that it was written for Passover/Massot. Neither argument is strong, though traditional Jewish use of 136 at Passover/Massot is evidence in Kraus's favour. But both Deut. 31.10-13 and Neh. 8.1-12 indicate that there was a public reading of the whole Pentateuch at the autumn festival; the creation theme in vv. 4-9 is associated with Tabernacles; and the antiphonal singing of the LORD's praises 'for he is good, for his mercy *endureth for ever* toward Israel' took place at Tabernacles in Ezra 3. The same chorus is chanted at the same feast for the founding of the Temple by Solomon in 2 Chron.

5.13 and 7.3; and with the refrain running through the length of Psalm 136, it is difficult not to see it as a Tabernacles celebration.

Schedl, 'Struktur', saw an arithmetical structure underlying the psalm: its 26 verses corresponded to the numerical value of יהוה, the 22 letters of the alphabet framed by vv. 1-3, 26 which open הודו, and so on. The suggestion is possible, though it seems fanciful.

PSALM 137

1   By the rivers of Babylon,
       There we sat down, yea, we wept,
       When we remembered Zion.
2   Upon the willows in the midst thereof
       We hanged up our harps.
3   For there they that led us captive required of us words of song,
       And our tormentors *required of us* mirth, *saying,*
       Sing us one of the songs of Zion.
4   How shall we sing the LORD's song
       In a strange land?
5   If I forget thee, O Jerusalem,
       Let my right hand forget *her cunning.*
6   Let my tongue cleave to the roof of my mouth,
       If I remember thee not;
       If I prefer not Jerusalem
       Above my chief joy.
7   Remember, O LORD, against the children of Edom
       The day of Jerusalem;
       Who said, Rase it, rase it,
       Even to the foundation thereof.
8   O daughter of Babylon, that art laid waste,
       Happy shall he be, that rewardeth thee
       As thou hast served us.
9   Happy shall he be, that taketh and dasheth thy little ones
       Against the rock.

The apparently straightforward text masks a series of problems.

(1) Where does the speaker live? It is not in Babylon (*There we sat...there they that led us captive required of us...*). But nor is it easily in Jerusalem, for those who live there are unlikely to *forget thee/remember thee not*. It was in Babylon that *we remembered Zion* in v. 1. Gunkel suggested the Diaspora, but a simpler solution might be that the singer has arrived recently in Jerusalem: he had *remembered Zion* in Babylonia, and did not intend now ever to *forget* her.

(2) How had the psalmist's group come to be *sitting and weeping by the rivers of Babylon?* Delitzsch and Kirkpatrick drew pathetic pictures of a melancholy gathering of pious Jews watching the flow of alien waters, and listening to the monotonous splashing of the waves. But Kraus more plausibly takes up a suggestion of Ewald that the gathering had been a formal lament. Some of the phrasing may be taken either way. The traditional posture for mourning, whether individual or corporate, was *sitting* on the ground (Isa. 47.1, 5; Lam. 1.1; Ezra 9.4). The word for *weeping*, בכינו, similarly, is that used both for informal and for ritual weeping, for example at Judg. 2.4-5, where the name for the site (Bethel) is given as בכים, Weepers.

But liturgical weeping was also traditionally symbolized by the pouring out of water, as when Samuel held a fast at Mizpah, and 'they drew water and poured it out before the LORD' (1 Sam. 7.6); hence a gathering *by the rivers* of Babylonia would be pointful, as well as providing for any ritual washing. Also it seems that some communal chanting of a lament was intended, since *harps* have been brought along. Liturgical gatherings during the Exile seem to be implied by 1 Kgs 8.46-49, 'If they sin against thee... and thou deliver them to the enemy, so that they carry them away captive... yet if they shall bethink themselves in the land whither they are carried captive, and turn again and make supplication unto thee...' No mention is made of synagogues, and such are not to be thought of; but ritual mourning by a river ('that runneth to Ahava') is mentioned for a large group of Jews in Ezra 8.21, and services by the river are still expected in Acts 16.13. It may be that Ezekiel had his first vision publicly among the exiles by the river Chebar (Ezek. 1.1); בתוך־הגולה may imply a vision during worship.

The hypothesis of a formal mourning ritual is criticized by Kellermann, 'Psalm 137', pp. 55-57, on various grounds: (a) the worship of other gods was respected in the ancient Near East for superstitious reasons; (b) there is no evidence of worship in the open air, nor of worship by water until later; (c) Psalm 137 is a modified form of *Zionslied*, and was expressly *not* to be sung in a strange, that is, unclean land. The first objection is curious, since Kellermann himself, like almost all critics, understands the request for a song of Zion as mockery. Formal fasting rituals in the open air go back as early as Samuel (1 Sam. 7.6), and the community prayers mentioned in 1 Kings 8 can hardly be indoors. Ezra 'proclaimed a fast' to the people encamped by the river running to Ahava (8.21, 15); the same phrase is used in 2 Chron. 20.3, and a detailed description is given of the public ritual. For the *Zionslied* argument, see below, p. 227.

(3) Why did they *hang up their harps upon the willows* there? Kraus thinks of even insensible things as expressing the community's grief, like the ways to Zion in Lam. 1.4; and the following sentence seems to suggest a connection (*For...*) with the derisive request for a song of Zion. It would be a gesture to tie the lyres to the foliage, and take them home a couple of hours later; a more dramatic gesture to leave them there permanently, to *hang them up* as a retiring boxer hangs up his gloves.

(4) When are we to date the psalm? In v. 8 the daughter of Babylon is described as הַשְּׁדוּדָה, RVmg *that art laid waste*. The parallel with *the children of Edom* in v. 7, *Who said Rase it, rase it*, leads the reader to expect the active, *that layest waste*; and indeed Symmachus's ἡ λῃστρίς, the Syriac and the Targum provide this (from a hypothetical הַשּׁוֹדְדָה?). But this looks like the intrusion of an easier reading, and many critics hold to the MT. However, this still leaves matters open. Delitzsch and others render with *vastanda* rather than *vastata*: the destruction is fixed by God and is assured, even if it lies in the future. This allows for the most popular dating, between 537 BCE when Cyrus authorized the Return, and 516, when the walls of Babylon were at least partly destroyed.

It is difficult to think this cogent. Behind it lies the impression on some (like Weiser) that the vividness of the memories in vv. 7-9 implies that some of the speaker's group had been there in 587 BCE, or at least were living not long after. But such an approach is naive. Serbs remember the Field of Blackbirds, their defeat by the Turks at Kosovo in 1389; and I am afraid that many Protestant Ulstermen insist each July on remembering King Billy's victory at the Boyne in 1690. Bitter minorities need long memories. Edom was to occupy the lands of southern Judah for centuries, and Babylon was an enormous and prosperous city when Herodotus visited it (*Hist.* 1.178-79), the home to an imperilled colony of Jews for many years. So even if it were partly devastated for its rebellions under Darius I, it might seem to a providentialist Jew to be due for more adequate retribution.

Nor can anything be inferred from שׁוֹבֵינוּ, *they that led us captive*, תוֹלָלֵינוּ, *our tormentors*, and their derisive request. It was the Babylonians who had deported the psalmist's community, and Gentiles in power have derided and tormented Jews in our own century. Kraus is quite mistaken in holding this psalm to be the only one clearly datable.

⁴ Any time from 537 BCE would be possible, perhaps till 400. The three שֶׁ's in vv. 8-9 suggest the fifth century.

Kellermann, 'Psalm 137', pp. 51-52, gives 445 BCE, Nehemiah's rebuilding of the walls, as the latest date; but Psalm 137 does not mention the walls, and most of the city was still in ruins when he had rebuilt them.

(5) How is the form of the psalm to be described? Gunkel and Mowinckel called it a cursing psalm, laying the stress on the last three verses; but we may think the more widely urged Communal Lament more adequate. The laments in Lamentations open with a description of the survivors' piteous plight, and tend to close with a curse on those responsible (1.21-22, 3.64-66, 4.21-22 specifically mentioning Edom). Psalm 137 is used in traditional Jewish liturgy as the psalm for 9 Ab, the anniversary of the city's fall in 587 BCE (and 70 CE). Eaton and Anderson suggest that it might have been written for one of the fasts mentioned in Zech. 7.1-5.

Mowinckel, *Psalmenstudien*, III, p. 54, V, pp. 83-84, saw 137 as a cursing psalm written for use at the annual fast on 9 Ab; Kellermann, 'Psalm 137', pp. 53-55, argues forcefully in favour of this.

Psalm 137.1-4. The psalmist and his colleagues have made the great journey from Babylon to Jerusalem. They had been used to meet by the waterside for prayer, and had held a formal service of lament, sitting on the ground and weeping; very likely a fast on some such anniversary as 9 Ab. The solemnity was interrupted by derisive requests from hostile local people. In earlier troubles it had been asked, 'Where is thy God?' (Ps. 42.11, 79.10); now, more subtly, *Sing us one of the songs of Zion!* The requirement is for *mirth*, שִׂמחה, so the mockers must have been familiar with more cheerful hymns. We need not think, as is so often suggested, of Gunkel's category, *Zionslieder*, 46, 48, 76, 87, 122, etc., but of joyful Jerusalem psalms more generally.

Allen and others claim that the כנור was a joyful instrument, and that the flute was used for laments. It is true that strings are often mentioned in connection with praise; but 55 and 61, both laments, are to be accompanied by strings (נגינת), and often a lament is headed מזמור. The celebrations of 81.3 are led by the כנור נעים, perhaps distinguished from the more usual lyre; and in Psalm 137 the instruments had presumably been brought in order to be used.

תוללינו in v. 3 is a *hapax*. It is usually derived as hiphil of ילל, *those who make us howl*, hence RVmg *our tormentors*; but Kellermann, 'Psalm 137', p. 45, prefers a suggestion by A. Guillaume that the root is cognate with the classical Arabic *talla*, to 'lead captive', cf. LXX οἱ ἀπαγαγόντες ἡμᾶς, a better parallel. The psalmist uses the form for the echo with תלינו in v. 2.

Such demands were the final straw. The worshippers symbolized their abhorrence by tying their instruments to the boughs of the trees, where their perpetual silence would form a reproachful dirge more eloquent even than Psalm 137. Delitzsch identified the trees as Euphrates poplars, though this is disputed by Jacquet. How could any loyal Jew accede to such a demand? The psalmist says *in a strange land*, על אדמת נכר, better 'on heathen soil'. His objection is not to worship on non-Israelite land, for he has brought his lyre out to play it, and the bystanders have heard him sing *the LORD's song* before. It is that the place where his group had gathered for their lamentation had been desecrated, made heathen soil, by the interruptions.

Psalm 137.5-6. Babylonia is now *there*, far away; the faithful Jews have left their living there, with its security, prosperity and enjoyments, in order to settle back in Jerusalem. The psalmist vows never to *forget* the holy city, at the cost of a curse on himself—if he does, may his *right hand* lose its memory for action, his *tongue stick to his palate*. Whatever his *chief joy* may have been, friendships, business success, family who have stayed behind, he has vowed to *prefer Jerusalem*. This is the spirit which has enabled the Jewish people to survive.

The psalmist has sacrificed substance to form with his *If I forget thee, O Jerusalem, Let my right hand forget!* We must supply *[its action]* in parallel with v. 6. There אזכרכי has the appended hireq, as in many postexilic psalms.

Psalm 137.7-9. As with the laments in Lamentations, the singer closes with a curse on those who have brought such destruction on his beloved city. The Edomites, who might have been looked to as blood-brothers and allies, had called for the city to be levelled with the ground, and much of such ruin is no doubt still visible; the annihilation of their larger neighbour had left them free to annex most of the land of southern Judah with impunity. The Babylonians, who had the chief responsibility for so much suffering, and for the horrifying slaughter of babes in arms, may expect condign punishment when their *Day* comes. Their devastation has only begun: vengeance is mine, saith the LORD, I will repay. Commentators like Gunkel should beware of too easy a contrast with the spirit of the New Testament; as Robert Carroll has observed, it is shorter, but with its novel doctrine of eternal punishment in hell, worse. Eaton notes more carefully that such vindictiveness is counterbalanced by a teaching of grace and forgiveness in both Testaments.

For all its colourfulness and eloquence, Psalm 137 gives us no clear indication of its temporal provenance. We might think of the 'ascent' of Sheshbazzar's company from Babylonia (בבל) in Ezra 1.11, though the tradition gives no hint of any fasting, or the hanging of lyres on the poplars. We could also think of the ascent of Ezra himself from בבל in Ezra 7.6, 8.1; in his case we do have a fast and it does take place by the river above Ahava (8.15, 21), but there is again nothing about lyres and poplars—we should have to think that such an incident seemed a little *infra dig.* to the author of the Ezra memoir. Or of course the psalmist's company might be one of many who have left not a name, whose memorial is perished with them.

Mowinckel, *Psalmenstudien*, V, pp. 83-84, followed by Kellermann and many, believed that the last three verses all referred in the original text to Edom, and that Babylon (and v. 8c) were later glosses. The arguments are forceful, but not, I think, cogent. An element of *inclusio* is common in psalms (cf. 139.1, 23), and we might expect a psalm which has begun with an insult to Yahweh by Babylonians to end with his punishment of their bestiality. For hesitations about the iniquity of Edom, cf. Bartlett, *Edom*, pp. 151-56.

The threefold ש in these verses (only one of which falls within the suspected gloss) is an indication of a late date. It occurs in some early texts with north Israelite affiliations, but becomes common in the period after the Exile: four times in sixth century Lamentations, ten times in fifth-century Songs of Ascents, nine times in various psalms between 135 and 150, 200 times in the Song of Songs, 68 times in Qoheleth. It is absent from all earlier parts of the Psalter, including Psalms 107–119.

PSALM 138

The specific detail of Psalm 137 limits scholarly disagreement, but there is no such limit with 138. Here three quite different lines of interpretation dispute the field:

(1) Kirkpatrick and Anderson, following Olshausen and other nineteenth-century exegetes, see the speaker as Israel, or its representative, giving thanks for God's lovingkindness in delivering the people from the Exile. The kings of the earth are to give thanks for this, following the thought of Second and Third Isaiah. Jewish tradition supported such a view: some MSS of the LXX add to the Heading ['Αγγαιου και] Ζαχαριου.

(2) Gunkel, Kraus and many moderns classify the psalm as an Individual Thanksgiving. The author has been delivered from some great personal peril, probably sickness, to his amazement; and speaks in exalted terms of praise *before the gods*, and of *all the kings of the earth* joining in his thanksgiving. He is but a *lowly* layman, but God has been true to his word, and is looked to to continue in his care for him.

(3) Mowinckel, Eaton and Dahood note similarities with Psalm 18 and other royal psalms. The speaker is the king, speaking of himself as *lowly,* as David so often saw himself as Yahweh's servant, poor and needy; but he sees himself as consorting with *all the kings of the earth.* He prays *towards thy holy temple* as he offers sacrifice at the great altar before it.

Psalm 138

A psalm of David.
1   I will give thee thanks with my whole heart:
     Before the gods will I sing praises unto thee.
2   I will worship toward thy holy temple,
     And give thanks unto thy name for thy lovingkindness and for thy truth:
     For thou hast magnified thy word above every name [read שֵׁם for שִׁמְךָ].

3 In the day that I called thou answeredst me,
  Thou didst encourage me with strength in my soul.
4 All the kings of the earth shall give thee thanks, O LORD,
  For they have heard the words of thy mouth.
5 Yea, they shall sing in the ways (בדרכי) of the LORD;
  For great is the glory of the LORD.
6 For though the LORD be high, yet hath he respect unto the lowly:
  But the haughty he knoweth from afar.
7 Though I walk in the midst of trouble, thou wilt give me life (תחיני);
  Thou shalt stretch forth thine hand against the wrath of mine enemies,
  And thy right hand shall save me.
8 The LORD will perfect that which concerneth me:
  Thy mercy, O LORD, *endureth* for ever;
  Forsake not the works of thine own hands.

Psalm 138.1-3. It is not surprising that the psalm is headed *For David*: v. 1a is very close to Ps. 9.2 and 111.1; v. 2b is identical with Ps. 5.8; *giving thanks* among the Gentiles comes in 57.10, and God's *mercy and truth* in 57.4, and he *perfects* (גמר) in 57.3. With these and other 'Davidic' echoes, the tradition might properly feel that this was an (adapted) psalm of David.

While it is not uncommon for psalmists to summon the Gentile world, rhetorically, to join in the worship of Yahweh, Psalm 138 is unique in promising praise *before the gods*, נגד אלהים. Psalm 82 is no true parallel, for there the אלהים are clearly understood to be inferior divine spirits, subordinate to God, עליון, that is, Yahweh. Here the heartfelt gratitude is to be expressed in the presence of *the gods*; it is implied, in defiance of them. There were no such idols in Jerusalem, so we are driven to think that the psalmist is not in the land of Israel. This seems to be confirmed by v. 2a, *I will worship toward* (אל) *thy holy temple.* Solomon was said to have prayed that God would hear his people in exile 'if they return unto thee *with all their heart* and with all their soul in the land of their enemies, which carried them captive, and pray unto thee toward (דרך)...the house which I have built for *thy name*' (1 Kgs 8.48). Daniel's windows in his chamber were open toward Jerusalem (Dan. 6.10), and Sarah the daughter of Raguel prayed by the window with her face toward the Lord (Tob. 3.11-12). The impression given is thus that 138 is the psalm of a faithful Jew in exile, living among heathen temples and praying towards the house of God in Jerusalem. As the היכל קדשך is spoken of as in existence, the psalm would have to be dated after 516 BCE.

Kraus offers three options for understanding נגד אלהים: (1) it is carried over from the old contrast of Yahweh with the gods of Canaan, as in Exod. 15.11, 'Who is like unto thee, O LORD, among the gods?'; (2) *the gods* are just angels, as understood by LXX. He sees that neither of these ideas is convincing, and prefers (3), under the influence of Second Isaiah, *the gods* of Babylon are seen as risible beside the powerful and gracious action of Yahweh. As Kraus thinks the psalmist is thanking Yahweh in Jerusalem for his recovery, the 'concretizing' of Second Isaiah's prophecies about heathen gods seems rather far-fetched. Dahood more realistically posits an Israelite king on campaign, away from Jerusalem, and praying towards the Temple; but our evidence of prayer towards the Temple dates from the Deuteronomistic history.

The wording of v. 2a recurs in Ps. 5.8, and this suggests to Gunkel that the psalmist is offering his personal thanks in the Temple forecourt. But Psalm 5 is not offered *before the gods*, and it is easy to think that a phrase from a familiar psalm has been used with a rather different meaning. Eaton, *Kingship,* p. 63, sees the king as the speaker of Psalm 138 as he offers his sacrifice by the altar *toward thy holy Temple*; but there is no suggestion of any sacrifice in the psalm. (Sacrifice is sometimes understood as accompanying Ps. 5; בקר אערך לך is translated by RSV *In the morning I prepare a sacrifice for thee.*) He takes *the gods* as 'heavenly beings subordinate to the one true God', as in Psalm 82.

The Hebrew of v. 2c seems insoluble: *For thou hast magnified thy word above all thy name* (על־כל־שמך אמרתך). Eaton comments, 'in all the self-revelation of God it is his fidelity to his promise which now appears most glorious'. But it is doubtful if a Jew could have spoken of anything, even God's *word*, as greater than his *name*. A number of emendations have been suggested, but I have not found what seems to me the most simple and probable. Verse 2b promises thanks to *thy name*, שמך, and the phrase is extremely common in the psalms. The context of *worship before the gods*, and away from Jerusalem, suggests that the original ran הגדלת על־כל־שם אמרתך, the additional ך being added to שם under the influence of the same word in v. 2b: *thou hast magnified thy word above every name*, that is to say, above all the gods of v. 1b. We may even think that St Paul was familiar with such a form of the text when he wrote Phil. 2.9, 'the name which is *above every name*' (cf. Eph. 1.21, Heb. 1.4). An early copyist has supplied ך in line with v. 2b, understanding what Kirkpatrick calls a harsh asyndeton, *Thou hast magnified thy name [and] thy word above all.*

The Hebrew of v. 3b is difficult also, where תרהבני, the hiphil of רהב, might be expected to mean 'overwhelm' as in Cant. 6.5. Delitzsch renders *Thou dost inspire me with courage*, and takes the following בנפשי עז separately, *a lofty feeling permeated my soul.* But this is cumbrous, and Anderson, with many, follows the ancient versions reading תרבני, 'Thou didst increase strength in my soul'.

The psalmist is giving thanks for the LORD's חסד ואמת, evident in the magnifying of his אמרה. We have seen how often Yahweh's חסד, his covenanted love, has been the cause of thanksgiving in Psalms 107–118, in the deliverance from exile; and אמרה similarly implies that he has kept his promise. The associations of Psalm 138 with Deutero- and Trito-Isaiah—the powerlessness of *the gods*, the worship of Yahweh by *the kings of the earth,* His concern for the *lowly* (Isa. 57.15), His *glory*—suggests that it is the prophecies of the exilic period (and perhaps the Deuteronomic historian's Prayer of Solomon) which constitute *thy word*, and which have *encouraged* the singer/ *increased strength in his soul.*

Delitzsch, almost alone until contemporary critics, links Psalm 138 to 137, and it is likely that it has been set after its predecessor for some reason. We may think that the connection lies in the two psalms involving the praise of Yahweh in the lands of the exile. In 137 the Jews sat down and wept in Babylonia, praying for their ruined city, Jerusalem; in 138 they give thanks for the LORD's lovingkindness in magnifying his word of deliverance *before the [Babylonian] gods.* Things have moved forward. The editor of the Psalter may be thinking that *In the day that I called thou answerest me* refers to the prayers in mourning of 137.1.

Psalm 138.4-8. The same context seems to be implied by the following verses. *All the kings of the earth shall give thee thanks, O LORD, For they have heard the words of thy mouth.* The change from imperfect to perfect suggests that some cognizance of Yahweh has been taken by the Persian kings; nor should this be dismissed as high-flown language, as it is by Gunkel, for our biblical tradition describes three occasions when Yahweh demonstrated his lovingkindness by a 'going up' to Jerusalem, and in each case they were sanctioned by a Persian king, under Sheshbazzar, Nehemiah and Ezra. Cyrus's cylnder and Nehemiah's Testimony are evidence that these traditions are historical; and the same is probably true of Ezra's ascent, since it is unlikely that any considerable group of Jews could 'go up' without official permission. So *the kings of the earth*, Artaxerxes perhaps and his predecessors, *have heard the words of thy mouth*, they have taken seriously the petitions based on the exilic prophecies; and in time it may be expected that, as in Isaiah 52 and 60, they will shut their mouths and come with tribute to the brightness of Zion's rising. Such a pilgrimage seems to be implied by בדרכי in v. 5: *they shall sing in the ways of the LORD, For great is the glory of the LORD.* שׁיר בּ־ would be unique in the meaning 'sing of': rather we should think of the kings joining in the pilgrimage psalms as they proceed along the roads of Yahweh's land towards his Temple. The combination of such a royal procession with the phrase כבוד יהוה (cf. Isa. 60.1) makes it likely that Isaiah 60 is in the psalmist's mind; so again the psalm should be dated in the fifth century.

The suggested translation 'in the ways of the LORD' is made by Eaton.

A couple of chapters before, Third Isaiah had promised God's restoration of the *lowly*: 'For thus saith the *high* (רם) and lofty One...I dwell in the high and holy place with him also that is of a contrite and *lowly* (שׁפל) spirit, to revive the heart of *the lowly ones* (שׁפלים)' (Isa. 57.15), while by contrast there is no peace to the wicked. The recurrence of רם יהוה in Ps. 138.6, alongside the uncommon שׁפל suggests that Third Isaiah is in mind still. The שׁפל to whom he has respect is the humbled Jew of the Exile, who has turned to Yahweh *with all his heart*, with mourning and weeping by the rivers. But not all Jews were so, and God can tell *the haughty* a mile off.

שׁפל, used as a substantive, is found in these two passages and in Prov. 29.23, and see 16.19.

J.A. Emerton, 'Some Alleged Meanings', follows D. Winton Thomas in arguing for a second root ידע, 'to humble'; but (1) it is more natural to say God *knows the haughty from afar* than that he *humbles* them *from afar*, and (2) 'knows' makes a good parallel with יראה, 'sees' (*has respect unto*). The form יֵידָע is irregular: Delitzsch compares Isa. 16.7 ייליל, and Job 24.21, ייטיב.

The psalmist is wholeheartedly thankful for divine deliverance; but his problems are not over—*Though I walk in the midst of trouble...* Dahood thought אלך was not metaphorical, but referred to a king's marching; we may think rather of some such scenario as is portrayed in Nehemiah and Ezra, with the exiles' long march home. *The kings of the earth have hearkened to the words of* the LORD's *mouth,* and have given permission for the ascent; the LORD's *mercy and truth* are clearly in evidence. But there remains the perilous journey home, on roads beset with robbers, disease and wild animals. Nehemiah had an

escort of cavalry sent by the king (Neh. 2.9), but the more religious
Ezra was ashamed to ask for military protection, and put his trust in
God (Ezra 8.21-23), like the author of Psalm 138. The latter also felt
himself to be in peril of his life, for he says תחיני, *thou wilt make me
live*, תושיעני, *shall save me*. He has to go *in the midst of trouble*, in
face of *the wrath of mine enemies*. Perhaps the latter are jealous
enemies in Babylonia, or perhaps plain highwaymen; or they could be
of the type of Sanballat and Tobiah on arrival.

Of one thing the religious man is confident: what Yahweh has begun
he will perfect, bring to completion. He prays in line with the divine
will that God *forsake not the works of thine own hands*—the LORD
has initiated great works, and he has chosen to do it on behalf of the
speaker, בעדי. Third Isaiah speaks of Israel as *the work of my hands*,
מעשה ידי (Isa. 60.21—Isa. 60 again; 64.8), but Psalm 138 has the
plural מעשי, the mighty works of the Restoration. He describes the
divine enterprise once more in the words of the exiles' refrain (Pss.
106.1; 107.1; 118.1, 29; 136 throughout), *Thy mercy, O LORD,
[endureth] for ever*.

Dahood, followed by Allen, renders גמר with 'wreak vengeance', in line with
Ugaritic evidence and LXX; but the verb comes three times elsewhere in the Psalter
meaning 'complete, perform' in addition to 57.3. Emendations of מעשי to מעשה
should be resisted: we have to do with a complex of divine *works* in the Return, not
the healing of a single sick man.

Psalm 138 may thus be seen to justify Kirkpatrick's approach. Worship of Yahweh before the gods, toward his temple from a distance,
suggests an exiled leader in Babylon. That kings have heard Yahweh's
word, which he has magnified above every name, again seems to
imply a setting such as is found in Ezra–Nehemiah. God's covenanted
love, his response to prayer and the use of the exiles' refrain from
Ezra 3.11 confirm the impression that it is the Restoration which is at
issue; as do the repeated echoes of (largely) Third Isaiah—the kings
who will sing of Yahweh's glory on his ways, the exalted God who
regards the lowly. The speaker's labours have only begun, and he may
be thought to have a journey before him, beset with enemies.

The assertion of royal assent (v. 4) limits our choice of a likely setting to the three ascents described in Ezra–Nehemiah, each of which
had the sanction of the Great King. But v. 2 implies that *thy holy
temple* is in existence, and this rules out Sheshbazzar's going up; as do

the repeated references to Third Isaiah. Nor is Nehemiah's ascent a very likely background; Nehemiah seems unaware of Third Isaiah, and the piety of his Testimony, and of the Songs of Ascents which go with it, is more practical than that of [137–]138. This must raise the possibility of a working hypothesis: perhaps 135–150 are a sequence of psalms, just as 105–119 and 120–134 were. Psalms 105–119 were a sequence celebrating the first Return under Sheshbazzar, Zerubbabel and Jeshua; 120-134 were a sequence celebrating the rebuilding of the walls under Nehemiah; 135–150 could be a sequence celebrating the return under Ezra with the establishment of the full Torah. There were 14 psalms, 105–118, for the feast of Passover when the Temple was rebuilt in 516 BCE, with 119 for Pentecost; there were 15 psalms, 120–134, for the feast of Tabernacles when the walls were rebuilt in 445 BCE; and there are 16 psalms, 135–150, for an eight-day festival such as Ezra is said to have presided over in Neh. 8.16-18.

The detail of Psalms 137–138 in this hypothetical final collection seems to favour an Ezra setting. (1) Ezra held a fast before setting forth (Ezra 8.15, 21), as did the community of 137.1. (2) Ezra's fast was held by the river above Ahava, as 137's was by the rivers of Babylon. (3) Ezra went up from Babylon (Ezra 7.6, 8.1), where the community of Psalm 137 lived, whereas Nehemiah had been in Susa. (4) Ezra brought rich gifts for the Jerusalem temple (Ezra 7–8); the psalmist of 138 worshipped towards the Jerusalem temple. (5) Ezra went up with King Artaxerxes' blessing (Ezra 7); 138 speaks of kings having hearkened to Yahweh's word. (6) Ezra went up without military escort 'against the enemy in the way' (Ezra 8.22), trusting in God alone, as 138 knows he must go in the midst of trouble from the wrath of his enemies, trusting in God to save him and keep him alive. (7) Ezra was zealous for the law of Yahweh (Ezra 7.10 and passim); 138 twice speaks of Yahweh's word, his written word, which is not mentioned in Nehemiah's testimony or in Psalms 120–134.

Our knowledge of the historical Ezra is much more limited than of Nehemiah: we can do little more than descry three phases in Ezra's mission. In Ezra 7–8 he leads a considerable body of exiles from Babylon to Jerusalem; in Ezra 9–10 he contends with a contumacious opposition in Judah, and enforces strict rules on intermarriage; in Nehemiah 8 he establishes the developed Torah as known in Babylon as the law for Israel, and symbolizes this with a new style of celebration for Tabernacles. We shall find the same pattern in Psalms

137–150. In 137–138 the psalmist is, in memory, still in Babylon. Psalms 138–145 are Psalms of David, and the speaker is much beset by enemies, while protesting his own purity. Psalms 145–150 are hymns of praise, a suitable climax for a final festal celebration.

PSALM 139

Psalm 139 has had an unfortunate exegetical history. The sense of religious nobility conveyed by the first three-quarters of the psalm has made it a classic of spiritual experience: E. Reuss said it would be among the most beautiful psalms in the Psalter if it had finished at the third strophe (cited by E. Würthwein, 'Erwägungen', p. 170). This has led to a devaluing of vv. 19-22, which were on a less high plane; perhaps they were a later addition by the same author (Schmidt, Gunkel), or at least they are not the main purport of the psalm. Gunkel's influence has been especially baleful. Psalm 139 was a rare thing, an individual's hymn, followed by a brief lament; elements which did not fit its high spiritual tone were emended, and almost all subsequent commentators have followed him in improving the text. A minority have given the last verses their due: Mowinckel saw the psalm as an assertion of the speaker's innocence (*Psalms in Israel's Worship*, II, pp. 74-75), and Eaton says vv. 19-24 are the goal of the psalm, with a national leader beset by fierce enemies. It may be thought that both of these approaches have more to be said for them.

Psalm 139

For the Chief Musician. A Psalm of David.
1   O LORD, thou has searched me, and known *me*.
2   Thou knowest my downsitting and mine uprising,
      Thou understandest my thought afar off.
3   Thou winnowest my path and my lying down,
      And art acquainted with all my ways.
4   For there is not a word in my tongue,
      But, lo, O LORD, thou knowest it altogether.
5   Thou hast beset me behind and before,
      And laid thine hand upon me.
6   *Such* knowledge is too wonderful for me;
      It is high, I cannot attain unto it.

7   Whither shall I go from thy spirit?
Or whither shall I flee from thy presence?

8   If I ascend up into heaven, thou art there:
If I make my bed in Sheol, thou art there.

9   If I take the wings of the morning,
And dwell in the uttermost parts of the sea;

10   Even there shall thy hand lead me,
And thy right hand shall hold me.

11   If I say, Surely the darkness shall cover me,
Then the night shall be light about me;

12   Even the darkness hideth not from thee,
But the night shineth as the day;
The darkness and light are both alike *[to thee]*.

13   For thou hast formed my reins:
Thou hast knit me together in my mother's womb.

14   I will give thanks unto thee, for I have been set apart for
a fearful destiny (נוראות נפליתי):
Wonderful are thy works;
And that my soul knoweth right well.

15   My frame was not hidden from thee,
When I was made in secret,
And curiously wrought in the lowest parts of the earth.

16   Thine eyes did see my unperfect substance,
And in thy book they were all written,
Even the days that were ordained,
When as yet there was none of them.

17   How precious also are thy thoughts unto me, O God!
How great is the sum of them!

18   If I should count them, they are more in number than the sand:
When I awake, I am still with thee.

19   Oh that thou wouldest slay the wicked man (רשע), O God—
Depart from me therefore, ye men of blood (אנשי דמים)—

20   Who utters thy name for his purposes (אשר יאמרך למזמה,
pointing יֹאמְרֻךָ: for יֹאמְרֻךָ);
He has taken thy cities for vanity (נשא לשוא עריך, pointing נָשָׂא for נָשֻׂא).

21   Do not I hate them, O LORD, that hate thee?
And do not I loathe those that rise up against thee?

22   I hate them with a perfect hatred:
I count them mine enemies.

23   Search me, O God, and know my heart:
Try me, and know my thoughts.

24   And see if there be any way of grief in me,
And lead me in the way everlasting.

If we steadfastly try to make sense of the MT, which as usual is the more difficult text, two things emerge: 139 is an evening psalm, and it has an internal political orientation.

The evening setting comes through from the beginning. *Yahweh knows* my *settling down* (שׁבתי, Holman 'Analysis', pp. 41-43) *and my getting up* (קומי), at night and in the morning (v. 2); he *winnows my path and my lying down* (רבעי, v. 3). When the psalmist considers how to escape the divine spirit, he thinks, *If I make my bed* (אציעה) *in Sheol…* (v. 8); why should he need a bed in Sheol if it is not in the night? Or he might as the night ends *take the wings of the morning* (v. 9). But his main hope would be the darkness now drawing on: *If I say, Surely the darkness shall cover me, Then the night shall be light about me. Even the darkness hideth not from thee, But the night shineth as the day*. The passage ends כחשׁיכה כאורה, *Like darkness like light*: the Hebrew does not add RVmg's pious addition, ['to thee']—the psalmist cannot get away in the night, dark and light are the same. The accumulation of these references to lying down, bed and darkness are sufficient to make an evening setting likely; but the matter is made plain by v. 18b, *When I awake, I am still with thee* (or perhaps, *I shall be still with thee*, Hebrew, עודי עמך). More than once the psalmist makes an excursus, here vv. 13-18a on the wonder of God's creation of him, later in v. 19b and vv. 19-22; v. 18b completes the thought of vv. 7-12. He cannot flee in the night the absolute paternal care That will not leave him, but prevents him everywhere; when he awakes in the morning, God will still be at his side. Gunkel, and even Rashi, destroyed the evidence by revocalizing.

MT has הֱקִיצֹתִי, *I have awoken*; Gunkel proposed הֲקִצֹּתִי, 'I come to the end'. Allen notes that this requires the postulating of a second stem קצץ as a hiphil denominative from קץ.

An even more important removal of the evidence is the frequent rejection of עריך in v. 20: Gunkel says it is meaningless, and so it is if the psalm must be the hymn of a religious individual, with unfortunate slipping of standard towards the end. The psalmist is up against *men of blood* (אנשׁי דמים), violent men who are part of his community, because he can say, *Depart from me!* If we take the consonants literally, the following clause, *Who says thee for a purpose*, suggests that the wicked man worships Yahweh with his lips (either *he addresses thee*, or *he speaks of thee*), but has intentions (מזמה, usually wicked intentions or devices) of his own. The speaker wishes *that thou would-est slay the wicked man* (רשע, sing.) in v. 19a, and he again uses the singular consonants in v. 20b, following his excursus into the plural for the men of blood. *The wicked man* has *taken* God's *cities for vanity* (נשׂא לשׁוא עריך); he is the governor of Judaea, or such, and he has permitted, or encouraged, the breaking of the divine law. He and his associates are nominally Yahweh worshippers, but their heart is not right with God. The psalmist asks to be examined *if there be any way of grief in* him, that is, any lapse from obedience to God's revealed will; the suggestion is that such *ways* are endemic among the *men of blood*.

MT has the vocalization יֹאמְרֻךָ and נָשֻׂא; it looks as if the consonants followed the singular רשׁע in v. 19a. and a half-hearted attempt has been made to fit with the plural of v. 19b, with two ˙s in place of ˙s: v. 19b will thus be a brief parenthesis, an apostrophe. נשׂא לשׁוא is used of 'taking God's name for vanity' in the third commandment (Exod. 20.7), and of 'lifting one's soul to vanity' in Ps. 24.4. It is probable that both of these passsages refer to idolatry, as שׁוא does in other contexts (cf. Goulder, *Asaph*, p. 296). The principal difficulty is עריך, understood by LXX as 'thy cities' (τὰς πόλεις σου), and by Aquila, Symmachus, Jerome and the Targum as 'thy enemies': ער means 'enemy' at 1 Sam. 28.16 and Sir. (Heb.) 37.5, 47.7. The latter, commended by Delitzsch and Allen, involves a cumbrous syntax: 'they have lifted [their voice] to vanity [as] thine enemies' (Allen), or 'lift [themselves] up [against thee] for vanity, thine enemies' (RVmg). But a less strained sense is available with *thy cities* as object. Jerusalem is often a symbol for the people of Israel in their relation to God/idols, for example, Isa. 1.21, 'How is the faithful city become an harlot!'; we may think that Psalm 139 is written at a time when Jerusalem is still only partially rebuilt, as in the fifth century, and most Jews live in *thy towns* around. To *take thy towns for vanity* will then mean to lead God's people into false religion; cf. H. Junker, 'Einige Rätsel'. The difficulty of the syntax with 'enemies', and the inappropriateness of 'cities' to standard interpretations of the psalm, have led to unenthusiastic changes of the text. An emendation to שׁמך here is a long way from the MT, and would leave the present consonants unexplained. Gunkel suggests עליך, 'rise falsely against you'.

A setting for the psalm then becomes apparent. The speaker is a reformist Jewish leader, embattled against the incumbent authority, whom he sees as determined to frustrate the divine will and impose an alien religious law on the cities of the land. He protests his own purity of life, which Yahweh has known through and through. Whatever he did, he could never escape from Yahweh, who would guide his feet and hold him by the hand. Yahweh has in fact formed him from before his birth, and set him apart for his vocation. The law-breaking governor and his men are God's enemies, and hence his own enemies, and he prays for their death. He closes with a prayer that God will search his every thought, and finding nothing amiss will guide him on the ordained road to the future. He is a man in some such situation as Jeremiah found himself in the seventh century, or Ezra in the fifth; the many Aramaisms in the text suggest the later date.

E. Würthwein, 'Erwägungen', expounded a suggestion of A. Bentzen that the psalmist had been falsely accused by his enemies of idolatry (an alternative translation of עצב, v. 24): he protests his innocence (cf. Mowinckel), and prays for their destruction. It is possible that the *searching* took the form of an ordeal. This suggestion has been quite widely taken up, especially by Kraus. But quite apart from its treatment of the text (see above, p. 241), it gives little force to the second and third sections of the psalm; and in Kraus's exposition depends on parallels with other psalms like 26, which are dubiously interpreted as prayers of an individual, at the expense of similar thinking in Jeremiah. Eaton properly highlights the personal language as fitted to a national leader; but his insistence on the king as speaker seems to go against the grain of the late language.

Psalm 139.1-6. The psalm is the second of a sequence, 138–145, *For David*: the continual reference to *trouble* and *enemies* recalls the David psalms of 51–72 and 3–41, with a psalm of praise (145) to close. The call for Yahweh to try his heart, together with a disavowal of the wicked, recalls Psalm 26 especially; there are *men of blood* in 55.24 and a *book* of destiny at 56.9. The more imperilled tone may account for the מזמור of 139–143 (משכיל in the case of 142). למנצח, *For the Chief Musician*, prefaces Psalms 139 and 140, and is probably connected with the *Selah*'s in the latter psalm (*q.v.*).

The psalm was written as a whole: it begins with an assertion of Yahweh's *searching* and *knowing* the singer's whole life (vv. 1, 2a), and ends with a prayer for the *searching* and *knowing* to continue (v. 23); God's hand will *lead* him (vv. 10, 24) *in the way* (vv. 3, 24). The divine gaze penetrates every action and every word, from his *settling* and *lying down* at night to his *uprising* in the morning. The mention of *my path* (Hebrew ארחי, perhaps an infinitive construct, 'my journeying', like its pair, ורבעי [Holman, 'Analysis', pp. 43-44; Anderson]), and *all my ways*, may suggest travelling, as in an *aliya*, but the words are often a metaphor for any activities. God *knows completely* every *word in my tongue*. Everything he says and does is open to Yahweh, and all is in accordance with his Law; he is pure.

God has *beset* him *behind and before,* like a besieging army, as he did with Job (Job 19.8); he has laid his hand on him, like a magistrate restraining someone from wrongdoing (Job 9.33). He has never been able to go wrong. Like Job he marvels at the divine providence (Job 42.3). In v. 19 the word for *God* is אלוה, as often in Job. The particular phrases, no less than God's profound awareness of his purity of life (Job 10.7 and *passim*), recall the book of Job.

But Psalm 139 is unlike Job in that the speaker does not feel God's hand upon him to be in the least hostile (*contra* Weiser). Rather he is like Jeremiah: 'But *thou, O LORD, knowest me; thou seest* me, and *triest* mine heart toward thee' (12.3), 'I *the LORD search* the heart, I *try the reins*' (17.10). The same protestation of purity of heart comes in Jer. 11.20 and 20.12. Like the prophet, the psalmist knows himself to be under continuous divine scrutiny, and he knows that he is a good man. He has enemies within the community, also like the prophet, because he is God's spokesman, demanding a full righteousness.

Aramaic words include רע, 'thought, aspiration', which occurs only here and in v. 17 in the Hebrew Bible; and רבע, 'to lie down', a hapax. ל in v. 2b may signal an accusative as in Aramaic; compare 135.11, 136.19-20. God's *laying his hand* in v. 5b is in restraint, as in v. 5a, not in blessing (Gen. 48.14, 17; *contra* Anderson).

Psalm 139.7-12. The presence of the All-Seeing Eye is not felt to be oppressive: rather *such knowledge is wonderful.* The speaker could not get away from it in *heaven* above or *in Sheol* beneath. The Dawn (שחר) had been a Canaanite god, and is still thought of as a lesser power in heaven, rising in the east and flying westwards; even if he might *take its wings* as night ended, and settle beyond Gibraltar, God would still be there to *lead* him and to *hold* him by the hand. There is no thought of escape from a Hound of Heaven, as in the book of Jonah; Hopkins's 'O mastering me God' is far from his mind. God has a destiny for him in which he will lead him and hold him, and which he is entirely willing to fulfil. Day and night, waking and sleeping, God is with him unceasingly.

Again there are echoes of the prophetic vocation. Jeremiah wrote, 'Am I a God at hand, saith the LORD, and not a God *afar off* (מרחק)? Can any hide himself in secret places that I cannot *see* him?' (23.23-24). The thought of ascending to heaven or going down to Sheol to escape God is a standard prophetic conceit (Amos 9.2). It comes in Job 26.6, and the Dawn is personified with 'eyelids' in Job 3.9 and

41.18, though these are no more taken literally than her rosy fingers by Homer.

Weiser is not untypical in seeing the psalm as a testimony to religious experience; but the experience is of a particular kind. Allen says helpfully, 'The psalmist is not engaged in a quiet reverie on a divine attribute... A polemical element is implicit from the outset' (*Psalms 101–150*, p. 261). He is conscious of two things in relation to God. First God knows him totally, and knows that he is dedicated to God's will, that is his Torah: *search* as he may, he will find no *way of grief* in him. He is pure. Secondly, God has a destiny for him, a vocation in which he will be led and sustained, and from which there is no escape even if he wished such. So the religion of the psalm is not the soul's silent awareness of God in prayer. It is the Jewish religion with its optimistic *mens conscia recti* so offensive to the disciples of St Augustine; and it is a providentialist faith open to the doubts of the sophisticated. Never mind: this is the religion that has changed the course of history.

A further Aramaism is אסק in v. 8, from סלק. With most exegetes I have followed what seems the natural division of the psalm into four six-verse units: for a more complex rhetorical analysis see Holman, 'Analysis' (1970) and 'Structure' (1971), and comments by Allen.

Psalm 139.13-18. A third section of the psalm celebrates the wonder of the psalmist's *forming*, קנית, by God, his *knitting together*, סכך, *in his mother's womb*. But the force of this thanksgiving (v. 14a) is lost if we render with RV and commentators generally, *I am fearfully and wonderfully made*. MT has נוראות נפליתי; Hebrew has two distinct roots פלא, niphal 'to be wonderful', and פלה, niphal 'to be distinct, separate'. With no א but a י, נפליתי is the niph. of the second, and means *I have been separated*. נוראות, usually taken adverbially, 'awesomely', should be understood as an adverbial phrase, '[for] awesome things, for an awesome destiny'. The assonance of the two roots suggests the second hemistich, מעשיך נפלאים, *wonderful are thy doings*; the psalmist adds, *And that my soul knoweth right well*—he has already experienced Yahweh's providential care in fulfilling his vocation hitherto.

The niphal of פלה occurs in Exod. 33.16 meaning 'be separated'; the more common hiphil, 'to make separate, set apart', comes in Exod. 8.18, 9.4, 11.7;

Ps. 4.4, 17.7. Our passage is the only other use. Jewish tradition supports *wonderfully made*, with the exception of Yephet Ben Eli, 'because you accomplish awesome deeds from the moment when I was separated [that is, from the womb]'. (I am grateful to Dr Gerard Norton for this reference.)

Again there is a parallel in Jeremiah: 'Before I formed thee *in the belly* I *knew* thee, and before thou camest forth out of the womb I sanctified thee' (Jer. 1.5). The prophet's predestination took place before he was born, in the womb; and indeed even before that. Yahweh sanctified him, set him apart, right from the beginning. We have the same two-part pre-destiny in Ps. 139.13-18. In vv. 13-14 the thought is of the psalmist's formation in his mother's womb; but in vv. 15-16 it moves back to a pre-embryonic stage, when his skeleton (עצמי) was curiously wrought in the lowest parts of the earth, when God saw his raw substance (גלמי), and his days to come were written by the moving finger in heaven. The Jews knew that embryos grew from sexual union; but they also saw the dead go back to dust, and held a second belief of human origins (Gen. 2.7, 3.19). Here, as less obviously in Jer. 1.5, the two explanations are held side by side, unreconciled. The same dissonance is found in Job 10.8-11. In 10.8-9 the prophet was fashioned as clay, and will go back to dust, as in Gen. 2-3; in v. 11 he is clothed with skin and flesh, and knit together (סככ) with bones and sinews, presumably in the womb; in v. 10 some attempt is made at reconciliation, 'Hast thou not poured me out as milk, And curdled me like cheese?' Or in Job 1.21, 'Naked came I out of my mother's womb, and naked shall I return thither': *thither?*

The notion of fixed *days* for human destinies is also found in Job. At 14.5 'his days are determined, the number of his months is with thee', and in ch. 3 the day of his birth is cursed for extinction. A book in which these things are pre-recorded is a natural extension of the idea. David's wanderings and tears were thought to be pre-written in God's book in Ps. 56.9, and there is a more general book of life for the faithful in Ps. 69.29 and elsewhere. But what makes *God's thoughts*, inscribed so, *precious* to the psalmist is their relevance to himself. It is overwhelming to think of the complexity of the divine purposes, so *great in sum, more in number than the sand*. But they are not the subject of meditation *in vacuo*: when the night is over and *I awake, I am still with thee*. He has been set apart for a crucial role in these purposes, and he is going to have to contend with enemies determined to frustrate them.

Psalm 139.19-22. With v. 19 the high calling of the pure-hearted reformer descends to the realities of a corrupt society. There is a *wicked man* (רשע), with an armed retinue, *men of blood*; who claims to be a Yahweh-worshipper; though in fact *he utters thy name for his purposes* (למזמה), *he takes thy cities for vanity*—he is governor of the province, and he is administering it on principles which fall well short of the *halaka* known as Torah to the psalmist. Such people are *thine enemies*, and need *slaying*; as they evidently *hate Yahweh and rise up against* him, his loyal follower naturally *hates them* too, and *loathes them with a perfect* (not self-regarding) *hatred* as his own enemies.

Psalm 139.23-24. The psalmist closes on a more positive note, as is normal. He is confident in his righteousness, and prays for a final *searching* and *trying*; he knows that his *thoughts* will pass muster, and that God will *see no way of grief in* him. What he really wants is divine guidance, to be *led*. There is a *way of permanence,* דרך עולם, the high road of history which God has planned ahead in his book; and that is where the speaker wishes to set his feet.

The parallel with Jeremiah continues to the end: we may cite Jer. 12.1-3, 'Wherefore doth *the way* of *the wicked* prosper?...But thou, *O LORD, knowest me; thou seest me and triest my heart* toward thee: pull them out like sheep for the slaughter, and sanctify them for the day of slaughter'. Jeremiah has all four themes of Psalm 139: God's knowledge of his purity, the inescapable eye of Yahweh, his preordaining of his servant to a frightening vocation, and his prayer for the slaughter of the wicked. God's enemies were indeed Jeremiah's enemies; only the prophet's prayer was probably more effective than the psalmist's—Hananiah the son of Azzur actually did die (Jer. 28.17).

We have a detailed contemporary account of Nehemiah's struggle with God's enemies, and some old traditions of the enemies faced by the first returning exiles. For Ezra we are less well placed. All we have is an account of his journey to Jerusalem (Ezra 7–8), the story of his ban on foreign intermarriage (Ezra 9–10), and his celebration of the New Year/Tabernacles ritual as found in the Holiness code in Leviticus 23 (Neh. 8). The impression given is that he carried all before him without significant opposition; and no doubt that is the impression we are supposed to receive. But there are hints that all was not quite so easy. The first to be named as having married strange women are sons of the priests, 'of the sons of Jeshua the son of Jozadak, and his brethren, Maaseiah, and Eliezer, and Jarib, and Gedaliah' (Ezra 10.19). Joshua ben Jozadak is implied to be the national leader in Zechariah 3 and 6, and Psalm 110 seems to hail him as 'a priest for ever after the order of Melchizedek' (see above, pp. 147-51); and his family succeeded him as rulers of the community after him (Neh. 12.9-10). Nor is it at all likely that so powerful a clan would meekly give way to a dogmatic 'Johnny-come-lately', resigning their position of national leadership and divorcing their wives. A further suspicious feature of the tale is that not only [some] of Jeshua's sons but also no less than four of his brothers have married Gentile women; attractive Jewish girls certainly seem to have been in short supply.

The brief account masks a power struggle of which the reality is quite likely evidenced in Psalms 139–145. One of Jeshua's descendants—Johanan perhaps (Neh. 12.22)—was high priest and administrator of the little Judaean enclave, his power resting in part on Persian sanction, and in practice on the prestige of his family and on an armed guard, the *men of blood*. They maintained traditional Yahwism as handed down in the Deuteronomistic corpus, though there may have been one or two lapses into foreign marriage, as encouraged by the authors of Ruth and [later] the Song of Songs. Ezra (if it was he) came with the more developed Priestly and Holiness traditions, in the confidence and zeal of a Jeremiah. The high priest was a *wicked man*, like the Wicked Priest in the Qumran documents, because he did not observe the true Law. He *uttered God's name for his own purposes, and* seduced God's *towns into vanity.* He is thus God's enemy, and so will be Ezra's. As emerges from later psalms, this was but the beginning of birth-pangs. But in the end the reformers won, and the losing hierarchy were stigmatized as law-breakers with strange wives, virtually the lot of them; the man of God had them dismiss these temptresses and expiate their sin with a guilt offering.

PSALM 140

Kirkpatrick noted a number of features which held Psalms 140–143 together. They were psalms *of David*, with David-type heading notes like מזמור, or משכיל, with the occasional סלה in the text, even with a 'historical' note for 142—all elements of the David collections in Books I and II, but hardly present elsewhere. They shared a good number of phrases, even whole verses, in common. They had a common situation with enemies conspiring to hunt the psalmist down, and pleas to Yahweh not to permit this. Kirkpatrick inferred a common author, and in view of a number of post-biblical words saw the collection as set in the period of postexilic disorder; the author had drawn on themes from the two old David collections to express his own trials.

Gunkel saw a different perspective on the group. They were laments of an individual, and Gunkel thought it noteworthy that there is no mention of his sickness. The enemies are a stock feature of such psalms. The Individual Lament theory sometimes sees the speaker as a target for widespread slander (Weiser), or as being falsely accused (Schmidt, Kraus, Anderson, Allen). The latter hypothesis may extend to some form of cultic ordeal to reveal Yahweh's judgment, though it might be thought that few accusers would be willing to submit to a shower of red hot coals, followed by a run through a trench of fire, as Schmidt suggested.

The Individual Lament view seemed to Birkeland, *Feinde*, pp. 74-76, as weak in its explanation of the references to *battle* and *arms* in vv. 3, 8, and he takes the psalm rather to be a communal lament, with the speaker a national leader. In this he is followed by Mowinckel, *Psalms in Israel's Worship*, I, p. 220, and Eaton, *Kingship*, pp. 63-64. The psalmist addresses God as 'my God', an expression apparently reserved for kings, priests and prophets, and gives thanks for personal preservation in battle; and has great confidence that his prayer will be heard.

Kirkpatrick's position can be combined with Eaton's, and can be further refined. The *battle* and *arms* in vv. 3, 8, imply something more than false accusations; but it is the poisonous talk of the evil and violent men which is the first concern, and suggests that they come from the psalmist's own community, like the men of blood in 139.19. It is not likely that a sick or persecuted individual would have thought it suitable to take over language attributed to the greatest of Israel's kings; rather such usage would be suited to a new aspiring national leader. But the references to earlier psalms in 140 are heavily concentrated on the second David collection (51–72), the Prayers of David (72.20), where the king's enemies were for ever sharpening their tongues against him and setting traps for him. Now Psalm 139 was also a *Psalm of David* with conspiring enemies, with *men of blood*, as in 55.24, *rising up against* him as in 59.2, and the psalmist's future written in God's *book* as in 56.9. So the sequence may be taken to begin with 139, not 140.

Psalm 140

1   For the Chief Musician. A Psalm of David.
2   Deliver me, O LORD, from the evil man;
    Preserve me from the violent man:
3   Which imagine mischiefs in their heart:
    Continually do they stir up battles (מלחמות).
4   They have sharpened their tongue like a serpent;
    Adders' poison is under their lips.   [Selah
5   Keep me, O LORD, from the hands of the wicked;
    Preserve me from the violent man:
    Who have purposed to thrust down my steps.
6   The proud have hid a snare for me, [see below]
    And have spread cords as a net;
    By the way side they have set gins for me.   [Selah
7   I said unto the LORD, Thou art my God:
    Give ear unto the voice of my supplications, O LORD.
8   O GOD the Lord, the strength of my salvation,
    Thou hast covered my head in the day of arms (נשק).
9   Grant not, O LORD, the desires of the wicked;
    Further not his evil devices;
    That they exalt themselves (ירומו).   [Selah
10 As for the head of those that compassed me about (מסבי),
    Let the mischief of their own lips cover them.

11   Let burning coals fall upon them, with fire (באש):
      Let them be cast into floods, that they rise not up again.
12   The man of tongue shall not be established in the land (בארץ):
      Evil shall hunt the violent man to overthrow him.
13   I know that the LORD will maintain the cause of the afflicted,
      And the right of the needy.
14   Surely the righteous shall give thanks unto thy name:
      The upright shall dwell in thy presence.

We do not learn much more about the psalmist's rivals than we did from 139. There seems to be an *evil man* (איש רע, v. 2), a *wicked man* (רשע) with *his evil devices* (זממו, v. 9), *a man of tongue* (איש לשון, v. 12), supported by *men of violence* (איש חמסים, vv. 2, 5, followed by plural verbs; v. 12). In 139.19-20 there was a רשע who addressed Yahweh for his מזמה, supported by אנשי דמים. Here *they imagine mischiefs in their heart, they have sharpened their tongue, Adders' poison is under their lips*, and the psalmist's prayer is *Let the mischief of their own lips cover them*. In other words they do not like the psalmist and his policies, and have sensibly been taking counsel together to resist him. Thus far the situation might be compared to a normal election in a modern democracy; one party leader might feel the same about the other's staff—indeed, some of the latter's more religious supporters might well be using Psalm 140 at their daily Prayer Meetings.

It is a contested question how much more than this is going on. There are three references to *violent men*, and in v. 5 they *have purposed to thrust aside my steps*. We hear of *a snare, cords, a net* and *gins* (v. 6), and it is difficult to think that all these images stand for no more than scheming in committee rooms. Even in moments of deepest anguish we cannot see Republicans calling down on Democrats such fate as is voiced in vv. 10-11. Furthermore the mention of *battles* (מלחמות, v. 3), and of *covering/protecting my head in the day of arms* (נשק, v. 8), suggests real violence. The situation is not quite as gentlemanly as a 1996 U.S. Election: it is more like the days when guns were used for Martin Luther King and the Kennedy brothers—there were *men of blood* then. It may perhaps be ventured as a general rule that when a group's legitimating dogma is threatened, like White Supremacy or the Deuteronomic Torah, resistance to change will go beyond words.

Psalm 140.1-4. In this psalm there are echoes of the Psalms of David, Psalms 52–71, in almost every verse; and 140 is a מזמור, a lament accompanied by strings like Psalms 62, 63 and 64. In the Psalms of Asaph there was a high correlation between the occurrence of למנצח in the Heading and סלה in the text (Goulder, *Asaph*, pp. 82-83), and we find the same here. *For the Chief Musician* is followed by three *Selah*s, after vv. 4, 6, 9. I suggested in each of my previous *Studies in the Psalter* that 'Selah' indicated a break in the psalm (διάψαλμα), in which a cantor (מנצח) lifted up (סלל) his voice to chant a relevant narrative; for instance, the Selah in 'Glorious things are spoken of thee, O city of God. Selah' (87.4) indicates that at this point the foundation legend, the 'glorious things', of the city of God were recited in a cantillation. The intrusion of Selahs enables the victor of an intra-community quarrel to have his version of events enshrined in the liturgy; but with time these trivia cease to interest the worshippers, and drop away. There are Selahs in Psalm 140 because, unlike 139, the psalm reflects an actual violent incident, as becomes clear.

The psalm opens with an appeal to Yahweh for deliverance, like 59.2. The נ has been retained unassimilated in תנצרני as in 61.8. The enemies *stir up battles* as in 56.7, 59.4 (יגורו in each case). They *have sharpened their tongue* as in 52.3, 64.4, see also 55.22, 57.5; their slanders are compared to *a serpent's poison*, as in 58.5. While some of these themes are to be found in Book I, all are concentrated here in the Prayers of David, and suggest a continuity with the references to the same group of psalms noted above in 139.

There are three Selahs in the psalm, as there are several in Psalm 55 or 59, and these correspond with the movement of the text. Verses 2-4 are entirely concerned with the plotting: the enemy *imagine mischiefs in their heart, gather themselves together for battles,* and *sharpen their tongue.* In vv. 5-6 the plots are put into action: they *purpose to thrust aside my steps, hide a snare, spread a net* and *set gins.* In vv. 7-9 their devices are foiled: *Yahweh* proves himself *the strength of my salvation,* and *covers my head in the day of arms.* After the third Selah the psalmist turns to cursing the men of violence, and to asserting confidently Yahweh's support of the righteous. So we may think that the Selah after v. 4 gave some account of the scheming of *the evil man* and his supporters, like the scheming of Absalom and Ahitophel in 2 Sam. 15.7-12.

Verse 2. Most critics take both אדם רע and איש חמסים as collectives, and the latter must so be, with plural verbs following; but Kirkpatrick takes the former to be an individual, as is suggested by singular verbs in vv. 9, 12, and as is the case in 139.19-20. *Verse 3.* Again יָגוּרוּ is commonly repointed יְגָרוּ from גרה, 'stir up': this meaning is supported by LXX, the Syriac and Targums, and gives sense to the context. It is unclear what meaning should be given to גור: it occurs in the same form, יָגוּרוּ, at 56.7, 59.4, where RV renders 'they gather themselves'; BDB and RVmg translate our text 'they stir up'; *DCH* gives 'attack', which does not fit with ירומו. But 140's heavy dependence on the Prayers of David suggests that our psalmist has taken יגורו over from 56.7 and 59.4, both of which imply ambushes. The following *battles* suggests that he thought it meant 'stir up': compare notes below on ימיטו, ירומו.

Psalm 140.5-6. After the first Selah the psalmist resumes with a virtual duplicate of v. 2; but this time the enemy has *spread a net to thrust aside his steps*, just as he prepared a net for the steps of David in 57.7, and he has *hidden a snare* and *set gins*, just as he hid gins in 64.6. The imagery of trapping is common in the Prayers of David, and there are a snare and gins at 69.23. But there are also echoes of Psalm 18, where there are *cords* of death and Sheol (vv. 5-6), and *burning coals* (v. 9).

In view of what is to come in the following section it is a mistake to reduce all this language to metaphor. What has happened is an ambush. The authorities, spoken of as גאים, *the proud*, have had enough of the pretensions of the arrogant newcomer with his claims of a higher Law; they have a party of armed men waiting *by the wayside* for him and his friends. Traps for animals are not set by the wayside (ליד־מעגל), but in the path itself, or they would never catch anything; it is ambushes for cocky critics that are set behind the rocks or the bushes, beside the path. It is not said, as it often is in 52–71 that they sought after the speaker's life; they are said to be *men of violence, who have purposed to overthrow my steps*—they were merely intending to beat him up. Perhaps the house of Jozadak were not above a little rough stuff to teach the opposition a lesson, but we need not think they would descend to murder. So the second Selah will have revealed the disposition of their forces.

RV renders, *The proud have hid a snare for me, and cords*; but וחבלים is unnatural after לי, and almost all critics wish to emend. But the חבלים come in Psalm 18, and should be retained; perhaps they are a late thought by the author when he thought of the *burning coals*. My translation involves moving the stop from מעגל.

Psalm 140.7-9. As David prayed, Thou art my God (אלי אתה, 63.2), so prayed our psalmist (*I said*) in the hour of the attack, *Thou art my God: Give ear unto the voice of my supplications*. The latter words almost reproduce the Davidic 28.2, and God as *the strength of my salvation* is similar to 18.3 and 62.3,7. In the event the providential hand which oversaw David's trials was in evidence here too; for even if the speaker received a few bruises, God *covered his head in the day of arms*. Perhaps the נשק were no more than clubs and staves; but in any case he has emerged without serious damage. He prays sensibly that any renewal of the assault—*the desires of the wicked man, his evil devices*—be frustrated. So the third Selah will have described the failure of the ambush.

The loose ירומו before the Selah is widely suspected of displacement; or perhaps אל has dropped out. But again we should look to the Prayers of David before altering the MT. In 66.7 the *qere* and many MSS of the *kethib* read ירומו, where also it is followed by Selah, 'Let not the rebellious *exalt themselves*'; the psalmist has taken the expression over to follow זממו, *his evil devices that they exalt themselves*. He has done a similar thing with יגורו in v. 3, and ימוטו in v. 11.

Psalm 140.10-12. David had turned on occasion from his complaint to a curse on his foes (58.7-10; 69.23-29), and so now does his successor. The tale of the ambush is told: now for a little *talio*. They tried to hit his *head*: so *As for the head of those who encircled me* (מְסִבָּי), *Let the mischief of their own lips cover them*. The ambushers will have surrounded him, and planned to lay him low; so now let just such violence fall on their own head. In 18.8-16 God delivered his anointed in a storm: 'the Most High uttered his voice; Hailstones and *coals of fire* (גחלי אש)...the channels of waters appeared, And the foundations of the world were laid bare' (18.14, 16). So what could be more suitable to be toppled on to the heads of the assailants than a load of *burning coals with fire* (גחלים באש), followed by drowning in the subterranean *floods*? The slightly surprising ימיטו, 'let them cause to totter', is taken over, like so much else, from the Prayers of David: 55.4, 'they cast (ימיטו, "topple") iniquity upon me'.

So much for the lewd fellows of the baser sort who had carried out the attack: but what about the *man of tongue, the violent man* who had master-minded it? Those who have faith in divine justice are assured that he *shall not be established in the land*: he will not be high priest and governor much longer. *Evil shall hunt him in double time* (למדחפת): God will see him off before long by one means or another.

The Hebrew is difficult in these verses, partly through the use of *hapaxes*, partly from the importation of words from earlier psalms in different contexts. *Verse 11.* Delitzsch took the hiphil ימיטו to indicate a suppressed subject—'Let [the angels] cause coals to fall...' Allen defends MT in the light of LXX πεσοῦνται, Syriac, and post-biblical hithpolel, 'sink'; but the fundamental reason for using the word is its occurrence—identically as first word of the verse—in 55.4. Dahood explains גחלים באש as linked by a ב *comitatus*, in line with LXX^A ἐν πυρί ['A Sea of Troubles', p. 607 n. 10]. מחמרות is a *hapax*, but is found in Ugaritic texts meaning 'watery depths'; the combination with coals of fire in Psalm 18 is striking. The post-biblical/ Aramaic דחף, 'to push, thrust', suggests that the *hapax* מדחפת means a forced march.

Psalm 140.13-14. It was a long tradition to end a psalm on a more positive note; and in particular the curses of 69.23-29 were followed by 'But I am *afflicted* (עני)...the LORD heareth the *needy* (אביון)' (69.30, 34). So does our psalmist *know that the LORD will maintain the cause of the* עני, *and the right of the* אביון. The tradition of David's afflictions and lack of resources during Absalom's rebellion seems to be all too clearly mirrored in the powerlessness and physical beating endured by his successor. David ended Psalm 56, '*I know* (ידעתי) that God is for me...That I may walk *before* God' (56.10-14); and similarly closed 64 with v. 11, 'The *righteous* shall be glad in the LORD...And all the *upright* in heart shall glory'. 61.8 also boasted that the king '*shall dwell* (ישב) *before* God for ever'. So does our psalm end, *The righteous shall give thanks unto thy name, And the upright shall dwell in thy presence.* At the moment worship in the Temple is in other hands; but the time is coming soon when the reformers will take over the running of the liturgy from them, in perpetuity. The wording is more meaningful, and more menacing, that the normal exegeses allow.

PSALM 141

With Psalm 141 we move on to a development in the situation adum-
brated in 139 and 140. In 140.8 the psalmist prayed, 'Give ear unto
the voice of my supplications'; at 141.1, *Give ear unto my voice*. At
140.6 the proud had hidden a snare for him, spreading a net and setting gins; at 141.9 he prays, *Keep me from the snare which they have
laid for me, And from the gins of the workers of iniquity: Let the
wicked fall into his own nets together.* The last colon echoes the curse
of 140.10, 'Let the mischief of their own lips cover them'. The rare
combination יהוה אדני comes in 140.8 and 141.8. But for all the similarities, things are not quite the same: the text reveals a complex of
new incidents.

Commentators agree in finding vv. 5-7 'difficult'. Perhaps the psalm is composed
from pieces of psalms going back to the days of Absalom (Delitzsch, Jacquet); or the
three mysterious verses could have been inserted from a quite different context
(Kirkpatrick). To Gunkel the psalm is a straightforward Individual Lament, but the
price is high, more than 20 emendations; and such a line is taken also by Kraus,
Anderson and Allen. Kraus thinks of Torah piety, and Anderson entitles the psalm,
'The Danger of Bad Company'. Other more imaginative scenarios are proposed.
Eaton, *Kingship*, pp. 84-85, sees Psalm 141 as the prayer of a king whose forces
have been fighting the Edomites (at סלע); Dahood thinks of Israelites exiled to
Phoenicia after 722 BCE, in view of the supposed Phoenician turns of language. No
one can do without serious changes to MT's 'corrupt' text. But such draconian solutions are not necessary: we may form a reasonable conjecture of what has happened
from the MT against the background that has already emerged from the preceding
psalms.

When Ezra came to Jerusalem, he found a varied reaction to his
reformist proposals. The princes (שרים), according to Ezra 9.1-2,
came reporting the widespread taking of foreign wives, especially by
the 'princes and deputies' (השרים והסגנים), including the priests and
Levites; and Ezra 10.18 gives the first of these as the family of Jeshua
ben Jozadak. We may have general confidence in the picture presented,

even if the history has been artificially compressed into the intermarriage issue. Any reformer from Babylon would find resistance
from vested priestly interests; and no reformer from Babylon could
have been successful without enlisting some support from influential
resident notables.

The text of Psalm 141 suggests that three things have happened
which have not been recorded by the compiler of Ezra (to whom
Jeshua ben Jozadak is the hero of chs. 3–6). (1) The sympathetic
princes have delivered a sharp warning to the psalmist, *smiting* him,
reproving him; and he has fully appreciated this as *lovingkindness, oil
upon the head* (v. 5). They told him to be careful: his rash claims for
the Priestly and Holiness codes were an infringement of what the
priesthood saw as the Law of God, the Deuteronomistic code, and this
could lead to charges of blasphemy. (2) Unfortunately some of these
sympathizers had themselves spoken in favour of the new Law, and
had in consequence been tried and executed. The method of stoning
prescribed in the Mishnah was already in place, and *their judges were
thrown down by the side of the rock* (v. 6), causing *our bones to be
scattered at the mouth of Sheol* (v. 7: the psalmist aligns himself with
the martyrs of his cause). (3) Having satisfactorily disposed of their
principal rivals, the house of Jozadak have welcomed the psalmist to
join their party, with a symbolic invitation to dine; but he has no
intention of being *occupied in deeds of wickedness with* them, or of
eating their dainties (v. 4).

No reconstruction of this kind can yield certainty; but it is important to see that it is based on inference and not speculation. No ancient
text can be understood without an element of inference from the
wording, and such inferences may always be wrong; but it is better to
infer uncertainly than to despair or to rewrite the psalm. In this case
the inference gains in plausibility from its explanation of all the
'difficult' phrasing on a single hypothesis, and that in line with both
the neighbouring psalms and (to a limited extent) the book of Ezra.

Psalm 141

1   A Psalm of David.
     LORD, I have called upon thee; make haste unto me:
     Give ear unto my voice, when I call unto thee.
2   Let my prayer be accepted (תכון) as incense before thee;
     The lifting up of my hands as the evening oblation.

3   Set a watch, O LORD, before my mouth;
     Keep the door of my lips.
4   Incline not my heart to any evil word (דבר),
     To be occupied in deeds of wickedness
     With men that work iniquity:
     And let me not eat of their dainties.
5   Let the righteous smite me, *it shall be a* kindness;
     And let him reprove me, *it shall be as* oil upon the head;
     Let not my head refuse it;
     For still is my prayer against their calamities.
6   Their judges are thrown down by the sides of the rock;
     But (ו) they shall hear my words, for they are sweet.
7   As when one splitteth and cleaveth (פלח ובקע) on the earth,
     Our bones are scattered at the mouth of Sheol.
8   For mine eyes are unto thee, O God the LORD:
     In thee do I put my trust; pour thou not out my life.
9   Keep me from the snare which they have laid for me,
     And from the gins of the workers of iniquity.
10   Let the wicked fall into his own nets (מכמריו) together (יחד),
     Whilst that I pass over.

Psalm 141.1-4. The psalmist prayed before that *Yahweh* would *give ear to* his *voice* (140.7); we should render v. 1a better therefore, *Lord, I called upon thee.* But matters have now become urgent: *make haste unto me, Give ear unto my voice when I call unto thee.* As a number of his leading supporters have just been executed, it is not surprising that some divine haste should be called for. Once more he has recourse to the language of the Prayers of David: *make haste unto me* is drawn from 70.6, and *calling unto* God from 57.3.

The psalmist is not in a position to offer *incense before thee,* or to preside over *the evening oblation*; but he hopes that his prayer may ascend to heaven like the clouds of burning frankincense, his hands raised like those of the priest with the sundown meal offering. He needs his prayer *to be established* (תכון) *before* Yahweh, that is, *to be effectual,* before worse befall. David had earlier promised to 'lift up my hands in thy name' all his days (63.5), with the smoke (קטרת) of rams (66.15). But קטרת here means incense (whether mixed with meal as in Exod. 29.38-42, or on its own as in Exod. 30.7-8), paired with the מנחה as bloodless offerings in Isa. 1.13 and (near to our period) Neh. 13.5, 9.

It is a question why the psalmist should think of the *evening* oblation; and we may notice that following the report of the princes in

Ezra 9.1-2, Ezra sat astonied until the evening oblation (למנחת הערב),
and at the evening oblation he spread out his hands (כפי) to the LORD
(9.4-5). It may be that the compiler of the history has decided to sup-
press any tensions between the heroes of his story, and especially any
judicial murders; and to present a (virtually) united front. Ezra as a
priest would have wished to offer incense and meal offering, and that
wish is latent in this psalm; but the occasion of his great prayer has
been shifted from the internecine struggle over the Law to the more
generally acceptable confession of national sin. Psalm 141 has been
used as an evening prayer in the church since at least the third century
(*Apostolic Constitutions* 2.59, 8.35), and no doubt was so intended
from the beginning. The historical Ezra might suitably have sat
astonied on hearing of his friends' death, and led intercession at
sundown.

The urgent prayer is for the maintenance of the speaker's integrity,
that he should not be drawn into collaboration with the evil-doers.
The wording is often compared with 39.1 where the psalmist vowed
silence in the presence of the wicked, but voiced a long complaint to
God when alone; or 34.14 where the tongue is merely to be kept from
deceit. But here it is a prayer for *a watch before my mouth, the*
guarding of the door of my lips; God is to prevent any *evil word*
from being spoken. The authorities have been involved in *deeds of*
wickedness, most scandalously the execution of the *judges* of another
party; the psalmist does not wish to be drawn into *doing* (התעולל) such
deeds, or accepting their hospitality, *eating of their dainties*.

What kind of *evil word* is implied here, and why should the
authorities take action against the *judges* while cultivating the
psalmist? The situation recalls something familiar from more recent
history. Mary Tudor, Queen of England, burned some 300 of her
subjects alive for Protestant heresy, but spared her temporizing half-
sister. Elizabeth walked delicately, knowing there was but a step
between her and death; but she guarded the door of her lips, neither
affirming Catholicism nor denying it, and her status as princess was
her protection. So we may think here: local leaders who sided with the
new Law exposed themselves to charges of blasphemy and paid for
their rashness; Ezra carried letters from the Great King, and it was
thought more prudent to win him over by subtlety. But he would not
accept their overtures, nor collude with their crimes, nor surrender
his convictions.

Verse 3. דַּל is a unique form for דֶּלֶת, and has a Phoenician parallel; but Allen thinks the survival may be accidental. The psalmist seems fond of apocopated forms, as in חַט, 'incline' (imper.), v. 4; יְנִי for יָנִיא, 'refuse', v. 5; תְּעַר, pour out, v. 8. They may be an expression of his feelings of urgency. RV translates דבר in v. 4 as 'thing', but the stress on speaking in v. 3 makes 'word' more likely.

Psalm 141.5-7. Let the righteous smite me, [it is a] kindness means *If the righteous smite me, [I take it as a] kindness.* Some local supporters have upbraided the singer, and he appreciates it; the men have *reproved* him, and he is not going to *refuse* what is the equivalent of a festal *anointing of his head. For* such candour was a blessing to him, and when he sees *their calamities*, the disasters which have befallen his local allies, he is determined to continue (עוד) *praying* for them. The צדיק is a collective, like the man of violence in Psalm 140, and *their calamities* (רעותיהם) are the calamities of *the righteous*, that is, the speaker's friends: to wit the execution of their leaders. The rebuke was clearly a considerable affront to the psalmist, or he would not consider ceasing to pray for them, nor make such a parade of his virtue in accepting it. It may be that he resented the criticism at the time, and it did actually come to a blow; but הלם is a strong word, used of a hammer on an anvil, and perhaps we should take it metaphorically, 'Let the righteous hammer me'.

The Hebrew of v. 5c runs כי. עוד ותפלתי ברעותיהם gives the evidence of the psalmist's forgiving spirit; you can tell that he has accepted the humiliation *for he is still praying for them.* ברעותיהם, 'in their evils', does not mean *in their [the authorities'] wickednesses* (RV), but *in their [the righteous men's] calamities* (RVmg). With the surprising ו, *For still and my prayer...*, compare Prov. 24.27, ו אחר (GKC 126.1). The difficulty of vv. 5-7 has led to numerous attempts to recover an earlier form of the Hebrew: so Pautrel, 'Absorpti sunt juncti', and Tournay, 'Le Psaume 141'. Burns, 'Interpretation', sees v. 7b as carrying over the Ugaritic myth of the monster Mot devouring the dead.

Execution by hurling over a cliff is testified in 2 Chron. 25.12 (for Edomite prisoners of war), and it was the standard form of stoning in the Mishnah (*Sanh.* 6.4). The guilty person was stripped and pushed over a twelve-foot drop; if he survived, a boulder was dropped on him. It was instituted for cases of blasphemy (Lev. 24.16), and we find it still invoked in New Testament times in the case of Stephen (Acts 7.58). Stephen had 'spoken blasphemous words against Moses and against God' (Acts 6.11), and we may think that a similar charge would be brought against anyone who proposed a revision of the Law of God as handed down by the Deuteronomists. At all events *Their judges*, that is the leaders of the *righteous*, the psalmist's allies, have been *thrown down by the sides of the rock*. However, *they* (the surviving righteous) *shall hear my words*, his prayer for them as in v. 5c, *for they are sweet*—they will be a comfort to them in their distress.

MT reads *Our bones are scattered at the mouth of Sheol*, and it is likely that the reading of the Syriac and some Greek MSS, 'their bones', is a correction to give an easier sense. In fact the psalmist is identifying himself with his supporters. He is a newly returned exile, they are local people, so the third person has been used so far: now that their lives have been given, they are one with him, and the shattered bodies at the foot of the rock are *Our bones*. The pathetic sight suggests a simile: *Like a splitter and a cleaver on the earth*. Kirkpatrick notes the use of פלח in 2 Kgs 4.39 to mean cutting gourds, and of בקע in Eccl. 10.9 for cleaving logs, and his translation above gives force to the image: as the chips and sections of wood fall on the ground higgledy piggledy, so lie the corpses of the murdered martyrs. This seems a more apt comparison than RV's *As when one ploweth and cleaveth the earth*.

Psalm 141.8-10. The speaker's repeated claims to be praying for his friends (vv. 5, 6) are now confirmed: *For mine eyes are unto thee, O GOD the Lord, In thee have I put my trust* (בכה חסיתי). We can hear the voice of David again, 'Mine eyes are ever toward the LORD' (25.15), 'In thee has my soul put its trust' (בך חסיתי נפשי, 57.2). But the praying is principally for himself. He fears that he may join the *judges*: *pour thou not out my life* (נפשי). The snare and gins which were so real in Psalm 140 are still feared, whether in physical or conversational form; one false step and he will be (as we shall see in Psalm 142) in trouble. He asks, *Let the wicked fall into his own nets together*, as David prayed, 'Let their table before them become a snare' (69.23), while he himself *walks over* (אעבור) the trap.

Verse 10. מכמריו has singular suffix, perhaps the 'nets' of their anonymous leader. MT has atnah at רשעים, but יחד belongs with the first hemistich, where the sense is clear, against RV.

PSALM 142

Matters have deteriorated further in Psalm 142: the hidden snares which have been such a feature in 140 and 141 have closed upon the psalmist, who is now in prison.

For once there is not much space for learned disagreement: what we have is plainly the lament of an individual, and his imprisonment (if intended literally) implies that he is accused and awaiting judgment. Kirkpatrick thought 'prison' was meant metaphorically, and Gunkel thought it might be a figure for sickness. Many critics haver between a literal and a metaphorical view, while Schmidt, Kraus and Anderson see it as real imprisonment, in view of the speaker's lack of support. Eaton takes the Davidic heading and the confidence that prayer will be heard as signs that the speaker is the king; though these features might also point to any national leader confident of his vocation.

Psalm 142

1   Maskil of David, when he was in the cave; a Prayer.
2   I cry with my voice unto the LORD;
     With my voice unto the LORD do I make supplication.
3   I pour out my complaint before him;
     I shew before him my trouble.
4   When my spirit fainted within me, thou knewest my path.
     In the way wherein I walk have they hidden a snare for me.
5   Look on *my* right hand, and see; for there is no man that knoweth me:
     Flight (מנוס) hath failed me; no man careth for my soul.
6   I cried unto thee, O LORD;
     I said, Thou art my refuge,
     My portion in the land of the living.
7   Attend unto my cry; for I am brought very low:
     Deliver me from my persecutors; for they are stronger than I.
8   Bring my soul out of prison, that I may give thanks unto thy name:
     The righteous shall crown themselves because of me;
     For thou shalt deal bountifully with me.

Psalm 142.1 Once more the psalmist sees his plight as a repetition of the trials of David under Saul; the psalm is a mosaic of phrases from the established psalter. Its editor expands on his usual brief heading: this is a *Maschil of David* like Psalms 52, 53, 54 and 55; and 57.7, 'They have prepared a net for my steps; My soul is bowed down...' recalls 142.4, 7, and suggests the same historical context as (claimed for) Psalm 57, 'When he fled from Saul, in the cave'. For further possibilities see the interesting suggestions of Slomovic, 'Toward an Understanding'. משכיל originally meant a 'clever' psalm, with a pun on the name of the chief character, like Hoshea in Psalm 44 or Jehoiachin in 89 (Goulder, *Korah*, pp. 88-91), but this technicality has been forgotten.

Psalm 142.2-4. The speaker is alone in prison, and is desperate; his only hope is the God whom he has spent his life serving. The *trouble* of which he *speaks before* Yahweh is indeed one which might make his *spirit faint*, though God knew every step of his path. What was the precise *snare* with which they trapped him was known to Yahweh, but is unfortunately not revealed to us. We may think that the authorities ('they') gradually isolated him. At first they thought to intimidate him with a beating (140.3, 8); then they arrested, tried and executed his leading supporters (141.7-8); then, like Herod with Peter, they stretched out their hands to take him also. The same accusations of blasphemy, in changing the Law of God, would serve against him, and with greater justification.

The language echoes earlier psalms. Psalm 77.2 had, *'I will cry unto God with my voice; even unto God with my voice'*: קולי stands first in both clauses without preposition, as here, and צעק is used for 'cry', like 142's זעק. A similar form ending אתחנן is found at 30.9. Psalm 64.2 had *my complaint*, and 62.9 *'pour out* your heart *before him'*; 77.4 has *'I complain* and *my spirit faints'*. Parallels with both 77.2 and 77.4 suggest that that psalm, also the lament of a leader, is directly in mind. עלי recalls 42.5. Psalm 140.6 had *'They have hidden a snare for me'*, word for word.

Psalm 142.5-6. It is *on* his *right hand* that an accused man looks for a powerful friend to defend him (16.8, 109.6, 110.5), and God is called on to see that there is no one there who will stand by the psalmist. Any hope of flight (מנוס) is gone, and there is no one willing to take action to save his life. In the moment of arrest he cried to Yahweh and prayed: God alone was his *refuge*, and all he had, his *portion*, in this world, *in the land of the living.*

Again much of the phrasing is from 'David': Psalm 16 supplies not only the thought of Yahweh standing at the speaker's *right hand* (16.8), but also of his being his *portion* (16.5). The absence of supporters comes in 31.12, 69.21, and elsewhere; *the land of the living* occurs in that Maschil of David, 52.7. But as in Psalm 139, an important force also is the image of Jeremiah, the prophet who was thrown into prison for his faith. *Flight hath perished from me* recalls Jer. 25.35, '*Flight hath perished from* the shepherds' (אבד מנוס מן); *no man careth for my soul* echoes Jer. 30.17, 'It is Zion, whom *no man careth for*' (דרש אין לה); *Thou art my refuge* repeats Jer. 17.17, אתה מחסי. It may be that we should think that the psalmist was a priest: priests had no land, but Yahweh said to Aaron, 'I am thy *portion*' (Num. 18.20, חלקך). For him in his hour of despair, these words might be a deep reality.

Verse 5. The versions and Targum, and 11QPs³ read *I looked...saw*; but this seems to be both the easier reading and less forceful than MT (Kirkpatrick).

Psalm 142.7-8. Verse 6 was the psalmist's prayer (*I said*) at the time of his arrest: his petition is now insistent, *Attend to my cry... Deliver me...* His *persecutors* are indeed *stronger than* him; they are the government, and he is a recently come troublemaker whose principal allies have just been pushed from the site of execution to their death. The same fate is likely to await him. But hope, that will-o'-the-wisp, still flickers; and Jeremiah came alive out of his imprisonment. So the prayer becomes specific, *Bring my soul out of prison*, with the customary vow, *that I may give thanks unto thy name.* Nor are things quite so bleak as the petition had led us to think. There are outside a good band of sympathizers, צדיקים, *the righteous*, who may be using their influence for him; and they will hold triumph when he is let out. Prov. 14.18 says that the prudent *are crowned with* knowledge (כתר, hiphil), and so here in a more literal way will his friends *crown themselves* with festal garlands *because of* him.

David's influence perseveres. *Attend unto my cry* (הקשיבה אל-רנתי) takes up 17.1, '*attend* unto *my cry*' (הקשיבה רנתי); *for they are stronger than I* repeats 18.18, כי אמצו ממני. The proximity of these two echoes to those from Psalm 16 in the previous verses is significant. There are a succession of echoes of Psalm 18 in 145, when the psalmist is delivered, and they have begun here. Psalms 16–18 are

seen as a succession of psalms, David's response first to his troubles
and then his deliverance (cf. the Heading of Ps. 18), and the psalmist
sees himself as following in the king's steps. There was a similar serial
interpretation of these psalms in 115–118 (see above, pp. 168-91), and
this may account for the two echoes here of Psalm 116: *I am brought
low* (דלותי) comes in 116.6, and *For thou shalt deal bountifully with
me* (כי תגמל עלי) follows 116.7, *for Yahweh hath dealt bountifully
with thee,* כי-יהוה גמל עליכי.

Verse 8. The force of יכתרו is unclear. RVtext, and many, render 'shall compass
me about', NEB 'shall crown me with garlands'. But the general sense is clear: the
psalmist's supporters will celebrate his release.

PSALM 143

The darkness deepens with Psalm 143. The psalmist still languishes in prison, *in dark places, as those that have been long dead*, but now he awaits with trepidation the sentence which is about to be pronounced.

Such a context follows from taking Psalms 140–143 as a unity. The relation to 142 is marked: *my spirit faints within me* (142.4; 143.4), *the way wherein I walk* (142.4; 143.8), *deliver me from mine enemies/persecutors* (142.7; 143.9), *bring my soul out of trouble/prison* (142.8; 143.11). Without such a framework the psalm's setting has seemed vague. The *dark places* may be metaphorical: Mowinckel, *Psalmenstudien*, I, p. 124, thought the speaker was sick, though Schmidt supposed that he was an accused man in prison. Eaton, *Kingship*, p. 64, noted the many indications that he was a national leader (for Eaton, the king): the Heading *for David*, the covenantal relationship implied by God's *righteousness* and *lovingkindness*, the confidence that prayer will be heard, the personal address *my God*, the status suggested by *thy servant*, the guidance by God's *good spirit*. But the extensive use of earlier psalms, including the alphabetical Psalm 25, suggests a postexilic date, and these expressions might have been used by some such figure as Ezra who saw himself as a latter-day David.

Psalm 143

1   A Psalm of David.
    Hear my prayer, O LORD; give ear to my supplications:
    In thy faithfulness answer me, [*and*] in thy righteousness.
2   And enter not into judgement with thy servant;
    For in thy sight shall no man living be justified.
3   For the enemy hath persecuted my soul;
    He hath smitten my life down to the ground:
    He hath made me to dwell in dark places, as those that are
    dead for ever (כמתי עולם).
4   Therefore my spirit fainteth within me;
    My heart within me is desolate.
5   I remember the days of old;
    I meditate on all thy doings:
    I muse on the work of thy hands.

266 *The Psalms of the Return (Book V, Psalms 107–150)*

6   I spread forth my hands unto thee:
     My soul *thirsteth* after thee as a weary land.   [Selah

7   Make haste to answer me, O LORD; my spirit faileth:
     Hide not thy face from me;
     Lest I become like them that go down into the pit.

8   Cause me to hear thy lovingkindness in the morning;
     For in thee do I trust:
     Cause me to know the way wherein I should walk;
     For I lift up my soul unto thee.

9   Deliver me, O LORD, from mine enemies:
     Unto thee have I hidden.

10   Teach me to do thy will; for thou art my God:
     Let thy good spirit lead me in a land of uprightness (RVtext).

11   Make me to live (תחיני) , O LORD, for thy name's sake:
     In thy righteousness bring my soul out of trouble.

12   And in thy lovingkindness cut off mine enemies,
     And destroy all them that afflict my soul:
     For I am thy servant.

Psalm 143.1-3. We feel here movingly the pathos of faith. The psalmist cried unto the LORD at his arrest (142.6); with his voice he cried again from prison (142.1), and asked God to attend unto his cry (142.7). Now he asks humbly that Yahweh will *hear, give ear*, and *answer* him. The survival of his psalm, and the continuation of the series, assure us that his soul was indeed brought out of prison—but how many more used such petitions and died? The appeal to Yahweh's אמנה, his צדקה, is a sign that the psalmist is conscious of a special vocation. He is God's עבד, his minister charged with his Lord's business; and when such a Lord has given responsibility, his servant may depend on his providential protection. The unlinked באמנתך...בצדקתך emphasize the claim, and the urgency.

The hour of his trial is approaching, and in a human court of law one may hope that justice will be done and the innocent acquitted (יצדק). With God one can but pray for mercy, for if he should be extreme to mark what is done amiss, who may abide it? The early Hebrew's confidence in his own faithfulness (44.18-23) has been eroded by the sad course of history, and there is the ever-present fear that God may set our secret sins in the light of his countenance. If that should happen, tomorrow will be the end.

Imperilled oligarchies do not change their ways greatly through history, and the experiences of the Israelite reformer in prison will not have been so different from those of a Soviet dissident in the

Lubyanka. *The enemy hath persecuted my soul*: plots, violence, arrest, intent to see him down the sides of the rock. *He hath smitten my life down to the ground*: beating, kicking, maltreatment. *He hath made me to dwell in dark places, as those who are dead for ever*: like Jeremiah, he has been thrown into a dungeon—and ancient dungeon-builders saw no need for light and air. The place is like the tomb, all too suggestive of the fate that may lie in store *in the morning*.

Verse 2 echoes many texts in Job, such as 9.32-33, 'For he is not a man, as I am, that I should answer him, That we should come together in judgement. There is no umpire betwixt us...'; compare Job 14.3, 22.3. Verse 3a takes up the words of the Davidic Ps. 7.6, 'Let *the enemy pursue my soul*, and overtake it: Yea, let him tread *my life* down *to the ground*'. Verse 3b repeats word for word the Lamentations of Jer. 3.6, '*He hath made me to dwell in dark places, as those that have been long dead*'. A reference by the psalmist to the fate of Jeremiah in the court of the guard is probably intended. The significance of עולם is disputed: Delitzsch prefers 'those who are dead for ever'.

Psalm 143.4-6. In view of such treatment it is not surprising that the psalmist's *spirit fainteth within* him, and his *heart within* him *is desolate*. His mind turns to Psalm 77, where an earlier Israelite leader found himself in perplexity, and cried, '*My spirit fainteth*' (77.4). Psalm 143.5, *I remember the days of old; I meditate on all thy doings: I muse on the work of thy hands*, recalls Psalm 77, '*I remember* God...I have considered *the days of old...I will meditate on all thy work, And muse on thy* doings' (77.4, 7, 13). Psalm 143.6, *I spread forth my hands unto thee*, echoes 77.3, '*My hand* was stretched out in the night'. Like 77, 143 is a night-time psalm, praying for deliverance *in the morning* (v. 8); its author also finds his faith on the stretch, and takes comfort in the thought of the deliverance of the Exodus (77.16-21), *all thy work, thy doings*. Those who aspire to lead the people of God do not despair of his power to work miracles. *My soul* is *for thee as a weary land* takes up 63.2, '*My soul* thirsteth *for thee*...in a dry and *weary land*'.

There is a Selah after v. 6, and once more we find the preceding verse making reference to some matter behind the text. There were three Selah's in Psalm 77, all apparently with the Song of the Sea (Exod. 15.1-21) in mind (Goulder, *Asaph*, pp. 97-106); and it is likely that this, or some other account of the Exodus, was recited at this point.

Verse 4. Delitzsch points to the hithpael יִשְׁתּוֹמֵם as a late form; and now see 1QH 7.3, 18.20.

Psalm 143.7-9. The psalmist fights down rising panic: *Make haste to answer me, O Lord; my spirit faileth: Hide not thy face from me.* He has already in his prison *become like them that go down into the pit,* and tomorrow's trial may make him even more like them. Trials often took place at dawn in the ancient world (cf. Mk 15.1) to allow time for execution, and he hopes to *hear* Yahweh's *lovingkindness in the morning,* that is a verdict of acquittal. In Yahweh *he trusts* for such an issue, and he *lifts up his soul unto* him with that in mind. What happens in the trial will depend upon the wisdom with which he speaks and conducts his case, and that is why he prays, *Cause me to know the way wherein I should walk.* He is not in quest of abstract virtue, but of a pragmatic effective defence. Only so can he be *delivered from his enemies, hiding himself* under the mantle of his divine counsel.

The approaching crisis draws the speaker's mind to earlier sequences of Davidic psalms. Psalm 69.18 has, *'hide not thy face from thy servant...make haste to answer me'.* Psalm 25 opens, *'Unto thee, O Lord, do I lift up my soul. O my God, in thee have I trusted... Make me to know thy ways'* (25.1-2, 4). Psalm 27.9 has *'Hide not thy face from me',* and 28.1 prays to the LORD *'Lest...I become like them that go down into the pit'.* Psalm 143.8a, *Cause me to hear thy lovingkindness in the morning,* הַשְׁמִיעֵנִי בַבֹּקֶר חַסְדְּךָ, is a play on the non-Davidic 90.14, 'Satisfy *us with thy lovingkindness in the morning',* בַבֹּקֶר חַסְדֶּךָ שַׂבְּעֵנוּ. The older psalm looked for God's renewed blessing on the year in the coming morning of the festival: our psalmist has a more limited but more urgent need, to *hear* the blessed words, 'Not guilty'.

Various explanations have been offered for *in the morning.* Johnson (*Cultic Prophet,* p. 270), suggested incubation in the Temple, as is probable for Psalm 77, and McKay, 'Psalms of Vigil', supposed a vigil; but the text gives no hint of either of these practices. A general metaphorical understanding, that Yahweh gave deliverance in the morning, is weak: in texts like 49.15 God acts in the morning because ancient battles, like modern ones, started at dawn. Anderson is better in judging that v. 8 implies an evening hymn. But it is too much to infer a location in the Temple from *Unto thee have I hidden.* The last expression is not easy: Delitzsch justifies *Apud te abscondidi [me].* Kraus thinks of Yahweh as *answering* in an oracle, and is followed by Anderson, Allen and others. The speakers of Kraus's individual laments often seem content with an oracle, where one might expect them to desire some more substantial deliverance.

Psalm 143.10-12. The petitions should be taken together, and seen against the context of Psalms 140–143 as a whole. In a capital trial, faced with able and unprincipled accusers, themselves under threat, everything depends on the conduct of the defence: we may think, as a parallel, of Thomas More brought from the Tower to face Secretary Cromwell. But for the psalmist as for More the issue will not turn on his cleverness but on inspiration from heaven: *Teach me, lead me, make me live* (תחיני), *bring my soul out of trouble.* The wording may sound like Psalm 119 (*'Quicken me'*) and an aspiration to live a godly life, but the context is otherwise. *Teach me to do thy will, for thou art my God*: every move in the defence needs to be as directed by God's will, for he is the God on whose business his servant is engaged. *Let thy good spirit lead me in a land of uprightness*: his acquittal will depend on two things—first the divine guidance, and secondly some willingness of the court to be fair—בארץ מישור, in the modern cliché, a level playing field. *Let me live, O LORD, for thy name's sake*: his condemnation and death will be a disgrace to Yahweh himself, whose bidding he has come to do. *In thy righteousness bring my soul out of trouble*: the saints have lived by the faith that where God guides he provides, and appeal can be made to his righteousness to see that his servant is not put to death.

In ancient Judah as in Tudor England it was *vae victis*. More's fall took him to the scaffold, and Cromwell's in his turn; and the psalmist knows that the other side of his vindication must be the death of his opponents. So, as the Muslim warriors of old charged their enemies to the cry, Allah is merciful, he prays, *In thy lovingkindness cut off mine enemies.* His acquittal turns on Yahweh's אמנה, צדקה, חסד, *For* he is *thy servant*, whose commission guarantees his protection; and that acquittal must end in *destroying all them that afflict my soul.*

The phrasing is in large part determined by reminiscences of earlier psalms. Psalm 27.11, continuing the chain of echoes from Psalms 25 to 28, has 'Teach *me thy* way, *O LORD*, And *lead me in a plain* path'. As with v. 8 and 90.14 there is a play on words. Psalm 27 sought guidance in life, ארח, נחני בארח מישור the path of levelness/equity: the speaker of Psalm 143 is on trial for his life and asks, תנחני בארץ מישור—in a *land* of levelness/equity, where one may expect justice. 25.17 has, '*The troubles* of my heart are enlarged: O *bring thou me out of my* distresses'. David's *enemies* are *destroyed* in God's *truth* in 54.7.

There is probably an echo of Psalm 143 in Nehemiah 9, when following Ezra's institution of the Holiness code autumn festal liturgy, the Levites make confession, including Neh. 9.20, 'Thou gavest *thy good spirit* to instruct them'. This is the only other occurrence of the phrase.

PSALM 144

Psalms 140–143 saw the psalmist brought progressively low: to violence, to the execution of his supporters, to prison, to panic. Whoever placed Psalm 144 after them, and then the stream of praises in 145–150, saw these psalms as a series. With 144 the psalmist goes to face his foes in court, and his mind goes back to David's great thanksgiving for deliverance in Psalm 18, whose language dominates the new text. He vows that when God has similarly rescued him, he will sing a new song of praise to him; and the psalm ends with such a paean.

Most critics have ascribed the body of the psalm to the royal period, and vv. 12-15 were seen by Delitzsch, Kirkpatrick and Gunkel as a different piece appended; though more recent commentators, Eaton, Weiser, Kraus, Anderson, have pointed to Psalm 72 as a parallel, and defend the psalm's unity. The king's blessing should extend not only to his victory in battle (vv. 1-11), but to the nation's prosperity in peace (vv. 12-15). But if the psalm is a unity, a pre-exilic date in the monarchy becomes problematic. Verses 1-11 certainly follow closely the royal Psalm 18, but this could be a post-monarchical adaptation, and the variations therefrom suggest a postexilic date; this is even more true of the closing verses, where זן (v. 13) is a late/Aramaic word, as is שׁ־, 'that', which comes twice in v. 15. Verse 9 reflects several phrases from Ps. 33.2-3, and v. 15b is close to 33.12, which suggests the same author for both parts of the psalm. The sharp difference of tone between the two sections is underlined by the numerous parallels with Psalm 18 and other psalms in the first, and their virtual absence in the second. But then the psalmist promised *a new song*.

The presence of so much late language makes the classification of 144 as a royal psalm difficult: Kirkpatrick suggests a Judaean leader from after the Exile. Eaton, *Kingship*, pp. 127-29, and others, view the psalm as a unity, citing Psalm 72 as a parallel: for Eaton it is a festival prayer for the king's deliverance from all kinds of enemies, expressed through a ritual humiliation, and the overflow of blessing through him on to the world of nature. But such a world-view, so plausible, could hardly be suspended when there was no king. The mention of kings and of David in v. 10 does not imply that there are kings reigning currently; the participles, *[God] the giver of victory to kings, the rescuer of David...*, are part of the broad appeal to the God of Psalm 18 who saved David. Later generations naturally saw themselves as David's successors (Isa. 55.3; Ps. 122.5; 1 Chronicles).

Psalm 144

1 *A Psalm* of David.
   Blessed be the LORD my rock,
   Which teacheth my hands to war,
   And my fingers to fight:

2 My lovingkindness and my fortress,
   My high tower and my deliverer;
   My shield, and he in whom I trust;
   Who subdueth my people under me.

3 LORD, what is man that thou takest knowledge of him?
   Or the son of man that thou makest account of him?

4 Man is like to a breath:
   His days are as a shadow that passeth away.

5 Bow thy heavens, O LORD, and come down:
   Touch the mountains, and they shall smoke.

6 Cast forth thy lightning, and scatter them;
   Send out thine arrows, and discomfit them.

7 Stretch forth thine hand from above;
   Rescue me, and deliver me out of great waters,
   Out of the hand of strangers;

8 Whose mouth speaketh vanity,
   And their right hand is a right hand of falsehood.

9 I will sing a new song unto thee, O God:
   Upon a psaltery of ten strings will I sing praises unto thee,

10 The giver (הנותן) of salvation unto kings:
   The rescuer (הפוצה) of David his servant from the hurtful sword.

11 Rescue me, and deliver me out of the hand of strangers,
   Whose mouth speaketh vanity,
   And their right hand is a right hand of falsehood.

12 ʾ(אשׁר) Our sons shall be as plants grown up in their youth;
   And our daughters as corner stones hewn after the fashion of a palace;

13 Our garners full, affording all manner of store;
   Our sheep bringing forth thousands and ten thousands in our fields;

14 Our oxen well laden;
   No outbreak (פרץ), and no miscarriage (יוצאת),
   And no outcry in our streets;

15 Happy is the people, that is in such a case:
   Yea, happy is the people whose God is the LORD'.

(RV has inserted a series of *When*…'s in vv. 13-14 which are not in the Hebrew, and have been omitted in the above version.)

In his prison lament, Psalm 142, the psalmist saw himself as a later David-in-persecution: the Lord was his portion (16.5), on his right hand (16.8); he prayed, 'Attend to my cry' (17.1), 'Deliver me from my persecutors; for they are stronger than I' (18.18). It was in Psalm 18 that David had uttered his great thanksgiving for deliverance, and he had virtually repeated this great prayer at the end of his life (2 Sam. 22.2-51): the Heading of Psalm 18 already associated it with deliverance from Saul and other enemies. So, as the hour of judgment approaches, the psalmist makes the king's petition his own.

Psalm 144.1-4. 144.1 draws on 18.47, '*Blessed be my rock*' and 18.3, '*The Lord* is *my rock*', and 18.35, '*He teacheth my hands to war*'. 144.2 comes from 18.3, '*my fortress, and my deliverer*'; My God my strong rock, *in him will I trust; my shield*, and the horn of my salvation, *my high tower*', and 18.48, 'And subdueth *peoples under me*'. It is noticeable that Psalm 144 has 'my people' for 'peoples' (עמי for עמים): where David aspired to foreign conquests, his successor hopes only to gain the rule over his own people. He turns aside for a moment to other psalm-texts which stress God's grace in caring for him: 144.3 takes up 8.5, 'Lord, *what is man that thou* art mindful *of him? And the son of man that thou* visitest *him?*'; 144.4 echoes 39.5, 'every *man is* altogether *a breath*', with 102.12, 'My *days are as a shadow that* is stretched out'. He knows that his life could be snuffed out in a moment, and that all depends on his divine protector.

In several details the wording is closer to the 2 Samuel 22 version of Psalm 18, a later modification: מפלטי לי, *my deliverer for me*, comes in 2 Sam. 22.2, and the verb רדד, 'subdue', probably follows מוריד in 2 Sam. 22.48. רדד is a violent verb: it will take some resolute action to make himself the master of Judah. The surprising חסדי should not be emended: v. 2a-c has three pairs of phrases, each with one personal and one material predicate. There is plenty of support, both Hebrew and in the versions, for עמים in v. 2d, following Ps. 18.35; but if this were the original, why should anyone write עמי? The thread of thought between vv. 1-2 and 3-4 is probably David's words in 2 Sam. 7.18, 'Who am I, O Lord God, and what is my house…?' (Kirkpatrick). Psalm 8.5 uses the slightly menacing verbs זכר, 'remember', פקד, 'visit', for which 144 substitutes the less ambiguous ידע, 'take knowledge of', חשב, 'consider'. Delitzsch says that 8.5's בן־אדם has been changed to בן־אנוש 'Aramaizingly'.

Psalm 144.5-11. Verse 5 returns to Psalm 18: 'He *bowed the heavens also and came down*' (18.10), with a second colon from 104.32, 'He *toucheth the mountains, and they smoke*'. The latter is a brief form of the darkness, storm-clouds and thunder of 18.10b-14, with a suggestion of the smoke of Sinai. Verse 6 takes up 18.15, 'he *sent out his arrows, and scattered them;* And he shot out *lightnings, and discomfited them*'. Verse 7 follows 18.17, 'He *sent from on high,* he took *me*; He drew me *out of great waters*'. The third colon combines 18.18a, 'He *delivered me from* my strong enemy', with the two references to *strangers* as the enemy in 18.45-46; their *speaking vanity* echoes 12.2. Verses 10-11 close the main section of the psalm with wording similar to the last verse of Psalm 18, 'Great *salvations giveth he to* his *king*; And sheweth lovingkindness to his anointed, To *David* and to his seed for evermore' (18.51). Verse 11 is a reprise of vv. 7b-8.

When the wording of Psalm 144 follows 18 so closely, the variations from it are significant. It is noticeable (1) that the indicatives of Psalm 18 have become imperatives in 144. The psalmist sees himself as David's successor, but, unlike the king, he is not yet out of the wood: for him the hour of trial lies still ahead. (2) The concentration of parallels is in 18.1-18; most of 18.19-44 is passed over. But the *strangers*, בני נכר, of 18.45-46 are taken up twice, in 144.7, 11; and this tells us something which has not come out of the previous psalms. Some of the speaker's principal enemies are non-Jews: we should think naturally of Persian governors like Tattenai and Sanballat, or powerful Gentiles like Tobiah and Geshem. It would always be against the interest of such people for there to be a religio-nationalist reformist movement in Judah, such as were sponsored by the three great עליות.

It is also to be noted (3) that the strong military tones of 18.33-49 are almost suppressed. The king was to smite the peoples through so that they came cringing out of their close places: all that remains of this is 144.1b, *Which teacheth my hands to war,* adding for parallel, *my fingers to fight.* The psalmist's fighting is not to be done with arms, but with his wits. The only sword mentioned is *the hurtful sword* from which David was rescued, and which corresponds to the execution which may await the singer. But the real arms he has to fear are the tendentious arguments of the prosecution, *Whose mouth speaketh vanity, And their right hand is a right hand of falsehood*; these are serious, and are mentioned twice (144.8, 11).

Finally (4) the speaker is not (despite many commentators) a king. 18.51 gave thanks for Yahweh's deliverance of 'his king', showing חסד to 'his anointed, to David and his seed': Psalm 18 is about what God did for King David, and by association for the later kings of his dynasty. In Psalm 144 *God* is *the giver of* (הנותן) *salvations unto kings, the rescuer of* (הפוצה) *David his servant from the hurtful sword*; the psalmist continues, *Rescue me, and deliver me*. Yahweh was the deliverer of David and the kings who followed him (participles); now he should deliver *his servant* (143.2, 12), called in his turn to lead his people. Other later leaders like Nehemiah might speak of themselves as *thy servant* (Neh. 1.6, 11).

Verse 5. The double 'them' are the enemies mentioned in 18.4-15 but not in our psalm. *Verse 7*. פצה, 'rescue', is used only here and in vv. 10, 11 in the Bible, but is common in Aramaic. *Verse 9*. The address אלהים is unique in Book V, outside Psalm 108, which is a compound of two psalms from the Elohistic Book II. Perhaps this is due to the four occurrences of אלהי, 'my God', in 18, or to 18.48, *the God of my salvations*; or even 19.1, 'The heavens declare the glory of *God*'.

Verse 9 leaves the shadow of Psalm 18 for a moment, but v. 10 returns to 18.50, the psalm's ending, and v. 11 repeats vv. 7bc-8. Verse 12 then opens with a surprising אשר, a change of theme (the blessing of nature), and the absence of any further psalm echoes. RV's series of *When*...s, leading up to an apodosis in v. 15, is clumsy; Eaton's *So that our sons shall be*...(cf. BDB, p. 83, 8b) is possible. But the change of topic and the independence from earlier psalms suggest that vv. 12-15 are in fact an earnest of the *new song* promised in v. 9: the אשר will then mean *which is*, introducing the new celebration. The follow-on from v. 9 is obscured by the intervening vv. 10-11.

Psalm 144.12-15. Yahweh's servant may not be a king, but he certainly sees himself in charge of affairs. On his deliverance he will *sing praises* in *a new song*, accompanied by a *psaltery of ten strings,* such as were to be sung in Ps. 33.2-3; so impressive a hymn is surely to be part of the public liturgy. His present psalm concludes with a short sketch of the utopia which is to follow his vindication. The community's *sons shall be as plants grown up in their youth*, shooting up healthily like runner beans in summer; their *daughters* will be as *corner stones hewn* as for *a palace*—it sounds as if someone has seen a caryatid. The *garners* will be *full*, the *sheep* will multiply astronomically, the *oxen* will be well fed, with big loads to pull. Verse 14 is ambiguous, but a continuing series of farm images is most likely. The *oxen* are masculine, and so *well laden* rather than pregnant. The absence of פֶּרֶץ will then be of any *outbreak* of disease: in 106.29 plague *broke out* (פֶּרֶץ) on the Egyptians. The absence of יוֹצֵאת will be of a cow *bringing forth* in miscarriage. Such things happen in a drought, and Jer. 14.2 speaks of the 'cry', צְוָחָה, of Jerusalem going up in a drought: we may contrast the absence of such a *cry*, צְוָחָה, *in our streets*. All this will follow the takeover by the new government, because the LORD will be on their side: *happy is the people that is in such a case*.

An alternative view of v. 14, taken by RV, is that the reference is to a town: there will be no פֶּרֶץ, 'breach' in its walls, and no יוֹצֵאת, 'sallying', to take the enemy by surprise. The Hebrew of the last verses is abnormal: אַלּוּפֵינוּ where we should expect אֲלָפֵינוּ; 'oxen', צֹאונוּ, where we should expect no ו (anyhow misplaced); נְטֻעִים where we should expect נְטֻעִים. No caryatids have been found in Syria/Palestine, so maybe we should think unromantically of polished cornerstones; but Allen translates 'corner pillars carved for the structure of a palace'.

PSALM 145

With Psalm 145 the last part of Book V takes a dramatic turn. In Psalms 139–143 the psalmist—the same psalmist—was beset by enemies who attacked him verbally and physically, who imprisoned him, killed his friends and threatened his life. In 144 the same psalmist (for he adapted Ps. 18 to his predicament, as Pss. 16–18 had been used in 143) prays for divine deliverance as the hour of crisis is at hand. With 145 goes up a great paean of praise at God's faithfulness in answering the speaker's prayer, a paean that will continue to the end of the book. Psalm 145, like 138–144, is headed *For David*, the last of the David series: whoever set the psalm here saw it as the culmination of the sequence, the response of the same psalmist who has been speaking all along, and now sees his trials at an end. To celebrate the wonder of his victory he has adopted the alphabetic format, which indeed dignifies the poem even as it constricts its expression. We may think, however, that the composition was spontaneous and impromptu, for it is missing a verse beginning with נ, an omission which must have been repaired at once in the Hebrew (as it has been in the Qumran form, and in the versions) had it dropped out by accident.

11QPs[a], LXX, and the Syriac supply the missing v. 13b, 'Faithful (נאמן) is the Lord in all his doings, and gracious in all his works', which has been composed by changing the first word of v. 17 for the נ, and turning דרכיו into דבריו. No one capable of reading Hebrew could fail to notice the absence of a נ-verse out of an alphabetic psalm. The composition of Psalm 145 has been much easier than 111 and 112 with their more compressed (half-verse) structure, or 119, and it is accordingly more natural and flowing. It could in fact have been written by a second year student (ג for גדול, ט for טוב, צ for צדיק, etc.). Its feeling of triumphant praise has made it one of the most widely used of all psalms, and its joyful spontaneity suggests that it was composed impromptu, with a slip at נ. Barnabas Lindars, 'The Structure of Ps. 145', defends the authenticity of the נ-verse, proposing a somewhat elaborate chiastic structure for the psalm.

There is thus an obvious similarity of the third section of Book V, Psalms 135–150, to Psalms 105–118: first two historical psalms (105–106, 135–136); then a celebration of the return from Exile (107, 137); then a sequence of psalms *For David*, drawing on the older Davidic laments (108–110, 138–144); next a turn to praise in acrostic form (111–112, 145); and finally a series of praises marked out with *Hallelujah*s at beginning or ending. So sustained a parallel can hardly be fortuitous. Psalms 135–150 are (a century) later than 105–118, and are modelled on the earlier group.

Psalm 145

1   *A psalm of* praise; of David.
   א   I will extol thee, my God, O King;
      And I will bless thy name for ever and ever.

2   ב   Every day will I bless thee;
      And I will praise thy name for ever and ever.

3   ג   Great is the LORD, and highly to be praised;
      And his greatness is unsearchable.

4   ד   One generation shall laud thy works unto another,
      And shall declare thy mighty acts.

5   ה   Of the glorious majesty of thine honour,
      And of thy works will I meditate.

6   ו   And men shall speak of the might of thy terrible acts;
      And I will declare thy greatness.

7   ז   They shall utter the memory of thy great goodness,
      And shall sing of thy righteousness.

8   ח   The LORD is gracious, and full of compassion;
      Slow to anger, and of great mercy.

9   ט   The LORD is good to all;
      And his tender mercies are over all his works.

10   י   All thy works shall give thanks unto thee, O LORD;
      And thy saints shall bless thee.

11   כ   They shall speak of the glory of thy kingdom,
      And talk of thy power;

12   ל   To make known to the sons of men his mighty acts,
      And the glory of the majesty of his kingdom.

13   מ   Thy kingdom is an everlasting kingdom,
      And thy dominion *endureth* throughout all generations.

14   ס   The LORD upholdeth all that fall,
      And raiseth up all those that be bowed down.

15   ע   The eyes of all wait upon thee;
      And thou givest them their meat in due season.

16   פ   Thou openest thine hand,
            And satisfiest every living thing with favour.
17   צ   The LORD is righteous in all his ways,
            And gracious in all his works.
18   ק   The LORD is nigh unto all them that call upon him,
            To all that call upon him in truth.
19   ר   He will fulfil the desire of them that fear him;
            He also will hear their cry, and will save them.
20   ש   The LORD preserveth all them that love him;
            But all the wicked will he destroy.
21   ת   My mouth shall speak the praise of the LORD;
            And let all flesh bless his holy name for ever and ever.

The link with the preceding psalms is not in the imagination of the
ordering editor: the anguished prayers of 144 and earlier psalms have
been heard. *The LORD is nigh unto all them that call upon him, To all
that call upon him in truth*, as the psalmist has done. He *fears* Yahweh
and *loves* him; and *He will fulfil the desire of* such, *He also will hear
their cry, and will save/preserve* them. *Save* (ישׁע) is a strong word;
the speaker, as in Psalms 140–144, has been, like *David*, in peril of his
life. He has been among those *that fall, that be bowed down* in prison
awaiting trial; and Yahweh has *upheld* him and *raised* him *up* to freedom and vindication. Ancient prisoners were not well fed (Jer. 37.21;
38.9), and could only *wait on* Yahweh, but one may trust in him: he
*gives them their food in due season, He opens his hand, And satisfies
every living thing with favour.*

Psalm 146.8 takes up the otherwise unique יהוה זקף כפופים, 'Yahweh raises up
them that be bowed down', and puts this in the context of the previous verse, '(the
LORD) giveth food to the hungry, the LORD looseth the prisoners' (146.7). Verses
15-16 have suggested to Weiser and others that the psalm is in part praise for the
harvest, but the impression arises from these two verses alone, which are an adaptation of Ps. 104.27-28, where the thought is of God's creative providence more generally. It does not fit well with the tone of excited thanks for prayer answered, or
with such words as *fall, bowed down, save, all the wicked will he destroy*, who for
Weiser require a hypothesis of foreign magicians. But זקף in v. 14 and לכל in v. 16
have convinced most critics that the psalm is late—too late for foreign curses.

Despite the formal arrangement, the gratitude of the speaker is
heartfelt and moving: *I will extol thee, my God, O King, And I will
bless thy name for ever and ever. Every day will I bless thee, And I
will praise thy name for ever and ever. Great is the LORD, and highly*

to be praised... God has been true to his character, declared in
Exod. 34.6, *The LORD is gracious, and full of compassion, Slow to
anger, and of great mercy*. It is that חסד, that loyalty to his promise of
protection, it is the fact that he is *righteous in all His ways*, צדיק, one
who vindicates his own, which draws the repeated ovation. God promised the psalmist he would look after him in his service, and he has
not let him down. The whole Psalter carries the Hebrew title תהלים,
but 145 is the only single psalm with the heading note תהלה, 'praise'.

Exodus 34.6 was often used in late biblical liturgy: it comes twice in Ezra's confession, at Neh. 9.17, 31. The repeated *for ever and ever* (145.1, 2, 21) is devo-
tional hyperbole, and binds the psalm's close to its beginning. 11QPsᵃ provides a
refrain, 'Blessed be Yahweh, and blessed be his name for ever and ever', after each
verse: the Qumran community not only improved the text in several places, but supplied a missing נ-verse and a refrain for choral response.

The psalmist is the community's leader. At the beginning and the
end of the psalm it is he who utters the praise of God: *I will extol
thee...I will bless thy name...I will praise thy name* (vv. 1-2); *I will
declare thy righteousness* (v. 6); *My mouth shall speak the praise of
the LORD* (v. 21). But his praises will be taken up by the people: *One
generation shall laud thy works to another, And shall declare thy
mighty acts...Men shall speak of the might of thy terrible acts...They
shall utter the memory of thy great goodness* (vv. 4-7). These celebrations are said then to extend to the whole world: *All thy works
shall give thanks unto thee...And thy* [Israelite] *saints shall bless thee.
They shall speak of the glory of thy kingdom...To make known to the
sons of men his mighty acts* (vv. 10-12); *let all flesh bless his holy
name for ever and ever* (v. 21). The mood is of high optimism. The
psalmist will lead the nation's worship now, with the enthusiastic response of the people (חסידיך, *thy saints*, v. 10; and the parallel *All thy
works* will here mean *All thy [Israelite] works*); they will testify to *the
sons of men*, the Gentile world, and in the course of time they too, *all
flesh*, will join in the adoration. It will be like old times, when Ahab's
priests sang Psalm 47.

All thy works in v. 10, and *all flesh* in v. 21, are sometimes interpreted to include
nature as well as humanity, but this is fanciful: *thy saints* in v. 10 *make known* Yahweh's *mighty acts to the sons of men* in v. 12. God is said in v. 16 to *satisfy every
living thing with favour*, but the living things in mind are *all them that call upon him*
in v. 18.

But what are *thy mighty acts, thy wondrous works, thy awesome acts* (נוראותיך), by which God has demonstrated his *great goodness, righteousness, compassion* and *great mercy*? Certainly a major part of them will be the national deliverances at the Exodus and in the Desert, as is testified by the citation of Exod. 34.6 in v. 8. But these classic divine acts cannot be the whole inspiration of the psalm. God is the God who has acted in our generation as he did in the days of Pharaoh: *The LORD upholdeth all that fall, And raiseth up all those that be bowed down... The LORD preserveth all them that love him.* As a modern Jew celebrating Pesach can never forget that those round his table have been delivered from the Holocaust, so the psalmist is giving urgent, heartfelt thanks to the God who has brought his community out of the Exile, and delivered him from personal perils. He preserves *all* them that love him.

Verse 5 is problematic: MT gives *on the majesty of the glory of thy honour, and the matters* (ודברי) *of thy wonders will I meditate.* The Qerib and LXX read the easier ידברו, 'they will speak'. This overloads the first half of the line, and leaves the second without a connecting ו. MT should be maintained. Eighteen of the other 20 verses in the psalm open the second half with ו; the psalmist will meditate, not on Yahweh's (unseen) wonderful actions, but on their effects, דברים.

A further indication of the centrality of present deliverances is the novel stress upon God's kingship, a theme not found in any of our earlier psalms: *I will extol thee, my God, O King* (v. 1); *They shall speak of the glory of thy kingdom* (v. 11); *To make known...the glory of the majesty of his kingdom. Thy kingdom is an everlasting kingdom, And thy dominion throughout all generations* (vv. 12-13). The opening verse does not use the standard *my king and my God*, but the apparently clumsy אלהי המלך; the psalmist, as leader of the community, addresses Yahweh as *my God*, but he is now *my God, the King*—his kingdom has become a reality. מלכות is the normal expression for a secular kingdom in the Old Testament (1 Sam. 20.31; 1 Kgs 2.12, etc.), and it is a mistake to introduce (ill-based) theories about the New Testament 'kingship of God' (Weiser). Israel is to become a theocracy. God is going to be the king henceforth, in place of the wicked who will be destroyed, and his kingdom will be different in kind. It will have *the glory of majesty*; and it will be a permanency, *for ever and ever, throughout all generations*. There were similar Utopian dreams in Christendom in the seventeenth century.

These expressions raise two further questions: what historical background is implied by the novel assertion of a theocracy? And how are we to explain the *bouleversement* between the dire situation of Psalms 140–143 and the triumph of 145? It is difficult not to return to the figure of Ezra, whom we have seen to be suggested by the riverside scene in Babylon in Psalm 137 and other details. The first exiles saw themselves as fulfilling the prophecies of Deutero-Isaiah and returning to the Land to rebuild the Temple (Pss. 105–118). Nehemiah saw himself as called to rebuild the walls of Jerusalem, and to re-establish the city as a thriving community, and the Temple as a properly resourced centre of worship (Pss. 120–134). But Judaism began with Ezra: there was a divine law which he had brought with him, and properly learned Levites to expound it. This law was to be observed and enforced, and was to be the way of life for all Jews in future, with the full calendrical ritual (Neh. 8) and the full social *torah* (Ezra 9–10). In some real sense Ezra did institute a theocracy which has endured throughout all generations from that day to this.

If that is right, Psalm 145 tells us that Ezra won; but no hint is given of how he won. The stress is entirely on his thanksgiving that Yahweh has heard his prayer, saved him, acted wonderfully and awesomely, and established his kingdom. If we had nothing but the psalm we should be reduced to speculating on how he won power. But we have the evidence of the book of Ezra, and for all its limitations we may think that it tells us the central issue on which he won the day. Nehemiah 13 reveals that intermarriage with Gentiles had been endemic in the 440s BCE, even among the priesthood, and that he took action against the offenders. The same question recurs in Ezra 9–10, and is the sole socio-ethical issue on which the new regime insisted, again in face of opposition from the highest priestly families. It is easy then to think that this was how Ezra prevailed, even if less smoothly than his chronicler suggests. His accusers charged him perhaps with attempting to introduce a new law, exceeding the established Deuteronomic code; to which Ezra might well reply, 'But you do not keep the established Deuteronomic code yourselves. What about Deut. 7.3-4, "neither shalt thou make marriages with them; thy daughter shalt thou not give unto his son, nor his daughter shalt thou take unto thy son. For he will turn away thy son from following me, that they may serve other gods"?' This verse is in fact cited in Ezra 9.2, and is referred to as 'the law' in Ezra 10.3. Such an argument would be unanswerable, and might easily lead to the harsh enforcement of the law described in Ezra 10. For a fuller discussion see Appendix on pp. 306-24.

As befits a final David psalm, there are many echoes from earlier psalms: its opening recalls 30.2 and 34.2 (also an alphabetic psalm), and there is the virtual citation of 104.27-28 in vv. 15-16. מְהֻלָּל in v. 3 echoes our old friend Psalm 18 (v. 4). Psalm 19.3, 'Day unto day uttereth (יַבִּיעַ)' seems to lie behind 145.4, *Generation unto generation shall laud*, with v. 7, *They shall utter (יַבִּיעוּ) the memory*. Yahweh's *greatness* is praised in 20.7, and the king is promised life *for ever and ever* in 21.5. These references may suggest that we have the same psalmist as the one who applied Psalms 16–18 in 143–144, but the echoes are not frequent enough for assurance. There are plenty of other parallels.

The LORD's providence in the provision of food has made the psalm a favourite for grace before meals, and from early centuries it was used before the midday meal in the church. But for Jewish people the main meal was in the evening, when work was done: perhaps 145 was at first an evening psalm, like 139, 141 and 143.

PSALM 146

The praise of 145 continues into the sequence of five Hallelujah psalms that close the Psalter. Each of the five, 146–150, begins and ends with הַלְלוּ־יָהּ. Gunkel called 146 an individual's hymn, but most recent critics have seen it as for liturgical use, with *Put not your trust in princes*, and such an opening and closing.

Psalm 146

1   Hallelujah.
     Praise the LORD, O my soul.
2   While I live will I praise the LORD:
     I will sing praises unto my God while I have any being.
3   Put not your trust in princes,
     Nor in the son of man, in whom there is no help.
4   His breath goeth forth, he returneth to his earth;
     In that very day his purposes perish.
5   Happy is he that hath the God of Jacob for his help,
     Whose hope is in the LORD his God:
6   Which made heaven and earth,
     The sea, and all that in them is;
     Which keepeth truth for ever.
7   Which executeth judgement for the oppressed;
     Which giveth food to the hungry:
     The LORD looseth the prisoners;
8   The LORD openeth *the eyes of* the blind;
     The LORD raiseth up them that are bowed down;
     The LORD loveth the righteous;
9   The LORD preserveth the strangers;
     He upholdeth the fatherless and widow;
     But the way of the wicked he maketh crooked.
10   The LORD shall reign for ever,
     Thy God, O Zion, unto all generations.
     Hallelujah.

Psalm 146 has notable verbal and thematic links with 145. אהללה (v. 2) came in 145.2; שברו, *his hope* (v. 5), a late Hebrew word (Ps. 119.116 is the only other use), is echoed by the verb ישברו in 145.15; נתן לחם לרעבים is close to 145.15-16, נותן להם אכלם; the otherwise unique זקף כפופים came in 145.14; ימלך לעולם...לדר ודר in v. 10 follows 145.13. Both psalms praise Yahweh for his deliverance of the hungry, bowed down, righteous Israelite, his confounding of the wicked (briefly), and his permanent kingdom. Delitzsch says correctly that they come from the same author.

This author has framed his poem on the model of earlier psalmody. The first collection in Book V followed a short series of David psalms (108–110) with a sequence of Hallelujah psalms (111–118), just as the David series 138–145 is now succeeded by the Hallelujahs of 146–150. Book IV had closed with 103–104 (see above, pp. 16, 194). So now *Praise the LORD, O my soul* follows the opening of 103, 'Bless *the LORD, O my soul*', and the same at 104.1; 104 ends with the same words followed by Hallelujah (v. 35). Psalm 104.33 has '*I will sing unto the LORD as long as I live: I will sing praises to my God while I have any being*', as in 146.2. Psalm 104.29 has 'Thou takest away their *breath*, they die, and *return to their* dust', which is followed by 146.4, *His breath goeth forth, he returneth to his earth*. Psalm 103.6 has 'The LORD *executeth* righteous acts, And *judgements for* all *that are oppressed* (לעשוקים)', like 146.7. 146 is in line with the earlier psalms in the series, which have drawn on specific clusters of psalms.

But the psalm is not a vacuous cento of earlier sentiments. Our psalmist means to *sing praises to my God while I have any being*, just as he promised in 145.1 to bless his name for ever and ever, because he has his personal deliverance to be grateful for. Yahweh *keepeth truth for ever* (v. 6), as he showed himself righteous in all his ways in 145.17, in that he kept his word to the singer. The latter was *oppressed*, on a capital charge, and Yahweh *executed judgement for him*, saw him vindicated in court. He was *hungry* and a *prisoner*, and Yahweh *gave* him *food* and *released* him. An ancient dungeon was in total darkness ('in darkness and in the shadow of death', 107.10, 14), and release into the light was experienced as the *opening of blindness*. The prisoner who had been *bowed down*, crouching on the filthy floor, was now *raised up* to stand his full height. Surely *the LORD loveth the righteous*: God does indeed look after those whom he sends.

286   *The Psalms of the Return (Book V, Psalms 107–150)*

Verse 8, *The LORD openeth [the eyes of] the blind,* is not thought of as a miracle like those on Bartimaeus and the blind man of Bethsaida in Mark's Gospel. Recovery of sight is linked with release from prison in Isa. 42.7, 'to open the blind eyes, to bring out the prisoners from the dungeon', and 61.1, 'to proclaim liberty to the captives, and the opening *of the eyes* to them that are bound'. פקח is used for the *opening* of eyes and ears.

It is not immediately obvious that so personal a reference is intended. Kraus and Allen take the primary allusion to be metaphorical, the same images of hunger, prison and darkness being used of the exile in Psalm 107, and in Second Isaiah, and of the Exodus before; and it cannot be said that the experience of deliverance from Babylonia is excluded. But this leaves a difficulty with vv. 3-4, which have been put at the head of the psalm. Why should Israel be warned, *Put not your trust in princes*, whose *purposes perish* with them, when it had never trusted Pharaoh, and Cyrus and Artaxerxes had proved trustworthy and their purposes a blessing? The thought is rather of the local authorities, the נדיבים both Israelite and Gentile, who have been the speaker's enemies through the series; the wicked man and his men of blood of 139.19, the evil and violent men of 140.2 with their pits and traps, who threw the judges down by the sides of the rock in 141.6, and set the speaker in prison, in dark places, in 142.7 and 143.3. It is they who have hitherto been *trusted* to rule God's people, but their *purposes* have been evil, 'to thrust aside my steps' (140.5) with their 'evil devices' (140.9). But they are mortal, *sons of Adam* soon to return to earth (אדמה), and their plots with them. There is no salvation (תשועה) in them: *Happy is he,* by contrast, *who has the God of Jacob for his help.*

The God of Jacob is a phrase from the old northern psalms, the Dan psalms, 46 and 84, the Bethel psalms, 75, 76, 77, 81; but in all these cases אלהי יעקב. It is אל here. The slightly surprising בעזרו, *he of whom the God of Jacob is in his help*, is explained either as a dittography (two בs, BHS), or better a *beth essentiae* (GKC 119i). But the play on the names of Israelite leaders (Solomon, Jehoshaphat, Nabal; cf. on משכיל, p. 262 above) suggests that there may be a similar possibility here: the God of Jacob is acting in his servant Ezra, עזרא.

From the time of Israel's weakness appeal was made to Yahweh's power in creation: *Which made heaven and earth, The sea, and all that in them is.* We had the same in 135.6-7 and 136.4-9, and it is an important theme of the rest of the collection. The wording is close to the prayer of Ezra (or his Levites) in Neh. 9.6, 'Thou *hast made heaven...the earth...the seas, and all that is in* them'. In v. 9 God's saving action opens to include the traditional *stranger, fatherless and widow* of Exod. 22.22, and elsewhere, and the frustrating of *the wicked*. But as in Psalm 145, the final note is one of triumph: the days of misrule are over—henceforward it is Yahweh, Zion's God, who will rule in a theocracy that will not end with some *son of Adam*, but will continue in perpetuity, *unto all generations*.

The late Hebrew/Aramaic ‑שׁ, זקף, עשׁתנת, שׁבר are evidence of a late date.

PSALM 147

The concluding Hallelujah cycle continues with Psalm 147.

1   Hallelujah.
     Surely (כִּי) it is good to sing praises unto our God;
     Surely (כִּי) it is pleasant to make comely praise (נָאוָה תְהִלָּה).

2   The LORD doth build up Jerusalem;
     He gathereth together the outcasts of Israel.

3   He healeth the broken in heart,
     And bindeth up their sorrows.

4   He telleth the number of the stars;
     He giveth them all their names.

5   Great is our Lord, and mighty in power;
     His understanding is infinite.

6   The LORD upholdeth the meek:
     He bringeth the wicked down to the ground.

7   Sing unto the LORD with thanksgiving;
     Sing praises upon the harp unto our God:

8   Who covereth the heaven with clouds,
     Who prepareth rain for the earth,
     Who maketh grass to grow upon the mountains.

9   He giveth to the beast his food,
     And to the young ravens which cry.

10   He delighteth not in the strength of the horse:
     He taketh no pleasure in the legs of a man.

11   The LORD taketh pleasure in them that fear him,
     In those that hope in his mercy.

12   Praise the LORD, O Jerusalem;
     Praise thy God, O Zion.

13   For he hath strengthened the bars of thy gates;
     He hath blessed thy children within thee.

14   He maketh thy border peace;
     He filleth thee with the fat of wheat.

15   He sendeth out his commandment upon earth;
     His word runneth very swiftly.

16   He giveth snow like wool;
     He scattereth the hoar frost like ashes.

17 He casteth forth his ice like morsels:
   Who can stand before his cold?
18 He sendeth out his word, and melteth them:
   He causeth his wind to blow, and the waters flow.
19 He sheweth his word unto Jacob,
   His statutes and judgements unto Israel.
20 He hath not dealt so with any nation:
   And as for his judgements, they have not known them.
   Hallelujah.

The setting of Psalm 147 is the period of Nehemiah and Ezra. *For he hath strengthened the bars of thy gates* shows that we are beyond the erection of gates and walls in 445 BCE (Neh. 7.1-5; Ps. 127): *He hath blessed thy children within thee* suggests that the repopulation of the city (Neh. 11.1-2; Ps. 128) has proceeded and been successful. *The LORD is the builder* (בּוֹנֵה) *of Jerusalem* may also imply that Nehemiah's schemes are bearing fruit. *He gathereth together the outcasts of Israel* would be a suitable comment on any of the three major 'ascents', but perhaps more particularly on the first and third, when more considerable numbers were involved. Further, there seems to be a period of peace and prosperity, such as there was not in Nehemiah's troubled governorship: *He maketh thy border peace; He filleth thee with the fat of wheat.* There is also a keen pride in God's *shewing his statutes and judgments unto Israel,* such as we might associate with Ezra. So the psalm would be most at home in Ezra's time, if Ezra may be taken to come after Nehemiah.

Delitzsch and Kirkpatrick were confident that the psalm belonged in the time of Ezra and Nehemiah, whom they took to be co-evals; and sited it in the celebrations described in Neh. 12.27-45. But there were celebrations every year at Tabernacles, and new psalms might be written to praise God's more recent marvels. In more modern times Anderson says it is 'not certain that the psalm must have been written shortly after the rebuilding of the walls in Nehemiah's time'. Weiser kept open a much earlier date with the *outcasts* as the refugees from northern Israel after 722 BCE; but the references to Isaiah 40 and 61, and to Psalms 33 and 104, make this impossible.

Psalm 147.1-6. The psalm is notable, like others in its sequence, for aligning Yahweh's present acts of providence with his works in creation. What moves the people to praise is his evident blessing on their lives. Jerusalem, so long a ruin, is growing again to be a thriving city under *the LORD's building*; immigrants from the Exile stream in, wave after wave, as he *gathereth together the outcasts of Israel.* The *heartbreak,* so eloquently expressed in the Lamentations, is now *healed* in the happiness of a nation renewed, and the wounds of *sorrow are bound up.* This is the work of the majestic Creator: he can *count the number of the stars, and name them all,* he is *great and mighty in power, and his understanding is infinite.* How marvellous then that he has been true to us in our undoing (עֲנוּיִם)! That he has *upheld* us, and *brought the wicked,* our hitherto rulers, *down to the ground!*

Verse 2. בּוֹנֵה, not בּוֹנָה, a noun not a participle, is followed by the imperfect יְכַנֵּס: *Yahweh, the (re)builder of Jerusalem, gathers the outcasts of Israel.* The suggestion is that the rebuilding is a continuous process (Anderson).

The psalmist, as heretofore, draws on earlier formulations. נָאוָה תְהִלָּה, *comely praise,* is a phrase from Ps. 33.1. Second Isaiah comforts the exiles by bidding them raise their eyes to the stars: Yahweh brings them out by *number, and calleth them all by name, for he is great in power; there is no* limit to *his understanding* (Isa. 40.26-28). He gathers *the outcasts of Israel* in Isa. 56.8, 11.12. He sends good tidings to the עֲנוּיִם in Isa. 61.1, to *bind up the broken in heart*; the same text spoke of release from prison and the opening of the captives' eyes for 146.7-8. Yahweh's limitless power was praised in 145.3, and his *upholding* of the downtrodden in 146.9, psalms in our present sequence.

Verse 1 is difficult. The opening *Hallelujah* stands independent at the beginning of the other psalms in the sequence. Anderson translates, *Surely it is good...Surely it is pleasant to make a fitting praise*: he argues plausibly that נָאוָה is an infinitive like זִמְרָה, following Blau, 'Lobpreisen'. For the form, see Lev. 26.18, יָסַרְתִּי.

Psalm 147.7-11. The call to praise is renewed: Yahweh brings the life-giving rain-*clouds* which produce *grass* over the *hillsides* without the farmer's labour. So the *cattle* are fed, and even the nestlings of the *raven,* who croak their prayer to him, and are of no use to anyone. But he takes no delight in powerful war-*horses,* or in the muscles of the soldier, swelled by miles of marching. What gladdens his heart is the obedience of *them that fear him, and hope in his* promised *mercy,* in faithful Israel. It is for us, his people, that all this provision is made.

Psalm 104, which supplied so much of the language of 146, is drawn on once more: 'He watereth the *mountains...He causeth grass to grow for the cattle*' (104.13-14). Verses 10-11 turn again to Psalm 33, 'A mighty man is not delivered by great strength; An *horse* is a vain thing for safety...Behold, the eye of the LORD is upon *them that fear him*, Upon *them that hope in his mercy*' (33.16-18).

Psalm 147.12-20. The call to praise is renewed a second time, with the same pattern of thought: first God's evident care for his people in their city, and then to his boundless power in nature—but this time there is a twist in the tail. Nehemiah's walls, and the gates he set so carefully in them (Neh. 7.1-3, 13.19) have stood the test of time: children have been born, and the population has grown. The Sanballats and Tobiahs have faded away; the harvests have been good, the wheatears fat, thanks to Yahweh's rain-clouds. When he *sendeth out his commandment upon earth*, it is performed in double time. At his *word the snow* covers the land as with soft flakes of *wool*, or the *frost* does, as with a dusting of white *ashes*. The hailstones come down like gobbets of food; *who can stand before his cold?* But *he sends out his word and melts* the little balls of ice; he blows with his warm west wind, and the thaw sets in. But the thought of the LORD's *word* stirs a deeper concern: *he sheweth his word unto Jacob, his statutes and his judgements unto Israel.* The Torah *is* the divine *Word*, and is our supreme privilege; it is unknown to any other nation.

The address, *thy God, O Zion*, came also in 146.10. Psalm 33 is again in the background: 'By *the word of the Lord* were the heavens made... *He* commanded, and it stood fast' (33.6, 9). *He maketh thy border peace* is probably indebted to Isa. 60.17-18, 'I will also *make thy* officers *peace...* Violence shall no more be heard in thy land, nor destruction within thy *borders*'. *The fat of wheat* comes in Ps. 81.17. It is often thought that the psalmist is drawing on the book of Job. In Job 38.41 God provides food for the *raven*, and there are *snow, ice* and *cold* in Job 37.6-10, and a war-*horse* in 39.19; but there is no echo of the Job phrasing in the way there is with Psalms 33 and 104 or Isaiah 40 and 61, and it is better to think that the psalmist has thought about these things for himself.

Verse 17b, יעמד מי, *who will stand?* is often emended to יעמדו מים, *the waters stand [frozen]*. Allen traces the proposal back to Derenbourg in 1885, and says it has the ring of certainty; for both cola of v. 18 describe a thaw, but the only *ice* in v. 17 has been the hail. However this may be too confident. The MT is supported by all the versions, and we should be involved in two emendations. The singular form יעמד comes in 33.9, and our psalmist has elsewhere taken forms from earlier Scripture and changed their meaning (נאוה תהלה from 33.1!). There is enough *ice* in v. 17a for him to have inferred a freeze.

LXX divides the psalm into two psalms, with a division after v. 11; most critics support MT, but Duhm and Dahood split the text (Duhm into three). In favour of unity are (1) the similarity of vv. 2-3 and 13-14 in the rather rare theme of the success and peace of the Return; and (2) the echoes in both halves of Psalm 33 and Isaiah 60–61. LXX needed a subdivision if it was to have 150 psalms like the Hebrew, and the point of division was chosen intelligently.

PSALM 148

In a fine climax of praise the psalmist broadens his appeal to include all creation.

1   Hallelujah.
    Praise ye the LORD from the heavens:
    Praise him in the heights.
2   Praise ye him, all his angels:
    Praise ye him, all his host.
3   Praise ye him, sun and moon:
    Praise him, all ye stars of light.
4   Praise him, ye heavens of heavens,
    And ye waters that be above the heavens.
5   Let them praise the name of the LORD:
    For he commanded, and they were created.
6   He hath also stablished them for ever and ever:
    He hath made a decree which none shall transgress.
7   Praise the LORD from the earth,
    Ye sea-monsters and all deeps:
8   Fire and hail, snow and vapour;
    Stormy wind fulfilling his word:
9   Mountains and all hills;
    Fruitful trees and all cedars:
10 Beasts and all cattle;
    Creeping things and flying fowl:
11 Kings of the earth and all peoples;
    Princes and all judges of the earth:
12 Both young men and maidens;
    Old men and children:
13 Let them praise the name of the LORD;
    For his name alone is exalted:
    His glory is above the earth and heaven.
14 And he hath lifted up the horn of his people,
    The praise of all his saints;
    Even of the children of Israel, a people near unto him.
    Hallelujah.

Book IV reached a crescendo of praise in Psalms 103 and 104, the latter an account of Yahweh's authoritative rule in heaven and his providential rule on earth: and so does our sequence, with 148.1-6 summoning the heavenly beings, and vv. 7-12 the creatures of earth, to his praise. Psalms 103 and 104 are pre-exilic psalms, somewhere between the mythical creation picture of Psalm 74 and the sober *fiat*s of Genesis 1; and Psalm 148 strives to combine their fervour with the more demythologized modernity of the P creation narrative.

Psalm 148.1-6. Psalm 103 ended, 'Bless the LORD, ye *angels*...Bless the LORD, *all* ye *his hosts*' (103.20-21). Psalm 104 closed with *Hallelujah*: it began with Yahweh robed in *light*, with the *winds his angels*, and *fire* and flame his ministers. His chambers were above *the waters; the waters* stood above the *mountains*, until at his thundering rebuke they went down to their appointed place. There is no rebuking or flight of the waters in Psalm 148: the serenity of the priestly tradition is ubiquitous. In the beginning God *created the heavens* (vv. 1-6) *and the earth* (vv. 7-12). *In the heights* balances *from the heavens*, and the denizens of heaven, *his angels/his host* then extend naturally to *sun and moon/stars of light*, themselves so often viewed as astral angels (Job 38.7; Rev. 1.20).

Thence to the second day of creation: the *heavens of heavens* are the untold splendours beyond the dome we mortals see (later numbered to three [2 Cor. 12.3], or seven, eight and nine in the Hekhalot writings); *the waters that be above the heavens* (הַמַּיִם אֲשֶׁר מֵעַל הַשָּׁמַיִם) are taken from Gen. 2.7 '*the waters that be above the* firmament' (הַמַּיִם אֲשֶׁר מֵעַל לָרָקִיעַ). With v. 5 the psalmist returns to Psalm 33, so often his text in 147: *he commanded* (הוּא צִוָּה) *and they were created* follows 33.9, '*he commanded* (הוּא־צִוָּה) *and* it stood fast'. Psalm 33 ascribes creation to 'the word of the Lord', like Genesis 1. נִבְרָאוּ is taken from Genesis 1: Ps. 148.6 opens *He also made them stand fast*, וַיַּעֲמִידֵם coming from 33.9 again. God's unbreakable *decree*, חֹק, for the heavens comes in Jer. 31.36, 33.25, where it is compared with his covenant with Israel.

Gerhard von Rad, in a well-known essay, 'Job XXXVIII and Egyptian Wisdom' (1955), suggested that the sequence of beings called to praise Yahweh derived from the Egyptian catalogue of praise to Ptah; he was followed by Kraus and others. More recently, however, Hillers, 'A Study of Psalm 148' (1978), objects that the scale of the Egyptian document is enormously larger than that of the psalm, and the coincidences of order, taken overall, are not impressive.

Psalm 148.7-12. The second section calls for praise from *the earth*. First come the *sea-monsters*, תנינים, once God's enemies in Ps. 74.14, but comfortably playing in his ocean in 104.26 (Leviathan), and in number in Gen. 1.21. They are paired with *all deeps*, תהמות, from 'the deep', תהום, of Gen. 1.2, itself once the monster Tiamat. The *mountains* are in 104.18 and the *cedars* in 104.16, with fruit trees specified in Gen. 1.11. Wild *beasts*, חיה, *and all cattle*, בהמה, with *creeping things*, רמש, all come in Gen. 1.24, with the *winged* birds in 1.21. But not only is all nature, above and below, to join in the great hymn: especially all humankind is to render its tribute of praise, and that includes the king of Persia and his satraps and governors, *Kings of the earth and all peoples, Princes and all judges of the earth.* It is the same vision of universal homage at the Jerusalem Temple which goes back to Ps. 68.30 and will continue to Zech. 14.16-19; and Israelites of all ages and both sexes, *young men and maidens, Old men and children* are to lead the worship.

Psalm 148.13-14. But for what are all these assembled beings to *praise the name of the* LORD? It is for the restoration of Israel. In v. 13b *his name alone is exalted*: in v. 14a *he hath lifted up the horn of his people*. In v. 13c *His glory is above the earth and heaven*: in v. 14b what is lifted up is *the praise of his devoted ones, Even of the children of Israel, a people near unto him.* The psalmist speaks no more than the truth: Yahweh's glory and the repute of his people go hand in hand—his name is only exalted when the people *near unto him*, under his mantle, is successful. In practice the *lifting up* of *his people's horn* probably means military success in a small way: *the praise of all his saints* in Ps. 148.14 is in close parallel to *the honour of all his saints* in 149.9, in a clearly military context. We may compare the rising reputation of Judah, and so of Yahweh, as Nehemiah completes the wall: 'all the heathen that were about us feared...for they perceived that this work was wrought of our God' (Neh. 6.16).

Gunkel and Kraus drew a line at v. 14a, and regarded v. 14bc, *The praise...*, as an *Unterschrift*. But Allen points out the careful parallel between vv. 13 and 14; and the closely similar Deut. 26.19, 'to make thee high above all nations which he hath made, for a praise (לתהלה), and for a name, and for an honour'; see also Jer. 13.11, 33.9. Delitzsch notes the parallel with 149.9, and attributes the two psalms to the same author.

So Psalm 148, like 147, draws on Psalms 33 and 104. It shares the same form as 147, with opening and closing *Hallelujah*s. It celebrates the same happy situation, the return of Israel to prosperity and international respect, with the raised horn of a victorious army. The two psalms are from the same hand, from the fifth century.

PSALM 149

The Hallelujah sequence continues towards its climax. There are a number of links to earlier psalms in the series: *Sing unto the LORD a new song* (v. 1) fulfils the vow of 144.9; *the LORD taketh pleasure in them that fear him* (v. 4) virtually repeats 147.11; the *kingship* of God (v. 2) was the theme of 145 and 146; *honour for all his saints* (v. 9) echoes *praise for all his saints* (148.14). Also significant are the common passages of earlier scripture drawn upon: Psalm 33 (v. 1) was a central text for Psalms 147 and 148; Isa. 61.1-3, which inspired references to *the broken in heart* (147.3) and to the *opening of eyes to the prisoners* (146.7-8), now lies behind the words פאר, נקמה, רצה, ענוים, and ציון, with משפט from 61.8.

Psalm 149

1 Hallelujah.
   Sing unto the LORD a new song,
   And his praise in the assembly of the saints.
2 Let Israel rejoice in him that made him:
   Let the children of Zion be joyful in their King.
3 Let them praise his name in the dance:
   Let them sing praises to him with the timbrel and harp.
4 For the LORD taketh pleasure in his people:
   He will beautify the meek with victory.
5 Let the saints exult in glory:
   Let them sing for joy upon their beds.
6 *Let* the high praises of God *be* in their throat,
   And a two-edged sword in their hand;
7 To execute vengeance upon the nations,
   And punishments upon the peoples;
8 To bind their kings with chains,
   And their nobles with fetters of iron;
9 To execute upon them the judgement written:
   This honour have all his saints (RVtext).
   Hallelujah.

Psalm 149.1-4 National confidence is rising. This is a new age of obedience and blessing, and it calls for *a new song*, like the new songs Psalms 96 and 98, which celebrated God's judgment upon the nations; or the psalmist's favourite, 33, with its similar theme—'*Praise the Lord with the lyre... Sing to him a new song*' (33.2-3). It is to be sung before *the assembly of the devoted ones*, the festal gathering of all Israel at Tabernacles. There *Israel* may *rejoice in the powers that made him*, shouting their *Hallelujah*s, though Israel is now no more than *the children of Zion*. They will indeed *be joyful in their king*, now that he is making his kingdom a reality by force of their arms. *For the LORD is taking pleasure in his people*—רֹצֶה, present participle: life has taken a strong turn for the better. *He will beautify the meek with victory*: the Jews, so long the wretched of the earth, עֲנָוִים, may now look forward to being adorned with triumph as their armies sweep to victory after victory to establish the kingdom of God. We may compare the feelings in modern Israel when the עֲנָוִים had suffered such terrible things in the Holocaust, and then found in 1948 that they could drive out the British and defeat the Arabs. The ideas of God's *pleasure*, רָצוֹן, and his *beautifying*, פָּאַר, *the meek*, עֲנָוִים, of Zion are found in Isa. 61.1-3 (cf. also 60.7, 9, 10, 13).

Many scholars place all the thought of the psalm in the future, either entirely in the fantasy world of eschatology (Gunkel), or in the not very different fantasy world of the cult (Mowinckel, Eaton, Weiser, Kraus). Delitzsch and Kirkpatrick thought of a more realistic setting as Israel regained self-respect in the time of Ezra and Nehemiah; and this seems to be implied by the present רֹצֶה in v. 4, as well as in 148.14, 'And he hath lifted up a horn for his people', which they both saw as linked to Psalm 149. However Gunkel sought a setting for the psalm in a victory festival following a real victory, pointing to the dancing (by the women) and the hymns sung by the men in arms in Jdt. 15.12-13, with Judith's psalm following in 16.1-17; most other critics have preferred Tabernacles as the natural *assembly of the saints*. Those who see the psalm as a cultic celebration of God's victory over enemies above and below have usually kept open the possibility of a pre-exilic date (Mowinckel, *Psalmenstudien*, II, pp. 193-95); but Allen objects effectively that Psalm 149 is heavily influenced by Isa. 60-61.

Verse 2. עֹשָׂיו is plural, 'those that made him'. Many commentators explain as a plural of majesty; GKC 124i as a retention of י in place of the defective ה. But such plurals seem to be concentrated on verbs of creation: יֹשֵׁי at Isa. 54.5, Job 35.10; בֹּרְא at Qoh. 12.1. It may be that the company of heaven was included in the work of creation, as in Job 38.6.

Psalm 149.5-6 give us a glimpse of the celebrations. *The saints*, that is the united people with whom Yahweh has made his covenant, are to *exult in glory*: for once they know the elation of having won in battle, and expecting to win again—glory, that most heady and most destructive of potions. They are to utter great cries of joy, ירננו, their vast Hallelujahs, רוממות אל, rising from their *throats*. But the surprise is that these shouts come from *their beds*: the worshippers are spending the dry September night in the Temple court, and between periods of celebration may snatch an hour's sleep on the bed-rolls they have brought with them, משכבותם. From early times Israel had come by night to intercede in trouble: 'they have not cried unto me with their heart, but they howl upon their beds, they assemble themselves for corn and wine' (Hos. 7.14). During the Assyrian invasions Hoshea 'stretched out his hand in the night, and slacked not' (Ps. 77.3: Goulder, *Asaph*, pp. 97-100). The 119th psalmist remembered the Lord's name in the night (v. 55), but not continuously: he rose at midnight to give thanks (v. 62). Vigils were normally held because of crises, and are associated with tears (Ps. 6.6); but Psalm 4 commends quiet prayer, trust and peace upon one's bed (4.5, 9), and in 149, in contrast to usual practice, the celebrants are to shout with joy on their beds. 149 is a night psalm.

The beds have been a puzzle. Anderson, followed by Allen (cf. NEB 'as they kneel before him'), translates 'their places of lying', that is, prostration; but this seems forced, and without parallel. Gunkel and Kraus emend the text as 'meaningless', but this is unimaginative: Psalm 134 saw Yahweh's servants 'standing by nights' in his house, but they must have slept some time.

Psalm 149.6b-9. The night-time liturgy is no sleepy head-nodding. There is *dancing*, and chanting praise to the tambourine and lyre. The dances include the warlike sword dance, as the victorious infantryman swings his double-edged weapon against an imaginary enemy. We may think of the fire dance at Tabernacles described in the Mishnah: 'They made wicks from the worn out drawers and girdles of the priests, and with them they set the candlesticks alight, and there was not a courtyard in Jerusalem that did not reflect the light of the Beth-She'ubah. Men of piety and good works used to dance before them with burning torches in their hands, singing songs and praises; and countless Levites played on harps, lyres, cymbals and trumpets...' (*m. Suk.* 5.3-4). It reads like a demilitarized version of Psalm 149.

The psalmist would not be human if he did not see the turn in his country's fortunes as an opportunity for *revenge on the nations* who had humbled Israel so long. *The peoples* are to be *punished*, no doubt with enslavement (Isa. 61). There will be a victory procession with *their kings* paraded *in chains, and their nobles in fetters of iron*; culminating in their *execution*, following the prescriptions of Deut. 7.1-2, or the example of Josh. 10. In Ps. 68.22, 24 the hairy scalp of God's enemies was beaten in, and the victors dipped their feet in the blood; some such edifying picture is in view. We have come a long way from Nehemiah: 'Pray for the peace of Jerusalem...Peace be within thee'. The gentle pilgrim in modern Israel may visit Tiberias on the Lake of Galilee, and stand before the memorial to the Jewish dead of 1948, a carved stone field gun. There is an inscription on it from the Psalms, and he may puzzle out the Hebrew: will it be 'Peace be upon Israel', perhaps, from Psalm 128, or one of the sentences of praise to God? No: the words are the Hebrew of Ps. 2.9, 'Thou shalt break them with a rod of iron; Thou shalt dash them in pieces like a potter's vessel'.

RVmg translates v. 9b 'He is the honour of all his saints'; but the הוא refers naturally to the judgment of v. 9a, which conveys הדר *to all his saints*, as the raising of their horn in 148.14 brought תהלה to all his saints.

PSALM 150

The final psalm of the series—and of the Psalter—is the most triumphant of all. It is linked to its predecessors in a small way: 150.1
calls for the praise of אל, as did 149.6; *in the firmament of his power*,
following Gen. 1.6, and 'the heaven of heavens, the waters that be
above the heavens' of 148.4. Psalm 150.2 asks for praise of God's
mighty acts, גבורת, as in 145.4, 11, 12. They are to be celebrated with
harp, timbrel and dance in 150.3-4 as in 149.3. With its opening and
closing Hallelujah, 150 is but a glorious expansion of the joys of its
preceding series, Psalms 146–150.

Psalm 150

1   Hallelujah.
    Praise God in his sanctuary:
    Praise him in the firmament of his power.
2   Praise him for his mighty acts:
    Praise him according to his excellent greatness.
3   Praise him with the sound of the trumpet:
    Praise him with the psaltery and harp.
4   Praise him with the timbrel and dance:
    Praise him with the stringed instruments and the pipe.
5   Praise him upon the loud cymbals:
    Praise him upon the high-sounding cymbals.
6   Let everything that hath breath praise Jah.
    Hallelujah.

Let us leave so splendid and so perspicuous a climax in silence, and
ask a more general question. Psalm 150 was a hymn of praise, the last
of a related series of hymns of praise, thought by some commentators
(and by myself) to come from the same hand: how are we to imagine
the original setting of this sequence, and of the psalms that go before
it? For Psalms 135–150 displayed the same progression as 105–118
(pp. 14-17): two historical psalms, a psalm celebrating the Return, a

series of psalms 'for David', and a Hallel sequence. It is not likely that such a serial parallel is an accident.

Our study of the Ascents group, and of the first Return group, Psalm 105–118, seemed to confirm the suspicion roused by Psalms 1–8 and by Book IV: there was in all these four groups an alternation, with the suggestion of an evening–morning usage at a festival. We may begin therefore by putting the same question to 135–150: how far is there any sign of an evening–morning alternation here? In this sequence, in contrast to 105–118, we have found no evidence of a morning psalm; but there seemed to be evidence of four evening psalms.

Psalm 139 seemed to be an evening psalm. 'Thou knowest my settling down (שבתי) and mine uprising...Thou winnowest my path and my lying down' (139.2-3) are but vague hints; 'If I say, Surely the darkness shall cover me, then the night shall be light about me' (v. 11) is not much clearer. But 'If I make *my bed* in Sheol' (v. 8) appears to suggest the night; and 'When I awake, I am still with thee' (v. 18) is a similar indication. The theme of Psalm 139 is Yahweh's total knowledge of his follower: he cannot escape the LORD, even through the darkness of the coming night.

Psalm 141 is a traditional night psalm, used by the church for Compline: 'Let my prayer be set forth as the incense before thee; The lifting up of my hands as the evening oblation' (v. 2). The speaker does not say he is praying at night, but there would be no point in his reference to the מנחת־ערב unless that were the time of his petition.

Psalm 143 is less clear, but is still likely to be an evening psalm. 'Cause me to hear thy lovingkindness in the morning' (v. 8) suggests that there is a contrast between the troubles experienced now and the hoped for action of Yahweh בבקר. It is as in 90.14 where the similar phrase is used, 'satisfy us with thy lovingkindness in the morning', and which I have also taken to be a night psalm. One may compare the texts cited above (p. 299) on 149.5, where intercession was made on 'beds' in time of trouble.

Finally, Psalm 149, with its 'Let [the saints] sing for joy upon their beds' (v. 5), seemed to be a night-time psalm: this time not a lament but self-consciously a hymn of triumph.

So the series includes four likely evening hymns; and all four of them fall on odd numbers, 139, 141, 143 and 149. The series begins at 135, and if it consisted of an alternation of evening and morning psalms we should have a psalmody for eight days, the evenings preceding the mornings as in Genesis 1, and in Psalms 90–106, 120–134 and 105–118. The time-references in Psalms 3–8 would also follow the evening–morning sequence if they began with Psalm 2.

But there were 14 psalms in the series 105–118, and 15 Songs of Ascents (120–134), and now we have 16 psalms in 135–150; and there are 17 psalms in Book IV, and in Book III (73–89). How can these small disparities be accounted for?

The old festivals were of seven days under the Deuteronomic law. 'Seven days shalt thou eat unleavened bread...Six days thou shalt eat unleavened bread, and on the seventh day shall be a solemn assembly' (Deut. 16.3, 8). Unleavened Bread begins on 15 Abib/Nisan as the sun goes down, and ends on 21 Abib/Nisan. 'Thou shalt keep the feast of booths seven days... Seven days shalt thou keep a feast unto the LORD thy God' (Deut. 16.13, 15). Tabernacles begins on 15 Ethanim/Tishri, and finishes on the twenty-first. So seven-day festivals with worship at evening and morning (Ps. 92.2) might seem to need 14 psalms; and there were 14 psalms, 105–118, for the Passover/Massot of the Temple thanksgiving of Ezra 6 (pp. 194-96); and there were 14 testimonies of Nehemiah for the Walls thanksgiving of Nehemiah 12 (pp. 108-11). But it might soon be felt suitable to close the final day with a suitable psalm: so the Songs of Ascents end Tabernacles with an extra brief Song, 134; and Book IV closed, before the Exile, with the hymn to the Creator, 104—fifteen psalms in all, 90–104. Such was not so requisite at the end of Unleavened Bread, because the feast is in a sense not of seven days but of seven weeks, and can close with the magnificence of the Pentecostal Psalm 119.

Some expansions were made to the sacred calendar in Babylon, and these appear in Leviticus 23. Passover/Massot was left alone (23.4-8), but there was to be a special New Year on 1 Tishri (23.23-25), and a special Day of Atonement on 10 Tishri (23.26-32), and Tabernacles was now to be eight days: 'Seven days ye shall offer an offering made by fire unto the LORD; on the eighth day shall be a holy convocation unto you...a closing festival' (23.36). These extensions to the festal year are instituted in Jerusalem, according to the Chroniclers, by Ezra. In Nehemiah 8 he first proclaims observance of New Year's Day (8.2, 9-12), in a long reading of 'the book of the law'; and in 8.13-18 Tabernacles is to be observed according to the detail of Leviticus 23, with olive and myrtle and palm branches. 'And they kept the feast seven days; and on the eighth day was a closing festival, according unto the ordinance' (8.18). Once this extension of the festival was in place, two further psalms would be needed; and we find in our final sequence, 135–150, sixteen psalms. There is minimal reference in the series to the Exodus (135.8-9; 136.10-15), but recurring emphasis on creation (135.5-7; 136.4-9; 139.13-18; 147.4-5, 15-18; 148.1-10; 149.2); so the series is more likely to be intended for Tabernacles than for Unleavened Bread. The new extended Tabernacles also required the poaching of Psalms 105 and 106 to make Book IV into a full eight-day (seventeen-psalm) psalmody; and the Asaph collection, Psalms 73–83, was filled out with old Korah psalms and others to make 17 (73–90).

The authors of Psalms 135–150 used the first Return series, 105–118, as their model. They wrote two new 'historical' psalms, 135 and 136, like 105 and 106; but they are happier psalms, less fixated on the *Vergeltungsdogma* that dominated the sixth century, more concerned with the promise of the Land, which they hope now to assist the LORD in redeeming. They followed this with a psalm to celebrate their return from Babylon to Jerusalem, Psalm 137: a shorter, more confident, more vengeful version of 107. But just as the first returning exiles had experienced the opposition and discouragement that underlie Psalms 108–110, so had the new *aliyah*, and in a more murderous shape, hinted at in 138–145. These two series of first-person singular laments were composed on the model of David's laments in his times of trial, especially those in the 50s and 30s; and the superscription *For David* was applied to both groups. Heaviness may endure for a period, but joy cometh in the morning; and as the Levites of the first Ascent were able to celebrate the completion of the Second Temple with a long Hallel for Passover/Massot in 516 BCE, so were those of the third Ascent able to crown their success with the triumphal hymn-series, Psalms 146–150.

By 400 BCE, we must think, the Jerusalem Temple had all our 150 psalms to use, if it chose, in its festal liturgies; but Book V was the latest, and therefore the best suited to popular feeling. It provided for the three traditional festivals. Psalms 105–118 were the psalms for Passover/Massot. Psalm 119 provided for the Pentecostal vigil. But for Tabernacles there was an alternative. For some of the Levite singers, Nehemiah was still a hero, and his exploits could be retold to the accompaniment of the Songs of Ascents, 120–134. For others there was a more recent *aliyah* to celebrate, with an eight-day festal tradition, and a psalmody familiar with Genesis 1 (148; 150.1b). I have hinted more than once that this third Ascent may be that led by Ezra; but the matter needs more serious consideration, which is given in the Appendix following.

We may end with a more speculative question. I noted (pp. 15-16) that just as the Paschal sequence Psalms 105–118 was followed by 119, a psalm glorifying the Torah, so was the Tabernacles sequence, 135–150 followed, in a manner of speaking, by the only other psalm given entirely to glorifying the Torah, Psalm 1. Both of these psalms begin with a blessing (אשרי) on those who walk in the way of the Lord. The Jewish tradition is to read the Torah in an annual cycle, ending on עצרת, the eighth day of Tabernacles: Deuteronomy 34 is read, and then Genesis 1, so that the *lectio continua* is never broken. Our third-Ascent psalmody provided 16 psalms, of which Psalm 150 fell for the morning of עצרת, a call to spend the day in musical (vv. 3-5) and verbal (v. 2) praise. Perhaps the evening might suggest a more sober and sustained 'way' for the righteous. Psalm 1 does not belong with the David psalms of Book I; and to early Western copyists of Acts 13.33 the text, 'Today I have begotten thee', was from the *first* psalm (τῷ πρώτῳ ψαλμῷ D it Origen; cf. τοῖς ψαλμοῖς 𝔓⁴⁵ Tert.). So there was a second-century CE tradition that the Psalter began with Psalm 2. If I were a fourth-century Levite arranging the Psalter, I think I would prefer to close the book on the high climax of 150, and use the earnest seventeenth psalm of the series as Psalm 1: to be the bridge for another *lectio continua*, and to introduce the whole book of Praises. But it looks as if the African churches and Origen knew another form of the Psalter, which ended with our Psalm 1.

APPENDIX

Ezra

Of the historical problems raised by the three Ascents, the most difficult are those concerning Ezra. For the first Ascent there are contemporary documents in Haggai and Zechariah 1–8, with occasional help from Isaiah 56–66 and Malachi. For Nehemiah there is the clearly reliable first-person testimony. In addition I have argued in this book that Psalms 105–119 are contemporary with the sixth-century Return, and 120–134 with Nehemiah. But for Ezra the principal evidence is the dubious and controverted narrative in Ezra 7–10 and Neh. 7.72b–8.18.

The Ezra story (ES—we should eschew the question-begging EM, 'Ezra Memoir') consists of three elements: the Ascent from Babylon to Jerusalem (Ezra 7–8); the mixed marriages controversy (Ezra 9–10); and the celebration of New Year and Tabernacles according to a law read out by Ezra (Neh. 8). These stories are partly told in the first person ('I/we'), Ezra 7.27–8.34, 9.1-15; and partly in the third person ('Ezra/he/they'), Ezra 7.1-11, 8.35-36, 10.1-44, Nehemiah 8. Ezra 7.12-26 consists of an Aramaic Edict of Artaxerxes authorizing Ezra's expedition.

Before any consideration can be given to historical questions, answers have to be found for literary ones. Of these, the three most pressing are the following. (1) Is the compiler of the ES 'the Chronicler'/'one of the Chroniclers', or not? (2) What sort of a source did this compiler have? (3) What sort of a writing is the ES, and to whom was it addressed? It is only when we feel satisfied on these issues that we can move on to ask what may be thought actually to have happened.

Of the numerous hypotheses offered to answer the first two questions, we may isolate the following as distinctive:

(1) The whole narrative from start to finish is a fiction, composed by the Chronicler with no underlying tradition (Torrey, *Composition* [1896], *Ezra Studies* [1910]).

(2) The ES is largely the composition of 'Chronicle circles', but is based upon memories of a historical Ezra (Noth, *Studien* [1943]; Kapelrud, *Authorship* [1944]).

(3) The Aramaic Edict is in large part genuine, and the ES has been composed as a series of edifying legends/'midrash' to turn the Edict into history (S. Mowinckel, *Esrageschichte* [1965]; Kellermann, 'Esragesetz' [1968]; In der Smitten, *Esra* [1973]). Mowinckel thought the legends were composed by an independent author about 370 BCE, and later edited by the Chronicler. Kellermann and In der Smitten give a central position to the Chronicler, but allow for a series of redactors.

(4) There was a continuous source for the ES, written by Ezra himself in the first person, and this was in time edited (rather heavily) by the Chronicler, who transposed some of the narrative into the third person (Rudolph, *Esra und Nehemia* [1949]; Blenkinsopp, *Ezra–Nehemiah* [1988]).

(5) The ES is substantially the work of Ezra himself, with minor editorial changes (Williamson, *Ezra, Nehemiah* [1985]).

For the third problem, answers vary in line with those to the first two. Rudolph, Blenkinsopp and Williamson all see an Ezra Memoir underlying the ES, and this will have been written as a report by Ezra to the Persian authorities: he was commissioned by the king, and he must have reported to the king. Mowinckel, on the other hand, sees the greater part of the ES as an edifying tale, whose sole intention was to inspire the Jews of the Return to godly living, in line with the Torah. It is the nature of edifying tales that they are mostly legend, even if the legends have some historical base.

I will not comment on the debate over the editor of Ezra–Nehemiah, and though I find myself convinced by the arguments of Blenkinsopp against Williamson and others: that we have to do with the Chronicler, or a leading member of the Chroniclers' community, as the main editor of the ES. But this only leads into the second problem. Most of the five Ezra chapters show signs of heavy over-writing by C [Blenkinsopp's Chronicler]: was C rewriting a written source, or series of sources, as is supposed by Blenkinsopp himself? Or was he dependent on some rather vaguer oral traditions going back a generation and more? The total scepsis urged by Torrey finds no support today: it would be unbelievable for Ezra never to have existed.

The influence of C is so pervasive in these chapters that it is often hard to see what sort of source remains when the editing has been removed: I think therefore that positions (2) and (3) are closer to being right than those of more trustful modern critics. For the issue between position (2) (Kapelrud) and (3) (Mowinckel), we may take as a critical instance Ezra 7.12-26, the decree of Artaxerxes; this is given in Aramaic, and is most usually appealed to as a written source.[1] Only then will it be sensible to consider the broader question of the nature and purpose of the ES, and its basis in history.

Is Artaxerxes' Edict Authentic?

One notices at once the extraordinary importance which Artaxerxes is supposed to give to Ezra's mission. Ezra is 'scribe of the law of the God of heaven' (7.12), there being only one God with one law, that is the Jewish law, which is 'perfect and so forth';[2] he has been the subject of a cabinet meeting, 'sent by the king and his seven counsellors' (7.14, like the seven princes of Persia in Est. 1.14); he is to 'carry the silver and gold, which the king and his counsellors have freely offered' (7.15); this is to be supplemented by 'all the silver and gold that thou shalt find in all the province

---

1. 'The authenticity of the edict was formerly questioned by a number of scholars (e.g. Batten, Torrey), but is now acknowledged in outline, at least, by nearly all' (Williamson, *Ezra, Nehemiah*, p. 98). Williamson might have mentioned Kapelrud as a further sceptic: 'the rescript, at any rate in its present shape, cannot be genuine' (*Authorship*, p. 42).
2. The meaning of this expression is disputed.

of Babylon', which is separate from 'the freewill offering of the [Jewish] people' (7.16); Ezra has carte blanche in the spending of this treasure once the prescribed sacrifices have been paid for (7.18); the king also provides vessels for the house of God (7.19); the royal treasury is available for anything further that may be needful (7.20); and Ezra may apply to the treasurers beyond the river for anything additional he wants (7.21),[3] with a limit of three and a half tons of silver (7.22); all details specified in the Torah are to be carried through exactly, lest 'the God of heaven' be angry (7.23); all Temple personnel are exempt from taxes for life (7.24); Ezra himself is appointed Commissioner for Jewish Affairs, with power to appoint magistrates throughout the empire beyond the River, over the heads of any satraps (7.25); and finally, anyone disobeying shall be punished by death, confiscation, imprisonment or eradication (7.26). Rather a generous edict, one might think: a Jew might have written it himself.

A Jew has written a good deal of it, to wit the Chronicler. Those going of their own free will follow in the steps of the first Ascent in Ezra 1.4; the public donations follow those made under King David in 1 Chron. 29.6-9; the sacrificial animals are in the order of Num. 15.1-16 and 1 Chron. 29.21, 2 Chron. 29.21, 32, Ezra 6.9; the sacred vessels follow those in Ezra 1.7-11, 5.14-15, 6.5, and the freedom to requisition from the royal treasury follows Ezra 6.4; the fear of divine anger (using the technical Hebrew root, קצף) follows 2 Chron. 19.10; the Temple personnel follow the same order as in Ezra 2; the appointment of judges to teach the law follows the story of Jehoshaphat in 2 Chron. 19.4-11, with God's law and the king's set side by side in 19.11 as in Ezra 7.26. There are besides turns of phrase characteristic of C, such as 'the people of Israel' for the laity, 'Judah and Jerusalem', 'which is in thine hand'. The word for Ezra *the priest* is כהנא, the standard Hebrew כהן, not the normal Aramaic כמרא; and the *magistrates* in 7.25 are שפטין, the standard Hebrew שפטים.

All these points are noted by Blenkinsopp,[4] who nevertheless holds to an underlying source. He argues for this on three grounds. First, the Edict contains a number of Persian phrases. It is introduced as a *copy of a memorandum* (פרשגן הנשתון, 7.11, not in the Edict itself). It speaks of Artaxerxes as *king of kings*, and of his treasury as *the house of the king's treasure*, Old Persian expressions. The law is דתא, and the king's bidding is to be done אספרנא, *with all diligence*, both Persian loan-words. Secondly, it adopts policies known from other Persian texts. It was the policy of the early Achaemenids to encourage local worship, partly to foster loyalty, partly for superstitious reasons. Darius I sent one Udjahorresnet on a mission to Egypt similar to Ezra's, with the remission of taxes for the Egyptian clergy. The punishments threatened in v. 26 include imprisonment, which was not a normal Jewish penalty, and perhaps flogging, which was limited in Israel.[5] Thirdly, there is an apparent

---

3.   Ezra 7.21-24 slip into an address to the treasurers beyond the River: this 'may have been copied from a separate decree forwarded directly to the satrapy' (Blenkinsopp, *Ezra–Nehemiah*, p. 146).

4.   Blenkinsopp, *Ezra–Nehemiah*, pp. 146-52.

5.   Blenkinsopp derives the Aramaic שרשו from the Old Persian *sraushya*, 'flogging'; RVmg takes it as a genuine Aramaic word associated with Hebrew שרש, 'rooting out'—it could be death for

disparity between the Edict and what Ezra actually does, to which I will return shortly.[6]

The first two arguments are not weighty. Any Jew who had read or heard an official Persian firman would be capable of writing one of his own with phrases like 'king of kings' or 'the house of the king's treasures' or 'with all diligence'; I am not a lawyer, but I could deceive the simple if I wrote long enough sentences full of 'Whereas' and 'hereinafter', and without commas—and I know some Old Persian words like *firman* if it came to that. The author of the ES knew about early Persian policy on local cults (Ezra 1–6), and he very likely knew what Persian punishments were like. But it is perilous to argue that the Edict was typical of Achaemenid treatment of local sanctuaries. If it were a general policy to treat them as Jerusalem is treated in the ES, the empire would have been bankrupt in a fortnight.

The disparity argument is often repeated, but is equally flawed. The Edict makes four provisions, each of which is carried out in the way appropriate. (1) Any Jew who wishes, and any priest and Levite, may go with Ezra in the Ascent (7.13). This is carried out in Ezra 8: specific mention is made of 12 chief priests who took care of the treasures (8.26), and of the Levites who had to be specially summoned (8.15-19). (2) Ezra himself is sent 'to inquire concerning Judah and Jerusalem, according to the law of thy God which is in thine hand' (7.14). Williamson, *Ezra, Nehemiah*, p. 101, says this is 'unfortunately not clear', but the reason for the obscurity seems clear enough: the ES is going to describe Ezra's discovery of widespread mixed marriages (9–10), and the Edict needs to make a vague general commission for him to do this. He is therefore empowered to make enquiry (לבקרא) over (על) 'Judah-and-Jerusalem', by (ב) the law 'which-is-in-thy-hand', which includes the ban on mixed marriages in Deut. 7.3-4.

The Edict continues with (3) the command to take the various treasures specified to Jerusalem, and to buy and sacrifice the requisite animals in the Temple (7.15-20). Ezra carefully weighs the treasure and the vessels, and hands them over to the priests and Levites (8.23-30), and they are duly handed over to the Temple authorities (8.33-34), and the sacrifices offered (8.35).

The problem has arisen principally over the final clauses of the Edict: these provide (4) for Ezra to exercise a wider authority. He may draw large subventions from 'all the treasurers which are beyond the river' (7.21-22), so that every detail of the sacrificial laws may be followed (7.23), with no taxation on the clergy to hinder their holy ministry (7.24). He is further to appoint magistrates and judges for 'all the [Jewish] people that are beyond the river', some of whom 'know the laws of thy God', and others not: for the latter, 'teach ye him that knoweth them not' (7.25).

the offender alone, or for his whole family. Williamson, *Ezra, Nehemiah*, p. 97, is sceptical about the flogging interpretation, and prefers the traditional 'banishment'.

6.   Mowinckel, *Esra*, p. 13, rejects authorship by C of the ES for two further reasons: (1) C was insistent on Jerusalem as the sole legitimate place of worship, and would not have mentioned 'the place [of worship, מקום] Casiphia'; (2) the list of names 8.1-14 is a gloss, which C would have wished to include in his narrative. The arguments are puzzling. C *has* mentioned the מקום anyhow, in Mowinckel's view, since he makes C the editor of the ES; and it is obscure *when* the gloss 8.1-14 was included.

These verses give him a double commission. He is to contact the local authorities in various centres in the Abar-Nahara for money, and for the enforcement of the Torah for their Jewish communities; and he is to ensure that the full law (that is in his hand) is taught to those who know it not. The first of these commissions he fulfils in 8.36: 'And they delivered the king's commissions unto the king's satraps, and to the governors beyond the river, and they furthered (וְנִשְּׂאוּ) the people and the house of God' (8.36). The teaching of those who know not the laws is done, with the aid of various experts, in Nehemiah 8.

Williamson (*Ezra, Nehemiah*, p. xxxi) follows many others in objecting to 'the lack of any reference to the appointment of "magistrates and judges"'; but this cannot be a serious difficulty. The ES sets out to tell the story of Ezra, and the reformation which he achieved in 'Judah and Jerusalem'. We could not expect that we should hear of visitations he paid to Damascus and Elephantine. Nor could we expect that every detail in the Edict should be precisely referred to in the narrative. Ezra 8.35 is a sufficient account of the sacrifices offered; we do not need to be told that 'their meal offerings and their drink offerings' (7.17) were included. We are not told specifically that Ezra collected offerings from Jews and others in Babylon (7.16), or that he pressed home the tax exemptions. We simply hear that his followers delivered the king's commissions to the local governors, and 'raised up' (וְנִשְּׂאוּ) the people and the house of God—that is, they produced the necessary money and exemptions to provide for the worship ('the house of God'), and they advanced the Jewish religion among 'the people'. The hearer knows that this involves the appointment of שֹׁפְטִים, as provided in Deuteronomy 16, on the model of Jehoshaphat's actions in 2 Chronicles 19, and as specified in the Edict.

Although Blenkinsopp concurs in the general view that the Edict is (fundamentally) authentic, he is noticeably less emphatic about the disparity argument; for his parallels with 2 Chronicles 19 effectively undermine it. There Jehoshaphat selected leading clergy and laity as judges (שֹׁפְטִים, 19.5) 'for the judgment of the LORD, and for controversies' (19.8)—for two areas of law, religious (לְמִשְׁפַּט יהוה) and civil (לָרִיב). This was to be done 'lest wrath (קֶצֶף) come upon you and upon your brethren' (19.10). One Amariah is to be in charge 'in all matters of the LORD', and a certain Zebadiah 'in all the king's matters'. Ezra's Edict has already provided lest 'there be wrath (קְצַף) against the realm of the king and of his sons' (Ezra 7.23). Now, 'according to the wisdom of thy God that is in thine hand' (that is, Deut. 16.18), he is to appoint two kinds of magistrates, שָׁפְטִין וְדַיָּנִין (like the שֹׁפְטִים וְשֹׁטְרִים of Deuteronomy) for the two areas of law specified by Jehoshaphat (7.25); and these two areas are then named as 'the law of thy God and the law of the king' in 7.26. So the whole of Ezra 7.25 is formed on the basis of texts in Deuteronomy and Chronicles, and cannot be an argument for an authentic Edict.

Williamson has a harder fight than Blenkinsopp, for he denies the influence of the Chronicler, and has recourse to older hypotheses. 'Scribe' originally meant 'Secretary of State for Jewish Affairs', and has been reinterpreted to mean a scholar of the Torah (*Ezra, Nehemiah*, p. 98); the Edict is likely to have been drawn up in response to a written request by Ezra, and so used Ezra's own language (p. 99); the Achaemenids were concerned for the religious well-being of their subject peoples, so

Ezra may have been sent to enquire how closely Temple worship was related to the Torah (p. 101); the phrase 'which is in your hand' should not be pressed to imply that he had a new law-code (p. 101); perhaps a few of the nobility followed the royal example with gifts almost as a matter of course (p. 102); we must assume that there has been some error in the transmission of the large quantity of silver (p. 103). The reader may scent the musty odour of apologetic: most of the arguments were confuted by Mowinckel 20 years before.[7]

What is the Nature of the ES?

About half of the ES is in the first person, and this has led to its being dubbed the Ezra Memoir. But memoirs are an outcrop of the nineteenth and twentieth centuries CE; even Nehemiah's first-person narrative is not a memoir, but a series of testimonies in worship (Part I). The first-person element is a blind. The style is identical in the third-person chapters, and the two are interdependent as stories; the author follows a widespread habit of combining first- and third-person passages in his narrative, with the Nehemiah story, including the early addition of Nehemiah 3 on the wall-builders, as his model.[8]

Rudolph, Williamson and Blenkinsopp follow the tradition of explaining the ES as the (more or less heavily edited) report which Ezra made to the Persian authorities. He had received a commission; he must naturally expect to give an account of his actions. But it has to be conceded that the ES does not read like a report to the Persian king. Why would he want to know about Ezra's ancestry (7.1-5), with its names so prestigious in Jewish ears? Or about the fast by the river that runneth to Ahava in ch. 8? Would he expect to spend time reading a ten-verse prayer that Ezra had delivered in the Temple in ch. 9? Or the details of the festal celebrations in Nehemiah 8? Why is there no mention of the governor of the district, whom Ezra must have approached, and perhaps replaced? And if it is a report, why is the whole thing written in Hebrew when Persian authorities used Aramaic? And how would a report to a foreign occupying power get into the Bible? The whole idea is beset with implausibilities.

Against such a notion Mowinckel's magnificent literary analysis (*Esra*, pp. 17-75) seems overwhelming. The ES was composed for Jews, to edify: it set out an idealized story, part fact, part imagination, whose purpose was to unite the people in a new devotion. Ezra, a priest with ancestry going back to Aaron, courageously asked the Persian king for permission to take a caravan of exiles to Jerusalem; and

---

7.   Schäder's theory of a Persian Secretary for Jewish Affairs is confuted in Mowinckel's *Esra*, pp. 120-24; historical speculations about Ezra's enquiry into Temple procedures, or the gifts of the nobility, or the textual transmission of the figures for the treasure, are all shown to be misplaced by Mowinckel's general argument that the narrative is not history but edifying legend. Blenkinsopp's Chronicles parallels are a more satisfying explanation for the 'Jewish' (Chronicular) colouring of the Edict than E. Meyer's hypothesis of Ezra's hand behind the text of the Edict.

8.   Mowinckel gives an impressive list of such 'mixed' narratives from Mesopotamian, Egyptian and Israelite sources, pp. 88-94. But it is the Nehemiah Testimony that counts, for this alone we know to have been available to C, and indeed to have been the model for the ES.

the hand of the LORD his God was upon him throughout the endeavour (7.1-10). Accordingly the king granted his requests in full, and more than in full, in the Edict I have already examined (7.11-26), eliciting a thanksgiving of joy from the good man of God (7.27-8).

An impressive list of leaders joined his expedition, with numerous followers, perhaps 5000 in all (8.1-14). Ezra gathered them by the river, but found there were no Levites, so he boldly held up the departure until he had some volunteers of this important group (8.15-20). He then committed the venture into the hands of God with a fast, and set off without an armed escort, for he trusted in the LORD to protect them. He carefully weighed the treasure into the hands of 12 priests, and the party set off, duly arriving at Jerusalem (8.21-32). There the treasure was handed over to the Temple priesthood, the sacrifices were duly offered, and letters were sent to the authorities in surrounding areas to see the king's orders were carried out (8.33-36).

These matters were hardly complete when the princes approached Ezra with the sad news of widespread mixed marriages. The arrival of the holy man sparked off a mood of repentance at a sin which must imperil the whole future of the people. The saint was distracted with grief, went to the Temple, rent his clothes, tore out his beard, and sat on the ground all day in silent affliction. By evening a large circle of the devout had gathered round him, and at the time of the evening sacrifice he fell on his knees and uttered a moving prayer (ch. 9). This triggered public action. The offenders at once offered to divorce their foreign wives, with one or two exceptions. The whole Jewish community came in from the villages, and a meeting was held in heavy rain. A commission was appointed, and the whole problem was cleared up by the first day of the following year, with every foreign wife being dismissed. Such is the power of a single man of devotion (10.1-17, 19, 44b).

Israel's history was a series of lapses into disobedience and idolatry, but underneath the people's heart was good, and there had been reformations under Hezekiah and Josiah, both of whom had concluded their purges with a celebration of Passover/Massot in the full traditional form (Hezekiah in 2 Chron. 30, Josiah in 2 Chron. 35). So now does Ezra seal the people's renewed obedience with the celebration of the autumn festival in its full form, first with New Year, then with Tabernacles. The people weep at first, fearing they had not been properly observing the Law, but they are soon reassured. The leaders come the following morning to listen to the saint's explanation of what is to be done, and the full eight-day festival is then celebrated with great joy.[9]

I have compressed Mowinckel's fifty-page exposition into a few paragraphs, but I hope that the force of his argument may be apparent. The ES is, in his words, *erbauliche Geschichtserzählung:* he closes many paragraphs with such a sentence as 'So ought things to be in Israel'. He thinks that attachment to the Report hypothesis

---

9.   Mowinckel argues persuasively against Torrey's widely accepted speculation that Neh. 8 originally stood between Ezra 7–8 and 9–10. This arises from the common confusion between literary and historical issues. The ES means to represent Ezra's mission as a success, the crown of the whole history of Israel; not to end it on the bleak, unsatisfying note of Ezra 10, but with the great joy of renewed festal devotion.

is due to something like the physical law of inertia. We do not need to agree with all his conclusions to think that he has understood the main thrust of the ES correctly: Mowinckel is among the masters.[10]

How much Historical Memory Underlies the ES?

Mowinckel has destroyed the ES as a document from which one can read off the historical facts, but he is insistent that it cannot be dismissed as without any historical value. The ES is in fact only an extreme case of the difficulty any historian finds in distilling fact from legend. Sarah Gertrude Millin wrote a biography of Cecil Rhodes in 1933. Rhodes died in 1902, so she was able to interview many people who had known him. She comments, 'People remember the little personal details, not the great historical facts'.[11] We shall be well advised then to apply three criteria: (1) where we find 'little personal details'—names, dates, specific things—which are not explicable as edification, they are likely to be true memories; (2) it is not at all likely that major elements in the narrative are fictitious, only that their description and setting are given for reasons of edification, and are not reliable; and (3) any evidence from non-biblical sources, for or against the historicity of the ES, will be invaluable.

On this basis we may think that the following traditions were available to C: (1) Ezra came from Babylon, with permission from the Persian authorities, in line with the general liberal policy towards local religions in the empire (Ezra 7); (2) he began his journey with a fast at the Ahava canal, and sent for learned Levites from Casiphia, a 'place' of worship (8.15-21); (3) he led a considerable caravan, whose family leaders are perhaps named in Ezra 8.2-14; (4) he delivered donations from Babylonian Jewry to the Temple (8.33); (5) he was involved in a major controversy over mixed marriages, upon which he imposed strict rulings (9-10); (6) a large public meeting on this topic took place in a rainstorm on the 20 Kislev (10.9); (7) among the offenders were descendants of the high priest Jeshua ben Jozadak (10.18), and four named men, including two priests and a Levite, who opposed the reform (10.15); (8) he introduced the Babylonian form of the Torah, something approaching our Pentateuch, with a form of the autumn festival close to that provided in Leviticus 23, including a joyful New Year on 1 Tishri, and an eight-day Tabernacles with people 'dwelling in booths' (Neh. 8).

It is only the last point that may require justification. I have noted above the extensive use in Psalm 119 of Deuteronomic language, and the absence of reference to the ritual laws in the priestly material (pp. 204-206); and that Nehemiah would have Deuteronomic texts for his usury, intermarriage and sabbath rulings, as well as drawing widely on Deuteronomic language in his lament (Neh. 1), and elsewhere (p. 36). With no priestly material in Nehemiah, it seems likely that the form of Torah accepted in Jerusalem in the fifth century was Deuteronomic.

10. Mowinckel was wrong on two important issues. He denied that the Chronicler was the author of the ES, attributing it to a follower of Ezra who had been a young man at the time, writing his memories up about 370 BCE. He also denied that Ezra's law-book was introducing a new law—see below.

11. S.G. Millin, *Rhodes* (London: Chatto & Windus, 1933), p. 288.

The ES seems constantly to hint that Ezra had a different form of the Torah which he was to enforce. He was 'a ready scribe in the law of Moses, which the LORD, the God of Israel had given' (Ezra 7.6); he 'had set his heart to seek the law of the LORD, and to do it, and to teach in Israel statutes and judgements' (7.10). Ezra's law is the true divine version; it needed *seeking*, and he was a *ready* (מהיר) scribe, able to do the seeking; and his vocation was to *teach* its provisions where they were not familiar. This calling is restated in 7.11, where he is called 'the scribe of the words of the commandments of the LORD, and of his statutes to Israel', and in the opening words of the Edict,'the scribe of the law of the God of heaven, perfect and so forth' (7.12).

Ezra is sent 'to inquire concerning Judah and Jerusalem according to the law of thy God which is in thine hand' (7.14); it sounds as if this may be different from other inferior versions in circulation in the provinces. The sacrifices which he is to offer in 7.17 are those prescribed in the P legislation, in Num. 15.4-13. Ezra is again spoken of as 'the scribe of the law of the God of heaven' in 7.21, and in 7.25 he is, 'after the wisdom of thy God that is in thine hand', to appoint officers over the [Jewish] 'people that are beyond the river, all such as know the laws of thy God; and teach ye him that knoweth them not'. The divine wisdom in his hand presumably includes Deut. 16.18.

C's situation and interest seem evident. There are, in his day still, supporters of the old Deuteronomic law; while he himself is a champion of the full Pentateuchal version introduced by Ezra. This latter has been repeatedly ascribed to God (7.6, 10, 11, 12, 21, 25), and it is 'in [Ezra's] hand' (7.14, 25); it contains both Priestly elements (the sacrifices) and Deuteronomic ones (the judges). Some people are familiar with this Pentateuch ('such as know the laws of thy God', 7.25), but others are not, and need to be taught it—'Ezra had set his heart to seek the law of the Lord, and to do it, *and to teach in Israel statutes and judgements*' (7.10), and the king told him, '*teach ye him that knoweth them not*' (7.25). It is not that these people disobey God's statutes; they just do not know them. C wishes to give the impression that Ezra's reformation went smoothly from start to finish, with the people as a whole falling in behind his every move; so he suppresses any suggestion of resistance, or that there was an older form of the Torah which had competed with the Pentateuchal form, and still did.

In the following chapters Ezra shows his familiarity with both P and D traditions. The priests and the Temple vessels are 'holy unto the LORD' (8.28), as in Lev. 21.6, 22.2-3 (P). The mixed marriages have broken the interdict of Deut. 7.3-4 (Ezra 9–10, especially 9.11-12). But it is in Nehemiah 8 that the difference between the Jerusalem (D) tradition and the Babylonian (Pentateuchal) tradition comes into the open. Two festal variations come to light, first with New Year and then with Tabernacles.

The D tradition (Deut. 16) makes no provision for a New Year distinct from Tabernacles, which was itself the 'turning' or the 'going forth' of the year in the old calendars (Exod. 23.16, 34.22). The old Psalm 81 seems to speak of new year as 'At the full moon, on our solemn feast day' (81.4).[12] With Ezekiel we find a New

12. See Goulder, *Asaph*, pp. 149-51.

Year ritual *before* Tabernacles, but the rite is merely to purify the sanctuary (Ezek. 45.18-19). The first indication we have of a public New Year celebration, with a holiday 'in the seventh month [Tishri] on the first day of the month', is in the Priestly/Holiness calendar in Lev. 23.24; in place of the old Israelite calendar with the turn of the year in the autumn, the first month is now in the spring, as in Babylon, and New Year is in the seventh month. Nehemiah 7.72b opens 'And when the seventh month was come...', and Ezra brought 'the book of the law of Moses, which the Lord had commanded' to Israel' before the people, with great solemnity, 'upon the first day of the seventh month' (8.1-2). It is a big document, for he reads it 'from the light [of dawn] until midday' (8.3), and the people are attentive and responsive. They cry Amen, Amen, and prostrate themselves, and when the text has been expounded with an Aramaic translation (8.8), all the people wept (8.9); as King Josiah tore his clothes when the book of the law was found in the Temple (2 Chron. 34.19). For God's law has not been observed all these years, and his wrath may therefore be expected: *ignoratio legis neminem excusat.* But New Year was intended for celebration and joy, and the learned Levites reassure the pliant people of God.

On the 2 Tishri the leaders gather to Ezra 'to give attention to the words of the law. And they found written in the law, how that the LORD had commanded Moses, that the children of Israel should dwell in booths in the feast of the seventh month' (8.13-14). This provision is 'found' in Lev. 23.42, and they found it there, not having seen it before, in the book in Ezra's hand. It also provided for the cutting of branches of olive, wild olive, myrtle, palm and 'thick trees', to make booths, 'as it is written'. Leviticus 23.40, 42 said the people were to take '(the fruit of goodly trees, and) branches of palm trees and boughs of thick trees, and willows of the brook... Ye shall dwell in booths seven days'.[13] The festival is held for eight days, not the traditional seven, with a solemn assembly (עצרת) on the eighth day 'according unto the ordinance' (8.18); the 'ordinance' is in Lev. 23.36.

C wishes to press the claims of the full Pentateuch, but without suggesting that there was an older (and still respected) alternative; and he achieves this with subtlety. He makes it clear without exactly saying it that the Jerusalem leaders had never heard about booths or palm branches; but he does say that Ezra's version was Moses' version, the holy original (8.14), and he manages to imply that it had dropped out of regular use during the wild days of the Settlement—'since the days of Jeshua the son of Nun unto that day had not the children of Israel done so' (8.17). It was not a *new* version of the Torah at all, you see.

So it is possible to single out eight or so points where the historian can hope to have winnowed fact from legend. It is the relation between these hopeful 'facts' that are the problem. It seems altogether too good to be true that much of the Jerusalem leadership should have dismissed their 'strange' wives and children without a protest; and that a hierarchy whose authority rested on the ancient form of the Torah should have capitulated without a fight to the pretensions of a 'Johnny-come-lately'.

---

13. Mowinckel, *Esra*, pp. 169-70, notes the difference in the trees of Neh. 8 and Lev. 23, and explains these by the difference of geography: willows of the brook were common in well-watered Babylonia but unknown in dry Judah.

What Really Happened?

The Fifth Book of the Psalter falls into three sections. The first section, Psalms 107–118, with its two predecessors, 105 and 106, was the creation of the first *aliya*, led by Sheshbazzar, and later Joshua and Zerubbabel. It was not a selection but a series of psalms, reflecting on the events of the Ascent, from its crossing the desert (107), through the trials of opposition (108–110) to the triumph of the rebuilt Temple (111–118). The whole series was intended for the celebration of Passover/Massot in 517 BCE, evening and morning, with Psalm 119 as a conclusion through a vigil at Pentecost. The second section, Psalms 120–134, was the creation of the second *aliya*, led by Nehemiah. It too was a series, reflecting on the events of the Ascent, from the lament and journey (120–122) through the trials of opposition (123–131) to the triumph of the wall-building (132–134). The whole series was intended for the celebration of Tabernacles in 445 BCE, evening and morning, and was marked off as *The Songs of the Ascents*.

Psalms 135–150 are a third section, also a series, formed on the model of 105–118. They too reflect the experience of an *aliya*, from weeping by the waters of Babylon (137), through the trials of opposition (138–145) to a triumph marked with Hallelujahs (146–150). They too constitute an evening–morning sequence, and with 16 psalms would be suitable for an eight-day festival of Tabernacles. As Jewish tradition in Ezra–Nehemiah looked back on three *aliyot*, led by Sheshbazzar, Ezra and Nehemiah, there is a suggestion that the third psalm-section was the creation of the third Ascent, led by Ezra, and was intended for the celebration of the eight-day Tabernacles described in outline in Neh. 8.16-18.

This suggestion is strengthened by correspondences with the ES, both expressed and tacit. Ezra came with authorization from the Persian king in Ezra 7, and the leader of the *aliya* could hardly have survived the resentment expressed against him in Psalms 139–144 unless he had some official backing. Psalm 138 also gives thanks 'before the gods' and worships 'toward thy holy temple'; so the psalm was probably first composed in Babylonia, and expresses gratitude for Yahweh's answer 'in the day I called'. The occasion could suitably be some official, or royal, sanction for the expedition.

Ezra 8 describes three principal events. First, his caravan is thought of as considerable, whether the names and numbers of 8.1-14 bear relation to history or not. A parallel sense of triumph in Psalms 146–150 is inescapable. There are repeated references to *Yahweh's reign* (145.1, 11-13; 146.10; 149.2); he builds up Jerusalem, he gathers together the outcasts of Israel (147.2); he has strengthened the bars of her gates, he has blessed her children within her; he makes peace in her borders, he fills her with the fat of the wheat (147.13-14); he has lifted up the horn of his people (148.14); there are war-dances, with intent to execute vengeance upon the nations, to bind their kings in fetters (149.6-8). The cause of gratitude, and of rising confidence, is a sudden growth in national power, which has often suggested parallels above with the post-1945 growth of modern Israel. We should have some explanation for this surge of optimism if Ezra had brought with him a large influx of settlers, or indeed the first of a series of such influxes.

Ezra 8.14-21 speaks of a fast which the emigrants held 'by the river [canal] that runneth to Ahava', and the name seemed to indicate a historical reminiscence. The psalm-sequence began similarly, 'By the rivers of Babylon, There we sat down, yea, we wept, When we remembered Zion' (137.1). The psalm is written in Jerusalem, and the mood is far from the self-pity so often painted. The remembering of Zion was with the intention of going there; the sitting on the ground and weeping were a corporate mourning, without food, as in Ezra 10.6, to pray for the LORD's blessing on the expedition, and his vengeance on Edom and Babylon; they would sing the LORD's song in a strange land no more, but in his holy temple. We may take it for granted that any such expedition would have monetary support from Babylonian Jewry, such as is mentioned (in exaggerated figures) in Ezra 8.25-34.

A third historical echo is likely to be the summoning of Mahlite and other Levites from 'the place [of worship] Casiphia' (Ezra 8.17-20). Nehemiah mentions the support of Asaphite Levites (Neh. 12.35, cf. 13.13), and it is probable that 'the sons of Asaph' held sway in his day, and maintained the Deuteronomic traditions which are so often echoed in his Testimonies. There must have been learned Levites behind the expansion of the Torah in Babylonia, and these will have been in part from the old ex-Danite 'sons of Korah' who have come to dominate the books of the Chronicler, and in part the 'sons of Merari', the third Levite guild, including the Mahlites, who have imported Jerusalem traditions into what had been a northern monopoly.[14] These are the authorities behind the Pentateuchal version of the law which Ezra will read out in Nehemiah 8, and which provides for the autumn festival season in line with the Holiness code in Leviticus 23. It is an important indicator that for the first time in the Psalter we find in Psalms 135–150 clear echoes of the P creation story. These come in Psalm 136, especially vv. 7-9 on the creation of sun, moon and stars; in Ps. 148.7-10, the dragons and deeps, the trees and animals; and in Psalm 150, the firmament. It is our third psalm-section that has become familiarized with the fuller Pentateuch tradition, and this implies the accession to influence of Babylonian Levites such as are sent for in Ezra 8.

This brings us to Ezra 9–10, and the implausible docility of the errant hierarchs. Spontaneous repentance is a rare phenomenon, especially among the powerful; and the more so when it involves divorcing one's beloved wife and dismissing one's children. It would be more common for the imperilled oligarchs to make use of their strong arms, physical and forensic. What our generation has so often witnessed, in the Soviet Union, China, South Africa and elsewhere, is likely to have been the resource of Judah twenty-four centuries before. Many dissidents may be silenced by being beaten up; and for the obdurate there is the Lubyanka, the show trial, the labour camp and the firing squad.

That such a policy is no idle speculation is testified by the psalm-sequence. The ES gives the impression of a power vacuum: no reference is ever made to a governor, Persian or indigenous. But the psalmist makes constant reference to 'the

---

14.   For a fuller account I refer the reader to Chapters 14 and 15 of my *The Psalms of Asaph and the Pentateuch*, and to Chapter 3 of my *The Psalms of the Sons of Korah*.

wicked/evil man' and his 'men of blood', to 'my enemies/persecutors' (139.19-20; 140.1-5, 8-11; 141.4, 9-10; 142.6; 143.3, 9, 12). In Psalm 144.7, 11 we hear for the first time of 'strangers' who speak vanity and falsehood, and from whom the speaker needs to be delivered. The latter is likely to be the Persian government, while the 'evil man' of 139–143 is more probably the Jewish high-priest, to whom the day-to-day running of affairs was delegated. The situation has the feel of a Caiaphas-and-Pilate alliance, with the imperial prefect reserving to himself the *ius gladii* in a major trial. We may think that the high priest was called Jehohanan and the governor Bagohi.[15]

The 'Edict' of Ezra 7.12-26 does not make Ezra the governor of Judah, and there would be no reason for the high priest to resent the arrival of a large expedition of settlers coming with generous gifts. Ezra's offence is that he also brings the *soi-disant* law of Moses which the LORD had given, and which is at variance with that in force in Judah: indeed he thought that Jehohanan and his followers brought the towns of the province into idolatry (Ps. 139.20). That is fighting talk, and no hierarchy can tolerate the superseding of its document of legitimation.

Jehohanan began with a campaign of slander and defamation (Ps. 140.3), backed by physical attack. He set an ambush for Ezra and his friends (140.2, 4-5), but the scribe escaped with bruises, thanking God for 'covering his head in the day of battle' (140.7). Such physical assault preys upon Ezra's mind (141.9; 142.3), but the Sanhedrin (if we may so speak of it) has moved on to firmer policies. They isolate some of the reformer's senior supporters in the community, 'judges', accuse them and see them condemned; and there follows the edifying spectacle of a public execution as the dissidents are hurled to their death 'by the sides of the rock' (141.6-8). The authorities hope to silence Ezra by a two-pronged strategy: fear by the killing of his friends, and seduction by inviting him to their banquets (141.4).

The reformer was a man of principle, not easily bribed or frightened; so the Council was driven to yet firmer measures. They arrested him, and put him in gaol (142.7; 143.3), and asked the governor (the 'strangers' of 144.7, 11) to try him. Psalms 142–144 give a clear and moving impression of the man of God looking forward to what is likely to be a rigged trial; we are reminded of Sir Thomas More in similar circumstances.

Ezra came triumphant through the trial, and we have his celebration of the verdict in Psalm 145; but the psalm-sequence ascribes the glory to God, and we have to turn back to the ES for some explanation. It is not believable that the Chronicler has made up the whole tale of the mixed marriages, and this is likely to be the issue on which Ezra in fact turned the scale. If he were accused of importing a new law and stirring up the people, he might reasonably reply that the senior priesthood did not observe their own version of the Law, for they had been involved in marriages with Gentiles since the days of Nehemiah (Neh. 13.28), and four descendants of the high priest Joshua ben Jozadak had Gentile wives—Maaseiah, Eliezer, Jarib and Gedaliah (Ezra 10.18), not to speak of a dozen or so senior clergy (10.20-22; 9.1-2). This was

15. These are the names of the Jewish high priest and the Persian governor in the Elephantine letter *Aram. Pap.* 30, active about 410 BCE: see below, p. 319.

strictly forbidden in their own Deuteronomic code (Deut. 7.3-4). Perhaps we should credit the names of Jonathan[16] and Jahzeiah, two priests, who with one Meshullam and the Levite Shabbethai stood in opposition to Ezra (10.15); they could have been Ezra's prosecutors. But the Persian governor was of sterner stuff than Pilate, or perhaps wished to diminish the high priest's authority. He gave the case to Ezra, and it is to his honest or partial verdict that Judaism owes its existence.

Thus far the psalm-sequence may help the historian; for the rest he must use his judgment. Very likely the disgraced high priestly family withdrew to their homes, leaving Ezra to occupy their Temple office (10.6). Very likely Ezra called a public meeting to drive home his advantage, and it met in a rainstorm on the 20 Kislev (10.9, 13). Perhaps the mixed marriages commission completed its work by the first day of the first month following, twelve months precisely since the ES began (7.9). The reformers were able in any case to enforce the Torah on exogamy, and no one in public life could have defied them; a hundred compulsory divorces is not unbeliev-able. No doubt it was on the following New Year and Tabernacles that the Holiness code calendar was put into practice (Neh. 8). Psalms on their own cannot tell us much history; but they are contemporary documents, and being addressed to God are normally sincere. With their aid we can check and interpret the edifying tales told two generations later.

The Dating

If Nehemiah's testimonies are familiar with the D traditions only, while the ES presupposes that Ezra brought the Pentateuch, in some form, then it is very likely that Ezra came to Jerusalem later than Nehemiah. This is borne out by arguments used by older critics from certain names. In Ezra 10.6 the scribe 'rose up from before the house of God, and went into the chamber of Jehohanan the son of Eliashib'. There is an Eliashib the high priest in Neh. 3.1, 20; 13.28, who is involved in a matrimonial alliance with Sanballat, and who has the disposal of rooms in the Temple (13.4-7); an expansion in Neh. 12.22 speaks of an apparent succession of high priests as Eliashib, Joiada, Johanan; and in the following verse of 'the days of Johanan the son of Eliashib' (12.23). As the Elephantine papyri speak of a Johanan ben Eliashib as high priest around 410 BCE,[17] and Josephus speaks of him as still in office under Darius II, after 405,[18] it is very likely that it is this man who is the high priest in Ezra's day.[19] The ES may well mention Ezra's going to his room as a symbol of his taking over as the nation's senior authority, as when an African general takes over the President's office after a coup.[20]

16. There is a Jonathan ben Joiada ben Eliashib mentioned in Neh. 12.10-11; and 'one of the sons of Joiada the son of Eliashib the high priest was son-in-law to Sanballat' in Neh. 13.28.

17. *Aram. Pap.* 30.18: the letter is dated to 408 BCE, and Jehohanan was high priest three years before.

18. *Ant.* 11.7.1 §297.

19. Mowinckel, *Esra*, pp. 104-105, says there can be no serious doubt of the identification.

20. Further arguments are adduced from the name of Meremoth ben Uriah, who is building the wall in Neh. 3.4, and which reappears as that of a senior priest in Ezra 8.33; and from Ezra's refer-

This argument goes back to a series of articles by a Belgian scholar, A. van Hoonacker, from 1890. It is disputed in modern times by Blenkinsopp and William-son. Blenkinsopp (*Ezra–Nehemiah*, p. 143), argues (1) that Eliashib is a common name, occurring three times in the list of those who married Gentiles in Ezra 10.18-44, none of whom is the high priest; (2) that we should have expected the Jehohanan of 10.6 to be called 'the high priest' if such he was; (3) Ezra would hardly consort with the high priestly family, if it were tainted (since Nehemiah's time, *ex hypothesi*) with foreign wives. Williamson (*Ezra, Nehemiah*, pp. 151-54), adds further points: (4) the Eliashib of Neh. 13.4-7 was 'appointed over the chamber' in the Temple, a phrase suited to a caretaker; (5) the list of high priests in Neh. 12.22-23 does not specify their relationship; (6) where the relationships are given, in Neh. 12.10-11, Eliashib's son is Joiada and his grandson Jonathan, and no Jehohanan is mentioned; (7) Josephus's high priest Jehohanan should be dated to the reign of Artaxerxes III (358–338); (8) it is likely that the high priests called their children after their fathers (papponymy), and we may have to do with an earlier Jehohanan ben Eliashib.

None of these objections seems substantial. (1) If we limit ourselves to Ezra 10 for the commonness of names (and it would be less impressive with other lists in Ezra–Nehemiah), we may compute the likelihood of the Jehohanan ben Eliashib of Ezra 10.6 being other than the high priest of the Elephantine letter. There are 110 names in the list, three of which are Eliashib, so we may say that (on this evidence) one contemporary Jew in 37 was called Eliashib. That leaves 107 other names, and one of these is Jehohanan; so (on this evidence again) one contemporary Jew in a hundred was called Jehohanan. So it is likely that about one Jew in 3700 at the time was Jehohanan son of Eliashib. As the population of Judah will hardly have been 37,000 at the time, we are thinking in terms of perhaps ten people of this combination of names in the whole community; and it is not likely that two of them would have had offices in the Temple. We may note the point about papponymy here, since that would affect the argument. Unfortunately there is no instance of such a practice in all the lists in Ezra–Nehemiah; it is just a speculation, and there is no means of computing its likelihood.

(2) The Chronicler does not usually add the title 'the priest', unless there is a reason for it, and never adds 'the high priest', except for Aaron (7.5): 'Jeshua the son of Jozadak' appears without title in Ezra 3.1, 8 (but with 'and his brethren the priests'), and without any indication of status in 5.2. The Temple was the territory of the priests, and it was unnecessary to say that Jehohanan's room in the Temple was a priest's room.

(3) There is no question of Ezra 'consorting' with Jehohanan. After the reformer's impressive victory in 10.1-5, the high priest has made himself scarce: note the dig-nity of the MT's description, 'And Ezra arose from before the house of God, and went into the chamber (לשכת) of Jehohanan the son of Eliashib; and he went there, he ate no bread...' (10.6). He was taking possession of the centre of administration,

---

ence in prayer to God's mercy 'to set up the house of God... and to give us a fence in Judah and in Jerusalem' (Ezra 9.9), a possible reference to the building of the wall. But it is a mistake to support strong arguments with weak ones.

but in no triumphalist spirit. There is no mention of his spending the night there, an interpretative gloss of LXX. On arrival there 'he made proclamation' of a mass meeting (10.7); he had taken over the country.

(4) Nehemiah 13.4 speaks of 'Eliashib the priest who was appointed (נתון) over the chamber of the house of God'; the Hebrew does not in the least suggest that he was the caretaker. The 'chamber' (as in Ezra 10.6, לשכת) is singular, and might be spelt with a capital: it is the administrative centre from which Eliashib deals out his patronage, including the use of other Temple facilities. He is appointed to this by virtue of being (high) priest, in the same way that the Speaker of the House of Representatives is appointed to lead that Chamber.

(5) Nehemiah 12.22-33 speak of 'the days of Eliashib, Joiada and Johanan, and Jaddua... until the days of Johanan the son of Eliashib'. By general consent these will be the succession of high priests; and Neh. 13.28 speaks 'one of the sons of Joiada the son of Eliashib the high priest' as Sanballat's son-in-law. Mowinckel therefore concluded that Joiada was Eliashib's elder son, and J(eh)ohanan his younger son, and that the high priesthood was inherited within the family, as it had been from time immemorial. If he had a married grandson in 445 BCE, Eliashib will have been over 60 at the time. It would not be surprising if his elder son were dead by 410, the time of the Elephantine letter. But a younger brother, perhaps from a later marriage in an age when so many women died in childbirth, might well be holding the reins.

(6) Nehemiah 12.10-11 gives a succession of generations: Jeshua, Joiakim, Eliashib, Joiada, Jonathan, Jaddua. Nehemiah 12.1 mentions Jeshua, meaning ben Jozadak, and 12.8 mentions Jeshua a Levite; but the succession in 12.10-11 is too close to the high priestly line not to be related to the former. Joshua was in office around 520–510 BCE, so his grandson Eliashib could well have been born in the sixth century and been 60 in 445 BCE. There is no justification for the suggestion that Jonathan is the same as Johanan, as is sometimes asserted. If Jonathan died before his father, the high priesthood would have passed to his uncle Johanan during the minority of his son Jaddua.

We may also discount the frequent suggestion that some generations have been passed over in the Nehemiah 12 sequences. High priests may live as long as kings, and we have dates for the contemporary kings of Persia: it is possible to make a table of the corresponding Nehemiah 12 names, with plausible dates of birth:

Regnavit			*Floruit*	*Natus*
522–486	Darius I	Joshua	520–510	550
486–465	Xerxes	Joiakim	490–480	525
465-424	Artaxerxes I	Eliashib	460–440	500
		Joiada	440–420	475
424–404	Darius II	Johanan	420–400	460
		(Jonathan)		450
404–358	Artaxerxes II	Jaddua	390–370	425

(7) Josephus's evidence is subsidiary, and may be left by in the present discussion.

If then Ezra's *aliya* is later than Nehemiah's, and during the high priesthood of Jehohanan, we should probably date it around 420–410 BCE. C thought that Ezra came first, in the seventh year of Artaxerxes; which he can hardly have done if Ezra was half a century later than Nehemiah, in the often canvassed 397. Luke thought John the Baptist was conceived 'in the days of Herod the king' (Lk. 1.5), that is, before 4 BCE, and that Jesus was born (15 months later) during Quirinius' taxation of 7 CE (2.2); and he also makes Gamaliel say in a speech given about 33 CE, that there had been risings first by Theudas, and 'after him' by Judas the Galilaean (Acts 5.36-37)—Theudas's rebellion was in 44, Judas's in 9. But Luke was writing about 90, and he is much more accurate about events in his adult lifetime. So if C wrote about 360, he might well have confused the order of Ezra and Nehemiah similarly.

A date around 420 is also suggested by the Elephantine letter *Aram. Pap.* 21.[21] This shows that a Babylonian Jew, Hananiah, had come to Elephantine in the fifth year of Darius II, 419, with instructions to the Jewish colony there to bring their celebration of Massot into line with that in the east; the unleavened bread was to be eaten seven days, and no work was to be done till the evening of 21st. Deuteronomy specifies six days for eating Massot (16.8), while the P texts Exod. 12.29 and Lev. 23.6 require seven; so it is easy to see Hananiah coming like Ezra to impose a stricter, more developed Pentateuchal Torah from Babylon on a more isolated western community with the older practices intact.

What then is to be made of C's famous date for Ezra, 'in the seventh year of Artaxerxes the king' (Ezra 7.7)? C certainly means Artaxerxes I, and he is thinking of 458, for he sees Ezra's coming as before Nehemiah's, and the latter also speaks of Artaxerxes the king (2.1), but in the twentieth year (1.1) of his reign, 445 BCE. Nehemiah sought royal permission in the month Nisan (2.1), and Ezra similarly began action on the first day of the first month (Ezra 7.9), and he had settled the mixed marriage problem by the first day of the first month in the following year (10.17). It is likely then that the dating in the ES does not come from memories of 'personal details', but that, like many other points in the ES, it has been derived from the Nehemiah Testimony. If Nehemiah sought permission from Artaxerxes, then so did Ezra; indeed Artaxerxes was introduced rather surprisingly as the addressee of a similar petition in Ezra 4.7-16. If Nehemiah acted in the first month, then Ezra acted on the first day of the first month. If Nehemiah went up in the twentieth year, then Ezra went up a good time earlier. And what period is more likely for the learned scribe to have waited than a week of years? C's dating is as edifying as so much else about Ezra, and as historically valueless.

The Chroniclers' Enterprise

The Chroniclers were a family of Korahite Levites, who had control over the developing Book of Ezra–Nehemiah over a period of generations. Ezra–Nehemiah has been glossed repeatedly; and the Levites are the heroes of Chronicles–Ezra–Nehemiah ('the Chronicle') with the Korahite Levites regularly (but not invariably)

---

21.   See Mowinckel, *Esra*, pp. 172-74; J.A. Emerton, 'Did Ezra Go to Jerusalem in 428 BC?', *JTS* 17 (1966), pp. 1-19 (8-9); B. Porten, 'Aramaic Papyri and Parchments: A New Look', *BA* 42 (1979), pp. 74-104.

taking centre stage. They were writing around 375–325, when the sequence of fifth-century events had become blurred, and they could also have the impression that the population of the province was exclusively the גלה/'the sons of the exile'. Their enthusiasm for Ezra means that their family probably came over with that reformer; and their repeated commendation of Ezra's book of the Law means that their Torah was substantially our Torah.

Ezra won the battle in the 410s BCE, but his enemies, we may be sure, lived to fight another day. Jaddua, of the house of Eliashib, became high priest; and the Asaphite Levites had not died away, who had for so long kept the flame of national devotion burning. Their loyalty was to the old Deuteronomic tradition, and their latter-day hero was Nehemiah, whose exploits they might still recite at festivals, and chant the haunting psalms of his company. The Korahites had psalms from the days of their grandfather's *aliya*, but there was no Ezra Memoir, only a few scraps of family reminiscence: if the tale of Ezra's reformation was to be told, they must compose it themselves.

C, 'the Chronicler', saw Israel's history as a series of periods of national obedience slipping away into idolatry, with consequent divine anger and retribution. But the heart of the people was always in the last resort penitent, and time after time God had raised up heroes of the faith, David, Asa, Hezekiah, Josiah, who had re-established a pure worship in a purified Temple, and briefly introduced a golden age of obedience and blessing. The great retribution of the Exile had been answered by the heroism of the late sixth century, when the first *aliya* had issued in the rebuilding of the Temple, and a splendid Passover. Nehemiah had rendered service in his day, but one could trace no new liturgical reformation to him, and his loyalty to the D tradition was all too obvious. C decided therefore to pass him over in silence, as he had passed Elijah over in 2 Chronicles, and to form an Ezra Story on the basis of the Nehemiah Testimony, just as he styled King Abijah on the basis of Judges 9 and Joshua 6–8 (2 Chron. 13), or Hezekiah on Josiah (2 Chron. 30). His ES was to be the climax of the great Chronicle, the tale of the foundation of a permanently obedient and blessed Israel, worshipping in a rebuilt Temple according to the definitive Torah.

Mowinckel has set out the detail of the ES's concerns inimitably, and Blenkinsopp has seen the ES's function in the whole Chronicle most clearly; it is ironic that they should both deny the ES to C—only Kapelrud gives the full credit to the true author. Mowinckel was right in seeing Nehemiah 8 as the climax of the story, the last great festal renewal restoring the liturgy to its purity as in the days of Joshua ben Nun (8.17). C had two Ascents, each of five chapters, Ezra 1, 3–6 for the first, Ezra 7–10, Nehemiah 8 for the second. In each the faithful exiles set out from Babylon with royal permission, with generous financial contributions and Temple vessels; in both they overcome resistance, whether external (Jeshua) or internal (Ezra); in both they triumph, celebrating the renewed festival (Passover/Massot or New Year/Tabernacles) with conspicuous joy. C paints Ezra's story also on the model of the suppressed Nehemiah Testimony: he is more learned than Nehemiah (a scribe), more holy (a priest), with a proper royal Edict, not just a verbal permission, with a larger caravan, more trustful in God (no armed escort), with larger donations, with wider authority, more effective in dealing with the marriage crisis, more concerned for the true Torah. With such a paragon, who would miss the half-cock achievement of his predecessor? Mowinckel missed only one vital concern of C: his zeal to confirm the Babylonian Torah as the true law of Moses which the LORD gave unto Israel, against Asaphite conservatism.

The Chronicler has done his splendid best; but he cannot expel the Nehemiah Testimony with his fork. One of his fellow-Korahites (or perhaps he himself in a mellower mood) has sought a compromise by combining the two traditions. Ezra had come first, and put his foot down about mixed marriages; but then Nehemiah had also had trouble with the same problem. He came after Ezra, and built the walls (Neh. 1–2, 3.33–7.5a); but then he finished the walls on 25 Elul (6.15), less than a week before New Year. It will be at this point that Ezra (and Nehemiah, 8.9) introduced the new Ro'sh Hashanah liturgy (7.73–8.12), followed by the new Tabernacles observance (8.13-18). This will have been marked by the celebration for the completion of the wall, with the double procession going round each half, and meeting at the Temple (12.27-43). Nehemiah himself led the left circuit (12.38-39), and Hoshaiah (and Ezra, Neh. 12.33, 36) the other.

So the second Chronicler has reached the end of both his sources, the ES with Nehemiah 8, the Nehemiah Testimony with Neh. 12.27-43, in a combined Tabernacles thanksgiving. What then is he to do with all the intervening material—the repopulation scheme, the trouble with Tobiah, the infringements of sabbath, further mixed marriages? He cannot fit all this in before New Year, and it spoils his lovely climax. Perhaps it all took place in a second governorship by Nehemiah more than a dozen years later: as we have seen, there may be some tension between the historical and the liturgical sequence of events in the Nehemiah Testimony (pp. 74-76), but Neh. 5.14 speaks only of one twelve-year governorship.

BIBLIOGRAPHY

Ackroyd, P.R., *Exile and Restoration* (OTL; London: SCM Press, 1968).
—'The Jewish Community in Palestine in the Persian Period', *Cambridge History of Judaism*, I, pp. 130-61.
Allen, L.C., *Psalms 101–150* (WBC, 21; Waco, TX: Word Books, 1983).
Anderson, A.A., *Psalms I–II* (NCB; London: Oliphants, 1972).
Auffret, P., *La Sagesse a bâti sa maison: Etude de structures littéraires dans l'Ancien Testament* (OBO, 49; Freibourg/Göttingen: Universitätsverlag/Vandenhoeck & Ruprecht, 1982).
—'A Note on the Literary Structure of Psalm 134', *JSOT* 45 (1989), pp. 87-89.
Baker, J., and E.W. Nicholson (eds. and trans.), *The Commentary of Rabbi David Kimḥi on Psalms CXX–CL* (University of Cambridge Oriental Publications, 22; Cambridge: Cambridge University Press, 1973).
Barr, J., *The Semantics of Biblical Language* (Oxford: Oxford University Press, 1961).
Barré, M.L., 'Psalm 116: Its Structure and its Enigmas', *JBL* 109 (1990), pp. 61-78.
Bartlett, J.R., *Edom and the Edomites* (Sheffield: Sheffield Academic Press, 1989).
Becker, J., *Gottesfurcht im AT* (AnBib, 25; Rome: Pontifical Biblical Institute, 1965).
Becker, O., 'Psalm 118.12 קוצים כְּאֵשׁ דֹעֲכוּ', *ZAW* 70 (1958), p. 174.
Beckwith, R.T., *Calendar and Chronology, Jewish and Christian: Biblical, Intertestamental and Patristic Studies* (Leiden: E.J. Brill, 1996).
Beyerlin, W., *Werden und Wesen im 107. Psalm* (BZAW, 153; Berlin: W. de Gruyter, 1979).
Bickerman, E.J., 'En marge de l'écriture', *RB* 88 (1981), pp. 19-41.
Birkeland, H., *Die Feinde des Individuums in der israelitischen Psalmenliteratur: Ein Beitrag zur Kenntnis der semitischen Literatur- und Religionsgeschichte* (Oslo: Grøndahl, 1933).
Blau, J., '*Nawa thilla* (Ps. 147.1): Lobpreisen', *VT* 4 (1954), pp. 410-11.
Blenkinsopp, J., *Ezra–Nehemiah: A Commentary* (OTL; Philadelphia: Westminster Press, 1988).
Booij, T., 'Ps CX: "Rule in the midst of your Foes!"', *VT* 41 (1991), pp. 396-407.
—'Psalm 116, 10-11: The Account of an Inner Crisis', *Bib* 76 (1995), pp. 388-95.
Braude, W.G. (trans.), *The Midrash on the Psalms* (2 vols.; Yale Jewish Studies, 13; New Haven: Yale University Press, 1959).
Burns, J.B., 'An Interpretation of Ps. 141.7b', *VT* 22 (1972), pp. 245-46.
Ceresko, A.R., 'Poetry, Themes (Exodus, Conquest) and Social Function', *Bib* 67 (1987), pp. 177-94.
Crenshaw, J.L., 'Education in Ancient Israel', *JBL* 104 (1985), pp. 601-15.
Crow, L.D., *The Songs of Ascents (Psalms 120–134): Their Place in Israelite History and Religion* (SBLDS, 148; Atlanta: Scholars Press, 1996).

Crüsemann, F., *Studien zur Formgeschichte von Hymnus und Danklied in Israel* (WMANT, 32; Neukirchen–Vluyn: Neukirchener Verlag, 1969).

Dahood, M., *Psalms III: 101–150* (AB, 17A; New York: Doubleday, 1970).

—'A Sea of Troubles: Notes on Psalms 55.3-4 and 140.10-11', *CBQ* 41 (1979), pp. 604-607.

Dalman, G.H., *Arbeit und Sitte in Palästina, I–VII* (Gütersloh: Bertelsmann, 1928–).

Deissler, A., *Psalm 119 [118] und seine Theologie: Eine Beitrag zur Erforschung der anthologischen Stilgattung im AT* (Munich: Karl Zink, 1955).

Delitzsch, F., *Biblical Commentary on The Psalms* (3 vols.; ET; London: Hodder & Stoughton, 2nd edn, 1888 [1867]).

Driver, G.R., 'Studies in the Vocabulary of the Old Testament', *JTS* 31 (1930), pp. 275-84.

Duhm, B., *Die Psalmen* (HKAT, 14; Tübingen: J.C.B. Mohr, 2nd edn, 1922).

Eaton, J.H., *Psalms* (Torch; London: SCM Press, 1967).

—*Kingship and the Psalms* (The Biblical Seminar, 3; Sheffield; JSOT Press, 2nd edn, 1980).

—*Psalms of the Way and the Kingdom: A Conference with the Commentators* (JSOTSup, 193; Sheffield: Sheffield Academic Press, 1995).

Ellis, R., *Foundation Deposits in Ancient Mesopotamia* (New Haven: Yale University Press, 1968).

Emerton, J.A., 'Did Ezra Go to Jerusalem in 428 BC?', *JTS* 17 (1966), pp. 1-19.

—'A Consideration of Some Alleged Meanings of דֹּעַ in Hebrew', *JSS* 15 (1970), pp. 145-80.

—'The Riddle of Genesis XIV', *VT* 21 (1971), pp. 403-409.

—'The Meaning of *sena'* in Psalm 127.2', *VT* 24 (1974), pp. 15-31.

—'The Site of Salem the City of Melchizedek (Gen.xiv.18)', in *idem* (ed.), *Studies in the Pentateuch* (VTSup, 41; Leiden: E.J. Brill, 1990), pp. 45-71.

Estes, D.J., 'Like Arrows in the Hand of a Warrior (Psalm CXXVII)', *VT* 41 (1991), pp. 304-11.

Ewald, H., *Die poetische Bücher des Alten Bundes*. II. *Die Psalmen* (Göttingen: Vandenhoeck & Ruprecht, 1833).

Feigin, S., 'Etymological Notes', *AJSL* 43 (1926–27), p. 58.

Fleming, D.E., 'House/City: An Unrecognized Parallel Word-Pair', *JBL* 105 (1986), p. 689.

—'Psalm 127: Sleep for the Fearful, and Security in Sons', *ZAW* 107 (1995), pp. 435-44.

Frost, S.B., 'Asseveration by Thanksgiving', *VT* 8 (1958), pp. 580-90.

Goshen-Gottstein, M.H., 'The Psalms Scroll (11Q Ps^a): A Problem of Canon and Text', *Textus* 5 (1966), pp. 22-33.

Gosse, B., 'Le Psaume CXLIX', *VT* 44 (1994), pp. 259-63.

Goulder, M.D., 'The Fourth Book of the Psalter', *JTS* 26 (1975), pp. 269-89.

—*The Psalms of the Sons of Korah* (JSOTSup, 20; Sheffield: JSOT Press, 1982).

—*The Prayers of David (Psalms 51–72): Studies in the Psalter, II* (JSOTSup, 102; Sheffield: Sheffield Academic Press, 1990).

—*The Psalms of Asaph and the Pentateuch: Studies in the Psalter, III* (JSOTSup, 233; Sheffield: Sheffield Academic Press, 1996).

Grabbe, L.L., *Judaism from Cyrus to Hadrian*, I–II (Minneapolis: Fortress Press, 1992).

Gunkel, H., *Die Psalmen* (Meyer; Göttingen: Vandenhoeck & Ruprecht, 5th edn, 1929).

Gunneweg, A.H.J., 'Zur Interpretation der Bücher Esra–Nehemia: zugleich ein Beitrag zur Methode der Exegese', in J.A. Emerton (ed.), *Congress Volume, Vienna 1980* (VTSup, 33; Leiden: E.J. Brill, 1981).

Guthe, H., *Bibelatlas in 21 Haupt- und 30 Nebenkarten* (Leipzig: H. Wagner and E. Debes, 2nd edn, 1926).

Hillers, D.R., 'A Study of Psalm 148', *CBQ* 40 (1978), pp. 323-34.

Holman, J., 'Analysis of the Text of Ps. 139', *BZ* 14 (1970), pp. 37-71, 198-227.

—'The Structure of Psalm 139', *VT* 21 (1971), pp. 298-310.

In der Smitten, W.T., *Esra: Quellen, Überlieferung und Geschichte* (Studia Semitica Neerlandica, 15; Assen: van Gorcum, 1973).

Jacquet, L., *Les Psaumes et le coeur de l'homme: Etude textuelle, littéraire et doctrinale. III. Psaumes 101 à 150* (Gembloux: Duculot, 1979).

The Jewish Encyclopaedia, I–XII (ed. I. Singer; New York: Funk & Wagnalls, 1901–1906).

Johnson, A.R., *Sacral Kingship in Ancient Israel* (Cardiff: Cardiff University Press, 1955).

—*The Cultic Prophet in Israel's Psalmody* (Cardiff: Cardiff University Press, 1979).

Junker, H., 'Einige Rätsel im Urtext der Psalmen', *Bib* 30 (1949), pp. 197-212.

Kapelrud, A.S., *The Question of Authorship in the Ezra–Narrative: A lexical Investigation* (SUNVAO; Oslo: Jacob Dywbad, 1944).

Keet, C.C., *A Study of the Psalms of Ascents: A Critical and Exegetical Commentary upon Psalms CXX to CXXXIV* (London: Mitre Press, 1969).

Kellermann, U., *Nehemia: Quellen, Überlieferung und Geschichte* (BZAW, 102; Berlin: Alfred Töpelmann, 1967).

—'Erwägungen zum Problem der Esradatierung', *ZAW* 80 (1968), pp. 55-87.

—'Erwägungen zum Esragesetz', *ZAW* 80 (1968), pp. 373-85.

—'Psalm 137', *ZAW* 90 (1978), pp. 43-58.

Kilian, R., 'Der "Tau" in Ps. 110,3: Ein Missverständnis?', *ZAW* 102 (1990), pp. 417-19.

Kirkpatrick, A.F., *The Book of Psalms*. III. *(Psalms XC–CL)* (The Cambridge Bible for Schools and Colleges; Cambridge: Cambridge University Press, 1903).

Koch, K., Review of Deissler, *Psalm 119*, in *TLZ* 83 (1958), col. 186-87.

Kraus, H.-J., 'Gilgal: Ein Beitrag zur Kultusgeschichte Israels', *VT* 1 (1951), pp. 181-99.

—*Psalmen I–II* (BKAT, 15.1-2; Neukirchen–Vluyn: Neukirchener Verlag, 3rd edn, 1966).

—*Worship in Israel: A Cultic History of the Old Testament* (ET; Oxford: Basil Blackwell, 1966 [1962]).

Kruse, H., 'Psalm CXXXII and the Royal Zion Festival', *VT* 33 (1983), pp. 279-97.

Laato, A., 'Psalm 132 and the Royal Ideology', *CBQ* 54 (1992), pp. 49-88.

Levenson, J.D., 'The Sources of Torah: Psalm 119 and the Modes of Revelation in Second Temple Judaism', in Miller *et al.* (eds.), *Ancient Israelite Religion*, pp. 559-74.

Lindars, B., 'The Structure of Psalm 145', *VT* 39 (1989), pp. 23-30.

Lipinski, E., 'Macarismes et psaumes de congratulation', *RB* 75 (1968), pp. 321-67.

Loewenstamm, S.E., 'The Lord is My Strength and My Glory', *VT* 19 (1969), pp. 464-70.

Lubsczyk, H., 'Einheit und heilsgeschichtliche Bedeutung von Ps. 114/115 (113)', *BZ* 11 (1967), pp. 161-73.

Marrs, R.R., 'Psalm 122, 3.4: A New Reading', *Bib* 68 (1987), pp. 106-109.

—'A Cry from the Depths (Ps. 130)', *ZAW* 100 (1988), pp. 81-90.

McKay, J.W., 'Psalms of Vigil', *ZAW* 91 (1979), pp. 229-47.

Meyer, E., *Die Entstehung des Judenthums* (Halle: Max Niemeyer, 1896).

Meyers, C.L., and E.M. Meyers, *Haggai–Zechariah 1–8* (AB; New York: Doubleday, 1987).

Meyers, E.L., 'The Persian Period and the Judean Restoration: From Zerubbabel to Nehemiah', in Miller *et al.* (eds.), *Ancient Israelite Religion*, pp. 509-22.

Meysing, J., 'A Text-Reconstruction of Ps. 117 (118).27', *VT* 10 (1960), pp. 130-37.

Millard, M., *Die Komposition des Psalters* (FAT, 9; Tübingen: J.C.B. Mohr, 1994) .

Miller, P.D., 'The Beginning of the Psalter', in J.C. McCann (ed.), *The Shape and Shaping of the Psalter* (JSOTSup, 159; Sheffield: JSOT Press, 1993).

Miller, P.D. *et al.* (eds.), *Ancient Israelite Religion: Essays in Honor of Frank Moore Cross* (Philadelphia: Fortress Press, 1987).

Millin, S.G., *Rhodes* (London: Chatto & Windus, 1933).

Mowinckel, S., *Psalmenstudien I–VI* (repr.; Amsterdam, Schippers 1966 [1921–24]).

—*Studien zu dem Buche Esra–Nehemia*. II. *Die Nehemia-Denkschrift* (SUNVAO NS 2.7; Oslo: Universitetsforlaget, 1964).

—*Studien zu dem Buche Esra–Nehemia*. III. *Die Esrageschichte und das Gesetz Moses* (SUNVAO NS 2.7; Oslo: Universitetsforlaget, 1965).

—*The Psalms in Israel's Worship* (trans. D.R. Ap-Thomas; 2 vols.; Oxford: Basil Blackwell, 1967 [revd Norwegian edn. 1951]).

Noth, M., *Überlieferungsgeschichtliche Studien* (Halle: Max Niemeyer, 1943).

Olshausen, J., *Commentar zu den Psalmen* (Leipzig, 1853).

Pautrel, R., 'Absorpti sunt juncti petrae judices eorum', *RSR* 44 (1956), pp. 219-28.

Petuchowski, J.J., '"Hoshi'ah na" in Psalm 118.25: A Prayer for Rain', *VT* 5 (1955), pp. 266-71.

Porten, 'Aramaic Papyri and Parchments: A New Look', *BA* 49 (1979), pp. 74-104.

Porter, J.R., 'The Interpretation of 2 Samuel 6 and Psalm 132', *JTS* 5 (1954), pp. 161-73.

Potin, J., *La fête juive de la Pentecôte*, I–II (LD, 65; Paris: Cerf, 1971).

Prinsloo, W., 'Psalm 116: Disconnected Text or Symmetrical Whole?', *Bib* 74 (1993), pp. 71-82.

Rad, G. von, 'Job XXXVIII and Egyptian Wisdom', *VT* 5 (1955), pp. 293-301.

Rehm, M., *Der königliche Messias im Licht der Immanuel-Weissagungen des Buches Jesaja* (Eichstatter Studien NS, 1; Kevelaer: Butzon & Bercker, 1968).

Rodwell, J., 'Myth and Truth in Scientific Enquiry', in M.D. Goulder (ed.), *Incarnation and Myth* (London: SCM Press, 1979), pp. 64-73.

Rogerson, J.W., and J.W. McKay, *Psalms 101–150* (The Cambridge Commentary on the New English Bible; Cambridge: Cambridge University Press, 1979).

Rowley, H.H., 'Melchizedek and Zadok', in W. Baumgartner *et al.* (eds.), *Festschrift für A. Bertholet* (Tübingen: J.C.B. Mohr, 1950).

Rudolph, W., *Esra und Nehemia* (HAT, 20; Tübingen: J.C.B. Mohr, 1949).

Sanders, J.A., *The Psalms Scroll of Qumran Cave 11 (11Q Ps^a)* (DJD, 4; Oxford: Clarendon Press, 1965).

Schäder, H.H., *Esra der Schreiber* (Tübingen: J.C.B. Mohr, 1930).

Schedl, C., 'Die alphabetisch-arithmetische Struktur von Psalm CXXXVI', *VT* 36 (1986), pp. 489-94.

Schmidt, H., *Das Gebet der Angeklagten im Alten Testament* (BZAW, 49; Berlin: Alfred Töpelmann, 1928).

—*Die Psalmen* (HAT, 15; Tübingen: J.C.B. Mohr, 1934).

Schreiner, S., 'Psalm 110 und die Investitur des Hohen-priesters', *VT* 27 (1977), pp. 216-22.

Sedlmeier, F., '"Bei dir, da ist die Vergebung, damit du gefürchtet werdest": Überlegungen zu Psalm 130', *Bib* 73 (1992), pp. 473-95.

Seybold, K., *Die Wallfahrtspsalmen: Studien zur Entstehungsgeschichte von Psalm 120–134* (Neukirchen–Vluyn: Neukirchener Verlag, 1978).

Sherwood, S.K., 'Psalm 112: A Royal Psalm?', *CBQ* 51 (1989), pp. 50-64.

Skehan, P.W., 'A Liturgical Complex in 11Q Ps^a', *CBQ* 35 (1973), pp. 195-205.

—'Qumran and Old Testament Criticism', in M. Delcor (ed.), *Qumran: Sa piété, sa théologie et son milieu* (BETL, 46; Paris: Duculot, 1978), pp. 163-82.

Slomovic, E., 'Towards an Understanding of the Formation of Historical Titles in the Book of Psalms', *ZAW* 91 (1979), pp. 364-79.

Smith, M., *Palestinian Parties and Politics that Shaped the Old Testament* (London: SCM Press, 2nd edn, 1987).

Torrey, C.C., *The Composition and Historical Value of Ezra–Nehemiah* (BZAW, 2; Giessen: J. Ricker'sche Buchhandlung, 1896).

—*Ezra Studies* (Chicago: University of Chicago Press, 1910).

Tournay, R., 'Le Psaume 141', *VT* 9 (1959), pp. 58-64.

—'Le Psaume CXLIV: Structure et interprétation', *RB* 91 (1984), pp. 520-30.

—'Psaumes 57, 60 et 108: Analyse et interprétation', *RB* 96 (1989), pp. 5-26.

Tov, E., 'Excerpted and Abbreviated Biblical Texts from Qumran', *RevQ* 16 (1995), pp. 581-600.

Van der Wal, A.J.O., 'The Structure of Psalm CXXIX', *VT* 38 (1988), pp. 364-67.

Vaux, R. de, *Ancient Israel: Its Life and Institutions* (trans. J. McHugh; London: Darton, Longman & Todd, 1961).

Viviers, H., 'The Coherence of the Macalot Psalms (Psalms 120–134)', *ZAW* 106 (1994), pp. 275-89.

Weeks, S. *Early Israelite Wisdom* (Oxford: Clarendon Press, 1994).

Weiser, A., *The Psalms* (OTL; trans. H. Hartwell; Philadelphia: Westminster Press; London: SCM Press, 1962 [German edn, 1959]).

Westermann, C. *Genesis: A Commentary, I–III* (ET; Minneapolis: Augsburg Press 1984–86 [German edn., 1974–82]).

Wilkinson, J., *Egeria's Travels: Newly Translated with Supporting Documents and Notes* (London: SPCK, 1971).

Williamson, H.G.M., *Ezra, Nehemiah* (WBC; Waco, TX: Word Books, 1985).

Willis, J.T., 'The Song of Hannah and Psalm 113', *CBQ* 35 (1973), pp. 139-54.

—'An Attempt to Decipher Psalm 121.1b', *CBQ* 52 (1990), pp. 241-51.

Wilson, G.H., 'Understanding the Purposeful Arrangement of Psalms in the Psalter: Pitfalls and Promise', in J.C. McCann (ed.), *The Shape and Shaping of the Psalter* (JSOTSup, 159; Sheffield: Sheffield Academic Press, 1993).

Würthwein, E., 'Erwägungen zu Psalm 139', *VT* 7 (1957), pp. 165-82.

Yadin, Y., 'Another Fragment (E) of the Psalms Scroll from Qumran Cave 11 (11Q Ps^a)', *Textus* 5 (1966), pp. 1-10, with plates.

INDEXES

INDEX OF REFERENCES

OLD TESTAMENT

INDEX OF AUTHORS